Wakefield Press

Living and Loving in Diversity

Living and Loving in Diversity

An anthology of Australian multicultural queer adventures

Australian LGBTIQ Multicultural Council (AGMC)

Chief editor Maria Pallotta-Chiarolli

Wakefield
Press

Wakefield Press
16 Rose Street
Mile End
South Australia 5031
www.wakefieldpress.com.au

First published 2018

Black and white photos and images prepared by Rob Chiarolli,
www.photosthattell.com.
Some photos and images may lack clarity due to the quality of the originals.

Edited by Margot Lloyd, Wakefield Press
Text designed and typeset by Clinton Ellicott, Wakefield Press

ISBN 978 1 74305 595 3

NATIONAL LIBRARY OF AUSTRALIA
A catalogue record for this
book is available from the
National Library of Australia

AGMC
Australian GLBTIQ
Multicultural Council

VICTORIAN
multicultural
commission
strengthening our community

VICTORIA

CORIOLE
McLAREN VALE
Wakefield Press thanks
Coriole Vineyards for
continued support

My heart is moved by all I cannot save:
so much has been destroyed
I have to cast my lot with those
who age after age, perversely,
with no extraordinary power,
reconstitute the world.

Adrienne Rich

We dedicate this book to our multicultural multifaith (MCMF) queer elders and pioneers in Australia's queer history.

So many have been lost in history; so many like Eugenia Falleni, an Italian transman who endured incarceration, medical injury and maltreatment. So many like Margie Fischer, Happy Ho, Ana Kokkinos, Joan Nestle, Paul Van Reyk and William Yang, who create(d) cultural spaces and carve(d) out personal lives and communities of belonging.

We also dedicate this book to Rochelle Miller and Bridget Dunn, AGMC founding members who have now passed.

Finally, we dedicate this book to the MCMF queers of the future, however you will be labelled then, or maybe there will be no need for labels; whatever the AGMC will have evolved into, or maybe there will be no need for an AGMC . . .

Contents

Acknowledgments

First, we thank our captain, Cinzia Ambrosio. Without her, there would be no AGMC. Cinzia, you put into motion something larger than any of us could have imagined back in 2004. And, like many visionaries and creators, once you knew the compass was set and the AGMC was gaining momentum that would not be stopped, you left us to it. You sailed off into the horizon to pursue other passions and directions, as well as to deal with life's storms, such as the passing of your beloved partner, Bridget. We cannot count how many people, families, organisations have benefitted from your vision.

We wish to thank all our contributors. Some of you have patiently journeyed with us since the idea for this book was first conceived. Some of you have jumped on board this moving bookship with such encouraging enthusiasm.

We wish to thank the Victorian Department of Premier and Cabinet for its LGBTI Multicultural Grant that made this project possible. The AGMC is truly fortunate to be based in Victoria, the Equality State, where Minister Martin Foley (Equality Branch) and Minister Robin Scott (Multicultural Affairs and Social Cohesion), together with Commissioner for Gender and Sexuality Ro Allen, and Commisioner for Multiculturalism Helen Kapalos, advocate and enable truly inclusive policies, programs and support services.

We also wish to thank the dynamic Shoshana Silverman, Senior Policy Officer (MASC), who, together with Fiona Crosthwaite, administers grants and creates supportive forums and events, all with a deft, delicate and understanding touch that truly encourages and enables. Maria thanks Shoshana for her patience at the helm as the unexpected turbulences of life, death, illness got in the way of docking deadlines. Those warming cups of green tea and the chats about our fur-babies and fur-geriatrics comforted and encouraged.

At this point, Maria tears up and says *thanxxxxxxxxxxxxxx* to the AGMC. She says:

I have loved every moment at sea with you as the 'token academic', 'token straightie', 'the ally', 'the ditz with dyscalcula', 'the 'you don't look like/speak like/dress like a Dr Maria Pallotta-Chiarolli.' You are family, you are a home in a world of heteronorms, gendernorms, academia-norms that I'm apparently supposed to fit seamlessly into. May my privileges continue to be erased as we continue to navigate our way through tough, tender and tranquil waters.

Our thanks also to our publisher, Michael Bollen of Wakefield Press. From publishing Maria's AIDS biography *Someone You Know* in 1991 to Dino Hodge's *Colouring the Rainbow: Blak Queer and Trans perspectives* to now this book, we appreciate and applaud Wakefield Press's support of intersectionality and multiple marginalities. We also thank Margot Lloyd for her gracious and sensitive editing, Clinton Ellicott for his careful typesetting through numerous edits, and Rachel Harris for a wonderful cover.

Our thanks to Maryann McIntyre who gave her time and professional editorial eye to this book, and played bad sea-cop when having to cut words, reconfigure sentences and ask the tough questions.

Our thanks to Rob Chiarolli for his sensitive and careful work on the precious personal photos and significant images, sometimes time-worn, that arrived with the written pieces, making black and white convey the rainbow.

Finally, we wish to thank and acknowledge the many writers, artists, activists and social leaders who were unable to be part of this project. And, with awkward mortification, we offer our deepest apologies if we were unable to include you, did not manage to contact you despite our attempts, or somehow horribly missed you. Please jump on board at our website book link www.forum.agmc.org.au and add your works, your name, social media links, contact details, etc.., as this is a space for all multicultural multifaith queers to connect, be visible, and be contacted.

Thank you for all you have done and been, do and are, and will do and be: Anthony Callea, Tom Cho, Maria Dimopoulos, Mo Elleissy, Margot Fink, Sophie Ismael, MoJo Juju, Maria Katsonis, Kochava Sam Lilit, Erik Ly, Wayne Martino, Raina Peterson, Magda Szubanski and Penny Wong.

This is just the beginning of the journey . . .

Welcome to Country

Annette Xiberras

> *Wominjeka yearmann koondee biik Wurundjeri balluk*
> Welcome to the land of the Wurundjeri people
> Our language is the Woiworrung language

The Wurundjeri are known as the Manna Gum People. This book has been largely put together on our land and it is our custom to invite people to share in a welcome ceremony.

As contributors and readers of this book, imagine manna gum leaves being offered to you. Take a leaf from this book as you take the leaves of memories, experiences, pleasures and pains. You are welcome to everything from the tops of the trees to the roots of the earth. It means we become linked symbolically and that you join with us to honour the spirits of our ancestors who have nurtured this very land for many, many thousands of years.

I am a Wurundjeri Tribal Elder with a Maltese immigrant father. I want to tell you a little about my story, my family. I also want to acknowledge that the AGMC has worked alongside and in collaboration with Indigenous queer communities, but respectfully not incorporated or subsumed Indigenous LGBTIQ under the homogenising umbrella of multiculturalism, because of the differing histories of genocidal colonialism and migration.

My country is in Melbourne. I'm an archaeologist and I run an Aboriginal archaeological consultancy company. I'm a 57-year-old black gay woman and I'm proud. My partner Cathy, who is also Aboriginal, passed away nine years ago when our daughter Julia was five and our son Joey was three. Cathy was one of the most remarkable women I ever met. She looked after me, she looked after the kids. She helped me a lot in my human rights fights.

We speak a bit of Aboriginal at home. I also teach the children a little bit of Maltese. My religious background is Roman Catholic, which stems from both my father and mother. When she was little, my mother was one of the Aboriginal children who were taken into welfare to be taught how to be a good little black girl.

I come from a long line of Aboriginal activists. My great-great-grandmother, Jemima, was on Coranderrk, an Aboriginal reserve north-east of Melbourne. She was one of the women who led the rebellion to keep Coranderrk open.

She refused to move off when they closed it and stayed there until she died. Grannie Jemima's daughter Martha, my great-grandmother, was among those who started the Aboriginal Advancement League, which was initially illegal but is still running today. The next in line was my grandmother, Julia Jones. Julia also worked with the Aboriginal Advancement League, was a founding member of the Aboriginal Health Service and fought for Indigenous rights.

I remember one day in the mid 1960s sitting at the Aboriginal Advancement League with Nanna and some of the old ladies. My nanna worked a lot in the Health Service and the social services and also for traditional owners. Being naughty little kids, we got up to the roof window to listen to the women. They were crying because my grandmother had picked up a 14-year-old girl and taken her to the hospital to have her baby. They knew once they took her to the hospital she would never see her child again.

My mother followed in my grandmother's steps. She was the first woman to be a shop steward in the Metal Trades Union. I followed my grandmother on the picket lines for Aboriginal rights and my mother on the picket lines for human rights. I grew up on cans of Coke and sausages in bread with a bit of sauce eaten on those picket lines.

My father is from a little island near Malta called Valenta. He used to talk to me a lot about his people, who were similar to ours. I used to look at my nannas on both sides, and they'd be sitting there weaving fish traps. I found it really interesting that my family from an island and my Aboriginal side were both doing the same things.

Dad wasn't an activist, but he was very instrumental in supporting us. He told us that Aboriginal people, like his people, would never get anywhere with the Commonwealth Government because 'they're no good'. Malta had been owned by a succession of countries. They finally won their independence through the United Nations, not through the government process. I listened to what my Dad said about human rights, moving your people forward and getting them equality.

Many European migrants came to Australia in the 1950s and my dad was one of them. He was 16 years old and was meant to go to Sydney but he got off at the wrong port, in Melbourne, because he couldn't read and write. A lot of Aboriginal people married migrants because they had similar values about family, respecting your elders, and sharing. If one's in trouble, everybody's there. When we needed a house, all of Dad's family came here and built it. Everybody helps everybody. But there were differences. We couldn't understand concrete backyards and concrete houses, which was very European. We believed that you didn't need quantities of stuff. You took what you needed and then you left the rest for everybody else. We think, 'Why have all these other extra luxuries?'

Dad was with the Aboriginals. He was so dark the whitefellas used to make him go with all the Aboriginals in a little box in the back of the hotel instead of through the front door. A lot of people thought he was Aboriginal; he never said he wasn't. He lived with the racism and stuck with us. I'm proud of him; I love him. I recognise my Maltese father and respect him, and I never denied my Maltese heritage. But Dad knew and wanted me to identify as Aboriginal to fight for the rights of my people against racism and reclaim our dignity, culture and land from the colonisers.

I remember a time when I was doing reburials of Aboriginal people's bones back into the land. The bones of different bodies had been mixed up and kept in a museum. I was driving around with them in the back of my car. Dad wanted to go to the market up the freeway so he got a lift with me. As we're driving, Dad said, 'What's all them boxes in the back of the car?' I go, 'Dad, they're people.' He goes, 'Jesus, Annette, they're dead!' He was scared and freaked because he was very Catholic about death and the afterlife. He wanted to jump out of the car there and then. I go, 'What do you want me to do with them?' He goes, 'Put them in the garage. You shouldn't be driving around with them. This is terrible.' He made me drive all the way back home and put the burials in the shed.

Everybody has a creator, whether it's Bunjil the eagle which is my God, or God, or Allah. It doesn't matter. We all believe that a creator created us from the land. Even if you don't believe in a creator, if you believe in evolution, you believe that you come from the land, split as micro-organisms and evolved to where we are today. My people believe that the land is your mother, your country. We believe until you go back to the land then your whole cycle of life hasn't been completed. You're born, you become a mother, you die, you go back to the land, you become a mother again to give life to trees, to birds, to people. That's my spirituality: I come from the land, I go back to the land, I complete my cycle.

My mum passed away two years ago and my father passed away seven years ago. I came home to look after Mum and I didn't leave her because that's part of our culture. This is why I love Europeans and we get on so well because we're so similar. In most white culture and beliefs, elders are put in homes and institutions. My mum brought me into the world. It was my place to take her out. I looked after her at the end and did everything she needed. She died with her dignity and that was important.

We grew up in Broadmeadows, which was a pretty rough area. We were very poor. My mum and dad both worked very hard just to survive. Dad worked in a factory on the trucks and stuff got in his lungs; he ended up getting cancer and never went to work again. Mum worked in a factory and then sometimes, to get extra money, she'd work at the Royal Melbourne Show and wherever she could get extra jobs. I would get up at five in the morning and Mum would get me and my brother ready, drop us off at a babysitter and then pick us up at five that night. I worked from the age of 12 too. I felt bad that my parents worked to support me so as soon as I was old enough to make a quid I went out to work.

Going to school was horrible. There were a lot of white people there. Half of them picked on me for being European and the other half picked on me for being Aboriginal. Dad would make some European food and I wouldn't take it to school. I remember when I was real little, in grade prep, my mum worked and worked and worked to buy me a coat so I wouldn't be cold. The day I went to school with my coat on, other kids took it into the toilets. After someone had gone to the toilet, they used my coat to wipe themselves. I took it home and I washed it. Every time I went to school I put my coat on because my mum worked so hard for it and I didn't want to break her heart. Everybody would laugh and pick on me.

So I caught the double whammy. I used to get the shit kicked out of me from the kids. The nuns were so racist. I used to cop the feather duster and the Bible over the head. And when we played kiss-chasey, I'd chase the girls and kiss them, and boy did I get into trouble. In the 70s if you were gay, they thought there was something wrong with you. You needed psychiatry. Even Mum and Dad were very 'ick' for a while. Dad's Maltese family loved us. It was just when I came out gay that the whole family freaked.

My children know they're Aboriginal and they're proud of Mummy being a political activist. They think that they've got Maltese blood even though Cathy was their biological Mum. I took them back to Malta to meet the family. They've been brought up that they're Wurundjeri and Maltese. They haven't got the blood, but is that important? My kids are absolutely beautiful. Julia's light and they say to her, 'You're not Aboriginal.' She says, 'Yes I am.' They are being taught that racism is really bad but they get picked on a lot at school because Cathy and I were gay and we always taught the kids that that's okay. They loved Cathy and they love me. They would rather go through the bullying and intimidation of uneducated people than deny me, deny Cathy or deny our right as their mothers. Joey and Julia went through the first three years of school with no friends. They weren't happy but they weren't going to say that Cathy or I were not their mums.

I think some European migrants came with racism toward Indigenous people because of the misconceptions about Aboriginal people. They were coming to Australia where Aboriginal people didn't get citizenship until 1967. They had a preconception of us as a useless race, a waste, and this was reinforced in Australia by white Australians.

I think racism isn't going to stop until we mix everybody up. If you're cut, you bleed. If your mum dies, it hurts.

Sadly, migrant heritage and archaeological projects mostly copy colonial erasure by failing to consult and acknowledge local Aboriginal communities and histories. Although there were many like my dad who saw the similarities in our cultures, lived and loved with us, migrants and refugees of colour would mostly dissociate themselves and consider themselves superior to Aboriginal people as they built their new lives on our land; indeed they have been honoured for 'building the nation'.

So, I welcome you to this book. It challenges the heterosexing of multicultural Australian history and culture. It recognises that migration to Australia became complicit in the racial discrimination and colonial degradation of the First Peoples.

From my family, my community, my ancestors, from Bunjil, I now leave you with manna gum leaves as you turn the leaves of this book.

Left to Right: Annette, Joey, Cathy and Julia

Multicultural Queers Say Sorry

From its beginning, the AGMC has supported and honoured LGBTIQ Aboriginal and Torres Strait Islanders and acknowledged our migrant heritages as part of settler colonialism in Australian history. Vic Perri, a founding member of the AGMC, helped set up one of the first Indigenous Gay and Sistergirl Social Support Groups, OUTBLACK, in 1997 when he was a cross-cultural worker at the Victorian AIDS Council (VAC).*

For ATSI LGBTIQ histories and social/support networks, see:

Hodge, D. (ed), (2016) *Colouring the Rainbow: Blak Queer and Trans perspectives*, Adelaide: Wakefield Press.

Sistergirl and Brotherboys Australia: An online group for gender diverse Aboriginal sistergirls and brotherboys, their family, friends and supporters.

Black Rainbow: An Indigenous mental health support source for Aboriginal and Torres Strait LGBTI people.

OutBlack: For Indigenous Australians/Torres Strait Islander gay and transgender sistergirls living in Victoria.

Indigilez Women's Leadership and Support Group: Provides information, support, networking and social activities for Indigenous lesbians.

---

* Please note, in July 2018 VAC became Thorne Harbour Health. As all the pieces in this book refer to the organisation before this date, we have used VAC throughout.

Introduction

'We were always there'

Chief Editor
Maria Pallotta-Chiarolli

Editorial Committee
Shanton Chang
Anne Harris
Alyena Mohummadally
Tony Mordini
Tony Romanelli

We acknowledge the Traditional Custodians of Country and their enduring sovereignty; we bear witness to their diversity, strength, and resilience; honour the elders past and present; and the emerging elders to come.

Welcome to our exploration of Australian rainbows – a tapestry of stories of living and loving that represent the rich and diverse experiences of people who continue to inspire, challenge and celebrate what it means to be LGBTIQ, multicultural, multifaith and Australian. In stories, we learn about ourselves and society; our shortcomings, frustrations and also our victories, tears and loves. The stories come in different shapes, sizes and colours. Each rainbow has a unique beginning, their own journey to traverse and endings that are not what you expect, or perhaps their adventure continues today.

This book also forms part of our challenge to historical and cultural amnesia in relation to heteronormative multicultural histories and anthologies. It explores the lives, loves and losses interwoven, crossed or contested on the borders of and within communities. There has been no other contemporary dedicated edited text on multicultural/multifaith LGBTIQ Australia since Peter Jackson and Gerard Sullivan's pioneering work *Multicultural Queer: Australian narratives* (1999). This book answers that call.

The large number of contributors (including some of Australia's best-known media, arts, health and education personalities) attests to the great need for this volume. This book was originally initiated to mark the 10-year anniversary of the AGMC and its work on behalf of culturally, ethnically and religiously diverse Australians who identify as gay, lesbian, bisexual, transgender, intersex or queer. The AGMC is a member of both ILGA (International Lesbian, Gay, Bisexual, Trans and Intersex Association) and FECCA (Federation of Ethnic Communities Councils of Australia).

Since its inception in 2004 by the forthright and visionary Cinzia Ambrosio, the AGMC has produced its own research, recommendations and strategies for the inclusion of multicultural LGBTIQ identities and perspectives into multicultural, mainstream and LGBTIQ community policies, programmes and practices (Chang and Apostle, 2008; Pallotta-Chiarolli, 2008; Pallotta-Chiarolli and Rajkhowa, 2017). Increasingly, the AGMC has been recognised and supported in its work by the Department of Premier and Cabinet in Victoria, specifically including Commissioners Ro Allen and Helen Kapalos, and the offices of Ministers Foley and Scott (Pallotta-Chiarolli, 2016). These endeavours have been inspired by lived experiences and grassroots communities, and supported from the beginning by Phong Nguyen and the ECCV (Ethnic Communities Council of Victoria) despite some difficult reactions from some community leaders.

The first signs of life for this book came about in an AGMC meeting in early 2012. The excitement in the room was evident. The need for the book had become increasingly apparent the more the AGMC's outreach grew. Like anything we do, the discussions were deep and meaningful, bolstered by good food in Melbourne's multicultural eateries and by feasts prepared in our homes. Earnest and eager, Anne Harris and Alyena Mohummadally volunteered to take the main editorial role together and many long nights at each other's homes ensued. A skeleton for the book was created. Submissions were sought. Dropbox was a valued and trusted member of the editorial party and the book was beginning to become a reality.

And then, life got in the way and neither Anne nor Alyena were able to continue with the book. Alas, after 18 months of solid work, it paused for a couple of years. Thankfully, a successful grant application to the Department of Premier and Cabinet by Tony Mordini and Tony Romanelli for multicultural LGBTIQ projects gave us the financials to allow the book to resume. And the rebirth was glorious! Bigger and brighter! The book became a huge adventure as renowned artists, writers, activists and performers gave generously of their time, personal lives and insights. Long-term communities and contributors breathed a sigh of incredulous belief that the bookship was finally setting sail, and emerging writers and young queers climbed aboard with growing confidence. A monolith of magnificent work. A monument to multicultural/multifaith Australia.

This book acknowledges the central role played by the AGMC for almost 15 years in celebrating the contributions of culturally, ethnically and religiously diverse LGBTIQ Australians. Whether you have been involved with the AGMC, benefited from the AGMC, or simply wish to read stories of living and loving in diversity in Australia, we welcome you to these pages. As we were unable to include so many established pioneering MCMF LGBTIQ, although many are honoured in the following pieces, and as there are an increasing number of emerging MCMF LGBTIQ writers, artists and activists, we welcome you to send us your contribution online and via social media, and engage in the digital forums found at our website – http://www.forum.agmc.org.au.

We have chosen to order this book alphabetically by author, as there is such a wonderful variety and fluidity of themes in each piece that coding or separating into thematic sections would not do them justice. Alphabetical is also a more egalitarian (how Australian!) way of listing award-winning renowned contributors, wow-factor emerging writers, long-term dedicated contributors to the AGMC and inspirational activists who specialise in acting up rather than writing down. Readers can dip in and out or go from beginning to end, and always land on something new, challenging, and beautiful.

Finally, we have requested each contributor to provide a meaningful photo to add to their piece. Many chose the 'queer kids' theme – we were always there! But we are also deeply mindful that for trans and gender diverse contributors, a photo of their 'child-self' performing a gender that was not their 'queer kid self' does not show us who was really always there.

We sincerely hope and trust you will thoroughly enjoy our collection of rainbows, and look forward to having you share your adventures with us on the AGMC website.

Committee and some invited guests at the inaugural conference, 2004, St Kilda Town Hall

'You will never be happy until you come home'

Patrick Abboud, as told to Maria Pallotta-Chiarolli

My family has left and come home so many times in so many ways, and sometimes from and to me. So have I, to myself, from and to my family and community.

My father is Palestinian. He's a 1948 refugee. There was a mass exodus, also known as the Nakba, where more than 700,000 Palestinians were expelled from their homes. He ended up in Lebanon where he met my mother. They got married, had my two brothers in Lebanon and then came to Australia in the early 70s, leaving their homeland because it was being ravaged by civil war. They then had my brother and I in Blacktown in Western Sydney. We moved further out west of Sydney and I grew up in an extremely redneck working-class white community. Racism was rampant. I was severely bullied, ostracised and isolated.

I grew up in a very traditional Arab household. My parents are Catholic by lineage but we were not raised under strict religious ideals. We went to the Maronite Catholic Church with Mum when we were children and then it got to a point where Mum said, 'You know, this is something that you need to work out for yourself. If you feel that you need something, then come with me to the church and get what you want from it.' And out of all my siblings, I'm the only one who continued to go with her. I'm the youngest, and very close to my mum. By the age of 13 I didn't really identify with the church but I went because there was so much going on with me: trying to work out who I was, and being in a difficult school environment where I was very much an introvert, a loner.

I was the only Arab kid in the entire school.

I was one of literally three brown people in the entire school.

I really copped it so I hated school with a passion.

I wanted to get away from it as soon as I could.

Throughout high school, I got dragged through corridors, spat on and beaten up, mostly just because I looked different. And it was awful. My way of dealing with the bullying was becoming really studious. Reading books. Writing. Listening to music. Playing music. Finding creative outlets. It's not something I'd ever really talked about publicly until I made a documentary in 2016 about the epidemic of bullying in Australian schools, *Breaking Point: Bullying's deadly toll*. My supervising producer at the time convinced me to tell my own story. I'd never really put myself in a doco before.

I was kind of the golden child in my family, expected to excel at everything. I think that instilled in me this feeling of always having to achieve, with good enough never being good enough. My parents came from a place of love. They saw that I did well in school so they wanted to ensure I got the best education, something they never had the opportunity to do coming to Australia with nothing. There was this expectation that I'd follow in the footsteps of my oldest brother. He was a lawyer, and he and I were incredibly close. He essentially raised me because my parents worked so hard and I really didn't spend much time with my dad especially.

When I was starting high school, my brother's best friend was captain of the football team and he spent a lot of time at our house. He involved me in everything and he was a male figure who didn't write me off like the bullies at school. I was really drawn to him. As I got older, my feelings for him became more physical. I was thinking about him all the time but I didn't know what 'gay' was. I just thought what I was thinking and feeling for my brother's friend would go away; it would leave me.

What being gay meant was not on my radar at all. I grew up in a very sheltered family and community. There was nothing said at school in sex ed. I was incredibly naïve, so I knew something was different about me but I didn't really know what it was. When I became sexually active, I was having sex with girls and I had a girlfriend for years. I had several girlfriends actually, all through school, even university.

Obviously, with time, and being exposed to LGBTIQ communities more, I realised I was gay and that was okay. Culturally though I knew my family and my Arab community would really struggle with it. And that's when I became fixated on thoughts like, 'I've got to work this feeling out of my head because I can't ever, ever discuss it with my family. I can never be openly gay. I have to try harder to be straight. I'll lose everything. Without my family, I'm nothing.'

In my 20s, I became very politically active with the Palestinian cause. I guess a lot of the anger that I felt about the bullying and racism came out in my activism. I was at protests all the time, and it became my way of taking the focus away from being gay. I realised I wasn't alone.

My coming out story is really long and drawn out. I have to tell you another thing in order for it to make sense: when I was 17, my oldest brother died in a motorcycle accident. That loss totally shattered my life. He had met a woman who is now the closest person to me in the world. They were married for just weeks when the accident happened. They were on the bike together. She survived, he didn't. Basically, from that moment, my whole life became about keeping her alive. I wanted to be there for her.

Over the years, grieving with her created some space, and when she was a lot better a few years later and got her life back on track, I felt like I could go to the Middle East, something I'd wanted to do for many years. I had been in the beginning of my second year of communication studies when the accident happened so I had taken a lot of time off, and I had to finish my degree before I could make the big trip happen. I went to Lebanon in the year 2000. I was supposed to be there for six weeks. I ended up staying for 11 months. Then Syria and Palestine for long stints.

The first time I kissed a boy was in the Arab world, where then it was illegal to be gay. I just think it's incredibly ironic that I ended up falling in love for the first time there of all places. I was living in the gayest city in the world, Sydney, and yet I felt really uncomfortable with my identity. I didn't feel like I could come out because wherever I looked I didn't see myself. I saw Oxford Street; lots of white men with their shirts off. That stereotype was all I really saw in popular culture, too. I didn't identify with that mainstream image of what 'gay' was. So I just kept telling myself, 'Maybe I'm not gay, because that's not what I look like, or how I behave, and my interests are so different.'

In Lebanon, Palestine and Syria I met some incredible people and I felt comfortable in my skin for the first time in ages. I also went through my own grieving process for my brother, because I didn't really have the chance to do that in Australia. I guess because I'm the youngest of four boys, and the most level-headed in my family, I had to keep it together to keep everyone else together. In Lebanon, I realised that many years of suppressed anguish and anxiety had really taken their toll on my mental health and I had to move forward.

When I came back to Australia, I came out to my ex-girlfriend, and then I came out to my sister-in-law, and they were amazingly supportive. And from that point on, I lived as a gay man but still very deep in the closet. I met a guy here in Australia and we were in a relationship for a good three years before my parents cottoned on. During that period, my sister-in-law – who had always said she would never love again – oddly enough met a woman. And that came out of nowhere. I was really happy because she was alive again in a way. And then we became even closer. We moved in together and started this life where our home was like a refuge for so many closeted queer kids from ethnic backgrounds. For a few years we lived a tumultuous double life, but we managed it because we knew that we were doing good, helping others, and that helped us.

I started flying to Queensland every weekend for a few months as my partner at the time was working up there, and my dad started putting two and two together. He came into the lounge room one day when my sister-in-law was visiting my parents, and said to her, 'Tell me something, is Patrick queer?'

And he used that word, which was really strange, because I don't know how he would even have come across it. And she said, 'He's a bit weird, I guess, because he has different interests to other young boys his age, so of course he's a bit queer.'

Dad said, 'No, no. Tell me, is he a poofter?'

She just paused and said, 'Well, it's not my place to tell you.'

At this point the girl who she was seeing had moved into our house as well, and my mum and dad knew that. But now my mum said, 'So you live with this woman and you've lived with her for ages, but you're not a lesbian.'

And then she said to them, 'Well, actually, I am.'

That was it. That was basically my coming out. She unintentionally outed me to my parents by default after outing herself. She left my parents, called me, and it was just terrible. I went into crisis mode. I was booking flights to leave the country. I thought my brothers would try and kill my partner or something. I was genuinely scared. So we stayed up, came up with a plan, and then that evening one of my brothers called.

It was probably the most confronting phone call I've ever received in my life because I really didn't know what I was going to say. We're sitting around the kitchen table, my sister-in-law and myself, my partner and a few other people, just kind of sitting there, trying to work out what the hell to do. And you've got to remember, for me it was also about the feeling that my parents were losing another child. And I had worked hard emotionally to get into a really good place. There were so many reasons why I didn't want them to know.

So, I took the call from my brother and he was really funny. The first thing he said was a really crass 'faggot' thing and I just didn't know how to take it. Then he started laughing. It was weird, and then he just said, 'Look, this is really difficult for everyone. I think it's best if you get in the car, come to my house, we'll work out what to do, and we'll go see Mum and Dad together. Don't be scared. Nothing's going to happen to you. It's okay.'

So that was the turning point. I went to Mum and Dad's and the real challenge started. I walked into the room, my dad walked out of the room. My mum was wailing like when my brother died. It's like I'd died.

So I told them I'd been through some really difficult experiences, that I'd considered taking my life, and I wanted them to understand that their reacting this way really put me back there. I didn't want them to suffer, or me to suffer, so we really needed to find a way to come together on this.

Their biggest concern was what people were going to say. It was all about the Arab community. It was all about the shame or what we call *haram*. Remember, in their eyes I was this golden child and they were saying, 'You're on the road to such success and you're doing great things.' They finally recognised that I was writing a lot, getting published, being on television, having a strong voice in the media, doing lots of things they were really proud of, and they saw me as a spokesperson for the community, which I never intended to be. It just happened. And people had started interviewing me about the work I was doing. So my parents were like, 'This is going to jeopardise everything now,' and, 'It's okay, we'll fix it. We'll go to a psychologist. We'll find the right wife for you,' and all that stuff.

So I took off again. I moved to Europe for five years. That was really tough because I felt like I was running away from them, leaving them, but I had to because I knew that if I didn't, I could lose them forever. I needed them to understand that I was the same person.

I stayed in touch with my mum. We'd talk every couple of weeks but it always ended in tears. I was in a tumultuous relationship with a guy I didn't understand. I was in a foreign country. I was living in a bus (yes, a bus). I was trying to freelance, find my way, and work out what the fuck I was going to do with my life.

I did a lot of travelling, and slowly my family and I reconnected in a new way. They were living vicariously through my experiences overseas. And it was the best thing I could have done because it strengthened my relationship with them. They started to see me as an adult, not their baby boy. It was such a huge shift for us as a family.

So out of that time came really great change – a positive turning point – and I knew then that I really wanted to help other people turn their lives around. I realised through the work I was doing that I could potentially have a genuine social impact and give voice to many other young people like me who were not represented in the wider media landscape. I broke up with that difficult partner, and that was a good decision. I came back to Australia.

I was still not publicly 'out'. I kept that a secret outside the family home.

Even though my family had come around, they were still saying, 'Okay, we accept it now, but don't flaunt it. Just keep it to yourself.' I slowly started coming out to my work colleagues and they were really supportive. I started doing a bit more LGBTIQ-themed stories and docos, and made some good networks. I also started to get involved in Mardi Gras.

The first year that I hosted the SBS Mardi Gras broadcast, five years ago, I didn't tell my parents I was going to do it. They saw me on the telly and weren't over the moon about it at first. The overwhelmingly positive response from audiences gave me the confidence to go very public about my story. I spoke about being closeted as an Arab, about the liberation I felt when I came out, about all the people who were suffering living double lives, all these kinds of secret communities that existed. I became very vocal about how we needed to start seeing more of ourselves on screens and across the wider media landscape. On stages, in papers, on the radio . . . everywhere. More of us: people who were queer, people of colour, people who were queers of colour, people who weren't being represented or were being mostly misrep-resented in the media landscape. I'd been through that experience myself so often and it just pissed me off so deeply that I was like, 'Well then, I'd better change it,' by developing pathways for others to self-represent and tell their own stories on their own terms.

After I did Mardi Gras, my parents were freaking out, thinking, 'Oh my god, your uncles and aunties are going to find out. Everyone's going to know. What are we going to do about it?' It was like Coming Out Crisis Version 2.0. And this was five years after I'd actually come out.

I pitched and started a TV show from scratch, *The Feed*, on SBS television and my parents were like, 'Wow, how did you do that? How did you go to a network and say, "We need to change the landscape and we need to have more people like me on screen and we need to have more stories from these communities"?'

Then, Mum and Dad started talking to other people socially about my work. They had friends who were pretty homophobic and my dad would be like, 'Have you met a gay person? How can you say that? Because my son's gay, and he's still the same person.' It was incredible for me to hear that. It still makes me emotional now. It was such a massive reward for all that hardship, because not only had my life turned around, so had my parents, and they were now educating others.

Last year I went away for a few weekends with my parents and my partner (whom I adore – he is such an incredible man and I'm very lucky to have met him). And that is mind-blowing. I never thought I'd be going on holidays with my parents and my partner, openly out as a gay Arab.

My partner is also half Palestinian. My mum said something really poignant to me many, many years ago when I was travelling, and it really sums up where I'm at right now. She said, 'You will never be happy until you come home.' And now I get it. What she meant was there's something culturally about being with your own that makes you feel like you're home. And honestly, since I've been with my partner, I do feel that. I feel like I've come home. I feel like my heart is at home, and there's something to be said about culturally having this kind of mutual understanding, with his family and my family, around the identity stuff and sexuality. It's so empowering, because they adore him and I feel like I've finally got what my brothers have always had. I feel like we can have kids now and we will be supported.

These days, I'm doing the work that I want to be doing. I don't feel like I work. I feel like I'm making films and making docos, telling stories that perhaps wouldn't otherwise be shared. I want other people's lives to be better. I want other people's lives to be easier. I want the journey to not be so difficult. And not just for LGBTIQ people. I feel like we, as humans, need to be more connected and better to each other. And storytelling is such a powerful means to do that.

So I am really happy. When I'm home I'm happy. I've got a beautiful place to live. The only thing I want is a family. I can't wait to have children.

To young people out there: never stop believing in yourself and don't ever feel like it's not possible to have your community, your family, your sexuality, and your religious beliefs. You don't have to choose between any of those things. You can have them all. And you can be a wholesome, genuine, true person and be open about that with your family. I know it's not possible for everybody. Coming out is not even an option for some people. And you don't have to come out to have all that. You don't have to be public about your sexuality. What you need to do is recognise that who you are is unique and everybody has that uniqueness about them. And once you accept it internally, for yourself, nothing can break that. I know I'm super idealistic but I think without idealism change doesn't happen. You need to go to that place in your imagination where things feel possible, because somehow they'll materialise. That just seems to keep happening.

To my family: without you I'm nothing and honestly you are now my rock. I love my family so much and they love me unconditionally. They have been through such an incredible journey with me and together we've found a beautiful place of acceptance and understanding. Their continued support is what carries me, and us as a family, forward daily.

I honestly believe that if you work and live from a place of love, everything is possible.

'Brown, queer and mentally ill'

Asiel Adan

I had my first depressive episode when I was 17.

Every day, I would walk through a busy intersection on my way to school. It was a major road frequented by cars, buses and beast-like trucks. For three months, I could not shake the thought of walking right in front of them.

Reflecting on my mental health, it's difficult to choose which perspective to listen to. On the one hand, I'm a doctor: I've seen psychiatry from the inside, seen mental health from behind the couch, seen the holes in our services and the chasms in our knowledge. On the other hand, I've been diagnosed with depression myself; I've felt its weight well up inside and drag to the bottom of my feet. And further still, as a queer person of colour, I'm part of a minority group with extensive past and ongoing violence from psychiatric discourse, where my sense of self is pathologised by the very profession I wish to join. To make sense of my experience of mental health, I've had to stitch these perspectives together piece by piece.

Growing up in Mexico, there was no discourse on mental illness. Rural town, people of limited means, large sugar cane plantations, and old Catholic traditions mixed with local superstition. Depression was for white people, depression was for rich people, depression was for people idle enough to get depressed. We had no notion of it, particularly within my family. I remember when I was little, one of my aunts went to a psychologist and there was this big hoo-ha about it. *She should have gone to the priest. We've raised her right. Well, if she wasn't crazy before.* Grandma sometimes told me of her panic attacks and how she felt suffocated, terrified and tight in her chest, hoping that the budding doctor could provide a good old-fashioned remedy for it. *No pills though. That's for sick people.* Illness is never in your head. Try to think of mental health without the 'mental' bit, and then you can understand where I'm coming from.

When I began struggling with my mood, I could never conceptualise it as 'depression'. The longest episode came just before I started medicine. Before my admission interview, I spent two hours lying in bed, mustering up the will to go, trying to get my head to focus, trying to stop my thoughts from spiralling into worthlessness. For a solid month, there was an unrelenting anxiety about nothing. By all accounts, that depressive episode should not have happened. I was doing everything I'd tell my patients to do: exercising, going out, socialising and building my support networks. But all of a sudden there would be emotions everywhere and I was this tiny thing burning for a sense of meaning in the world.

This lasted four months and gave me a habit of crying in public.

Where my family had none, I had so many words for it. I called it shame, I called it poetic melancholy, I called it existential disease. But somehow depression was out of the question; it was too alien. Once I told my father I was struggling with my mood; he stiffened and told me in a stern voice whatever I was going through was no reason to be depressed. I had a roof over my head, food in my mouth and access to an education many would envy. I was expected to deal with whatever difficulties were thrown my way with unbridled machismo. I suppose a country with a 300-year history of colonisation had learned to restrain its sorrows.

Then there's my gender, my sexuality and my queerness to contend with. My relationship with gender has always been mediated by my heritage and this has been a tricky space to navigate. I'm non-binary. As nice as it sounds, the label betrays an uncomplicated simplicity underlined by a certain assumption that there's men, women and a morass of people in between. As a person of colour, being anything else than a man was not only seen as a failure of my masculinity, but also a failure of my culture. Any foray into feminine play would quickly be admonished with the threat of abandonment. Part of my depression stemmed from the sense of isolation this created. I was simultaneously too brown to be white and too queer to be brown. For many queer people of colour, culture and family become a source of trauma as much as a source of identity.

Many of the ideas surrounding sexuality and gender have been framed in Western, pathologising and medicalising terms. Let's not forget that *homosexual* and *transgender* were first uttered by white doctors attempting to cure their ailing subjects. Unfortunately, this violence lingers in today's terminology. We've come to know gender variance only under the guise of the medical gaze. Our sistergirls, brotherboys, hijra, muxes, fa'afafine, akava'ine, two-spirit, winkte, takapatui, bakla and many more Indigenous genders are rarely centred as legitimate. Pathologisation, psychiatric assessments and alienation from our heritage are not the way queer people of colour know ourselves. They're not the way we connect with our identity and our culture.

This is often where mental health fails those who are most vulnerable. By framing mental health in a way that is inaccessible to people of colour and pathologising people with diverse gender and sexualities, the medical profession alienates those whom it seeks to help out.

Our understanding of mental health must be expansive. It has to encompass all of our paradoxical selves. Diagnosis is not enough. Antidepressants are not enough. Similar to the attempt to unify quantum mechanics and general relativity, mental health faces the task of reconciling the minute, complex systems of genetics, neural circuits and biochemistry with the huge phenomena of human experience, society and its influence. The beauty of understanding mental health is its potential to encompass it all in one single breath.

The Baton Passes On!

Faustina Agolley

I'd like to pay my respects to the traditional owners of this land. And respects to those who have fallen on this Remembrance Day.
!

When I heard about the first annual LGBTI awards a few months ago, I was elated. I instantly thought, this is a much needed cultural event, and I was even more thrilled as the awards also champion the support and care of our straight allies. This matters, as we strive for inclusion.
!

I've spent much of the past few years in the US and I've been out for just two years. And I'm sure, like a lot of you if not all, I've been making sense of the events over the years, the past few months, and particularly the past few days.
!

My views are through the lens of being a woman of colour. Seeing what I've seen, travelling through the South where the Confederate flag still flies high, to seeing old slave shacks on former tobacco plantations. Then in more socially progressive states in the US, like marching at LA Pride the morning after the Orlando tragedy, all while being abreast of the news back home – like the delays in Marriage Equality.
!

It can easily feel like a burden being a minority. A struggle. And at times, very lonely. We all have our moments. And when 'our moments' intersect with news so defeating, it makes you numb – we want to throw in the towel. I had one of those moments this morning. But I told myself to show up.
!

In the US, I looked for hope. A lot of what I was reading wasn't helping. Soon my mind turned to a play I saw in 2011 on Broadway called *The Mountaintop* by Katori Hall. It's based in the black civil rights era, and I often compare that movement with gay rights.

!

There are two characters in this play, Martin Luther King (who was played by Samuel L. Jackson) and the motel maid, Camae (played by Angela Bassett). Although fictional, it's taken from real events the night before Martin Luther King's assassination.

!

Camae delivers a cup of coffee requested by Dr King. They end up having an hour of deep conversation and (sorry to those who haven't yet seen the play), Camae turns out to be an angel of death. She tells Dr King that he's to die the next day, and that she's been sent to take him to the other side.

!

Dr King pleads with Camae, saying how much work he still needs to get done for his vision to be complete. Then, accepting his fate, Dr King wants to see what the future looks like after he dies. He asks Camae, 'Is the future as beautiful as you?' Camae very wisely replies, 'Yes . . . and it's as ugly as me too.'

!

It's then that Camae rips into a stunning monologue paired with images of the decades that follow – the good, the bad, the ugly of America and the world, of legislation, events (Katrina, Sept. 11), African Americans (Spike Lee, Run DMC, Tupac, Oprah, Biggie), slogans, 'I'm black and I'm PROUD', to a black president! She exclaims:

!

'The baton passes on!
The baton passes on!
The baton passes on!
The baton passes on!'

!

And so here *we* are.

!

We're not at the Mountaintop. But when we look behind to see how far we've come in gay rights, a lot of baton passing has happened. It's passed from the people who were once silent and lives were taken, to those who risked their safety and their livelihoods in the first Mardi Gras gathering. To openly gay and thriving Australian politicians like Senator Penny Wong, the heart-felt apology from Victorian Premier Daniel Andrews, to gay formals for high school kids, to a rainbow Qantas logo, a gayer presence on mainstream media than we've ever seen, to cracker journalists like LGBTI reporter Lane Sainty at Buzzfeed, to Benjamin Law's literary genius, to seeing equal marriage in every English-speaking country – to championing for our own. To our first LGBTI Awards. Every bit matters. Every person matters. The baton passes on.

!

So thank you to Awards Director Silke Bader for accepting the baton once more, for adding to the celebrations in the way gay people know how. And thanks to you all for being here. There will always be ugliness but here's to more positive change; where we can feel a lot less lonely, where we can live in the world as true equals. Any step forward by our LGBTI community is a shared victory. The baton passes on.

LGBTI Awards press day speech, Sydney Opera House marquee, 11 November 2016.

Multiple Margins
Queer people of colour in the arts
Mama Alto

I will begin by acknowledging that I write these words, and live and work, on the lands and waters of the Wurundjeri and Bunurong people of the Kulin nations, and that the work of the AGMC is likewise conducted on the countries of First Nations people across this land. Sovereignty was never ceded.

Let me introduce myself – I am Mama Alto, a jazz singer, cabaret artiste, gender transcendent diva, and community activist. I am a proud non-binary trans femme person, and a proud person of colour (POC). My background is mixed race, with Javanese, Irish and Scottish bloodlines. As you can see, I exist outside of many binaries.

As the AGMC has grown, the presence and visibility of queer artists of colour in Australia has also grown – often slowly, and sometimes with back-lash and stigma. But we continue to make our presence felt and our messages heard locally, nationally and internationally.

Firstly, I will discuss why the arts appeal so strongly to queer POC, before attempting to review the contemporary lay of the land: the presence and impact of a selection of notable companies, collectives and solo artists I have encountered through my life and work.

It is hardly shocking to observe that the arts attract LGBTIQA+ people, and that a high proportion of those involved in the arts – both as artists and arts adjacent practitioners such as administrators, curators, technicians, educators and more – are LGBTIQA+. More intriguing and far less discussed is the observation that among queer POC, especially queer trans POC, a high proportion of the community identify as artists and exercise creative abilities or distribute creative output of some kind. I wonder why this is, and my thoughts turn to marginality.

LGBTIQA+ people in this country, and indeed worldwide, are marginalised in a social framework that is still heteronormative, as well as patriarchal. POC in Australia are marginalised under social constructions that naturalise whiteness – specifically Anglo-European whiteness – as the norm and characterise non-whiteness as the 'Other'. Sometimes this gatekeeping of a colonial 'us' and 'them' mentality will go so far as to cast non-whiteness as 'Un-Australian'. We can see then, that queer POC are doubly marginalised within such a social context.

However, the complicated layering of multiple margins does not end there. Within LGBTIQA+ communities, queer POC can face further stigma, prejudice and oppression under mainstream gay cultural norms which alternately fetishise or revile, hypersexualise or desexualise, and arbitrarily discriminate against, while simultaneously appropriating from, various ethnic identities. We can see the all-too-common online dating phrase of 'no spice, no rice' as one symptom of this oppression, or the unreasonably generalised expectations that certain racial groups should be well endowed and aggressively sexual while others should be submissive. Meanwhile, within POC communities, queer POC can experience severe backlash against their sexualities and gender identities in the face of cultural or religious norms. It may be worth noting that, in some circumstances, this ethnocultural homophobia, biphobia and transphobia stems from, or has been exacerbated by, colonisation and white supremacist systems.

Considering these multiple marginalities in the lives of queer POC, we can begin to understand the appeal of the arts as a mode of communication, a site of expression, and a medium of community building. In sharing stories, perspectives, questions and explorations, the arts can create empathy, nurture connections, build understanding, foster diversity and confront inequality while giving a platform for empowerment. We can observe that one of the vital but often subconscious roles of the arts in our society is as a site of meaning-making, where identities can be created, affirmed and cemented, and even interrogated, explored and questioned. And due to this function, the arts and artists have the ability to place the marginalised at the centre of culture and society – there are strong traditions and consistent history of both LGBTIQA+ and POC artists operating in this way.

This is not to say that the oppressions of marginalisation do not operate within the realm of the arts – often in the layers of presentation/re-presentation/representation, there is a tension between art as agency and expression, and the use of constructed representations as fetishisation, colonisation, ownership, consumption or exploitation. Sometimes we may be complicit in the latter as queer artists of colour, whether for strategic or subversive reasons, or sometimes for more practical concerns of economics and survival. However, it can be said that the journey of queer POC in the arts is one of carving out a niche for ourselves and, in this way, impacting society and our role within it through our prominence, visibility and platforms in the arts.

And there is no doubt that, despite an increasing climate of conservative racism and xenophobia in Australian politics, culture and broader society, the future of queer POC in the arts here grows brighter and brighter. This is not only due to our increasing presence in main stage and established companies, but in the emergence of new, youth-led collectives and initiatives that centre queerness and cultural diversity in their practice, as well as the fearless and determined trailblazing of solo artists.

The established companies in the worlds of circus, burlesque and cabaret can be seen as leaders within the performing arts when it comes to championing the voices, art and visibility of queer artists of colour. The revolutionary calls of the Hot Brown Honey burlesque troupe of First Nations Pacific women to 'Make noise!' and 'Decolonise and moisturise!' during their ongoing national and international tours speak volumes to the power that the arts have in reclaiming space for multicultural dialogue. While not all members of the troupe are queer identifying, the queer aesthetics and messages of solidarity (including a shout-out to all gender non-binary people in the audience) are similarly powerful and omnipresent. All-male revue Briefs places queer men of colour front and centre in its lineup of comedy, tease and drag, most notably the fierce Fez Fa'anana unapologetically celebrating queerness and relishing racial diversity in the frantically sexual, highly charged but empowering genre of boylesque performance. In a similar context, the fierce voguing of Boy RoRo in the YUMMY cabaret troupe places colour and queerness at the forefront of empowering spectacle.

Widely acclaimed production house Finucane & Smith is deeply committed to showcasing performers of colour within its sisterhood troupe as a part of its modus operandi. The company's predominantly queer politics, aesthetics and diverse identities, along with its mission statement to 'give audiences a discourse on social justice disguised as a fantastic night out', has resulted in prominent inclusion of several queer people of colour – including myself – in the nationally and internationally touring cabaret burlesque works. The fabulous ascendancy of gay Kamilaroi man Dale Woodbridge-Brown within Circus Oz, and his subsequent addition to the Briefs lineup, is another salient example in the cabaret and circus field. Interviewed by queer magazine *Star Observer*, Woodbridge-Brown observed that certain performing arts genres value diversity: 'Circus culture is quite accepting of queerness and drag . . . There are probably some people who don't like it, but they're staying in the shadows where they belong.'

When it comes to the major theatre companies, emerging theatremaker and Patrick White Award winner Kim Ho (2017) recently analysed the presence and visibility of POC across 10 main stage companies: Sydney Theatre Company, Melbourne Theatre Company, Queensland Theatre, State Theatre Company of South Australia, Black Swan State Theatre Company, Belvoir St Theatre, Malthouse Theatre, Ensemble Theatre, Griffin Theatre Company and La Boîte Theatre Company. His findings indicated 26.6 per cent of all main season productions were written or devised, and 16.84 per cent directed, by POC. While promising, when considering both these criteria in combination, only four of 95 productions were both written and directed by artists of colour, compared to 67 written and directed by white artists. While statistics concerning LGBTIQA+ identity in these companies are unavailable, the minority status of all POC within main stage theatre is clearly indicated by Kim Ho's research, as well as in important observations in the mainstream press by Nakkiah Lui (2014) and Candy Bowers (in Neutze, 2016). This situation reflects that very marginality I have suggested is in many complex ways central to the appeal of the arts for queer POC. However, our voices are at last beginning to be included in these main stage platforms – and this will only increase as our excellence continues to prove itself time and time again in the independent, fringe and emerging arts sectors. In mainstage contexts, the outstanding playwriting talent of Jean Tong and the production design innovation of Eugyeene Teh stand as an inspiring demonstration of queer POC excellence.

In the Melbourne independent scene, we see the Myriad collective, which prioritises trans and gender diverse queer artists of colour within their organisational structure, consistently sold-out performance lineups, and well-regarded visual art exhibitions. Arising from a student theatre context in Melbourne, groups such as DisColourNation aim to amplify culturally, racially and ethnically diverse experiences and to solely work with artists of colour, a significant proportion of whom are also queer-identifying. Meanwhile, the Sydney club scene and independent cabaret, live art and dance communities spawned bodies such as the Glitter Militia, which reclaims oppressive labels and concepts such as oddity and the bizarre, and recurring events such as Club Atè, helmed by Justin Shoulder and Bhenji Ra, which celebrates contemporary voices of the queer Asia-Pacific diaspora. Spanning multiple cities, both within Australia and the UK, the Cocoa Butter Club, under Melbourne production by Krishna Istha, showcases and celebrates performers of colour within cabaret to counteract the trivialisation, appropriation and misrepresentation of the culturally and linguistically diverse in cabaret and burlesque.

Nationwide, solo artists from multicultural queer perspectives manage to override niche appeal to become cult phenomena, including Phil Ferguson with his infamous crochet food creations, Mojo Juju's magnificent retro-flavoured music, Benjamin Law and his witty prose, and Mohini, who brings trans and gender diverse representation into the contemporary music circuit as one half of indie electro-pop duo Habits. Locally, many solo practitioners wield important influence and considerable popularity in their fields. There are packed out performances by drag queen D Flowers in Melbourne's Smith Street gay precinct, and galleries with art and curatorial approaches by Léuli Eshraghi informed by philosophies of global Indigenous knowledge-making. In poetry, we experience the biting analysis of Bobuq Sayed and the quiet empowerment of Asiel Yair Adan Sanchez; in dance, the Samoan traditions of fa'afafine Amao Leota Lu and the raucous burlesque of Beni Lola, the queered Kerala stylings of Raina Peterson and the multidisciplinary practice of poet and dancer Adolfo Aranjuez; in cabaret, the considered and musically sublime Margot Tanjutco and the consent-based practice of genderqueer drag king Dani Boi; in the realm of performance art and as a magician, emerging star Creatrix Tiara; and in illustration, the politically charged drawings of the idiosyncratic TextaQueen.

Indigenous LGBTIQA+ people in the arts continue to make far-reaching waves, and it is vital to recognise their presence and works in any reflection on the state of queer artists of colour in the lands now called Australia. In the visual arts, as I write this chapter we see Brook Andrew at the National Gallery of Victoria in a landmark career retrospective of powerful assemblage and bricolage works that reconstitute archives and mythologies into self-examining critiques, and Peter Waples-Crowe's metaphoric dingoes occupy Melbourne's Dirty Dozen gallery in the Flinders Street underpass as part of Yirramboi Festival, celebrating and exploring being marginalised on the outside and yet simultaneously native and integral to this country. In the performance realm, we see queer artists whose work delivers messages without seeming didactic, and which entertains and transports without compromising identity and culture. The hilarity of comedian Steven Oliver comes to mind, as well as national treasure opera singer Deborah Cheetham, and the resilience and exuberance of Uncle Jack Charles. In the realm of drag, we see 'black divas' such as Constantina Bush, who alternates from outrageous comedy to heartbreaking pathos with light speed timing and astounding clarity; the emerging talents of fabulous dancer and Indigenous linguist Ana Diction; and of course Miss Ellaneous and Marzi Panne, and their recent Black Divaz documentary subjects including Crystal Love and Nova Gina. Musician William Cooper, who shares the name but also the politics of an early Indigenous pioneer, encompasses intersecting identities of Aboriginality, neurodiversity, disability and queerness in their considered, layered compositions. And one of our most promising writers, advocates and public intellectuals is the astounding Nayuka Gorrie whose words are equal parts cynically comic, brutally honest, and deeply insightful.

Of course, in my survey of the state of queer POC in the arts today, I have not managed to include every example, every artist, every collective and every company. But I have endeavoured to discuss all the artists I have encountered through my life and work as a queer artist of colour in Melbourne and Sydney in the last 10 years. I deeply apologise for any oversights and omissions as a result. Let us all talk more about our queer artists of colour until we all know their names and works.

A final thought: many queer POC are drawn to the arts, and as I have suggested, this may be strongly influenced by the way the arts can place the marginalised in the centre once more. However, it is worth considering the strange situation of the arts and artists themselves: the contradiction of the arts being at the centre of society as culture makers, while simultaneously artists are marginalised as supposedly unproductive and inessential, and youth are often cautioned against pursuing the arts by authority figures in their lives. Perhaps, with queer POC already conscious and aware of their own overlapping intersections of marginalised identities, taking on the mantle of yet another margin – the arts – is no great leap.

Within multiple margins, then, queer POC in the arts embrace the contradictions of our situation to exist simultaneously outside and within; at once pushed to the margins of society, and yet central to creativity and culture which society surely could not flourish without. And lastly, I would say: we have been here all along, and we always will be.

Mama Alto photographed by Trent Pace

Mosaic

Gavriel Ansara

I am the Seven Wonders of the World,
A veritable map of East and West,
My flesh the site where borders are unfurled
In sandalwood and jasmine at my chest.

I sing the desert's ululating cry
Beneath a moon as black and gold as song,
That stains my fingers with ancestral dye,
Reminder that I've stalked this earth so long.

Before the wind first whispered through these fields
Or mountain fog birthed legends into fate,
I dreamed rice paddies bowed to violet sun,
And tasted hunger only East could sate.

My birth beneath the shifting desert sands
Forged in my bones the sweat of other soil,
The golden red of blazing sunset skies,
The musk of sunbaked mining towns and oil.

I danced my first bloodbath of Eastern rain
When women cradled tiny limbs in silk
And fed me from the bitter sea of dreams
In trances of progenitory ilk.

I am the olive tree in winter's field,
My blazing limbs too hot for any shade;
I am the midnight eyes of Turkish baths
That drench my lover's limbs in serenade.

I am the East meets West meets Borderlands
That slips like quicksand through your ethnic cage,
My eyes are ebony and scarlet seas
That drown imperialist ships with rage.

Drink deep the paradox within my song,
The Mecca and Jerusalem of days,
Before the war descends and brands me wrong,
A misfit to the world's unholy ways.

I am the Seven Wonders of the World,
A symphony of continents and stars;
Drink rich the heady potion of each hue,
Before my Border flesh succumbs to bars.

The Colour of Light (for Chanukah)

For J.

Gavriel Ansara

At five, he learned his primary colours. Red, blue, yellow. Except that the red wasn't truly red, but a pinkish red that he later learned was called magenta, and the blue wasn't really blue, but an electrical turquoise hue called cyan.

At 13, he learned the colour of longing when his family abandoned the arid, burnt sienna desert sands of his youth for the strange, green wildernesses of southern and north-eastern America. His mother had lied. The streets were not paved with gold. On cool, crisp mornings when strange ivory tears called snow had fallen from the sky, he would awaken from dreams of golden browns, oranges, and red like fire scorching the chalky earth of his youth, to find the streets paved with melting ice.

At 14, he believed that he knew all there was to know about colour, its gradations and complements. This belief lasted until the time that he described a friend's hair in exquisite detail, the dozens of tiny plaited strands that fell in ebony rivulets down her back. A citizen of the Land of Ivory Tears had interrupted him with a colour. Black. It had not been uttered as a compliment, and the unfamiliar usage of the word as an all-encompassing descriptor for another person stole a sort of colour from his world. His own skin was dark bronze in the desert summers, then deathly pale against the backdrop of the threadbare alabaster trees in the new green land. He learned that his skin was dangerous because it did not represent his race in any season.

Many people associate green with life and rebirth, but for him it represented the colour of uniformity, a military drab emblazoned with two types of insignias that cancelled his heritage out of the equation. White, black. Men in this new green land had slaughtered one another over the meanings of these terms; wars had been hard fought and won to ensure an uneasy peace that sometimes managed to pass for equality.

Men and women who shared his winter pallor would approach him periodically, assuming a conspiratorial tone as they recited a litany of complaints about people whom they reduced to mere colour. Black. At these moments, the colours of his childhood would vanish suddenly before his eyes. Cape Verdean, Ghanaian, Dominican, Haitian, Moroccan. Igbo, Yoruba, Fon.

He supposed that the allure of elemental colours was their simplicity. Perhaps it was easier for people to control what they believed they understood. Then there was the opposing colour, a word that had equal power to eradicate entire histories and narratives with an utterance. White. Celtic, Norse, Fleming, Sicilian, Finn. Pict, Lapp, Rom.

His border flesh refused either descriptor. Desert sun rendered him a wholesome brown that those unfamiliar with the colour wheel called black. Cold northern sky lent his skin the shade of freshly churned cream, a hue so pale he barely protested when it was termed white.

Even in religion, his winter skin was a passport to instant acceptance in this place, while the skin of his mother drew questions about blood and belonging, despite her ancestral Jewish lineage. Black. His lips hungered for another colour to describe the melted caramel sweetness of her face.

And so it was that he found himself remembering his experienced history of colour as he drew a cyan candle to the mouth of its magenta twin in a slow kiss of fire. Black and white vanished as the Menorah flames writhed in flickering dances that illuminated a variance of colour. Moss green, lavender, azure, midnight blue. He stayed silently mesmerised as the candles reminded him of the many colours of his soul. He watched until his eyes blurred and he could not distinguish anything but the colour of light.

From My Life to All Lives
From identity to representation

Tony Ayres

This article is a potted history of my career, which attempts, in a limited way, to chart the evolution of my thinking around identity, politics and representation. Clearly my cultural background has hugely influenced the creative work I've made. I'm of Chinese origin, born in Macau. My mother worked in nearby Hong Kong where she met my Australian stepfather, William George Ayres. We immigrated to Australia in the mid 60s, whereupon my mother left 'Uncle George' and we lived in the world of Chinese restaurants until my mother's death in 1972.

When I first went to art school (early 80s) and then later film school (late 80s, early 90s), my work was primarily around tales of growing up Chinese in a xenophobic Australia, being gay when homosexuality was still criminal, and coming from a working class/underclass Chinese restaurant community. These were the forces that shaped who I was. These were my stories.

My first screenwriting job after film school was a commission to develop an autobiographical piece called *The Long Ride* for the SBS anthology series, *Under the Skin*. It was about an epic taxi journey that my mother, my sister and I undertook from Perth to Bunbury, 175 km away. *The Long Ride* won the 1994 AFI award for best mini-series or TV movie, and the 1995 AWGIE (the Australian Writers Guild Award) for best screenplay in a TV series or mini-series. At the time, writing a Chinese-Australian story wasn't a self-consciously political act. I did what a lot of younger filmmakers do; I took a narrative from my own life because it was what I knew. Nevertheless, *The Long Ride* announced me to the Australian film and TV industry as 'the Chinese writer' and I got offered a whole bunch of jobs about the Chinese in Australia. It was my first experience of being 'generalised' from the 'particular', an uncomfortable irony given that I spoke neither Mandarin nor Cantonese and had to that point spent my entire adult life distancing myself from my ethnic origins. In short, I was the least qualified 'Chinese' writer you could find.

Around the same time, I was also making creative work about being gay.

Again, my experience was very particular. I didn't have a traumatic time coming out; it happened when I was 16 years old when I told my history teacher that I was gay. He randomly took me to an illegal casino to 'celebrate' (that's a longer story). By then, I was an orphan, so I didn't have to deal with the restrictive expectations of Chinese parents that burden so many Asian queers. Instead, my grappling with sexuality came in another form – the shocking way that I felt I was treated by other (predominantly white) gay men. While I aspirationally saw these men as my peers, they saw me as 'Asian', as Other, as undesirable. Another one of life's strange ironies – my most unequivocal experiences of racism in Australia have been within the male gay scene.

This took a fair bit of unpacking because it was like my different identities just didn't mesh. My way of interrogating this contradiction was to make work about it. I wrote a short story about a gay Chinese guy, titled *A Night Out with the Boys*, which was published in a number of gay-themed anthologies. I then wrote about my experiences of being gay and Chinese in essay form, which became the basis of a documentary, *China Dolls*, where I interviewed a number of other gay Asian men about their intersectional experiences and realised that the alienation I felt wasn't unique. The documentary explored ideas of 'racialised desire' and how this might be part of an unreconstructed colonialism at play in the Australian psyche. Interestingly, at the same time that I made *China Dolls*, there was a short drama made in England (*Yellow Fever*) and a documentary from Canada (*The Queen's Cantonese*) on similar topics. It seemed that in that historical moment (the mid 90s) there was a common recognition among gay Asian filmmakers living in Western cultures that we were being treated in a discriminatory way.

As an aside, I've kept track of issues of sexuality, race and desire over the years and I don't think they have gone away, although they have evolved. My sense is that pervasive unconscious bias against Asian men by white gay men will become increasingly untenable as we start recognising the need for racial diversity across society in general. Until fairly recently, gay men (being an oppressed minority) have had something of a 'hall pass' when it comes to the politics of race and desire, but there is a reckoning on its way (again, that's a longer story).

The last documentary I made, in 1999, dealt with race and sexuality from a different angle. It was called *Sadness*, a monologue performed by photographer William Yang, which explored a murder in his family many generations earlier, intersecting with stories of his friends who had died of AIDS-related complications. It was deceptively simple, a 50-minute visually stylised talk to camera, which screened on SBS and travelled around the world to many film festivals, winning a variety of prizes along the way. Making *Sadness* gave me a sense of completion – I felt that I had explored the intersection between race and sexuality (in this form at least) as much as I could, and that it was time to look at other subjects.

My next significant work was my first feature film, *Walking on Water*, which premiered at the 2001 Berlin Film Festival. The film was set in a pre-dominantly gay, white, inner-city world, and explored how a group of friends dealt with the death of their best friend. It was based upon the real-life experience of writer Roger Monk, which spoke of the extraordinary, intense train wreck of grief gay men were experiencing at that time. While it wasn't my personal story, I connected very deeply to the script because I had also lost quite a few of my nearest and dearest friends. The film was a huge learning curve and focused me on feature filmmaking for the next few years. *Walking on Water* also won a significant number of Australian film awards, although not that many people actually saw it, which was becoming a recurring theme in my career.

After a few false starts and a few detours into theatre and literature, I wrote and directed my second feature film, *The Home Song Stories*, which was the final instalment of a trilogy of autobiographical works which started with *The Long Ride* and progressed with a 50-minute TV drama called *Ghost Story* (for the 1996 ABC TV series *Naked*). *The Home Song Stories* again told the story of my mother, my sister and me, focusing on the year of my mother's death. Of all the work I had made to that point, this film was what I was most proud of. It was also the most acclaimed, winning 23 awards within Australia and internationally. And yet, it was simultaneously one of my most disappointing experiences. *The Home Song Stories* had a limited cinema release and negligible box office impact. Once again, I felt the paradox of speaking from the margins. By this time, I firmly believed that it was important that I do this – I was one of the few Asian-Australian filmmakers around. But it came at a cost. I felt my work would always be peripheral, its audience small, and that (awards aside) I would be largely ignored.

As well, although I had always operated within the broad spectrum of 'identity politics', I was increasingly aware of its limitations. Human beings are made up of a complex amalgam of identities, some coherent, others con-tradictory. To prioritise one identity over another is always a reductive act. For example, I may have had to face various kinds of oppressions because I come from an ethnic and sexual minority, however, this has been counterbalanced by the privileges I've experienced being cis-gendered, male, able-bodied, middle class (these days) and educated. Once you start prioritising one identity over another, you become limited and ideological in your view and you start mythologising what the world actually is. This is exactly the opposite of what I felt I needed to do as an artist. Our job as artists is to speak a different kind of 'truth to power'; we find the complicated, messy, human truths that intersect against and rupture the reductions and simplifications of ideologies (both of the Left and the Right).

While identity-based art at its best illuminates inconvenient truths about the tyranny of entrenched power structures and orthodoxies, it can (at its worst) become a kind of solipsism that posits the self (me, me, me) at the centre of all meaning. Nothing exists or is important beyond our own issues and what affects us as individuals. This leads to all kinds of distortions of scale. Suddenly our own oppressions and slights become more significant, more overwhelming than global inequalities, wars, genocides, famines. And this is not something that sits comfortably with me.

That's a longwinded way of saying that, after *The Home Song Stories*, my work shifted into a different direction. I started moving away from very personal work to looking at other themes and other lives. I co-produced an SBS comedy series with Rebel Wilson called *Bogan Pride*, about a fat, bogan Christian girl (played by Rebel). I directed a TV movie for SBS called *Saved*, starring Claudia Karvan and Osamah Sami, about a relationship between a refugee in detention and his married advocate. I produced a series of documentaries for the ABC called *Anatomy*, about the relationship between art and the human body. And I co-produced a feature film written and directed by Belinda Chayko, starring John Hurt, called *Lou*, about a young girl and her relationship with her dementia-addled grandfather who mistakes her for his wife.

Increasingly, I found myself working in television and it's without question that in this medium I found my greatest success. My first experience as a 'showrunner' (a US term for the producer who takes on the creative responsibilities for the entire TV series) was on Matchbox Pictures's adaptation of Christos Tsiolkas's bestselling novel, *The Slap*. *The Slap* was a watershed experience and hit the sweet spot that all filmmakers hope for. It rated incredibly well, reviewed sensationally, sold all over the world, got nominated for both a BAFTA and an International Emmy, and was remade in America (very badly). It also gave me many other opportunities to work in television. And because it was so successful, I think *The Slap* shifted the Australian TV industry's perception of me as someone who made worthy but marginal work, to someone who is capable of speaking to a broader audience.

For the past seven years, I've had a dream run in TV. I've created or co-created two high concept shows: *Nowhere Boys* (about to enter its fourth season) and *Glitch* (currently developing its third season). *Nowhere Boys* has been even more successful than *The Slap*, winning 18 Australian and international awards (with a further 23 nominations), including the 2015 International Kids Emmy for Best TV Series. And *Glitch* won Best Drama Series at both the 2015 Logies and AACTA Awards (our industry's highest honours). I've executive produced a number of popular TV shows, such as *Underground* for Channel 10, the ABC's *Old School*, and Channel 7's *Wanted* (which was also nominated for an International Emmy for Best Drama Series in 2017). I've worked in comedy (as executive producer of *Maximum Choppage* and *The Family Law*) and also in high-end literary adaptations (*Barracuda* and *Seven Types of Ambiguity*). As well, I've managed to direct a feature film, *Cut Snake* (which, true to form, hardly anyone saw), and executive produced another movie, *Ali's Wedding*, which punched well above its weight and was one of the most loved films of 2017. There is no doubt that I've moved from someone who was considered marginal at the beginning of my career, to someone who is considered mainstream these days.

But another of life's great ironies is that, even though I've superficially broadened the subject matter I deal with, in many ways I've pretty much stayed the same. I've always been interested in telling stories from the edge, stories about outsiders and that's pretty much what I still do. *Maximum Choppage* was the ABC's first mainly Asian comedy series, *The Family Law* is Australian TV's first all-Asian comedy, *Ali's Wedding* is Australia's first all-Muslim romantic comedy, and *Barracuda* was about a gay Greek swimmer. What has evolved has been my sense of purpose. I started out making work that was very personal, trying to resolve what was troubling me the most. Nowadays, I'm much more concerned with the politics of representation. It's important to tell stories from minority or invisible cultures because if those stories aren't told, those people do not come into existence except as stereotypes or clichés. And that's what good art can do – it can conjure up lives, it can make us feel for other people. It can be an act of compassion.

What's changed more significantly than my intentions, though, is the world itself. Diversity of representation is one of the key issues of our times. We are now in a universe where *Moonlight* can win an Oscar for Best Picture and *Transparent* can be one of the most celebrated of TV shows. Another way of thinking about it – we live in a world where there is so much content, so many TV shows, that coming from a distinct minority background can be an advantage. It can make your work stand out.

However, there's one big and important caveat to that. It has to be *good*.

And that's why I have always placed an emphasis on craft and, in particular, on writing (which is the foundation of most narrative screen arts). Knowing how to tell a story, how to affect an audience, understanding the necessity of suspense and intrigue, surprise and emotion, understanding the difference between mystery and confusion, between plot and story, between trope and cliché, are all crucial to the art of screen storytelling. Without command of the craft, whether your story connects with an audience is accidental.

Another important thing I've learned about telling stories from the margins is that while the cultural background may influence the texture, flavour and nuance of the central narrative, it is not *the* story. This is why it's called cultural *background* rather than cultural foreground. The true theme of the work you are making needs to both be deeply embedded in and simultaneously transcend its cultural roots, the way a tree grows beyond the earth that nurtured it.

In summary, I've had a blessed career, in that I've managed to work non-stop since my graduation from AFTRS in 1989, which is almost 30 years now. In that time, I've transitioned from making deeply personal and autobiographical work to work that is broader in scope and reach. Yet in that time, I think because of my emphasis on the quality of my work, I've managed to remain true to my core interests – telling stories from the margins that reflect Australia's cultural diversity.

Limitless Boundaries

Ayman Barbaresco

When life gives you lemons, you just want to squeeze them and make lemonade!
Well in my life, I have been given many lemons and am still squeezing them.

You see, I was born with a neurological disorder called Neurofibromatosis
Type 1 (NF1) and this was the start of a life that has always, still does, and
will always involve many doctor appointments, MRI scans, blood tests and
the list goes on.

I was born on Tuesday 14 February 1989 at 2.01 pm (yes, I am a Valentine's
baby) in Sydney, Australia, to an Italian mother and Middle Eastern father.
I am the youngest of two. My brother is three-and-a-half years older than
me. For the first two years of my life, we lived in Burwood, Sydney, and
then moved to the north coast of New South Wales to the beachside town
of Coffs Harbour. I went to a public primary school and three high schools,
one public, one co-educational private and then a senior college for Years 11
and 12.

For me, growing up in a regional town had mixed emotions. I mean, I
couldn't choose where I lived but I had many mixed experiences and that
wasn't just during my schooling years. The biggest thing that impacted me
was my identity. Growing up, especially having a disability and being sick as
a child, was confronting. I was always picked on at school because I was different. I was the odd sheep among the crowd.

Having NF1 means I have been diagnosed with numerous tumours. My
first brain tumour was diagnosed on my third birthday. This tumour sat on
my brain stem and was inoperable and I had less than 20 per cent chance
of survival. My doctors and specialists trialled a new regime of drugs. I was
given extreme doses of chemotherapy and radiotherapy and it eradicated
the tumour. I am damn well proud of where I have come from and where I
have been.

Growing up, my father was never really around. This made it very difficult
for my mum who was trying to look after me, deal with my treatments and

brain tumour as well as raise my older brother. Thankfully we had the beautiful and amazing support of my maternal grandparents who were there every step of the way and provided that much-needed support. For treatment, my mum and I would travel to Sydney with Ansett Airlines (yes that shows my age) every six weeks for an average of eight weeks. This process went on for almost two years. Even after I was given the all-clear, Mum and I would still spend many months travelling to Sydney for follow-up appointments, scans and tests.

Despite being sick and not really having a childhood, there were still many happy memories of my time in and out of hospital. I remember flying with Ansett in the 1990s and being lucky enough to be taken up to the cockpit and see the pilots fly the plane. This is a privilege that kids who are growing up today don't get to experience and I feel pretty special.

Another great part was staying at Ronald McDonald House in Camperdown, New South Wales (now Westmead). This amazing organisation provides a home-away-from-home for seriously ill children and their families who are more than 100 km away from their family unit. The atmosphere created within this house is truly remarkable and special. The bond that families have within these houses is special and because of the amazing support I received as a kid, this is one organisation that will always be in my heart. As I write this story, they are also one of the organisations that I volunteer for.

To date, I still live with many ongoing medical complications. I was diagnosed with scoliosis at the age of 12, diagnosed with my second brain tumour in 2012, and my third in 2016, and I know that my medical journey hasn't ended. The roller-coaster is still running. I am a little uncertain of where it will take me but I keep living my life, I keep being myself and having fun.

If my medical condition and everything I was going through wasn't enough, my sexuality came into play in 2001 when I was 12 years old. I realised I was gay. I liked guys. A lot of people ask me how I came to terms with my sexuality and for me, it was nothing. It was just another part of me. I mean, I have overcome childhood cancer and dealing with scoliosis, so my attitude was 'so what if I am gay'.

Throughout my work in the LGBTI community, I have heard many coming out stories. I have three different coming out stories. My first one was in 2001. I remember it was a Saturday afternoon when I walked up the stairs of the family home. My mum was in the lounge room and I said to her, 'Mum, I've got something to tell you. I'm gay.' And Mum says, 'I always knew,' and gave me the biggest hug.

My second one was to my best friend in high school. I was in year eight at a Catholic co-educational school. Not long after I told him, I was bedridden due to my scoliosis so I was stuck at home watching TV and not doing a lot. After that three-month bed stint, I returned to school where I had been outed by my best friend. He told everyone in my year and people at my old high school also found out.

My third coming out story is to my dad. I came out to him in 2004 when I was 15. See, my mum and dad divorced in 1996. When I came out to him, he told me, 'No, you're normal. You're going to have a wife and kids.' That was quite confronting for me. I thought my dad would accept me for who I am but in looking at it and knowing what I know now, because he is from a Muslim background, it was quite confronting and challenging. In saying this, just the other week (June 2017), he phoned me and said, 'I don't care that you're gay, I just want you to be happy.' He has accepted me 13 years later and that's quite nice to have some form of closure.

For me, growing up in a regional town and being gay was quite difficult. I had very little support and there was nothing around when I was growing up. We had a couple of services and groups that met, but after a while, it was the same people doing the same thing and got quite boring. There were very few support services online and I had a counsellor who was okay but not the best.

Young people these days are so much luckier than when I was coming out with all of the support services they have access to. There are online chat platforms and discussion groups. In Melbourne there are organisations like Minus 18, JOY 94.9, Headspace, Switchboard and the Victorian AIDS Council just to name a few. I had none of that. Yes, there's still the gay hate, which is horrible to see. And I still hear stories of kids being thrown out of home for being gay. I mean, who cares who you love? Whether you're gay, bi, trans, straight or you're asexual. So long as you love someone for who they are in the heart and not for what's between the legs, that's what matters. I think given enough time we will get there. I think whatever your sexuality is, your gender, whether you have a disability, you're from the deaf community, you're yellow, black, brown, whether you're male, female, or somewhere in between, the main thing I want people to do is to be themselves.

And there's still this whole misconception that people with a disability don't or can't have sex. So where do you go with that? I've been single my whole life, I've never had a boyfriend and I find that challenging, especially being gay with a disability, because there's this dominant perception in the gay community that you have to look a certain way, you have to act a certain way. Why is it that as a minority we victimise and reject a minority within a minority? You can't be 147 centimetres of energy like I am, you have to be six foot tall, dark and handsome with a gym-toned body. But what's wrong with someone who has a little character? I have a goddam awesome personality and a contagious sense of humour. Did I mention that I have an infectious smile? Who cares if they have a few kilos and they don't look like Prince Charming? I may not be who you expect (or want) me to be but spend just five minutes with me and you will find that I am just like that guy you swiped right. I am just like that guy you woofed at. My disability will not leave me. It will be by my side, as I lie beside you. I can't become someone else who will meet the 'gay hook up' checklist requirements that we all have in the back of our heads, because my disability won't let me. Nine times out of ten, I've had to pay for sex and that takes a lot of guts to acknowledge. The thing that I would love the most is intimacy. It's not necessarily about the sex but it's more about the cuddling and the intimate connection that I would love. My bed gets very cold during the long Melbourne winter.

In the 28 years I've been on the planet, I look at it as I'm healthy, I'm happy, I'm living a life that I never thought I would live, ever. I'm breathing, I feed myself, I clothe myself, I don't rely on anything or anyone to keep me alive. I'm so damn lucky! I'm a big believer that because I've gone through so much shit in my life, there must be a reason. There must be some underlying thing that's keeping me here. Life is what you make of it.

The main thing that I want you to know is that you should always be yourself, have fun and enjoy the ride, because you never know where the path will take you.

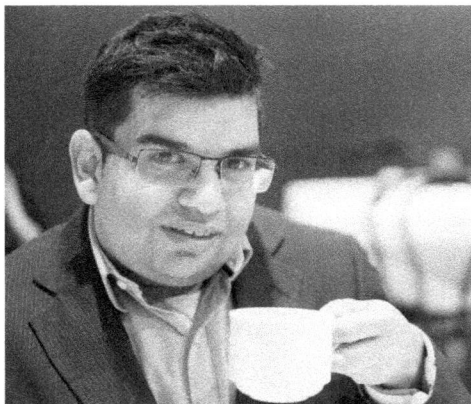

My Helmet

Roz Bellamy

There are two dramatic hair acts I contemplate from time to time.

The first is to chemically straighten my hair, which I consider when I pass Japanese or Korean hair salons. Some of these salons offer permanent hair straightening for $100, which I find both worryingly cheap and appealing.

I imagine the hairdressers laughing when I walk in. They might grab a handful of fuzzy curls and say, 'We don't do hair like this.'

The second is to shave it all off: number one on the clippers. I started considering this in my late 20s, years after coming out as queer.

While I am used to being teased over my curly hair, a shaved head would invite a new type of criticism. Short hair can be seen as an act of defiance: daring not to appear feminine. Perhaps I felt this pressure subconsciously; I never risked the clippers. A shaved head makes a statement that I have always felt too timid to make.

When I was growing up, my family told me repeatedly that my thick, curly hair was beautiful. I never believed them. My Russian grandmother would nod with approval when I wore it out. 'You could be a model,' she told me when I became a teenager.

'I don't think people want models who look like me,' I said.

My mother, who wrestles with her own curly hair, wanted to make the experience better for her daughters. She gave us luxurious hair treatments. She combed and styled our hair. None of it made a difference; I couldn't stand my curls.

There is a photo of my mother as a 14-year-old, taken after she arrived in Australia from the former Soviet Union. She has long, straight hair. She looks gorgeous in her 70s clothing, with her heart-shaped face and perfect hair. When I first saw the photo I was fascinated.

'You had *straight hair*?' I asked, like I had discovered she was royalty.

'I used to iron it,' she said regretfully. 'It's so bad for your hair. Sometimes I burnt it!'

I wasn't interested in the negative side of the story. 'Can we iron my hair?' I asked, and she shook her head.

In Odessa, where my mother grew up, curly hair wasn't unusual. Many people she knew had similar hair. It was only when she came to Australia that she felt different. Some of her relatives, who had migrated much earlier than her family, looked critically at her hair.

'You need to find a way to make it look more shiny,' a relative told her. 'There must be something you can do.'

That was when she discovered the iron.

My issues with my hair go beyond the regular shame some curly-haired women are taught to feel. I was bullied from the age of five, by a girl I met on my first day of school. She had opinions on how I looked and acted. She gave me orders, like I was in a boot camp:

Don't talk to anyone unless I give you permission.

This is how you should sit.

She had punishments if I didn't obey.

Her nickname for me was Fuzzball.

The bullying lasted, undetected, for three years, because at home I acted the same. I talked, just not about what was really going on. By the time my parents found out and the principal got involved, I had changed, becoming silent and submissive at school. Nobody noticed the contrast from the confident kid who had shown up on the first day.

I went to the same Jewish school for 13 years. The other girls had long, straight hair or shiny, bouncy curls. My hair curled up so tight it looked short, even when long, and was thick and frizzy.

In high school, I pulled back my hair as tight as I could. When I wore it in a braid, it stuck out at an angle. One of the boys in my year passed me as I walked to class. 'It looks like a stiffy!' he said, laughing with his friends. He reached out and touched my braid. 'It feels like pubes.'

My stomach took the brunt of his words. I learned a number of lessons about my hair at school, and this one was that I should feel shame. It worked.

I get the strongest sense of how I might have been different when I compare myself to my sister. We are alike in many ways, but she celebrates her curls and dresses boldly. In her words, 'leopard print is a neutral'. She cut her hair during university and ever since has worn it out, wild and bold.

The bullying I experienced at school is the only variable, the only difference in circumstances between us that could justify my lack of confidence. Being teased about something you already perceive as a fault only deepens the pain and shame. It adds a dangerous element to self-judgement: the knowledge that others are disgusted too. Without it, I may not have been a target for bullying at all. The popular girls with curly hair did not get this treatment; it was specifically for the shy girls. It was meant to make us feel inferior.

When I was 14, I started buying hair gel. Each morning I plastered down my hair. My sister watched the process reprovingly. Her hair was less tightly curled than mine, and she could wear her long waves out. 'Try not to use so much gel,' she said. 'It looks like a helmet.'

I couldn't stop using it. Once the gel hardened, I felt safe. I would tie my hair into a ponytail or bun, pinning back any pieces left unsmothered. If I was feeling really insecure, I would put on a thick velvet headband – school uniform regulation blue. I knew how ugly it was. But each morning I pulled it down over my glasses, lifted it around the circumference of my head, and then I was ready.

My father had wild curls in his early 20s. They suited him and his left-wing radical politics. He was carried out of the Vice-Chancellor's office at the University of Sydney for protesting the Vietnam War.

His hair was like him: striking, non-conformist, hard to ignore.

In his mid 20s, when he got married and started a full-time job, he cut his hair and has kept it short ever since. The curls disappeared.

People look from his hair to mine, confused.

'What is your background?' I'm asked. 'Where are you from?'

It is the question everyone with an unidentifiable race is asked. 'My mother is from Odessa, in the Ukraine, and my father is British,' I say.

'That doesn't explain it,' they reply. They insist on taking it further.

'I'm Jewish, if that helps,' I add. Some people – usually Americans, I find, courtesy of both Seth Rogan and *The OC* – understand the concept of a 'Jew-fro'. But mostly, when I mention my heritage, people look blank.

The magic word is Romania. As soon I mention the distant Romanian connection on my father's side, they are satisfied.

I am often mistaken for other cultures. A Lebanese café owner gave me free falafel and treated me like family. On Sydney Road in Brunswick I get offered mint in my tea, even when it isn't on the menu. Some assume I am Italian, Spanish or Greek, and start speaking to me in these languages. In Hawaii, an

African-American woman working at Macy's cast a look at my hair and skin and asked, 'Where are *you* from? You're black*ish*, right?'

When I wear my hair in a bland, helmet-like style, I fit in. I may not look particularly good, but with helmet hair I pass as Caucasian-ish. When I wear my hair out, it attracts words like 'wild' and 'exotic' and I no longer pass.

People have expectations and stereotypes for women with curls. They expect a big attitude. When I am loud and confident, the attitude accompanies my hair nicely. People are pleased. This has been a struggle, since I was exceedingly shy for years.

At one point, I got so sick of my hair that I insisted on a change. A local salon offered hair relaxing. After much pleading, my mother agreed to it. The owner, a man with leathery skin and a lot of attitude, fluffed my hair until it formed a mane around my head. 'You've got to feel it,' he cried out to his co-workers.

I was horrified but submissive. I let him lead me around the salon, stopping for the straight-haired customers to touch my hair. The treatment relaxed my hair, but not in the way I had planned. The curl was gone. The frizz increased exponentially. My hair had too much volume and too little life.

Another time, a popular girl in my year talked to me about curly hair. 'Have you tried mousse?' Her eyes roamed over my hair with judgement and pity. 'That's the only thing that makes it curly without frizz.'

Neither of us brought up the issue that her hair was, at most, lightly wavy, while mine was thick and tightly coiled. According to the Naturally Curly website, which has revolutionised the way curly hair is cut and styled, my hair texture type is somewhere between 3C ('Curly Coily') and 4C ('Coily Ziggly'). Most of the models for these categories are African American. The hair type is fine, tightly coiled, kinky and easily damaged, hence the frizz.

The girl who recommended mousse had hair the website would describe as 'Wavy Whirly'. Taylor Swift's pre-pop country look is the example.

I don't have to tell you that I went out and bought mousse, a number of bottles. It did nothing to my hair apart from making it white and soapy, like I had bathed it in shaving cream. It hung limply, feeling so sticky and coarse I didn't want to touch it. I added a new rule to my knowledge about curly hair: mousse only works in nice, loose waves.

In my senior years of high school, more kids were thinking about crushes than studying for exams. Some were in relationships or at least had a regular Saturday night make-out partner. What happens to those taught they are undesirable?

I believed nobody would find me attractive. Hollywood constantly reinforced my high school worries with modern-day versions of *The Taming of the Shrew*, including *Clueless*, *She's All That*, *10 Things I Hate About You*, *Never Been Kissed* and *The Princess Diaries*. The plot was always the same: beauty was achieved once curls were tamed and eyebrows shaped. Only then could the female character be considered attractive and, therefore, desirable.

I'm not surprised I experienced my first kiss when my hair was not in its natural form. I had it blow-dried straight and my sister patiently wove it into microbraids. It looked, from afar, like long straight hair. I felt confident and attractive and, for the first time ever, a boy showed interest. Despite the initial attraction, however, the braids had to go, and eventually so did the relationship.

After my first year of university, I fell in love with a woman and entered into a long-term relationship. Coming out as queer and coming to terms with my hair have involved similar processes of self-acceptance. Both have taken a long time and a considerable amount of work.

Rachel has spent years trying to help me to see that my hair is beautiful. Despite her love and support, I continued to struggle with my hair when I came out. When *The L Word* aired in 2004, it added another level to my complicated feelings about my hair. I looked at Shane and Tina, the characters we were meant to perceive as butch and femme, and felt, again, like I didn't fit in.

In 2006, to celebrate three years together, we planned a trip to the United States to overlap with the LGBT Pride Month festivities in June. While we were in New York City, we went to the world's largest LGBTI synagogue for a Friday night Shabbat service. The rabbi welcomed people to join their float in the Pride March to Greenwich Village on Sunday, where the Stonewall Riots occurred in 1969. We looked at each other nervously. We had planned to stand and watch the march anonymously, but participating in a float sounded appealing.

That Sunday, we turned up early and fortified ourselves with iced coffees. It was already over 30 degrees. Drag queens were pacing impatiently at the starting point, complaining about their hair and make-up. When we joined the float, we forgot about the heat and our anxieties. Dancing the Horah down Fifth Avenue, we felt kinship and acceptance. Rachel and I danced under a rainbow chuppah, the Jewish wedding canopy, to cheers from our fellow marchers. Back then, same-sex marriage was only a distant dream to us.

Toward the end of that trip, we flew to San Francisco. I met Sia Amma, an African-American woman who writes and performs shows and comedy, including *In Search of My Clitoris* and *What Mama Said About Down There*, to educate people about female genital mutilation in Africa. She supplements her artistic work and activism with hairdressing, offering African braids, weaves and extensions. It didn't occur to me until later how appropriate it is that her hairdressing demonstrates the beauty of black hair, while her writing, performing and activism aims to increase women's rights. Rachel and I bought tickets to her show and I made a hair appointment.

Sia drove me to a store that sold hair extensions. Back at her apartment, she weaved the deep red hair into mine, handling my thick hair with ease. In Australia, many hairdressers treat my hair like a wild animal, either terrified or violent with it. It took seven hours to braid my hair.

'Do you want me to style it for you?' Sia asked.

'Yes, please!' She styled my hair in a way I could never dream of replicating, gathered into a cool side-swept knotted bun. It was big, bold, colourful and feisty.

I kept the braids in as long as I could, until one day my poor hair couldn't handle the weight anymore. The final pieces of hair snapped off at the roots and a long braid fell off my head, hitting the floor of our apartment. I jumped, thinking a small animal had run past my feet. As I unwound the braids and removed the glue that held in the extensions, I saw the thick fuzzy hair underneath and my heart sank.

My time in New York City and San Francisco stands out as a short period where I felt positive about my sexuality and appearance. Before the trip, it hadn't occurred to me that I could be proud of my difference, the way I was when I marched down Fifth Avenue holding hands with Rachel or walked around San Francisco with my braided hair.

I don't know if I would braid my hair again. I now realise how ignorant I was about my white privilege. Even without braids, I used to call my hair an 'Afro'. It took me too long to understand that my experiences differ from those of women of colour, and that I need to be careful and intentional when I speak about my hair. The idea of 'choosing' my race, or fluidly fitting into different groups, is problematic. Being mistaken for a woman of colour does not mean I am one. I have had many privileges because my skin isn't darker.

My hair comes with its own identity and set of struggles; my Facebook photos from the last eight years look like a slideshow on my hair's progress that should be put to symphonic music.

Soon after our overseas trip, Rachel and I moved to Melbourne. I continued wearing my hair slick and pulled back for four more years. On the rare occasion that I had it straightened, I received profuse compliments. 'You look so pretty,' people gushed on social media or to my face, not realising the impact that had on me.

In 2011, we quit our jobs and went overseas. In 2012, we decided to get married. The year 2013, following the pattern of the previous two years, was eventful. In addition to our beautiful wedding, I started a Masters degree. I felt drawn to make changes as significant as the inner transformation I was experiencing.

I found a couple of curl-specialist hairdressers. One of them is Neel Morley, who opened Australia's first dedicated curly hair salon, Neel Loves Curls, in Fitzroy. The other is Cherry Bomb Hair in Collingwood. It is a friendly, alternative space, where the hairdressers' dogs sleep by your feet during your haircut. The hairdressers at both salons suggested trying short hair, which made me nervous.

Cutting my hair turned out to be liberating. The shorter cut is alternative enough that queer women identify me as one of them, but femme enough to pass as heterosexual. Better yet, my hair is cool during summer and quick-drying during winter.

Neel has studied curly hair in the United States, where they offer training in 'wavy, curly and multi-cultural hair'. He told me I am lucky to have this hair. When I first met him, he asked, 'You're not one of those crazy people who tries to straighten it, are you?'

When we talked about my hair on my first appointment, which felt like a mix between therapy and an empowering learn-to-love-your-hair session, I couldn't thank him enough.

'It's pretty amazing to have a job where you can make someone think that their hair is awesome, when most of their life they have struggled with it,' Neel told me.

Writing about my hair, I think I wanted to find clear answers. Was the judgement and teasing racial? Was it a form of self-hatred in the Jewish community, a rejection of historically being perceived as Other? Another part of me always found it sexist. The males I knew with curly hair didn't seem to spend all their time trying to 'define their curls'.

People love to make jokes about curly hair, and we are meant to laugh and agree that it is weird or ugly. As an adult, I have been told, 'You look like Sideshow Bob'. This was after having my hair styled specially for a wedding. My hair has been likened to dog fur, or called 'knotted' when it is knot free.

Even though I have gained confidence, I fight the urge to restrain my hair. Then I remind myself that it represents war protests, history and family, overcoming bullies, and bravery. I wear it out, try to ignore the comments and the people who come up uninvited to touch it, and think back to times when I felt accepted and happy being me.

In the week that I finished this essay, Rachel and I married again. On the day of our ceremony, I went to Cherry Bomb. I told my hairdresser, Kate, that I have become more and more tempted to shave my hair off.

'You should do it,' she said, 'even just once, to try it out.' Being a lovely and supportive hairdresser, she didn't push me to do it that day. 'How about we try a pixie cut?' she suggested, 'with soft edges.'

While she cut my hair, she told me that she found short haircuts to be very feminine.

'Why do you think that?' I asked.

'When you cut it, we can see your gorgeous face. Sometimes, hair is a way of hiding.'

With those words, I went to meet my wife.

Reproduced with kind permission from Going Down Swinging.

Thrilled to find a wedding hairdresser
who isn't afraid of my curls.

I'm a Lesbian from Lesbos

Maria Bololia

Being the firstborn came with the responsibility of looking after my three siblings, supporting my battered, overworked and unappreciated mum, serving in our milk bar, and dealing with a postwar tormented father. It became an interesting juggling act. By 10 years of age, I was a champion customer service operator in our North Fitzroy milk bar. My sister was too traumatised to even face strangers and never stepped foot in our small business.

My family was functional only in the way that saw my father working, not drinking or gambling. Both parents battled on without many resources, funds or life experience, surviving the only way they knew how. They worked separate jobs with alternating shifts in a marriage that showed signs of trouble right from the very start. Mum was 12 years younger than Dad. He was one of six and she the youngest of four. Neither really knew why they were marrying nor how to be functional, lacking emotional maturity or much relationship experience. Growing up for them was about survival, finding something to eat, somewhere to live, a job and nothing else. They didn't have the time or the luxury of hours or space in their day to discuss their feelings, voice their concerns. They didn't have mentors to teach them healthy boundaries, risk or protective factors. As a result, they ended up going through the motions, following societal expectations and mimicking what their parents had done.

Both of my parents suffered anxiety, had bouts of anger, were fearful of anything different or new, and had trauma-related issues. They worked hard, almost to the point of exhaustion, to ensure that their children wouldn't ever experience the hunger or lack of career and education opportunities that they had experienced. They purchased everything in bulk, filling their freezers and pantries. They allowed us to eat everything and anything we wanted. In addition, they made sure we always had the best of the best when it came to education, clothes etc. We grew up in a privileged home devoid of much quality time or open contact with our parents.

My relationship with my father was explosive. I was meant to be seen and not heard. I was a very strong young woman with alternative outlooks, beliefs and values. My father was traditional, expecting to be served by his wife and daughters. He tried beating me into submission. It never worked and that angered him even more. He was afraid that I would empower my mum to leave him.

We were sent to Greek school twice a week to learn their language of origin. Maintaining and passing down their culture to their offspring was key. My two brothers and sister and I protested, asking our parents 'Why do we have to go to two schools when everyone else doesn't?' After getting whacked across the behind with a slipper, we were swiftly accompanied around the corner to commence our Greek education. Thinking back, I thank my parents for their insistence and commitment to our language skill development. My current position is with a Greek community organisation working on an LGBTI project. Never could I have even dreamed up a position like this. It's both ironic and a bucket list dream all in one!!

Our first-generation parents had migrated to Australia, the land of opportunity, upholding everything that was Greek. They remained loyal to their country and their upbringing due to feelings of displacement, lack of family support, and unfamiliarity with anything Australian. Greece had moved along in leaps and bounds while they remained stuck in the mindset of yesteryear. Maybe this was their way of feeling connected to everything they had left behind. On the other hand, it was the only thing they had known. Mum came to Australia at 19 years of age, moving into her uncle's house and working for one year before Dad joined her. Their marriage was arranged and they wed immediately. Not long after, I came into the world. Mum was overjoyed with having a girl, my father was disappointed, and he didn't hold back making that known. Much to his dismay, the second child was also a girl, with 22 months the difference in age. After a couple of years, Dad became gravely ill, leaving an eight-year gap before child number three was born. Dad's wishes came true: he was jumping off the roof in joy announcing to the neighbourhood that he had a son. Life for all of us became much less bearable after this. Dad ignored us and treated us with great disdain. He cared only for his son and we became shadows in the distance. This only made me focus more on ensuring my sister's and mother's safety from his violent physical outbursts and emotional abuse.

Three years later my younger brother was born. If my sister and I thought we had it bad, he suffered the worst mistreatment. Dad favoured the older brother and gave next to no attention, time or anything else to the younger one. By this stage I was starting to grow tired of my parents' constant arguing, the dividing and conquering antics of my father, and just wanted out. I felt trapped in an explosive situation, often bordering on some kind of crazy. I was only 15 and wanted to leave home. I often told Mum that there were ways to leave, and women's refuges we could live in. Dad controlled all the money she made, leaving her penniless and powerless with no escape. I often closed myself in my bedroom reading copious volumes, listening to music in the very little spare time I had, finding anything to escape the chaos I was living in.

By the time I turned 16, I informed Mum that I was same-sex attracted. This went down like a lead balloon. Mum spat at me in the face and slapped me so hard that I had a red imprint of her hand on my cheek for days. Mum told me she would never accept my sexuality, as the Church and God forbade it. I was bemused and felt totally betrayed. My expectations weren't that she would embrace me or tell me that everything would be alright but we had been so close before I disclosed my sexuality. It caused our relationship to deteriorate and we became distant. Mum felt ashamed that I was so proudly lesbian and she didn't want our relatives to ever know. Ironically, she was born on the island of Lesbos and calls herself a Lesvia, as everyone from there does. I promptly explained how that word had other connotations in this country.

I was in Year 12 and left home without giving either of my parents an explanation, a clue or anything. I didn't take any of their money, only a small overnight bag of clothes.

Leaving home was the best day of my life and the pathway to my brilliant life. It didn't come without hard times or the times that had my relatives calling my parents frantically to report that I was spotted walking barefoot down a main street, on the television advocating and protesting Bob Hawke's plan to cut the under-18 dole, and so forth! After finding part-time work and moving into a friend's housing commission double-story townhouse, I was able to get on with my lovely lesbian life. This accommodation option was short-lived, as my friend's mother returned from overseas and we were all kicked out. This meant that I needed a place to stay asap.

Another friend asked me to move in with her for a short while in Clifton Hill. There was a period of about six months where I squatted. I joined the Squatters' Union and became passionately involved in the search for empty homes to house the homeless. Having come from a middle-class background, this was definitely a steep street-life learning curve. Times were tough, food and money scarce. This meant that I needed to become more resourceful, opportunistic and optimistic. I survived with the loving support of teachers and friends. They became my adopted family as my own didn't even come looking for me or enquire as to my whereabouts. I was appointed the head of the SRC at a school embracing diversity, with lesbian teachers and six other lesbian classmates. During a humanities class, I was even able to invite a male to female transgender person to facilitate an information session. In addition, I was an advocate for anti-bullying behaviours. The teachers asked me to mentor the younger students who were getting into trouble at school and partaking in risky activities. This helped me feel useful in a way that I had never felt before. I started to entertain the thought of pursuing a career in youth development, which has been my lifelong love.

Mum had a mini breakdown as the neighbours and the Greek community blamed, shamed and told her that I left home to prostitute in St Kilda. I was my mum's strength and biggest supporter. Life was so much more difficult for her without me. This weighed heavily on my young shoulders but I wasn't coping with my father's endless psychotic behaviours. I had gone through the motions of being a good responsible Greek girl and had taken as much as I could of being asked when I was going to marry, how many children I wanted to have, did I have a boyfriend. My answer to this day about when I will marry is, 'The month that doesn't have a Saturday, Sunday, Monday to Friday'. It became a question of my survival against my mother's. She had made her decisions and I had to make mine.

I became an activist, joining a lesbian support group facilitated by two social workers based at the former City of Brunswick called 'What Are Ya?'. We chose this name because most of the kids at school would say 'Why don't you have a boyfriend? What are ya, a lezzo or something?'. Jenny Pausacker (1987) wrote a book about us with the same title. I trained to be a radio console operator at 3CR. I had a weekly show playing my favourite tunes, discussing relevant issues and promoting our political causes. The universe also arranged for me to commence working in child care, setting up a small business running child care for women's conferences. This was followed by coordinating a childcare service in a multicultural women's centre. I also took some time out to manage a natural health and floatation centre as I have a personal interest in healing.

It was 1982, homosexuality was decriminalised and I was having a ball. My new-found freedom gave me the platform to exercise my alternative viewpoints, be a change-maker and live exactly the kind of life that I knew I was destined to. I became involved in the Youth Affairs Council of Victoria and co-wrote a short health and sexuality guide called *The Little Blue Book for Girls* (Charman, 1982). This was banned from school libraries due to the fact it included one paragraph on same-sex attraction and lesbianism. What a shame the relatives didn't find out about this. It would have really given them something to talk about.

I pursued my career in youth development, which included legal advocacy, leadership programs, arts, life skill development sessions, young women's empowerment programs, learner driver education and, the best of all, LGBTI programs. Young people were challenged by everything that was me. I was delighted by their transparency, curiosity and tenacity. They have this knack of saying exactly what they mean and meaning what they say. Some told me that I set a bad example due to my hair, piercing, tattoos and the clothes I wear. Others said I confused them because they couldn't work out if I was straight or bisexual. I was too comfortable with guys to be gay and too chilled about everything to be bisexual. This always made me laugh on the inside. I always replied with, 'I'm tri-sexual.' The young people thought that I was always on something as I seemed way too happy for someone who wasn't.

Thankfully, my mother has been supportive in terms of meeting my partners, accepting them at family functions and celebrations. Interestingly enough, the partner she has embraced the most is the Greek. Yet, she was the most difficult in that she was closeted, bottled up her feelings, gambled and had too much of a liking for the amber fluid.

Mum will never fully accept my sexuality due to her religious beliefs. I respect her right to believe what she must. When it comes to who she always runs to for support, it has and always will be her big proud lesbian daughter. I think the pride I take in rejoicing in my sexuality is what irks Mum the most. If I felt ashamed or remorseful for all that I am, she may have felt happier about it. But I love all that I am and the life I lead. Wouldn't change it for anything or everything in this whole wide world.

xxx

PS: My mum voted YES after vowing she never would! I downloaded the Marriage Equality YES campaign brochure and info pages in Greek and gave them to her to read. She did so after a couple of days.

My mum's first granddaughter and apple of her eye is also a lesbian and trying for an IVF baby. So I then asked Mum if she received an invitation to her granddaughter's big fat Greek gay wedding, would she go? Mum shot me a death stare and told me, 'She could get married in the park and no one's stopping her from doing so.'

I informed her that this had no legal grounds in Australia and didn't give us any of the rights that heterosexuals took for granted. In addition,

I explained how the YES vote was a civil or political union as the Europeans call them and not religious ones.

Mum informed me a couple of days later that she voted YES! Incredible for a mum who's so brainwashed by the Greek Orthodox Church.

But, after all, my mum was born in Lesbos!

Maria on her 19th birthday

The Hippocratic Oath, Western Medicine, and the Children of Hermes and Aphrodite

Tony Briffa

Multiculturalism defines Australia and what we think of as the Australian way of life. Our beliefs, values, aspirations and sense of community are all personally influenced by our own feelings of isolation or inclusion, our own feelings of being *apart from* or *a part of* the wider community in which we live. Australian values are really, with two notable exceptions, an average of the many values that generations before us brought with them to Australia when they travelled here.

Students of philosophy or ethics will tell you that truly ethical behaviour is an average of behaviours measured across all of society, not the subjectively measured personal moral standards of a few who hold themselves out as examples of proper behaviour. The wider the diversity of the population and therefore the variation of measured behaviours, the more meaningful the average and ethical standards of that society. By this measure, Australia should in theory be a world-leading nation, one that sets an example for others to follow. In practice we often fall short.

There are two exceptions to the rule that our Australian average of behaviour is built from our diverse cultural background. The first exception is the traditional owners of Australia, as we have not yet really begun to recognise and embrace their culture to the point where it has an impact on our overall sense of community and of community standards. This is sad for the isolation this must inevitably lead to for our traditional peoples and sad for the loss to the community of an important piece of the puzzle that binds us together as a single people with diverse and unique backgrounds.

Sad also then that the second group in our society that has not had the opportunity it might otherwise have had to positively impact on our values is the LGBTIQ community. The same tragic consequences of this have been our own sense of isolation and the lost opportunity for societal behaviour to more closely reflect the ethical ideal.

In my own case, the impact of multiculturalism upon behaviours accepted by society, and the consequences of failing to recognise and embrace this, has had a profound effect for another reason. As some of you will know, professional ethics that determine medical treatments in some instances are also influenced by wider societal beliefs and behaviours, often leading to doctors taking on a role that is as much societal constructionist as it is healer.

I am proud of my Maltese heritage. Both of my parents chose Australia as their new home during the 1950s and 1960s. They met and married here in Australia and settled down in Altona, which has been home to me my entire life. Like many traditional families of European background, they chose to share their new-found home of safety and acceptance with children of their own. I have two sisters and three brothers all with their own children now; your typically small Maltese family!

Depending on when it was you asked my parents about their children, they would tell you they had three girls and three boys or, more lately, two girls and four boys. When I was born one of twins at the local Altona hospital, the attending physician wasn't sure if I was a boy or a girl.

I would later learn that I was born with Partial Androgen Insensitivity Syndrome, or PAIS, one of what are now referred to by the medical profession as intersex variations. These variations result in the birth of children with reproductive anatomy or sex chromosomes that are neither exclusively male or female. The initial attending physician stated that she thought I was a boy, but that I would have to be taken to the Royal Children's Hospital in Melbourne for a specialist opinion.

At that stage of their lives, English was very much a second language for my parents, so they understood very little of what they were being told and even less what it all meant. They dutifully delivered me to the specialists at the Royal Children's Hospital for a second opinion. The opinion they received was that I should be surgically altered to make my genitals look like those of a girl, and that I should thereafter be raised as a girl.

Although at this point there were considerable cultural differences and a lack of medical understanding to be overcome, my parents had heard all they needed to realise that none of this sounded right. They told the doctors that they believed God had made me the way I was for a reason, and it was up to God to decide what should happen from here, not doctors. They took me home, untouched, trusting that their own cultural and religious beliefs and innate knowledge of what is best for their child would be all they needed to guide me through life.

As things turned out the specialists at the Royal Children's were not going to leave things as they were. They turned up at my parents' house later that night, arguing that God worked through doctors by giving them the knowledge to do what is right in cases like mine. Unfortunately, medical interpretations of the wishes of God can be wrong. Keep this thought as we will return to it and my story in a while.

The history of ethics is very much entwined with that of religion. It must be so, as to deny that religion had any place in moulding our current social framework would be very naïve. If we talk of the influence of religion, we are not talking solely of Christianity but of the many religions that have contributed to our modern understanding of ethics and society.

Those of you who have studied the history of modern ethics will realise the very important role the early Greek philosophers played in the development of modern conceptual understandings of ethics. In turn, many of their philosophical points of view were influenced by the roles Greek Gods played in the social cultures of the time.

At this point, it will be helpful to turn to the Hippocratic Oath, the oath taken by doctors that binds them to observe the code of behaviour and practice observed by Hippocrates, a Greek physician often called the father of modern medicine. The Oath is commonly cited in brief as 'first do no harm', but it is actually more involved than that. The original version of the Oath translated from Greek starts:

> I swear by Apollo Physician and Asclepius and Hygieia and Panaceia and all the gods and goddesses, making them my witnesses, that I will fulfil according to my ability and judgment this oath and this covenant.

Apollo was, among other things, God of healing power. Apollo is in good company when swearing this before all the Greek Gods as among them is Hermes, God of science, and Aphrodite, Goddess of beauty and love.

The modern version most often used now is not an oath made before the Greek Gods as witnesses. In its simplified form, however, the Hippocratic Oath warns of the evils of over-treatment and therapeutic neglect, and contains a reminder that a doctor is still a member of society with all the obligations and responsibilities this entails.

Returning to my story and the comments doctors made to my parents about their doing God's work, nowhere in either version of the Hippocratic Oath is this written. In fact, we find in the modern version of the Oath, 'Above all, I must not play at God.'

Interesting also that the original word for the term 'intersex' was *hermaphrodite*, coming from the Greek Hermaphroditus. Hermaphroditus was the son of Hermes and Aphrodite, all before whom the Hippocratic Oath is sworn.

Fable has it that the nymph Salmacis was so enamoured of Hermaphoditus that she wished 'the twain might become one flesh'. Her wish was granted by the gods and the two became one. Fable also has it that all persons who bathed in the fountain Salmacis in Caria became hermaphrodites.

People with intersex variations have been recorded in mythology, religious texts and more recently in medical and scientific records. Angels are said to be not exclusively of either sex. Some shamans, healers of the Mayan and other early advanced civilisations, were said to be chosen from those born neither male nor female because of the special healing power they were believed to possess.

How is it then that people who have long existed, been accepted, even revered in some cultures, are seen as something less than worthy by so-called educated Western doctors? How is it that these same doctors can swear an oath before God about the beloved child they are content to medically modify because it suits them to do so now that medical science is capable?

My parents were right when they believed I should be left as nature made me, a special person of both sexes for whom the gods had a special place. Their religious beliefs and cultural instincts, which led them to believe my path in life should be something for God to decide, were clearly the better choice for me, but regrettably not the path my life was to follow.

The medical profession was able to convince my parents that the correct path to take was to remove any part of my anatomy that might offend when raising a child as a girl. They convinced my parents that they knew better than to trust I would find my way in life without their intervention, something that my parents and I regret to this day.

Many now adult children and their parents for whom these decisions have been made also regret the outcome of similar decisions as their lives became a series of seemingly endless surgeries, medical check-ups, and roles as medical curiosities to both photograph and put on display for medical students. I am sure this was not what the gods had in mind for the child of Hermes and Aphrodite.

Culture is so much more than being of non-English speaking background, so much more than being a person indigenous to a particular place or region, so much more than skin colour, sex, sexual identity, sexual orientation, sex characteristics or even genetics as a whole. Culture is a rich mix of our collective experiences that has the potential to create a society of balance, acceptance and value.

As we have heard, part of the Hippocratic Oath is a reminder to the medical profession that they are still part of society. For the medical profession to be truly a part of society, they need to embrace the cultural differences that make up society as a whole, that decide what is truly ethical behaviour, and apply this to the professional ethics that guide them as physicians.

The importance of administering only that medical aid needed for the health and wellbeing of their patients seems to be getting lost in the modern age of advances of medical technology and technique. Doctors seem to be stepping over that fine line where therapeutic value is less important than the development of technical skills – the very line the Hippocratic Oath warns should not be crossed. In looking to increasing technical skill as an answer for social considerations, it seems doctors have designs of 'playing at God' rather than trusting that these children of Hermes and Aphrodite are of God's design. Again, the Hippocratic Oath warns against this.

A medical professional I know once rationalised the objections against medical intervention on people with intersex variations by stating they believed it was people with intersex variations with poor surgical outcomes who were dissatisfied. They believed that better surgical outcomes would reduce the number of complaints about medical intervention. This demonstrates, very regrettably in my view, that medical professionals are being encouraged to turn to better technical outcomes rather than to consider other cultural solutions that exist elsewhere in the world. It seems it is perfectly reasonable for those cultures to turn to Western medicine for solutions, but not the reverse.

It is not just the medical profession that needs to look outside narrowly defined cultural expectations to ensure society is allowed to prosper for the realisation of all hopes and the inclusion of all cultures. People who make and enforce laws, and people who use those laws to achieve outcomes, need to make sure they also look outside their own cultural beliefs.

Society is made up of many cultural backgrounds and attempts to subsume these for the sake of expedience or advantage, against the wishes and at the expense of these groups, is just another form of minority oppression. Likewise, we need to ensure we respect the differing experiences of other groups, and ensure we speak taking these views into account rather than on their behalf or using their experiences as our own.

I mentioned earlier that I am proud of my Maltese heritage; I am also proud of my intersex heritage. As a heritage that has a very long history, I believe having an intersex variation is nothing to be ashamed of despite the fact that some would have had my parents and I feel ashamed, as they still to this day try to convince others.

People with intersex variations have only relatively recently found their own voice. We work to ensure that the social and medical needs of those with intersex variations have a voice that is understood in its own right. It is often the cultural examples of other societies rather than Western understanding of intersex variations that is key to achieving the best way to approach treatment and so it would have been in my case.

Part of introducing these other cultural concepts into Western society is accepting that there are people born who in some way bridge the so-called divide between male and female. Many other groups in the LGBTIQ community would benefit from wider understanding of this concept.

I think this is a much more valuable role for the children of Hermes and Aphrodite than the one the Western medical profession currently has in mind for us.

Surviving Our Cabaret

Paul Capsis

I remember a month before Trump was elected, when it was definite we were doing the musical *Cabaret*, I said to the producer, 'You're clever. You're so smart.'

He went, 'Why?'

I went, 'Because of what's going on in the world.'

He went, 'Oh, I never thought about it.'

I went, 'You've timed it well, love.'

The day I read the script for *Cabaret* was the day Trump was elected.

I was in the library, Surry Hills, Sydney. I read it from beginning to end. It's quite a detailed little script, not an easy read. My hair was standing up. By the time I'd finished reading, my Facebook was full of, 'Oh my God, he's getting in! He's winning!' It was chilling because for me he has only displayed qualities you never want in a leader. And just when you think we're moving forward.

That's why I think it's so timely, doing *Cabaret*. It's a jewel and it has the politics and it has the ugliness of then and now. Like my character, the MC, says, 'Everything's beautiful,' and yet everything's also disturbing. When I was young and saw the film, I saw Joel Grey in the role. I found him very creepy. The ambiguity of him. You don't know where the MC sits. What is he politically? Is he a Nazi? Does he end up in the gas chambers as a Jew, as a queer? I actually think he escapes and lives a completely different life somewhere else because I think of him as like a cockroach. I think of the MC as a survivor and I identify with him as a survivor. I identify with him as a person who knows how to exist. We have people in our world, our Cabaret now, who don't know where they are politically, they don't know who they are for, and they trust people like Trump.

I want that ambiguity to come through on stage. The MC is humorous but the MC watches the audience. I'm observing the audience and making them think about their stage of the everyday, while they think they are watching us on stage. Gale Edwards, the director, said to me, 'You have to trick us. You have to pull us in, and then you give it to us. Paul, come out, sit there, watch.' I find it exhausting though. It makes the audience uncomfortable. I get the audience staring back at me.

I'm old enough to remember the progress we made and how we've gone back. Now we have Milo Yiannopoulos, openly gay, stating gay rights are detrimental to humanity, and that gay men should get back in the closet. That right-wing gay element has always been there. I read this extraordinary book by Otto Friedrich, *Before the Deluge* (1972), about the Weimar Republic and he says that a lot of the Nazis were gay. All the gays went to the gas chamber unless you were a Nazi gay and they were, in fact, the worst. If you were a gay Nazi and you saw some queen, effeminate, it was 'gas chamber, bitch'. If these right-wing, nasty gays could do that now, they would. They would put me in the gas chamber now if they could. Like Roy Cohn, leader of the CIA and J. Edgar Hoover, leader of the FBI, targeting gay men. The Jews did that too to each other. People will do anything to try and survive.

I'm a fighter. I always have been and I always will be. I think the one thing that people have to do is they have to be activated. When I was a young person I felt there were other young people who were totally unaware of what had gone on 20 years before us, queers who made it possible for us. There was a lack of knowledge or understanding that there were people responsible for what we managed to have. I remember I was still in high school, before AIDS, going on a march for our rights to exist as homosexuals, not to be thrown in prison; I remember thinking how dangerous it was that I could be on television, that my family might see me because I wasn't out, and how united we were underground when we faced danger on the surface. We existed underneath, we were a strong culture, we were naughty and we were bad, and we were revolutionary. In a funny way I accepted that about myself and about the world I was part of.

I remember when the laws changed, when we were allowed to be homosexuals and wouldn't go to gaol. That was extraordinary but it was short-lived, I felt, because then we got AIDS. To me it was the worst thing imaginable. It didn't garner any shame, even though I had a very strong religious upbringing. I never believed for a minute that this was God's punishment. I thought it was a scientific catastrophe. I was young; I didn't understand the whole idea of being homosexual, the whole idea of love and relationships. I had a heterosexual mythical idea of relationships. I thought: you meet a man, you fall in love, and you stay together and love each other forever. I found that wasn't the case and the AIDS epidemic was a heartless result of our lifestyle, which I hadn't really taken part in at that point in my life, which is kind of, maybe, a blessing, but I did lose a lot of friends. I went through a very difficult period psychologically, emotionally, because of what was happening all around me; people my age, people younger, people older. We were losing so many people. I was gripped with fear. I was certain that I was going to die as well. I was thinking, 'Why am I not going to die? I'm not better than anyone else so I'm going to die too.' By some miracle I didn't get it. I may have done less stuff but I wasn't a saint and I'm very lucky to be alive. I never believed in condemning people who had it.

So I've seen the legal change. I saw the gay community be a very political, extraordinary cultural energy in Sydney, and I then I saw it change. I became disappointed by the gay community that I thought I was a part of, because it was funny about people who were ethnic. It was a shock. I'm like, 'Wait a minute. I was born here. I'm Australian,' but they didn't see me like that. I got that exclusion pretty much until the film *Head On*. That was when my career and my life changed, from doing that film. It made me experience fame for a moment but I also realised that I was in a tiny box. I was always going to be seen as ethnic and as a person who has played a transgendered or trans-identified, or maybe transvestite, character and, therefore, I was put in that box. Forevermore my career was about playing those characters. It's only been in the last few years where I've played male roles like the MC, Quentin Crisp, Riff-Raff in the *Rocky Horror Show*, and my own show about my grandma, *Angela's Kitchen*.

With *Head On*, I had people from both ethnic and Anglo sides furious with me. I had Anglo gays come up to me and go, 'I hate that film. That film depicts us backwards and presents us as whores.' I'd say, 'But we are. That's who we are. Isn't it nice that they're showing an ethnic gay story for a change?' Their response was offensive to me. How dare they talk to me about how we should be presented! For me *Head On* is the TRUTH. These characters all exist. This community exists, this lifestyle exists, and these people are real. Ethnic homosexuals: we are here, we're part of this culture. My family wanted to be proud but it was difficult for them to be proud of this film. My Dad is Greek. He didn't condemn it or say anything negative, but I could sense it wasn't easy for him to watch it.

I have issues with the Marriage Equality movement because I think there's other shit going down that's far more important to talk about. I mean, yes,

I want it for those who want it but I can't help think it is part of this conservative Milo Yiannopoulos stuff. I'm happy to have Milo be just Milo. Milo can describe all those types of homosexuals who are like him, who think like him, who are money– and-class minded, feel racially superior, but they're not. I had a massive fight with somebody on Facebook when I put up anti-Trump stuff. This homosexual attacked my friends for their comments because he was anti-Hillary. I wrote this person a private message because there was a lot of verbal abuse coming from him. I said to him, 'If the right come to take us all away to the gas chambers, you'd be the first they'd take. Don't think for a minute that they're going to look after you.' Anyway, I cut him off. I got rid of him. Those right-wing homosexuals are thinking, 'I'm not like those other homosexuals. I'm better than them. I'm wise' or 'I'm Christian' or whatever. No, I say, 'You take it up the ass, bitch, and you're like everyone else. That's how they see you.'

I understand where they're coming from. They don't want to lose their power. I get that. They don't want to lose their position. I get that. I get the whole Trump thing, the Brexit thing. I've been here too long. I know what this thing is. I experienced this as a kid: 'You filthy wog bastard, get out of our country. You take our jobs, you take our homes.' I got it from teachers for the gay thing. The Greeks and Turkish hated me too because I had the homosexual thing going down. It was a hate fest. Bizarre. I went to Greece a couple years ago. Full on homophobia in my face. I said, 'I like the sea, the land, and the trees, the history, but not the people.' They were dreadful. They laughed in my face. I thought I was going to be drowned on this particular island in Greece. That's how much bad energy I got from the people.

I've found my people in the actor community. I cherish that. I found them by being persistent. I don't go, 'Oh, I want to be a big, commercial star like that person over there because they've got the right Anglo blood going on. The blue eyes.' We still keep doing period dramas where wogs don't exist in this country. Why do they keep doing that? Cos they never have to give me a gig? That's okay. I'm very critical when I see things that are made now about history where I don't see the people represented. For example, the film *The Dressmaker*. I left going, 'Great film. Judy Davis, great actress. But for 1950s Australia, that little country town they represented was the whitest place and I don't believe it.' I didn't believe anything about that film except the performances. They couldn't even do a story on television about the two famous crime queens in Australia: Diane Hurst and Kate Leigh from Surry Hills in *Razor*. They put two attractive women in it. My family knew Kate Leigh. She lived around the corner. This woman was rough. So was Tilly Devine. Surry Hills stank. It was rough. But instead they presented pretty people, skinny people, glamorous, glitzy, glossy; everything was shiny, everything was beautiful. I watched it and went, 'What a load of bullshit.' With the men, at least, they had a few wogs in there. Rough wogs, mafia. I guess that's something. I'm like, 'My family told me these stories. They never mentioned any gloss or glamour. They talked about the roughness and what these people got up to.' Why can't they tell those stories? Why can't they be honest? Because the white people are up there and they still have all the power. This is Trump, this is Brexit. 'We are still the power even if we're clinging and clawing to what's left because we fear it's all going. The last gasp.'

And all these wog names are starting to turn up on the bloody right side of politics! Cory Bernardi, 'Hey Italiano, where do you come from?' This is brainwashing by the white Australians: 'We're better. We're Christian. We're better than the Africans, Muslims, the Hindus, the Chinese.' I feel that we're going to get a wave of new conservatives: Asian, Muslim, coming through. The Anglos might not like your religion and your God but at least you're conservative. I have a feeling that a lot of the new migration is conservative. Even though whiteys don't like them. They rather that – the conservatism – than the lefties. Migrants have changed and are changing the face of our country, sometimes in a negative way. Just like there are the conservative Italians and the conservative nasty Greeks, there are conservative nasty Maltese. They think they're better than everyone else. They don't like the Asians, they don't like the Muslims. They use the same words that were used against them. My family has done that. They forget. Both my grandmothers, Maltese and Greek, used to remind me of how they were treated when they came to this country. My grandmother came here in 1948 from Malta, the Greek grandmother in 1958 from Egypt. They were not accepted. They were filth, even though people didn't know anything about their culture. Even though they were Christian, they were the Other, and they were coming here and changing the culture and Australians didn't like it. Like what's happening now.

I think a lot about racism, and where we all come from. I've always obsessively wondered about my Maltese grandmother, who had very dark skin and an Afro. I used to stare at her and think, 'She's got African blood.' I was fascinated with that. 'Why does my grandmother have hair that grows like that?' It was really hard, steel wool hair that was thick until the day she died. Two of her sons, Charlie and Tony, have very, very dark skin. In photos they all look Indigenous. I would look at Indigenous women and think, 'Why does my grandmother look like these Aboriginal women?'

I'm anti anything that's repressive. I don't care what religion it is. In fact, I don't care who your God is. If you repress women, if you repress homosexuals, I hate you, you're my enemy. And I know you, I'll identify you. My Greek side were kicked out of Egypt so you could say they were like refugees. My grandmother's siblings went all over the world. They didn't all go to Australia. She never saw her siblings again. I was fascinated with how many people identified with my Maltese grandmother in *Angela's Kitchen*: Irish, Italian, Greek. A Brazilian woman one night sat in the front row with her husband, I was only 15 minutes into the show, and she was doubled over crying. It was very distracting because I didn't know what was wrong with her. I thought maybe she was sick and she needed to leave the theatre. She looked identical to my cousin so I thought, 'She's definitely Maltese and she's responding to the story.' I came out after the show and went straight up to her, 'You're Maltese,' and she went, 'No, I'm Brazilian. That was my mother's story.'

When you do a one-person show you really notice things, people's reactions: whether the people are interested or hating it, or loving it. *Angela's Kitchen* was probably the most draining experience of my career. I've never been as depleted after a season of a show. It was like I had my grandmother with me all the time. And she is with me all the time, but in that play she was present, you know? That was difficult also because I miss her terribly. What was also draining is that I was meeting families, so many Maltese, I heard so many stories. I'll never forget the stories. Generations of people coming to the show. 'This is our grandmother. She's never been to the theatre before in Australia, and never in her life.' I got a lot of that. I got stories like, 'My grandmother killed an Italian in the war. The plane went down in Malta and she came with the frying pan. He was injured and she killed him'. I'll never forget that story. The war made people crazy. The constant bombing. Six years of bombing. My grandmother talked about that. People did crazy, crazy things. They're doing it now in different regions, different religions. We've seen that horror footage of a woman being shot in the head on the street by ISIS.

Fight, fight, fight, fight, fight! You've just got to keep going and suffer the consequences. I'm an artist and dedicated to my work, and I've paid a price for that and I'm fine with that. Because that's what I wanted. That's what I love. That's my passion. If it means I've lost stuff, I'm fine with that. Yes, I'm using the stage so we can all reflect on our stages, our Cabarets.

If I've lost things because I'm a homosexual, I'm good with that. If I've lost things because I'm a wog, I'm good with that. I embrace that. I want it to smother me, to cover me, to drown me. What I will never do is conform to whatever those others think of me. That's what I say to young people. You have to be strong in yourself and you will find your people.

Holy boy, 1971, Surry Hills Convent

'Everything changed except my mind'

Carolina

Hi, I'm Carolina, and I'd like to tell you my story. I'm a 25-year-old transgender Muslim refugee, born in Tehran, the capital city of Iran.

I had a very happy childhood, surrounded by a loving family and many friends. Sadly, by the time I was in high school, a single-sex boys' school, the problems began. In a country where you are expected to be a boy or girl, I no longer fitted in. The boys began to make fun of me, harassing and bullying me because they saw me as weak, with a feminine voice, and not what boys should be. I couldn't stand that school. I couldn't focus on my study so I was also very poor in my grades. I felt stuck in that school. The other students, even those I had grown up with, saw me as a new person, developing very, very differently to them during puberty.

I suffered a deep depression and I didn't finish my schooling. I just had to leave school because I was so distressed. But all the time I was at home, I remained so depressed. I thought, 'Why am I different to other people?' At home, some family and friends told me, 'Carolina, go to the doctor. Take a mild hormone, your voice will get masculine. Everything will change'.

Yes, everything changed. My voice changed. My body changed; it got hairy. My face got hairy and by then I was only 16. Everything changed except my mind. I was thinking like a girl and that didn't change.

I became even more depressed, and sometimes thought, 'I'll kill myself'. I didn't have a good time, a good life, outside in the community, always hiding like many transgender people in Iran.

Then my family took me to another doctor who confirmed I am transgender. She was kind and said, 'You need to take care of yourself, Carolina. There are other people the same as you, and you need to accept that, and you cannot help it.'

So I stopped using testosterone, and I started finding other transgender people. I wanted to go into the transgender community and I started to dress as a girl. In Iran, this means wearing a hijab. So I used to wear a hijab to go out, but the police caught me and arrested me for wearing a hijab and being homosexual. In Iran, if you are transgender, you have to have surgery and be in a heterosexual relationship. Otherwise, you are a homosexual and this is a very big crime. And if the police and government can find any evidence that you are a homosexual, they can harm you. They can kill you. But I was transgender and I didn't want the operation at that time, so the government gave me a very hard time, even coming in to my home to arrest me.

If I tried to go as a boy in the community, people would make fun of me, insult and bully me. So I was uncomfortable going outside as a boy. If I tried to go as a girl, the government would catch me and give me a very hard time.

That's why I made a decision: 'Okay, I am in a very oppressive country but this is more and more unsafe for me.' I made a very, very risky decision that I would come to Australia by boat, and yes, this is a very, very dangerous way to come to Australia. I would leave Iran illegally and come to Australia illegally. It was so frightening even thinking about this. But I had read in a book a long time before that if you cannot live freely where you are, you have to change where you are. It means you have to change your life; you may have to leave your country. But I also knew there was a 50 per cent chance that I would die in the ocean.

I left Iran and flew to Indonesia. I found a person who asked for a lot of money to send me from Indonesia to Christmas Island by fishing boat. I accepted. I gave a lot of money to him, and I accepted that I would either die or stay alive, and if I survived I would have a happy life. I could not return to Iran now, as I would be going back to die.

Oh my God, the boat journey was very bad because it was a very, very little boat, and it was like a very small house, with about 150 people, women and children, many cultures, like Afghan, Persian, African. We had to lie under covers in the boat. Everybody was crushing each other, and sometimes huge waves would come in from the ocean and people, children, were crying because the ocean is very wild and very scary. We were two days in the ocean and it was a very, very hard time. I had never been in the ocean and I got very seasick and I was trying to sleep all the time, and thinking, 'I cannot swim. If anything happens to the boat, I will die.' I had a life-jacket on but I kept thinking, 'How long am I going to survive in the ocean?' It was so scary, so scary.

I arrived on Christmas Island very weak. The Australian government caught me on Christmas Island and put me in the refugee camp. The Australian government was a little bit hard on me but they saw there were many Persian people in the refugee camp who did not accept me and made it very hard for me to be there. I was placed with families of women, men, children, because they didn't send me to the single refugees section because I was transgender.

So the government sent me to a special refugee camp in Adelaide where they were nice to me. It was like a gaol, yeah, it was hard not being allowed out of the refugee camp, but they were very respectful and they wanted me to pass these courses, where they interview you about why you came to Australia, and they did the ink-blot test, psychology tests. So many courses and I passed the system and was processed to come into the Australian community. They asked me where I wanted to go. I said Melbourne and after that they released me to the outside and I started living in Australia as a transgender refugee.

In Iran, I had the same language, same culture, family and some friends. That country was mine and then everybody forced me to leave. I love my country, I love Iran. It's my food, my language. I was living there most of my life with the Persian culture and people, but unfortunately I had to leave because of my government. In Australia, I didn't know any English. I didn't know any information about the country. I didn't know anything about the culture. I didn't know anything. After 20 years in my country, I was told I was no longer safe, and I decided to go to a country I don't know.

It was a very, very hard time in the beginning because I was really depressed. I couldn't speak with anyone. Always, when I was speaking with someone, I had to get an interpreter, and that was so uncomfortable for me as a transperson. I couldn't go to the English class because so many other refugees who hated me were also in the English class. That's why I tried to learn at home, reading books and using translations, and talking with people a little bit to practise my English. I was so lonely.

I had a good case manager from AMES who would ask me, 'Do you need to go to any doctors, a dentist, any health clinic?' If I wanted to book anything, needed to find a house or something, they used to help us because we didn't know anything and they used to teach us about Australian systems, but now there isn't much help anymore because the government doesn't support them as much. Everything gets less funding.

To be honest, transgender Muslims need more help because they are Muslim and transgender. It's a very big deal for the Muslim religion, because it doesn't permit these things at all. An example of a huge problem as a transgender Muslim is housing. It's very hard for me having to share a house with people because some people accept me, but so many people don't accept me. Since living in Australia the last five years, it's not easy for me to find somewhere to live. They either don't like that I am transgender or they don't like that I am a Muslim and a refugee, or they don't like the mixture of those things. For example, I ended up homeless for two months, and then the homelessness services found me a share house. They chose it for me, and said, 'It's a good house, a cheap house so go out there.' Now I don't judge any culture but this time it was Bangladeshi Muslims I was sharing with who made many problems for me. They dirtied my bed, messed up everything in my room, and told me they would make me leave.

I went somewhere else. Maybe I wasn't lucky in housing, because in this Muslim house, they also forced me to leave the house. I was very emotional and I went to my case manager again and they found me a house with a Vietnamese owner, and he was living there. I started living there, but unfortunately he just wanted to use me to do sex work for him. For example, one time I was sitting in my room, and he knocked and came in and said, 'Okay, this Indian guy's going to have sex with you. He will give you money. Let's have fun with him, and he will give you some money. It will be helpful for you.' I was shocked. To bring a customer to me, in the privacy of my house. I went to my counsellor and he said, 'It's a shocking thing.' They sent people to the house, and they asked the owner why he did that. He said, 'Oh, I just bring my friends to have fun, you know?'

I wish I was back in the time of my Islamic Persian culture, about 1,000 years ago, when there were transgender people and they were more accepted than they are now. I wish I could say to Imams, 'Please, say something about us, that we are good people. We are not bad people. Tell your people who respect you to respect us as well. We are not evil. We are just human, and your God created us. I didn't want to be trans, seriously. I wanted to be a boy or a girl. That's why when I was 16, I used the testosterone, and I damaged my body because I was trying to be a boy. It didn't work for me.'

I wish I could say to Australians, 'I don't want to hurt anyone. Muslim people are not dangerous. It's only because of politics, because of money that the governments are fighting with each other. Nothing else. The government doesn't care about community, we have to understand each other.' Governments just want oil, gas, and everybody says, 'Okay, Iran is bad because it is independent. We want their oil, everything.' No community is all bad or all good. There are good people and bad people. Islam is not bad. I'm Muslim transgender and I didn't change my religion. I'm happy that I'm Muslim, but you have decided to show Islam as very bad; as if to be a Muslim is to be bad. We love people, we love humanity and we respect all religions, all cultures.

I'm transgender. My religion doesn't quite accept me, but still I love my religion because this is an important part of my life. I'm connected to some accepting Muslim groups now to have a chat, not feel alone, which feels very good. When I grew up and found that I could choose my faith, I made the decision: 'Okay, I'm going to be Muslim. I choose this.'

www.irqr.net **IRQR** info@irqr.net

Iranian Railroad for Queer Refugees

From Alternate Dimensions

Paula Carpio and Naya Rizwan

A 25-year-old Sunni Muslim Pakistani born in the Punjab region.

A 30-year-old born into a Catholic family in the devoutly religious country of the Philippines.

We come from two completely different worlds – alternate dimensions, it sometimes feels. Never in our wildest dreams did we ever expect to fall in love (let alone cross paths). But here we are.

For both of us, coming to terms with and embracing our sexuality, owning our own gender, was more than just 'coming out'. It was (and still is for one of us) a hard-fought battle to be free of the conditioning we were subjected to from the day we were born.

Paula: I didn't grow up in quite as strict a background as Naya did. I have been out to my immediate and extended family since I was 16. It wasn't easy dealing with how my family reacted to these changes, but I still had the power and autonomy to press on and be me, so I never understood why Naya couldn't just stand up to her family. I never understood just how sensitive and complex her navigating this entire thing would be as the roots of culture and faith were so much deeper than they are in my family.

Naya: For me it was eye-opening that a family could be like Paula's because growing up having a boyfriend before you can be arranged to be married was a difficult enough thing. I always had cousins hiding their boyfriends from their parents, but being in a gay relationship was completely not even an option. Coming into Paula's family and seeing how they operate and how welcoming and open they are with each other was quite surprising. I was always questioning myself and my identity because I got to a certain age where I needed to have a boyfriend or felt like everyone had a boyfriend. Why didn't I have a boyfriend? Why didn't I feel attracted to guys? I found myself just going from one guy to another but none of the relationships worked because I just didn't feel right. Eventually, thank God for Tinder, there was a night where I just came across Paula. I couldn't go out there in the real world and meet girls. I knew I wanted to, I had a lot of lesbian friends at university and I always found myself really being able to be more friendly and be real around them, yet I had this entire different personality at home. Being able to safely do that behind a phone screen was easier.

I think Paula was lucky because she had all her family here. Her grandparents, uncles, and aunties, they all came together. With me, my dad was a skilled immigrant, he came here in the 90s. My parents left all their families in Pakistan and India, so when they came here it was just them. The Indian community and the Pakistani family in Melbourne became their family. It's hard because you may cause your family to lose their friends and community, and losing dignity and respect which is built on the success of their kids. If it wasn't the fear of being extradited from the community, being ostracised, and the shame, then my family would completely accept me. They've met Paula under other circumstances and they've loved her. They've commented on how great a person she is, which is ironic because they would never accept her as my partner, but if she was a male they would welcome her with open arms. She's successful, she's really caring, and respectable.

Paula's previous relationships were fairly easy in that she never had to go through so much and fight just to be with someone. I feel like my relationship is valid and the person I love is a valid person, and the love I feel for that person is valid, so I feel like it's important to make sure that people see that as valid. It's not just a lifestyle or a phase or this horrid brainwashing system or the result of the gay agenda.

Paula: We've come a long way. We've learnt so much and immersed ourselves in our communities. We've talked to others who come from the same or similar backgrounds. This was especially important for Naya as she realised that she was never alone in her journey. It was extremely valuable that she found the courage to reach out to the appropriate group of people (from the same faith who understand how to navigate the space). There was a sense of belonging finally, no longer having to feel the guilt of being who she is and loving who she loves. These people exist and they are fighting similar battles.

From our journey, we would love to share the message to anyone going through this same struggle: love who you are regardless of what others impose on you; spread the radical notion that family and love can be found in whoever your heart chooses. It is the biggest gift to now be part of a community that doesn't base our acceptance or inclusion on how much we can 'assimilate'. We want anyone who comes from the backgrounds and environments that we do to know that your ability to water down your true self and conform to someone else's idea of who you are is not the sum of who you are, and it can be a very lonely and sad place, but stay strong.

Coming to terms with our sexualities and reconciling it with the faiths that we were brought up in is a long, gruelling journey – but one that we go through each day with pride, abundance, love and gratitude.

Reach out if you feel ready and if it is safe. We all need support, belonging and the tools/education to help navigate these often scary and complicated spaces.

Pink balloon Paula, cheeky glasses Naya, image by Rob Chiarolli

'Bless me for I am gay'
My journey from activism to acceptance
Shanton Chang

I am a tea-loving, gayming, spiritually Catholic, moderate, middle-aged, gay-identifying, life-partnered, Australian Malaysian academic, who is also an oldest son in a Chinese family . . . and this is part of my story.

When I was asked to write this, I struggled to explain who I was. Focusing on the 'multicultural queer' aspects alone would have marginalised other intersections in my life. Therefore, I was reluctant to write this story because it meant I had to think about who I was, and that could be a very uncomfortable journey. I decided to start my story with my second journey to Australia, specifically Melbourne, when I had acknowledged my gay identity more fully. The year was 1997.

I wanted to be out so I could relax and be me. – Melissa Etheridge

A key reason for coming back to Melbourne after a brief stint during my undergraduate days in Perth was that I was offered a scholarship to study for a PhD. It helped to be able to financially and safely support myself in my journey in academia. The other major reason was to finally acknowledge, deep down, that I was gay. I owed it to myself, and also to the people I love, to explore and understand this aspect of my life. I thought it would have been difficult to do this in Malaysia or Singapore and, with the privilege of an opportunity too good to be true, I had to accept this as a sign from God.

Did I tell you that I believe in God?

This move coincided with the early days of the internet when it became possible to start looking for connections. I was lucky to find some mentors (and potential lovers) before I arrived in Melbourne. When I was asked by one of these eventual mentors what my hopes were, I remember saying, 'I just want to be able to walk down the supermarket aisle with my boyfriend, deciding what to buy. To be able to do this would make me so happy!'

Looking back, I think of both the simplicity and complexity of that wish. It was something so simple and yet something I didn't imagine could be a part of the norm. And so, that simple wish became a driving force. It belies the pain that I must have felt not being able to be myself.

The first time I came to Australia as an international student, I mostly hung out with other international students and being a representative and leader back then accentuated the need to be a big part of that social circle. The second journey was a bit different: I was determined to 'acquire' a social circle that had more of a domestic Australian flavour. This immediately exposed me to different ideas, some of which were illuminating while others were confounding.

Asian Chicken Salad? – Margaret Cho

The first of the confounding ideas was being 'Asian'. I never knew I was Asian till I came to Australia. In all my years in Malaysia and Singapore, I never referred to myself as Asian. Nor was I labelled Asian that much by anyone I came into contact with. Suddenly, in Australia, 'Asian' was everywhere! It was used to describe salads, students, restaurants, attitudes, and me! Suddenly my people included strangers from North Korea to Pakistan to the islands of the Philippines. By the way, I had never been to those three countries and still have not after all these years.

So basically, I knew I was gay before I knew was Asian.

Being queer is like being on a lifetime assignment as a secret agent in some foreign country. – Noretta Koertge

Despite acknowledging my gay identity, the second confounding idea was the concept of what it means to be gay. I was active in student politics while I was completing my studies in the late 1990s to early 2000s. In student politics, it seemed to me there was a particular way of being gay. Pride and coming out were the order of the day and if you were not part of that, you were not being true to yourself. Not only was I not ready for that, but I actually found it rather alienating. Although I was ready to come out to myself, I was not yet ready to come out to my family and community back in the 'old country'.

My solution to this was compartmentalisation. It was a lot easier to do in a time when Google and Facebook didn't exist. Compartmentalising, I realise now, is something I've done most of my life because of my sexuality. I became quite adept at showing only key parts of me to different groups of people: family, friends in Australia, friends back home, housemates, work colleagues, the gay community. I was definitely out to many of my friends in Australia but I separated them from my family back home.

The irony was that I played an active part in the gay community: marching in my first Mardi Gras in 1999, being a radio presenter on JOY 94.9 (Melbourne's Queer Radio Station); and performing with the Melbourne Gay and Lesbian Chorus. At the same time, I was a student activist but continued to keep my gay activism and student activism separate.

The gay Asian male on the gay scene comes to know himself sexually, to interpret his desirability, through multiple sites of racialised rejections, fetishisations and social interactions. – Dr Gilbert Caluya

In the 1990s, being a gay Asian male was often defined by non-Asians. Even today, you read and you hear people talk about gay Asian males as if they were one group with identical physiques, attitudes and outlooks. This was something I found incredibly frustrating and offensive. Any suggestions of racism within the gay community were swept under the umbrella term of 'preference'. I found this particularly confounding because I found (and still do) beauty and sexiness in men of all different origins.

As I began exploring and experiencing the gay scene, I saw my share of racism of all kinds. Ranging from 'No Asians' to 'Looking for Asians', I would only respond to online profiles that indicated they were 'Asian friendly', and even hesitated or ignored the profiles that did not specifically indicate they were looking for Asians. I learned to go to places where I perceived Asians were more desired. I also came to expect that when dining out, the wait staff would automatically assume that my 'white' partner (if that was who I was dining with) would be the one paying. I would do all this and at the same time railed against it. It didn't help that I was not the stereotypical gay Asian male being, shall we say, of fuller figure, hairier (including facial hair), and perhaps with an overblown confidence. Early on in the game, I remember saying to a friend who was himself a gay Asian male, 'It might have been easier if I conformed to the stereotype.'

It took a while before I could overcome that insecurity, purposefully go against the stereotype and revel in it. This was also helped by my discovery of the 'multicultural queer' community. The first time I came across this community was when I was interviewed by Maria Pallotta-Chiarolli (1999) for her report *'Too busy studying to have sex?': Homosexually active Asian male international students and sexual health*. I found it interesting that there was an assumption that international students were mostly asexual beings who were in Australia primarily to study. Sex was never talked about, whether among the students themselves (unsurprisingly) or by the support services they encountered through their educational institutions. Therefore, it was incredibly refreshing when I met Maria who was actually investigating the sex lives of international students! In some way, meeting her gave me a voice I had not thought was possible. Someone was actually interested in my story and, more significantly, felt that the story was an important one to tell as a way of challenging the status quo.

It was also around this time that a movie that was so important in my own journey screened for the first time. *Head On* is based on Christos Tsiolkas's book, *Loaded* (1995). It was groundbreaking in so many different ways with amazing performances by Alex Dimitriades and Paul Capsis. To me, it was a highly charged and sexual movie, which provided strong commentaries on gay men and ethnicities. More importantly, the one pivotal scene where Ari cruises a random Vietnamese man (acted by Allan Q) and proceeds to engage in sex in a public space hinted to me that perhaps Asian men could be desired too. It was not much but it was a start and something I could hang on to as a young gay Asian man trying to believe he could be desirable. When I watched the movie years later as a much more confident man, I found the scene to be slightly disturbing in that Ari was really only using the Vietnamese man for his lust with no interest in reciprocation. Since that movie, we haven't come very far in the media or even gay media in this area. This is why media representation is so crucial in a multicultural society and something that continues to be an issue.

In the late 1990s there are far more Asian men on the gay scenes in cities such as Sydney and Melbourne than ever before and there seems to be a greater intermingling of races than was the case even a few years ago, especially amongst younger gay men. – Tony Ayres

In 1998, when I first came across JOY 94.9, I was most excited about the idea of a radio station as a vehicle to mitigate isolation and fear but also to enable celebration and a coming together of minds. Yet, it was a forum where, again, the 'multicultural voice' was silent. It was, of course, going to remain silent, unless someone said something. So I did – six and a half years after stepping on to Australian shores. With Dr Kim Benton (who presented the psychology program on JOY), himself a Kiwi, we started *Orange Ribbon*. This was JOY's multicultural show. When JOY 94.9 finally achieved full-time status, *Orange Ribbon* became a weekly show and continued to 2012 with different hosts.

Orange Ribbon started out as a campaign at Flinders University against racism in response to Pauline Hanson. I argued for using the name Orange Ribbon as a way to highlight that racism in whatever shape was not welcome anywhere – including within the queer community. The idea was to introduce multiculturalism to the queer community, to challenge queer norms from a cultural perspective, to challenge the ideas of Pauline Hanson, to highlight and support the social ethnic queer groups, and to have a great time doing it.

The beauty of standing up for your rights is others see you standing and stand up as well. – Cassandra Duffy

In 2004, I was invited to be a part of an exciting initiative to organise Australia's first multicultural LGBTIQ conference in Melbourne. More than anything, the conference represented a coming together of the multicultural queer communities for the first time. We were learning from each other, arguing with each other and, most importantly, growing together. The theme of the conference was 'Living and Loving in Diversity' and we were looking at a celebration despite the challenges of the past and the ones to come. The conference united the community and gave it an energy that has continued in the form of the AGMC.

Two things have stayed with me from that time as one of the co-convenors:

The night before the conference, one of the sponsors' representatives told the committee that it was a mistake not to offer free alcoholic drinks at the opening, citing his extensive experience at organising conferences. Imagine a group including an Italian lesbian, a Malaysian Chinese gay man and a Maltese gay man saying almost together, 'Are you kidding!? We are wogs! The food is way more important than some cheap drinks!' As a concession, after a bit of an argument, the committee agreed to provide 50 vouchers to guests who could trade them in for an alcoholic drink. During the opening, all the food was finished within the first 30 minutes and by the end of the night only five vouchers had been traded in for alcohol. Perhaps this was a lesson that grassroots communities know their people best?

The second thing is a recommendation that came out of the conference, which achieved strong consensus: 'LGBTIQ events such as Mardi Gras and Midsumma need to be culturally aware and responsive. There should be no imposition of colonial perspectives on what is queer and how queer one must be. There is an urgent need for the LGBTIQ community to understand what prevents ethnic members from entering the "mainstream" gay scene.'

Nearly 15 years later, many of the recommendations from that first con-ference still ring true and need to be revisited. More importantly, the AGMC was formed at the end of the 2004 conference and continues to advocate and represent the views of cultural minority groups. The question remains as to how many mainstream services pay attention to their stories and wisdom.

Every gay person must come out . . . Once they realise we are indeed their children, we are indeed everywhere, every myth, every lie, every innuendo will be destroyed once and for all. – Harvey Milk

As I became an accidental activist in the gay community, the ability to compartmentalise my life became more difficult. In addition, by the mid 2000s, I had completed my studies, the internet was in full swing, I had been financially independent for a while, had a stable job and a stable partner. So, I brought my parents to Australia to visit for the first time. I saw them every year when I visited them in Singapore, leaving the 'gay' behind, and by this time there was a lot of 'gay' to leave behind. The first time they visited me, I continued to compartmentalise my life, not really introducing them to any of my friends, gay or straight.

It wasn't until 2008, during their second visit of three months, that the topic was finally brought up. You would think that after more than 10 years of being a gay activist, coming out to my Catholic Chinese family would have been easy. No! In fact, I did not come out at all! Rather, it was the amazing woman who is my mum who took matters into her own hands.

My parents had met some of my friends on this second visit, including my then partner, Michael. Because we weren't living together, Michael was patiently shunted to the side for a bit during that visit, though he did get to meet my parents (as a friend). Thankfully, Michael was a patient and chilled guy.

A month into their visit, Mum came into my room while I was reading, 'Son, is Michael gay?'

I looked up and with a perfectly straight face, 'Why don't you ask him the next time you see him, Mum?' I was a little shit! But the woman caught me off guard. Of course she was not about to let this go.

A week later, my parents and I were on a not-too-crowded tram going into the city. Mum decided this was the best time to ask, 'Are you gay?' This whole thing was suddenly a bit surreal as the tram turned from Clifton Hill into Collingwood (where many of the gay venues I used to go to were just up ahead). I couldn't very well say, 'Go ask Shanton'. She was asking Shanton, and then she followed up with, 'And is Michael your gay partner?' I had to say yes, and then we sat awkwardly on the tram as it zoomed along Smith Street in Collingwood.

Then my mum said, 'Okay, well not everyone is as understanding as me. Just keep this to yourself.' Well, that was simple; I had been doing that most of my life. She then proceeded to ask some questions that I will always remember: 'Do your other friends know? Do they mind? Does work know? Will it impact on your career and promotion?' I realised with these follow-up questions that, ultimately, she was worried about my future more than anything else. When I explained that my friends knew and that my workplace didn't particularly care, she relaxed visibly. It was also very Chinese – I mean, I had a good thing going at work and we don't want to mess that up! Dad just nodded in the background. His quiet support was both understated and powerful.

'I don't want you to tell your brothers,' Mum said after dinner a few days later. 'I am understanding but others may not be and I don't want them to respect you any less. You are my oldest and they must respect you.' I didn't tell her that in the age of the internet, my brothers had probably worked it out and might not have really cared that much. Nevertheless, I didn't tell my brothers and it was she who told them a month later when she went back to Singapore. My brothers were great about it.

More than nine years since that tram ride, my family is fully accepting of me and my current partner of eight years, Robbie. We've both gone back to Singapore and stayed with them and they have come to stay with us for long periods of time. Our families know each other and it all seems so normal. Yet, I know that in some ways, I had failed Harvey Milk! I didn't really come out: Mum took the initiative. But then, coming out is perhaps not for everyone of every culture?

However, one thing did become clear to me. Keeping families together and respecting each other is a family affair. Many Chinese families talk about this and how it is so important. Yet, one hears of Chinese parents who have disowned their children for being gay. I get so angry when I hear that because it's the parents who have broken up that family, not the child, and yet they blame the child. Filial piety in Chinese culture refers to the importance of children respecting their elders, and especially their parents. What is often forgotten is that this Confucian virtue of piety also indicates the reciprocal role of the parents in respecting their child and in being responsible for the wellbeing and material needs of all their children. The whole point is keeping the family united. Piety is also rooted in the importance of carrying on the family name and legacy. These days, enabling gay children and supporting them to have their own children is not an impossible dream. So, when a Chinese parent disowns their gay child or children, they abandon their own responsibilities. Gay children often are not the ones who seek a break from their family and their silence is evidence of their desire to respect their parents, keep the family together and maintain a sense of unity, at a serious cost to their own mental wellbeing. The dominant discourse of conservative Chinese parents that their gay child is unfilial needs to be challenged.

While I am not excusing my lack of courage in my own coming out, I applaud my parents' embrace of their role in this and in providing a space and love that kept our family together and extended it to Robbie's family. What greater unity could there be and how lucky am I? I am truly humbled by my family.

There are biological families, and then there are logical families. – Anna Madrigal, Armistead Maupin

A good friend of mine, Paul, talks about this a lot. I owe a lot to my logical family through the years when I was 'alone' in Australia. Finding people that I could trust and who would be my tribe members was crucial in keeping me sane. They provided the stability that one needs as one flits from lover to lover. Over the years, I managed to finally 'acquire' that social circle that had a more domestic 'Australian' flavour, but along the way I discovered that 'Australian' flavour was a very elusive thing. Having been naturalised in 2007, I realised that my logical Aussie family is truly diverse and I bathe in the warmth of their acceptance. If I had one piece of advice to my much younger self, 20 years ago, it would be, 'Find your tribe before you look for that super-market aisle companion.' Perhaps that is something I feel comfortable saying now because I have that in Robbie, and can judge my younger self.

I am trying to understand what it means to be a Christian without being religious. – Bishop John Shelby Spong

That logical family also presented some challenges. Most of my friends and the people in the gay community, because of their history and current experiences, find organised religion extremely alienating. I do not blame them but I am sad about it. The people who speak the loudest and claim to be Christians in Australia are also often the most bigoted and ungodly. Their self-righteous judgement, lack of charity, lack of compassion and their willingness to incite hate seem to know no bounds. Yet, at the same time, the opposing force of queer activism that understandably wants to fight back and ridicule the idea of God and of religion means that I am caught in the middle.

So, how do I find God in all this? The secret I am guessing is in my own personal relationship with my God, the first 'person' I came out to. How many Christians have tried to pray the gay away, rather than to accept it as a blessing from God? As it turns out, once I accepted that God was okay with me and continues to bless me, my love for God (rather than my fear) has grown. Anything and everything I do that is good, is by the grace of God. When I was a child, in catechism I learned that living a Christian life is not about saying what you believe but living what you believe. My actions need to embody my faith as I go on my personal journey of faith. This is not easy to explain to those who have been hurt by religion, and who religious leaders continue to hurt. I have learned that these so-called leaders are not intermediaries to my loving God.

We should indeed keep calm in the face of difference, and live our lives in a state of inclusion and wonder at the diversity of humanity. – George Hosato Takei

I am thankful that I have been relatively lucky in my experiences, and that I have led a relatively privileged existence even in the face of adversity. However, being thankful means giving back as well and helping out where I can. It is too simple when one sees another awful thing being said publicly about our community to think, 'It doesn't affect me; I don't care about that idiot! You can't expect everyone to like you.' If the people who I have quoted in this chapter had thought the same thing, I would not have had as easy a life as I do now. I am blessed by their actions. And if I can make life a bit better for just one young person coming out, that is what matters.

So, I will continue to speak out against homophobia. I will continue to speak out against racism and especially racism within the queer community where too many still think it's okay to say 'No blacks, no Asians, no rice, no curry, no fats, no fems, no trans'. No! It's not acceptable and it's not about preference, it's about the hurt you cause and the hate that you promote because you want a good time. I am not saying this because I'm complaining about someone not wanting to sleep with me. I don't particularly want to sleep with ugly souls. I am saying that within our community, we need to look out for each other and we don't need to make it worse for those who come after us.

Race, gender, religion, sexuality, we are all people and that's it. We're all people. We're all equal. – Connor Franta

I am hopeful that the next generation of queer community will be more open, more accepting and more inclusive. I also hope that the next generation of the human race will be more enlightened. I also urge us to continue to remember where we have come from and that we all stand on the shoulders of giants.

As I started writing this, the Marriage Equality debate was raging in Australia. It is one where the battles are being fought between generations of accepting decent Australians and conservative religious and political leaders of every culture. By the time this anthology was published, love had won, so there is hope here. However, it doesn't solve all our problems of racism, biphobia and transphobia. It would be dangerous to assume that all our social problems are solved because of Marriage Equality. The fact that an upper-middle-class white man could propose to his partner in parliament is to be celebrated but it doesn't change the fear and racism that thousands of kids continue to face when they think of coming out in our community and society.

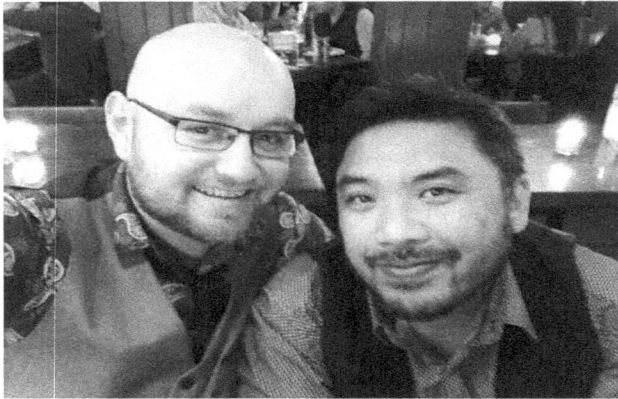

Robbie and Shanton between trips to supermarkets

Taking Our Liberation to Others – Let My People Go!

Dedicated to Peter Bonsall Boone

Joseph Chetcuti

I was not born to be a homosexual, let alone a gay activist.

As a toddler and a young boy, I played with small statues of saints. Aged around five, I ran off from my family home in Paola; the journey's end was a shop owned by a man known to us as Felić tal-Pasturi (Felix of the Figurines). I was back home in no time, having acquired my prized possessions – a few clay nativity figurines created from plaster moulds. They were crudely painted. Baby Jesus was made of wax. They might not have been great works of art, but the cross-eyed figurines provided a bridge to the divine.

Each year, I joined my father in assembling the Christmas crib. I can still smell the little brown beads of the carpenter's glue as they simmered away in a pot. My father applied the glue to old newspapers before assembling the crib. I helped him construct the houses and palm trees out of brown paper and cardboard. I carefully placed the figurines around the crib – their focus always on the Infant Jesus. There were also fairy lights to brighten the cardboard sky and the crib.

Weeks before Christmas, we collected empty cans which we filled with newspaper and cotton. We carefully placed seeds of wheat and vetch on top of the cotton, consigned the cans to dark cupboards, and regularly sprinkled them with water. We were careful not to expose them to any light. Weeks later, the delicate foliage adorned the sides of the crib.

When my family moved to Scots Street in Valletta, I took to displaying statues of saints on the window sill of one of the balconies. Occasionally, I gathered my friends – all boys – for a small procession around the streets of my neighbourhood. I made liturgical vestments out of butcher's paper for those taking part in the procession. A few boys were tasked with carrying the small statue as others followed prayerfully behind.

My boyhood dream was to become a priest, a Franciscan to be precise; and not just any Franciscan. I wanted to be a Friar Minor, the order entrusted with Valletta's Good Friday procession. I had no other ambition in life apart from those lapses when I toyed with becoming a horse rider or a trapeze artist at a circus. Entering the legal profession never crossed my mind. I fell into that profession in 1985 or thereabouts, almost by accident.

At 11 years of age, I joined the Legion of Mary. As a member, I carried the statue of Our Lady of the Miraculous Medal from home to home, hoping to promote devotion toward her. I attended and served mass, almost daily. Bishops travelling Malta during breaks from the Second Vatican Council urged me to become a priest (not that I needed any urging); some were from Australia.

In 1962, aged 14, I joined the Society of Christian Doctrine, known locally as tal-Mużew, a secular society of celibates, not an inappropriate home for someone with no interest in girls. I attended classes daily for prayer and study including church history. I had set prayers to recite throughout the day. I dressed modestly in accordance with the rules of the Society and I enjoyed the company of like-minded boys who took their religion seriously.

In 1965, my world fell apart when my father broke the news that we were migrating to Australia. His decision surprised everyone, including my mother. We had no relatives in Australia other than an uncle and an aunt and their families, both on my father's side. In Malta, my father was gainfully employed as a night editor of a leading newspaper (*Il-Berqa*). He also taught at Stella Maris College, a girls' secondary school in Imdina, and at two friaries run by the Franciscan Minor Conventuals. He earned in one day what most men earned in a week. Travelling to a heathen country was never on my agenda.

Flotta Lauro's *Sydney* set sail from Valletta on 27 April 1965. As *Sydney* steamed out of the Grand Harbour, my eyes remained fixed on the city's church steeples, the houses that gave me a sense of permanence, the streets I treaded and loved, and the relatives and friends I was leaving behind. It was the saddest day of my life. I was not sure what to make of my vocation to become a friar.

The ship stopped at Piraeus, Port Said and Aden, before reaching Fremantle. At Fremantle, from the deck of the ship, I spotted a good-looking young man, and I began to like my new surroundings. The ship sailed to Melbourne. My eyes were fixed on the many good-looking young men greeting the ship. I have often wondered if any of them were gay; maybe I had even stumbled onto a beat. When the ship entered Sydney Harbour, the bridge came in full view; we scrambled onto the deck to catch a sight of this new icon. There were also skyscrapers to gaze at, the AMP the tallest among them. Ziju Pawl and Ziju Nena were there to greet us, and take us to their home, providentially in Boundary Street, Paddington. We were in for a surprise as Zija Nena took her seat behind the wheel. My father was alarmed. He had survived four weeks on the sea; now he thought the end was near. He told her so, and we all laughed.

I was keen to join the workforce. Within a few weeks of arriving, I was working as a clerical assistant with the Department of Social Security in Carrington Street, Wynyard. Almost daily, I looked out of the office window at the P&O liners, wondering how long it would be before I saved enough money to return to Malta. At work, I stuck out like a sore thumb. I was different, but that difference had nothing to do with my ethnicity or sexuality (which I had not yet acknowledged). Religion made me different. Occasionally, workmates branded me a papist, but that was like water off a duck's back. I was a proud papist, a member of the one truth faith. And there was no sense of malice in what my workmates said. My strong suspicion is that they wanted me to be 'one of them'. I have wondered whether any of them were gay.

In November 1967, I transferred to the Eastern Command Registry of the Department of the Army, as a clerical assistant, at Paddington's Victoria Barracks. Each morning, I walked past two handsome soldiers guarding the entrance to the barracks. In June 1968, I was promoted to the position of clerk in the Command Pay Office. I resigned on 24 January 1969 to join the Franciscan Conventuals. Two workmates took me on a night out, stopping at a bar in Bondi Junction. I remember being startled at the sight of two men with their arms around each other. Perhaps my workmates guessed I was gay, and decided to drop in at Chez Ivy in the hope that I would reconsider my decision to become a Franciscan.

Religion was still at the core of my being. Days after arriving in Sydney I made my way to the Paddington branch of the Society of Christian Doctrine. The Society operated from rooms in the primary school alongside the Church of St Francis of Assisi in Oxford Street. I became a fully-fledged member of the Society on 28 December 1966, at Ryde's Holy Cross College. I did not see eye-to-eye with my superior. I gained a reputation of being a rebel even though I was no heretic. He also did not approve of the colour of my tie – a conservative brown. Black was the colour.

On 1 February 1969, I joined two prospective novices on an Alitalia flight to London. My boyhood dream was beginning to take shape. Two days later, Fr Richard the Provincial, a good friend of Michael Ramsey, then Archbishop of Canterbury, took us on a tour of London. One of the stops was Soho. He expected us to be surprised; he was not wrong, but he had an important point to make. He reminded us that as friars, we were required to attend to the needs of everyone, prostitutes and spruikers included. A new world was opening up.

The day after, Brother Francis drove us to St Bonaventure's Friary in Anglesey, North Wales. Friars came out to greet us, expecting to see three tall blond men. They were disappointed. I received my Franciscan habit on 14 February 1969. It was a proud moment in my life, one I still cherish. I took on the names of Robert John in honour of the Kennedys. Occasionally, the rudimentary studies in theology and philosophy turned to some interesting topics like *amicizia particolare* (particular friendships) and homosexuality, which Fr Robert, the novice master, denounced. He told us that religious life was no place for homosexuals. I gained the impression that he was talking directly to me. A good-looking friar, with whom I fell in love, unwittingly made me wonder whether there was more to my sexual temptations. Was it at all possible, I asked myself, that I was homosexual?

We returned to Australia in 1970. On 25 February 1970, I took simple vows at Kellyville's Our Lady of the Rosary Church. A moment of intimacy with another friar roused my sexuality: it was my Damascene experience. From then on, emotionally at least, I knew that same-sex love was not sinful; no theology could convince me otherwise, but that was another battle yet to be fought. The decision to abandon my vocation was painful. Liberation comes at a cost.

In 1972, I called on a psychologist priest at St Vincent's Hospital in Darlinghurst. I wished to be 'cured' of my sexuality, but the priest was not in the business of offering cures. His message was clear – I was neither a sinner nor a sick man, and I should simply accept myself as I was. I responded by quoting the Bible and the Church's teachings. He listened patiently, but then declared that 'the Church does not know what it is talking about'.

Before I left, he handed me the telephone number of CAMP's Church group, the Campaign Against Moral Persecution, Australia's first explicit lesbian and gay political organisation, and directed me to contact the organisation without delay. I requested another appointment; he bluntly refused to see me again until I had dropped in on CAMP. His parting words were, 'I don't think you'll need to see me again.'

I attempted to ring CAMP from a telephone booth at St Peters station; at the time, I was living in Goodsell Street, St Peters. Finally, in late 1972, I gathered the courage to stay on the line. I spoke to either Peter Bonsall Boone or Peter de Waal who invited me to a meeting of Cross+Section. I made my way to Terry Street, Balmain, frightened to knock on the door of the house. Images of transvestites and strange men flooded my mind. After some 45 minutes strolling up and down the street, I climbed the few stairs of the terrace house.

Inside, and for the first time in my life, I came face-to-face with a group of homosexuals. They were all boringly normal – except for Peter Bonsall Boone who looked like a hippie, complete with beads around his neck. My life had changed. I was now in the company of members of my own tribe.

I am not one for half-measures; I soon embarked on my work in the vineyard of gay liberation. I joined members of Cross+Section on their regular raids of public toilets with the aim of promoting Phone-A-Friend, CAMP's counselling service. A member of the group kept watch, making sure that no police were around; the rest of us occupied the cubicles. Our business, to put it delicately, was to stick the green Phone-A-Friend labels inside the walls of the cubicles. By September 1973, I was sufficiently self-assured of my sexuality to agree to be part of CAMP's response to the *Report on Homosexuality: Report of the Ethics and Social Questions Committee to the Synod of the Church of England Diocese of Sydney*. That year I also joined a political demonstration, possibly that of Gay Pride Week. I attended other political demonstrations and in 1978 I was also part of Sydney's first gay Mardi Gras that saw 53 people arrested.

I attempted, albeit unsuccessfully, to modify the conservative views of the Maltese community in Australia, a community that claimed to have assimilated into Australian society. In 1983, for example, I was asked to read poetry at the annual Maltese literary function at Melbourne's AMP theatrette. A few days before the event, the organiser asked me to show him what I was planning to read. He was surprised when he discovered I planned to make mention of my homosexuality. He reminded me that the Maltese community in Melbourne was conservative – as if I did not already know.

At Coburg's Philip Institute, a few students routinely criticised my choice of prescribed texts and they made their complaints known to the Director of Studies. They took aim at Oliver Friggieri's (1980) *L-Istramb* (*The Strange One*), a book that talked about prostitution and homosexuality. Friggieri is one of Malta's leading writers, and he is hardly a leftie! I flirted with the Maltese community, but was never really a part of it. Between 2006 and 2007, the unthinkable happened: I was elected president of the Maltese Literature Group (Victoria). My election caused a stir; the homophobes began plotting to remove me. As far as they were concerned, my election was an abomination.

As President, I planned to deliver a public lecture on 29 May 2007 at the Maltese Community Council of Victoria. The lecture was to consider social movement literature, hence the topic, 'Ten Years On: "The Pink Book: A sin, disorder and crime?" and the "birth" of the gay movement in Malta'. Hell hath no fury like a Maltese dared! (Maltese often see themselves as being very stubborn, the colonial version of the British bulldog.) The Council and the Missionary Society of St Paul were up in arms. The Council threatened to disaffiliate the Maltese Literature Group. The lecture was blocked and I left my post shortly thereafter, never to return to that homophobic institution, Parkville's Maltese Community Centre.

The Missionary Society of St Paul had good reason to thwart my lecture. In August 2011, Malta's courts found two of its priests guilty of sexually abusing 11 boys placed in their care at Santa Venera's St Joseph's Home. One priest had escaped from Canada in 1993 to evade police arrest on charges that he had abused a young boy for four years. The Society offered him refuge in Malta. Another member escaped legal prosecution because his alleged crimes were time-barred (Scicluna, 2016). A member of the Society who in the past had a lot to say on homosexuality is now noticeable by his silence. I am not suggesting that this priest has committed any criminal acts.

I continued to outrage the Maltese community in Australia, furious over an article I wrote for the second edition of *The Australian People: An encyclopedia of the nation, its people and their origins* (1988), where I made mention of homosexuality, the only reference to homosexuality in that encyclopedia. Surely, I was not the only gay ethnic in Australia. Leaders of the community disapproved of my contribution; they made their views known to James Jupp, the encyclopedia's editor. They accused me of blemishing the reputation of the Maltese in Australia, conveniently overlooking our profile in places like Soho and Kings Cross. Nothing should come in the way of the myth that represents us as model migrants, as politicians keep reminding us, politicians who are after our vote, and who repeat the same nonsense to other ethnic communities.

I managed to have the last laugh. In 2015, I was invited to be part of the IV Convention for the Maltese Living Abroad. By then, Malta had elected a new government. Prime Minister Joseph Muscat won the 2013 election by the biggest landslide since Malta's independence. He promptly went about entombing the legacy of his two arch-conservative predecessors, Eddie Fenech Adami and Lawrence Gonzi, into the dustbin of history. During Labor's first term in office, Malta enacted civil union legislation with all the rights of marriage. There were rumours that Malta's past president George Abela, a Labor man and a former catechist, refused to have anything to do with the law. He was also too busy to see me in 2010, even though he was addressing a conference I was attending. I planned to present him with a copy of *Queer Mediterranean Memories: Penetrating the secret history and silence of gay and lesbian disguise in the Maltese Archipelago* (2009).

At the 2015 convention, I spoke about my personal journey from assimilation to liberation. I argued that Australia's pluralism has ossified our community, a community that was already badly affected by a cultural freeze. I went on to claim that women's and gay liberation promoted other identities, often at the expense of our ethnicity. I asked the obvious question – why should Maltese Australians bother with their ethnic identity when many of our leaders are so out of touch with modern Australia?

I regularly visit Malta. Invariably, I make a point of calling in on gay bars. I was reluctant to take on an activist role there, but all that changed in 1995.

One evening, I was watching television with my late uncle (Guze Chetcuti), a well-known writer. A TV program (*Pjazza Tlieta*) was planning to discuss the taboo subject of homosexuality. My uncle counselled me to have nothing to do with it. He warned me that going public with my homosexuality would destroy all prospects of employment in Malta. I had never planned to work in Malta; nevertheless, I declined the station's invitation to be part of the program.

Mario Azzopardi, a writer and close friend of my uncle, telephoned me around two hours before the program went to air. He wanted to know why I had declined to appear on *Pjazza Tlieta*. He persuaded me to contact Lou Bondi, the program's presenter, and I agreed to appear. I was faced with the challenge of having to come out yet again but in a different country, and some 23 years after I came out in Australia. As it turned out, I became the first openly gay professional to appear on Maltese TV, and the first gay Maltese man to publicly debate a priest, a representative of the Maltese Roman Catholic curia. After the program, I joined Lou Bondi and some of his workers for a pizza at Paceville. The restaurant's patrons swarmed around us. We then made our way to Potters Bar, a gay bar in the same suburb, where we were welcomed as heroes.

I returned to Malta to launch *Il-Ktieb Roża: Dnub, diżordni u delitt? (The Pink Book: A sin, disorder and crime?)* (1997) and, some years later, *Queer Mediterranean Memories*. Sapienza Bookshop in Republic Street, Valletta, featured *Il-Ktieb Roża: Dnub, diżordni u delitt?* in its front widow. Conservatives were not amused. The book attracted extensive newspaper, radio and television coverage. Some experiences are worth mentioning.

On the morning after the launch of *Il-Ktieb Roża: Dnub, diżordni u delitt?* I was taken aback when an elderly man approached me in Sliema to thank me for my intervention. In Valletta, an elderly woman crossed the road to greet me. Years later, during Valletta's procession of Our Lady of Sorrows, I noticed a middle-aged woman, a veil covering her head, rosary beads in her hands, taking a second look at me. I was standing on the side of the road with an Australian friend, waiting for the procession to begin. A confrontation appeared imminent. I was in no mood for a quarrel, but I had no choice. She made a dash for me, and looked me straight in the eye. To my surprise, she extended her hand of friendship, and warmly thanked me for what I had done. She had one message for me, 'Thank God, someone has finally spoken. You do not know how many gay men in Malta are suffering in silence'. She left as quickly as she had come.

Queer Mediterranean Memories: Penetrating the secret history and silence of gay and lesbian disguise in the Maltese Archipelago saw conservatives come out of the woodwork. Malta was changing, and the changes were not to their liking. An archbishop condemned the book, but acknowledged he had not read it. A bishop accused me of promoting an agenda that was intended to harm the church. A government minister joined the chorus of condemnation. Some gay men and lesbians began to wonder why this 'foreigner' was causing trouble. Gay men and lesbians, they claimed, had nothing to fear in Malta so long as they did not publicise or promote their sexuality. Little did I know that by 2017, both Malta and Australia would enact Marriage Equality legislation, even if they went about it very differently.

There is no denying that difference can trigger depression, and bring about ostracism. Family and friends can desert you, and you are left with no choice but to cultivate 'families of choice'. But being culturally, ethnically and religiously different from an imagined mainstream is both a stumbling block and a stepping stone. It need not be a handicap; in fact, it can be a source of empowerment that brings with it opportunities that may be denied to others. For activists, including those who campaigned for Marriage Equality, difference brings with it the prospect of preaching the 'good news of liberation from heterosexism' to those who are not yet liberated.

Written on the Body

Margherita Coppolino and Steve Dow

Who's that laughing?

It's coming from the bathroom.

It's the early 70s, and tiny, barely teenage Margherita Coppolino is up from her bed, off to the toilet.

The lights in the dormitories of the St Catherine's Children's Home in Geelong, west of Melbourne, have long since been turned off.

Splash.

It's definitely coming from the bathroom.

The door is ajar. Young Margherita peeps through the crack.

Two nuns.

Off duty.

Having a bath together.

Sotto voce: Naked.

They're kind of . . . well, you know . . .

'It was like,' says Coppolino, having a drink with me near her office where she works as a disability advocate, 'why would two nuns be having a bath together?'

Good question; one that might earn you a smack. There were, after all, nuns who, until that point, had never shown non-facial flesh to Margherita and the other children in the home. They even normally had special large, flowing habits in which to swim. But there was not even a floatie in sight this night in the bathtub.

About the same time, young Margherita would sometimes climb into bed with a couple of the other girls when they should have been outside playing.

Instead, they were cuddling. Fondling. They had no name for what they were doing. Playing a game, maybe.

The boy residents were of course shipped out of the home at a young age to a boys' home. Why, sex could happen between these tender young wards of the state if their carers weren't too careful.

One day, a nun caught little Margherita in bed with one of the girls, and sent her to confession. But Margherita didn't know what she was meant to be confessing to, exactly.

Margherita Coppolino was not your average burgeoning lesbian – gay person, she prefers to call herself, though the labels are becoming less important as she gets older – and certainly with her (significantly) small stature, olive Italian looks and loopy earrings, she cuts quite a different figure.

At Coppolino's birth, her young mother and the medical staff knew the child was a dwarf.

Sometimes, you never escape being seen as disabled before you're ever seen as an adult. Once, outside a Shirley Bassey concert in Sydney, Margherita Coppolino and I asked for directions to the nearest taxi rank.

Three obviously well meaning, middle-aged women started speaking to her as though she were a child.

'Now, dear, you make sure those cab drivers don't take you the long way to get a bigger fare.' Voices pitched high. Mummy knows best.

I wanted to step in, but realised: no, that would be patronising behaviour too.

Let me backtrack . . .

In 1959, Coppolino's 19-year-old mother travelled from Sicily to Melbourne to join her father and help raise enough money to bring the rest of the family to Australia.

On the boat, the young woman was raped.

Two days after giving birth, the woman signed the adoption papers and left the child Margherita at Melbourne's Royal Women's Hospital. The welfare authorities never heard from the young woman again.

Grown up, Coppolino researched the cultural imperatives behind the mother's decision and found that a dwarf was said to have been a curse in some Italian villages.

'If she'd gone back, the community wouldn't have accepted her. She might have been killed. She would have at least been ostracised.'

Coppolino grew up a ward of the state in orphanages. Nuns and their habits – or lack thereof – were to play a key role in her maturing.

It's hardly a tearjerker of a story, though. Consider that Coppolino, as a consultant with the Change Initiative Company, has a portfolio that has included advising AMP and Westpac on disability issues, and project work in the community sector. Her ambition is to work internationally.

'I am "disabled" because of physical obstacles put in my way. People are "disabled" because of society's attitude.

'People have this idea that I live in a small house, where everything's fitted out.

'Do I have a single bed? No, I have a double bed, thank you. Most of my partners have been over my height.'

Which brings us to why (once again) I have asked my friend Margherita Coppolino to turn interviewee. To talk about the lesbian thing. And about being small. Both, preferably.

And whether there has ever been an expectation, maybe, that she might match up with someone else who was small.

'I always used to say the reason I'm not in a relationship is I haven't found women tall enough.' Of course. That's why she took me to see Bassey. Those legs.

And there have been relationships, always with taller women.

Very tall, and feminine, women. Not 'gay-looking' (read: butch) at all.

For a while, in her 20s, Coppolino would don all the hallmarks she thought went with lesbianism – very short hair, ties, and suits. Carrying a man's cigarette case. Holding doors open for women. A sort of kd lang in kd's lounge era, except she only came up to your belt buckle.

'I tried to be butch, but I never have been,' she says. 'Far from it.'

Coppolino left the orphanage at 18, and lived in a flat for a time. At 19, a gay male hairdresser took her to Melbourne's Universal Club, in Collins Street. It was 1979. You found out about this place through word of mouth. There were gays and lesbians aplenty.

'I remember looking around and thinking a load had been lifted from my shoulders.'

Yet there were misconceptions about her in the gay community that 'Margo' had to clear up. 'I had to tell a lot of people I was gay,' she says.

'Some gay people were surprised about that. I'd say, "Why do you think I'm hanging around the gay scene?" They'd say, "We thought you were hanging around the gay scene because you were comfortable and were accepted for your disability . . ."'

Then there were the lesbians who told Coppolino outright that they would never consider sex with her because they wouldn't be comfortable with her disability. Thus Coppolino relates more to gay men – a comfort zone perhaps – and prefers to call herself a gay person, relating less to the term 'lesbian'. She thinks gay men are 'less bitchy' than some lesbians she has encountered. (She has indeed been fortunate.)

But the attitudes among lesbians toward her, her height and her disability have become more positive in recent years.

'As I've become more comfortable with my own body within, and more comfortable with being gay, and understanding feminist issues, then yes. But it took a long time before I could say, "Yes, they've gotten over it."'

In August 2010, Coppolino celebrated her 50th birthday in an upstairs bar in Brunswick Street, Fitzroy. At the time, she was co-hosting the *Small Talk* radio program on 3CR, which gives a voice to people with dwarfism, a term she has never really minded. 'For the next 30 minutes, we invite you to see the world through our eyes: "Hey, down there."' She has also taken up photography with gusto, offering a unique perspective of angles from below the eyelines of many subjects.

Her costume for her 50th was a green GI hat and yellow scarf, like a tiny Gomer Pyle. The number of people moved to pay tribute to her was remarkable only if you don't know her, and plenty are keen to be her friend.

Excerpt with kind permission from Steve Dow, Gay: The tenth anniversary collection *(2011).*

Missy and Margherita

Immortal

Franco Di Chiera

On the night of 29 April 2017, I found myself at Xavier College in Melbourne's well-to-do suburb of Kew. It was emotional being in Tim Conigrave and John Caleo's old stomping ground. We'd been close friends, living together in Sydney during the mid 80s – a period marred by the arrival of the AIDS epidemic. Little did we know how much it would affect our lives and the lasting legacy Tim's book, *Holding the Man*, would have.

I'd come to the school's performing arts centre to attend a one-man show by Fabio Grossi and Leo Gullotta, *Reading Sicily*, focusing on the literature of the island's great authors. The choice of the former Jesuit-run college was rather apt; the Jesuits' first schools were established in Sicily in the 1500s.

As I waited for a mate to arrive, I took the liberty of wandering through the grounds. I'd heard a lot about the college from Tim and John and despite having driven past on numerous occasions I'd never visited before. Nor had I got to appreciate its full splendour until that night. At the top of a hill stood a beautifully lit sandstone basilica with Romanesque columns and a Mediterranean cypress by its side. One could be forgiven for thinking it was Italy – a suitably romantic setting for the birth of the country's most iconic gay love story.

I imagined Tim on stage in one of the school's productions or John playing football on the sports field below or the pair stealing a kiss behind the old boarding quarters. These were hallowed grounds for the many people who knew their story, especially young gays in the process of coming out. Reading Tim's book was something of a rite of passage. Tragic as it was, gay men needed to believe that their relationships could be just as deep and just as enduring as their heterosexual counterparts. The couple were the Romeo and Romeo of their time and Tim's memoirs, which he finished just before he died, an opus to their extraordinary devotion. Published posthumously in 1995, *Holding the Man* not only became a bestseller but an Australian literary classic that has since spawned a play, a feature film and, more recently, a documentary.

When Tim and John fell in love at Xavier College they were only 15 years old, staying together until AIDS finally ended John's life another 15 years later. My partner Steven Choo and I have just had our 15th anniversary and it's heartbreaking to think what it was like for Tim and John to have to say goodbye to each other under such physically and emotionally challenging circumstances. Tim and I had met on a film shoot in 1981 while I was a student at the Australian Film, Television and Radio School (AFTRS) in Sydney. He was one of the actors on Karl Steinberg's film *Purgatory* and I, the production manager. But Tim was sacked on the way to the film's location, Southern Lake Eyre, and was stuck with us in the middle of nowhere. With little to do, he became one of the writers as well as my assistant and we soon became lovers.

Not surprisingly, John wasn't at all pleased with our antics on the shoot. During his regular visits to Sydney when Tim was studying at the National Institute of Dramatic Arts (NIDA), he avoided all eye contact with me whenever we crossed paths. I didn't blame him; I probably would've done the same. Of course, it takes two to tango and Tim took some share of the responsibility. Regardless, I thought it only reasonable that I apologise and I did. Eventually, John too moved to Sydney and after some persistence on my part, we got to know each other. John had a heart big enough to let bygones be bygones, allowing me to enter their lives.

John was gorgeous, loving and caring but he was no shrinking violet. He was strong-willed like his Italian father, Bob. Tim's book and the adaptations that followed didn't paint a very positive picture of this conservative family man. It's based on what Tim witnessed, so I can only assume it's a valid account. At one point, Tim was appalled at what seemed like a callous grab by Bob for John's possessions while he was dying. Had it been a heterosexual relationship perhaps his father wouldn't have behaved the same way. It showed disrespect for them as partners of 15 years. But I also wondered whether it had partly to do with grief – a father grasping at straws at the loss of his son. It's not an excuse, merely an acknowledgement that grief often brings out the best and worst in people.

Sorrow was something that had impacted on my life at an early age. My mother died when I was eight and a half years old. After half a century, I'm still coming to terms with how it affected me. When I first moved to Melbourne in 1998, I hardly knew anyone. Although I felt fortunate to have had several long-term relationships, I found myself, aged 40, without a partner. I wasn't good at dating; I kept meeting the wrong men – the unavailable kind. Whether they came from another city, another country or had another partner, I was inexorably attracted to them. After decades of romantic disasters, seeking counselling and scouring self-help books, I had an epiphany: my mother dying had caused me to associate love with absence.

I grew up in the little country town of Waroona in Western Australia and moved to Perth with my family after my mum died. My burgeoning sexuality as a gay man combined with my Italo-Australian background subjected me to a fair share of name-calling and fistfights at school. Later, I attended Murdoch University, studying communication studies. It was there that I fully immersed myself in the heady gay activism of the 70s, including numerous marches and protests. Gay sex between consenting adults was still illegal in Western Australia as it was in other states, except for South Australia. A number of us had the role of giving talks on homosexuality at tertiary institutions, particularly to students of male-dominated disciplines, such as engineering, who were renowned for their homophobia. I recall that after one such event at the University of Western Australia, the engineering students spray-painted 'Ban the Bum!' on a huge wall outside of their faculty the next day. These were difficult but rewarding times. A couple of mates and I also helped establish Australia's first gay radio show, *Gays Weekly*, becoming the highest-rating program at community radio 6NR. It gave me a chance to make a difference, not to mention, a much-needed escape from my patriarchal homelife against which I frequently rebelled.

I took to wearing 'How dare you presume I'm heterosexual' badges at the dinner table, plastering gay rights and feminism posters on my bedroom walls and leaving gay books lying around, the covers of which I'd find turned over when I came home from university each day. It all came to a head one night when my father asked me if I was gay. I answered, 'Of course, I am.' I suggested we talk about it later as I was racing out 'to record my weekly gay radio show'. He insisted I wasn't going anywhere and that if I were really gay, he'd disown me. I stated that was his prerogative and left.

I decided to give him time to think it over, staying with my lesbian university friend Beck in Fremantle. After a week, he called saying, 'Franco, we miss you. Come home.' So I did. His only condition was that none of my gay friends were to phone or come by. While I respected I was living under his roof and he could dictate the terms, that wasn't acceptable to me and I told him so. That was the end of that; he never hassled me about it again. Years later, he adopted at least one of my boyfriends, Peter, letting him live with him and the family while I was studying at the AFTRS in Sydney. My father cried when Peter eventually left Perth to join me. People do sometimes change, if you give them a chance.

The vagaries of growing up gay in an Italian-Australian family influenced much of my work. My graduation film, *La Scala, Lo Scalone* (1984) was semi-autobiographical, centring on a young Italian boy growing up in Australia as he struggles to deal with the mysterious demands of the adult world. It explored notions of family, religion, sexuality and death. My intention was to make it in the Italian language. However, that meant using subtitles. As a directing student at AFTRS, I was allocated a small cash budget but because the subtitles had to be done optically, the cost was prohibitive. So I applied to a Special Projects Committee to subsidise the process. The Committee had a reputation of being a bit of a boys club, where additional funds were usually reserved for special effects – for 'boys with toys' as we used to call them. I was advised that subtitles were a waste of money and to just make it in English.

Naturally, I was disappointed. I felt it was my prerogative to tell this story in my family's mother tongue, adding to the authenticity. I couldn't see, for example, how an Italian nursery rhyme could be translated and delivered in English with the same sense of poetry. In the end, I was forced to use nearly all my annual budget on subtitles, leaving little funds for the other productions I was required to make in order to graduate. The film inspired other Italo-Australian student filmmakers to tell stories in their own language, including AFTRS's Monica Pellizzari (*Rabbit on the Moon*) and Swinburne Film and Television School's Luigi Acquisto (*Spaventapasseri*).

To some extent, *La Scala* defied categorisation. While it wasn't explicitly gay, it dealt with the learning of sexual difference against a background of Catholicism and cultural diversity. It was with some trepidation that I discovered the film was invited to open the 1985 Sydney Gay and Lesbian Film Festival, playing as the short to the feature documentary *Whoever Says the Truth Shall Die* (1981) about the death of Pier Paolo Pasolini by Philo Bregstein. While it received a good response, some of the audience was confused by its inclusion in a gay festival; apparently it wasn't 'gay' enough for them. The reaction was in contrast to the supposed inclusiveness of minority groups. I wasn't only gay but the son of immigrants, raised a Catholic, brought up in a working-class family and of non-English-speaking background. Why shouldn't those aspects of my life be part of the gay experience on screen?

For all my passionate advocacy in trying to get *La Scala* made, I wanted to lock it away never to be seen again. The reason: I received a heartbreaking letter from one of my sisters, revealing that our father had sexually molested her as a child. It was gut-wrenching news and ripped the family apart. The level of anger and hurt I felt on behalf of my sister was indescribable. She had carried this heavy burden alone for so much of her life.

I was also to discover that my sister had suffered decades of depression –

something I hadn't realised while growing up. Indeed, what made the situation worse was that her and her husband thought we all knew what had been going on and had turned a blind eye. Nothing could've been further from the truth and it posed an ethical dilemma for me as a filmmaker. Arguably, *La Scala, Lo Scalone* represented a lie, an image of my family that hadn't really existed when one looked below the surface. I felt I had been conned. Reflecting on it, I realised it was all that I was allowed to see as a child and realistically, all I was capable of understanding at the time.

I still find it hard to watch the film but when I do, I spot clues as to a harsher reality: the apparent non-existent relationship between my father and sister on screen, and the early death of my mother, possibly brought on by the discovery of the abuse. Remarkably, my sister eventually forgave my father, occasionally caring for him during his old age as his health deteriorated. Luigi De Chiera (born Di Chiera), father to Peter, Cecelia, Mary, John and I, passed away on 8 October 1996, one day short of his 86th birthday. I gather he didn't want to hang around for another party. My brother and sisters had been with him just prior to his death but he chose a brief moment when none of them were in the room to pass away. I'd spent the previous night by his side saying goodbye before flying back to Adelaide where I was in the middle of directing the miniseries *Three Forever* (1996). Made for SBS in Australia and RAI Uno Italy and starring Bud Spencer, the cast and crew gave me some time to compose myself after receiving the sad news on set.

I know my father was far from a perfect man, a monster in some people's eyes, but in the end, he admitted his dreadful failings and asked for forgiveness from the person he hurt, his daughter. And this was done in front of my sister's husband and children. It gave me the courage to share my own feelings in return. I told him that I thought I would never be able to say I had a father of whom I was proud but I acknowledged he had changed. In the last years of his life, he lived by example. My father's death was hardest on my sister because she felt she'd found the father she'd never had, only to have him taken away a few years later.

The concept of family is a malleable thing. Like relationships, there's no one definition. I've lived in all sorts of family situations, including gay ones; people who I regarded as much a family as my own. My time with Tim and John was one such example. The house in Sydney where we lived was located on Enmore Road, Edgecliff, beneath the eastern suburbs railway overpass. It was adjacent to the gentrified suburb of Paddington but still close enough to Kings Cross if you needed a good dose of sleaze. The fourth member of our household was Ben Drayton, a boy from Maitland who'd decided to pursue a career as a DJ. It was hardly a secure vocation but who were we to criticise? After all, I was a filmmaker and Tim an actor. John, it seemed, was the only sensible one – a chiropractor – setting up a clinic with a mate in Crows Nest. Ben proved us wrong. He's a celebrated Sydney DJ to this day.

Most of our social life was spent in the eastern suburbs including Sydney's Gay Golden Mile, Oxford Street. It may have been a magnet for the LBGTI+ community but it also attracted homophobes who regularly bashed and murdered gays with considerable immunity. From the big muscly bouncers to the churlish door bitches, Oxford Street's gay venues provided a safe haven from the ominous world outside. One of the most popular venues was the Midnight Shift where I filmed a scene for one of my early films *Bad News Bachelors* (1990). A parody of single life in Sydney, it tells the story of a gay man and straight woman, played by Nicholas Papademetriou and Helen Dallas, who meet regularly at coffee shops bemoaning their romantic disasters. A little ahead of its time, *Sex and the City* came along 8 years later with its own brand of sexual liberation – straight, gay and everything in between.

The representation of gay characters in cinema was thoroughly explored in Italian-American Vito Russo's brilliant book *The Celluloid Closet*. Vito visited Sydney in the mid 80s during the Sydney Gay and Lesbian Mardi Gras Film Festival. On the first occasion, he presented a series of lectures about gays in cinema. This was before his book was published. It was a liberating and fun-filled experience. Well, not so much for Vito though. He suffered a serious bout of sunstroke at one of the city's gay nude beaches, Lady Bay – known as 'Lady Jane' among the gay community – and spent the rest of his stay holed up in his hotel room with the curtains drawn. I called by with food and medical supplies, mainly creams to treat his burns. Applying them to his slender, fragile body was no mean feat. I was convinced he would never want to return to Australia after that. But he did, years later, for the release of his book.

This time I supervised his visit to Lady Bay!

When we got there, he undressed to reveal a pair of black leather swimming trunks, not at all suited to the humidity of Sydney's summer weather. Despite cloud cover, the sunrays were deceptively strong. I applied a thick layer of 30+ sunscreen for good measure. Vito was a delightful and intelligent person, full of gossip from Hollywood and New York, the latter being where he lived and spent most of his time. As we lazed about gawking at the 'featherless peacocks' on display, he told me his partner was sick in hospital with AIDS. He was worried about him and didn't know how long he should stay in Australia. He also confided about his own HIV status. It was upsetting, but revelations of this kind were so common back then that we quickly discussed it, sharing a sombre moment and moving on.

When I dropped Vito off at his hotel, there was an urgent message waiting for him – his partner had deteriorated and he needed to return to the US as soon as possible. Sometime later he wrote to say he didn't make it back in time – sadly, his boyfriend passed away before he got there. It must've been shattering. For all the horrible challenges Tim and John had faced before their deaths, they at least got to say goodbye. It was a small consolation given what a devastating thing it is to do. By the time the film version of *Celluloid Closet* was released in 1996, Vito had also died. Narrated by Lily Tomlin, the documentary was a fitting celebration of Vito's life and the contribution he made to gay representation on screen.

Living at Enmore Road was one of the most wonderful, and gloomy, times of my life. It was in 1985 that we debated having AIDS tests at the Albion Street AIDS Clinic in Darlinghurst. Young Ben didn't want to know his status. He rationalised that given there was no cure, getting an antibody positive result would only stress him out and hasten his decline. On the other hand, many health experts believed it was important to know one's status as it could motivate those with the virus to live healthier lifestyles. The aim: to survive long enough for an effective treatment to become available. I was the first to make an appointment and Tim and John soon followed. Ben stuck to his guns and bowed out.

My results were negative. The next week Tim and John were informed of theirs. Tim was antibody positive and John was initially told he was negative. But just as they were absorbing the shock, and this is well documented in *Holding the Man*, they discovered that John's results had been misread. Tragically, he too was antibody positive; tragic because in those days it was a death sentence. AIDS did finally take both their lives; John, seven years later in 1992 aged 31 and Tim in 1994, aged 34. Tim hung in just long enough to complete his book. I remember that when they returned home from the clinic, I knew the news wasn't good; they were white as ghosts. A distraught Tim quizzed me about my own status. He wanted to know if I was really antibody negative since we'd previously had sex. He thought I might have fabricated the story to avoid them worrying until they got their results. I confirmed I really was negative.

AIDS sufferers were relegated to the fringes of society; their eating utensils were thrown away and they were treated like lepers. It was the last thing I wanted Tim and John to feel. I walked up to them, kissing them both on the lips and giving them a long hug. I wanted to do all I could to comfort them.

As they retired to their bedroom upstairs, I quickly ran up the street to buy urgent supplies – tea and cake. On my return, I could hear them sobbing. I took a deep breath, climbed up to their room, knocked on their door and entered. We just looked at each other; words were superfluous. Tim and John's tears betrayed the implications of what they'd discovered, not the least of which was the fear and discrimination they would now have to face. Tea and cake may have been comforting, it was never going to be enough.

This was the environment in which anti-gay messages of politicians such as Rev Fred Nile and Franca Arena thrived. Coincidentally, in 1993 Arena launched the Sydney premiere of my music documentary, *The Joys of the Women*, a film that documents the journey of a young Italo-Australian musician Kavisha Paola Mazzella to establish the Fremantle Italian Women's Choir. It records the last vestiges of the traditional Italian folk music in Australia while telling the touching personal stories of the immigrant women involved. A member of the Australian Labour Party, Arena was the first woman from a non-English-speaking background to be elected to the New South Wales Parliament. She was incredibly supportive of young artists like myself wanting to explore their Italian cultural backgrounds.

Unfortunately, her charm, warmth and great intellect didn't always translate into her political life. She hit the national stage after naming retired judge David Yeldham and former New South Wales MP Frank Arkell as potential paedophiles under parliamentary privilege. Her relationship with the gay community was further strained when she headed a parliamentary enquiry into giving financial assistance to the 'innocent' victims of AIDS, namely those who'd contracted it medically through blood transfusions. It implied that gays and people who'd contracted the disease through intravenous drug use deserved it. This was despite the fact that the majority of them had become infected with the virus before anyone really knew anything about how it was transmitted. Like many others, Tim and John were victims of circumstance.

I was really disappointed by Arena's public pronouncements; that someone I knew and admired could be so ignorant. This selective compassion infuriated gay activists and the controversy escalated when Queer Nation publicly 'outed' her twin sons who were both well-known diplomats. I always wondered what Arena felt about me being gay. Maybe she didn't know because it was something we'd never discussed. Or perhaps she didn't want to know, just as she'd presumably done with her sons. Nonetheless, I was grateful for her role in introducing my film. Fortunately, that was before the controversies with which she became embroiled had reared their ugly heads. At the launch of *The Joys of the Women*, she gave a wonderfully generous speech, helping to put the film on the map. For all her faults, Arena was still a torchbearer for female immigrants.

The film catapulted Kavisha and the Choir onto the national stage, climaxing in a concert in Canberra to celebrate the 100th anniversary of Australian women winning the vote – in the presence of then Prime Minister Paul Keating. The women also recorded the theme song for the Fremantle Docker's football team and sang it at their grand final match in Perth, making front-page newspaper headlines. One of the members, Emma Ciccotosto, became an author, doing the rounds of television talk shows promoting her books including the award winning, *Emma: A translated life* (1990). A stage adaptation was a critical and box office success.

In 2013, we had the 20th anniversary screening of the film at the Luna Palace Cinema in Perth. Emma was reluctant to go but Kavisha and I persuaded her for old time's sake. As one of the few original choir members left, we really wanted her to be there. At the end of the screening, aged 85, she got up with Kavisha and the choir to perform to a full house, stealing the show with her infectious enthusiasm. Soon after, Emma died unexpectedly while having a routine medical procedure. The anniversary event not only became her swan song but marked the end of an era in the history of the choir. The new generation of members continue to celebrate Italian immigrant women in Australia and their multifaceted lives, symbolising a kick up the arse for ethnic stereotypes.

Franca Arena wasn't the only high-profile woman to become involved in the AIDS debate. Ita Buttrose was one of the more enlightened proponents of progressive policies designed to halt the spread of the disease. As teenagers, my sisters and I loved Ita. She was the founding editor of the ground-breaking magazine, *Cleo*, which not only discussed women's health issues such as abortion, female sexuality and other taboo subjects all in a very frank way, but also featured male nude centrefolds. Clearly, young women weren't the only ones responsible for its high circulation; gay men were also fans. Buttrose featured in the first Australian series of *Who Do You Think You Are?* (2007), which became one of SBS's highest rating local productions of all time. I was fortunate enough to write and direct a couple of the episodes including Ita's.

Ita was a trailblazer. She'd cracked the glass ceiling as the first female editor-in-chief of a major metropolitan newspaper in Australia, Sydney's *Daily Telegraph*. Everywhere one turned, there was Ita – in commercials, on billboards, on TV talk shows, in print media and on radio. The fact that she proudly allowed this exposure despite a speech impediment inspired women all over the country to have confidence in themselves. And for an

Italian-Australian gay man like myself, it proved that whoever you were, you could rise above disadvantage and shrug off the ridicule.

Inclusion was an issue close to my heart, motivating me to produce the 12-part anthology series *Under the Skin*. This package of dramas evolved out of a documentary series I produced five years earlier called *A Change of Face* (1988), which challenged notions of Australian identity on screen. It argued for a film and television industry inclusive of Australia's cultural diversity in front of and behind the camera. It caused a sensation and, according to *The SBS Story: The challenge of diversity* by Ien Ang, Gay Hawkins and Lamia Dabboussy, 'The coverage and controversy surrounding the series made it one of the most influential SBS Television has ever made.' However, decades on, audiences might still be asking: has anything really changed?

The *Under the Skin* drama series put into practice what *A Change of Face* had proposed. Shot around Australia, the stories were culturally diverse, including characters of Italian, Polish, Chinese, Fijian-Indian, Aboriginal, Greek and Vietnamese backgrounds as well those of Anglo-Saxon and Celtic origins. The diverse cast were wonderful. Many of them had agents but had been unable to get decent roles until *Under the Skin* came along. Diversity was also reflected among the writers and directors, including Chinese Australian Tony Ayres who wrote the episode *The Long Ride*. I'm also proud of the fact that the series featured two gay characters. Long before the American TV drama series *Six Feet Under*, writer/director Belinda Chayko conceived a gay mortician in the episode *Grandma's Teeth*, an idiosyncratic comedy. And Teresa Crea, an important figure of the Italian-Australian theatre scene, having established Doppio Teatro in Adelaide, wrote and directed *Windows* about two immigrant women cleaners who have an affair.

Launching the series in Sydney in 1994, Annita Keating, wife of the then prime minister, exclaimed, '*Under the Skin* is not about Australian multi-culturalism . . . it was possible because of it.' A former Dutch national, she understood only too well the potency of such a distinction. The industry nominated it for five Australian Film Institute Awards, winning Best Miniseries/Telefeature; an ATOM Award for Best TV Series; and four Australian Writers Guild Awards nominations, winning two of its categories. But the series was also credited with a much wider impact by SBS Independent's first general manager, Andy Lloyd James. In an interview with *Encore* magazine (18 April to 8 May edition, 1994), he acknowledged that it was one of the main catalysts for the formation of SBS Independent, finally enabling the network to commission independent filmmakers from a range of cultural backgrounds to tell their own stories, hear their own voices and see their own faces. Perhaps the most celebrated of these voices was Tony Ayres who went on to become one of the principals at the highly successful production house, Matchbox Pictures.

After *Under The Skin*, Tony and I worked together again while I was an executive producer at Film Australia. He adapted and directed William Yang's one-man show, *Sadness* (1999). I remember seeing another of William Yang's shows, *Blood Links*, when my partner Steven and I were living in Rome in 2004. The show had more than enough personal resonances for Steven who was Malaysian Chinese and had migrated to Australia with his family at the age of 15. Many people have speculated that the Chinese and the Italians have much in common, from their large family get togethers to their cuisines, not to mention the role of matriarchs in their children's lives, particularly those of their sons. Indeed, my feature comedy *Big Mamma's Boy* (2011) which was released theatrically and sold to Foxtel's Movie Network, could easily have been set in a Chinese-Australian family. That familiarity might partly explain why Yang's stage show played to packed houses in the Eternal City. To see a Chinese Australian performing a subtitled monologue with little more than slides and percussion instruments and attract a standing ovation in such an ancient city says more about the universality of human experience than the differences. Yang returned to Italy a few years later with another show but *Sadness* remains one of the pinnacles of his career.

Part of the reason I moved to Melbourne in 1998 was because of such sadness; there were too many memories of loss in Sydney from the AIDS era. When I got there, I wanted to visit John's grave but didn't know where it was located. Set among the thousands of tombs at Fawkner Cemetery in a grassy area with a discrete headstone, it was difficult to find. Intermittently over the years, Andrew, a friend of Tim and John's, and I have made the trip to Fawkner on the anniversary of John's passing, relying on a little divine intervention to lead us to his grave. Visiting is always full of mixed emotions, not the least of which is some regret that Tim was never buried with him. Instead, he was cremated and his ashes scattered elsewhere by his family.

Holding the Man's film production team managed to secure Tim and John's old school Xavier as a primary location. I remember Tim sharing his memories of the Catholic Jesuit Brothers who taught him and John and how they never got in the way of their budding relationship. Whether out of respect or because they were gay themselves, the brothers left the lovebirds to their own devices. That is, until John's father intervened, forbidding the boys from making any further contact with each other. But they always found a way. I didn't go to John's funeral – it was a private family affair. Things were already strained between Tim and John's father and the situation reached a climax at the service. Tim was sidelined, unable to sit among the people considered to be John's nearest and dearest. This was despite being John's loving and devoted partner and caring for him during his long illness. Nor did Tim, their relationship or AIDS rate a mention in the eulogies.

The deep emotional injury Tim suffered at the funeral still tears many of us apart. John's family may have felt the stigma associated with AIDS but there were no excuses for the failure to recognise and support his partner-in-life at his time of need. When I think about the ridiculous debate conducted around gay marriage and the hypocrisy of federal parliamentarians on both sides of politics procrastinating in the face of public support, their behaviour can only be described as appalling. The religious right would do well to remember that marriage vows are promises each partner makes 'to have and to hold, from this day forward, for better, for worse, for richer, for poorer, in sickness and in health, until death do us part'. Tim and John practised these fundamental principles as much as any strong straight marriage I've known.

Tim passed away several years later in 1994. At his wake, we were all asked to take one of his belongings to remember him by. Initially, I didn't want to participate. It was like dismantling what remained of Tim and John's lives and having to accept they were finally gone. In the end, I chose Tim's Mickey Mouse toy, which had accompanied him on his pilgrimage to the Aeolian Islands after John died, and featured in so many of Tim's holiday snaps. These and many other reminders continue for those of us left behind. The day before I visited Xavier College, I'd been to a little Italian café in Footscray, Cavallaro & Sons, to eat their prized Sicilian ricotta cannoli. Up on the wall was a photo of Lipari, where John's family came from. I may have escaped sad memories of the AIDS era in Sydney, but here in Melbourne Tim and John's story is ever present. When Tim visited Lipari, he caught glimpses of John in the faces of the locals who inhabited this dot of land in the middle of the Tyrrhenian Sea. I remember Tim recounting a story about a waiter that strongly resembled John – handsome and dark haired with long eyelashes and an angelic smile. It must've been both thrilling and heartbreaking for him to be reminded of his beloved man in such a physical and spiritual way.

A few days after seeing *Reading Sicily* at Tim and John's old school, I received DVD copies of the feature-length documentary *Remembering the Man*. It's a remarkable piece of work, using Tim's voice from an AIDS oral history project as the narration, complemented by contributions from friends. I was interviewed for the film but was somewhat of a bubbling mess. I asked the directors to edit out as much of my tears as they could; they kindly obliged.

On Sunday 30 July 2017, *Remembering the Man* was broadcast on ABC 2 in prime time, some 25 years after John's passing. It coincided with a turning point in the gay marriage debate as rogue federal government MPs argued over a conscience vote. While this political drama was playing out and Australia crawled toward a plebiscite to finally decide on the matter, Steven and I were invited to attend the wedding of gay friends Oscar and Stefano in Italy – the most Catholic nation on earth. This same right is now being exercised in more than 20 countries around the world, including Australia. Reflecting on Tim and John's lives, I realise they've played significant roles in the battle against AIDS, homophobia and marriage inequality. Their deaths, and those of so many in the gay community, have not been in vain. Creative forces have ensured their stories and characters live on, in the hearts and minds of those who knew and loved them or wished they had. They are immortal.

Franco at Kelmscott Primary School sports carnival
(aged 10) and fancy dress ball (aged 12)

'The earthen smell'

A coming out tale

Anton Enus

It was empowering to be out. All the confusion that had been part of my life vanished. When the whole world knew I was gay, I wasn't angry anymore. – Ian Roberts (2007)

I've led a charmed life. I've been fortunate enough to be out of the closet since the 1980s, first to my parents and close friends, then – in the 1990s when I had a bit of a media profile – in the more public sense.

Unlike Ian Roberts, my sometimes neighbour where I live in Sydney, I had experienced no anger in my hitherto closeted life. Anxiety, perhaps; frustration, certainly. There was a clear sense of burden, of being alone with this problem. The amazing thing about being out was this: it was liberating and explosively energising. I find it amusing to relate to friends that I've been outed not once, but twice in my life. What makes this particularly hilarious is that I had been 'out and proud' prior to both of these media reports, but no one had noticed. So, the 'news' of my being gay was, in fact, old hat, unremarkable, nothing more than a reporter's idea of spicing up a dull weekend.

The journalist in question, Eben Engelbrecht, a former colleague and the then husband of a friend, called me one day and said he was filing a report for the Afrikaans Sunday broadsheet, *Rapport*, in which he was going to reveal my homosexuality. At that point I was a fairly prominent TV news presenter on the SABC, the national broadcaster in South Africa.

That left me with a clear-cut, if invidious, choice. Ignore him and face the consequences of a potentially damaging newspaper report. Or, more strategically, engage him on the facts in the hope of softening the impact. I opted for the latter, figuring I'd rather be party to my own fate than put myself at the mercy of a deadline-driven reporter whose motives were not clear.

The Sunday came and went, the report entered the public domain, and the sky did not fall. No one – not even in God-fearing, communist-hating, family-values-driven* South Africa – seemed particularly put-out by my sexuality. The fact of the matter was that I had, by then, served on gay and lesbian community committees for years and had been a spokesman for Frontrunners and other sports organisations. I had done numerous radio interviews (including ones where I'd had to deal with inane questions such as, 'so what is gay sport exactly?'). I had even appeared on a TV panel discussion about sexuality in which I had been completely transparent about being gay. In other words, the spectre of doom had been overstated. To be fair, I had had some pretty anxious moments, imagining that my fledgling career as a news presenter was about to come crashing down, with the word 'SCANDAL' emblazoned across my picture in the press.

This thankfully anticlimactic response to my outing in the national press proved an interesting point: the threat of sanction, the fear of losing face, was always going to be greater than the real danger. However, it was now the 1990s and things had changed. Apartheid, that iniquitous source of oppression, was effectively dead. South Africa was on its way to a new, democratic future that sought genuinely to include all minorities, which it duly did.

In 1990, Johannesburg held its first ever Gay Pride March, a jumbled mass of community groups, loose political alliances, and individuals spilling out onto the streets of Braamfontein, Joubert Park and Hillbrow in the inner city. All of us, I'm sure, had well-founded feelings of uncertainty, such as about the hate-mongering Christian fundamentalists who sought to rain on our parade. Perhaps our greatest anxiety was the presence of the police. Long part of the apartheid repressive machinery, they were meant to protect and guide us on the streets, but would they? Or would they actively crack down on us?

Most fears were, happily, unfounded. The police were mainly concerned with managing the traffic and seemed wholly unconcerned with the tenor of the protest. The 'Turn-or-Burn' placarders were few in number and certainly no match for the colourful and – dare I say – performance-enhanced rhetoric of the dancing queens. We'd waited a long time, some for all our lives, for an opportunity to be out and proud. Loud and proud! And a minuscule group of misguided people, badly dressed and spouting hatred, was not going to stop us.

As a teenager I'd felt so very alone in trying to come to terms with how different I was to the other boys at school and in my social circles, like Scouts. If only I'd had someone to talk to, someone in a public position who could

---

* For the benefit of those of you – and I'm sure there are many – who are not *au fait* with South Africa's twentieth century history, this is meant to be a sarcastic reference to the apartheid establishment that ran the country.

reassure me that it was okay. So, later, when my turn came and I was able to build a public profile, I decided I would, for what it was worth, make it my goal to be visible and vocal. On the eve of one of the subsequent Gay Pride marches, I was part of a group of volunteers building a float in someone's backyard. We were making flower rosettes and attaching them to mesh wire, which in turn was going to transform into something magical. Beavering away alongside me was a friendly young guy and eventually we got chatting. After a while, he said he wanted to thank me. What for?, I wanted to know. Well, he said, he'd grown up in a small, conservative town in the Eastern Cape. There'd been absolutely no scope for his sexuality to be acknowledged, let alone nurtured. But, he said, he'd read in the newspaper that I had come out. So, there, every night on his television, he had someone he could relate to, someone who knew what his world was like. I gave him a hug, because if ever there was vindication for my being out and proud, this was it. That one person was enough as far as I was concerned – whose life was just a little better, whose outlook was a bit more positive.

My coming out happened in Grahamstown, a quaint, sometimes charming provincial town in the Eastern Cape province of South Africa. Rhodes University, named after a political giant of the colonial era, Cecil John Rhodes, occupied a prime cultural and economic – as well as beautiful geographical – position overlooking the town. Rhodes presented many hurdles for me to leap over, not the least of which was academic. There was also the political challenge of a race-driven society and its effects on me, a young dark-skinned kid attending a 'white' university. The federal education minister, in all his puffed-up importance, had deigned to grant me a permit to attend the university. The underlying message being hammered home was that I owed my presence there and my chances of a valuable education to the goodwill of the apartheid government. It left me feeling frustrated, but, if the truth be told, also under a self-imposed pressure to behave myself. It was always there at the back of my mind, the thought that a successful tenure on my part would help the next black student get in and enjoy the same opportunities. Or, put more succinctly, I felt all of us black students were on permanent probation. Naïve, I know, but there it is, a relic from apartheid South Africa.

When you have the door slammed continuously in your face, you learn not to take initiatives. You become less proactive, less creative and less innovative. You may become resigned to following orders. This may explain why whites, already used to being affirmed, jump at the slightest opportunity while blacks often wait to be asked to perform tasks. – Seepe (2004)

Before coming to Rhodes, I'd had no notable friendships across the colour line. You could say it was a triumph of *apartheid*, which, after all, means 'separate-ness'. So in 1980, the prospect of this unique brand of social separation being tested in my personal experience was at hand. It was a thought I approached with muted excitement, but also with a measure of unavoidable trepidation. The dilemma for me was the fear of being found out, coupled with the secret delight of being surrounded by 60 or so testosterone-enriched individuals in the men's residence where I now lived. There were the sporty types, lean frames in perfect balance as they set off for football or hockey training; the rugby players, hefty and thick of neck who strutted about, their masculinity on display, like Stanley Kowalski in *A Streetcar Named Desire*. There were the politically-sensitive arts students and their androgynous girlfriends; the must-impress wannabes with their overblown boasts of sexual escapades; the loudly obnoxious Eastern Cape brothers who were still strangely attractive; the blond Zimbabwean whose slight deafness – and muscular thighs – made him all the more appealing; the unreconstructed MCP (Male Chauvinist Pig) about whom I had discreet sexual fantasies (actually there were a few who fitted that description); these guys – teenagers some – exuded that essential maleness so maddeningly alluring when it's so out of reach.

What is it about men that so excites me and my kind? I'm not sure that I can adequately encapsulate that feeling, but it's akin to a primordial force, the unerring impulse of nature. It's philosophy, lust, admiration – many things rolled into one. All I know is that it's as powerful as anything I've ever felt, made even more so, perhaps, by the *verboten* quality imposed on it by generations of learned social oppression. Gay men everywhere know what it's like to be made to feel there are parts of ourselves – legitimate, essential, fundamental parts of ourselves – that are stuffed into dusty corners of our memories, relegated to a second tier of consciousness, because they are deemed shameful by those who wield power in our society.

I who knew what his body tasted like, the salt of his mouth, the earthen smell between his legs. – Mendelsohn (2000)

It was some time later in that transitional phase of university life that I finally found the courage to start the difficult, unavoidable process of coming out. It's the only time of my life that I've seriously thought of myself as being depressed. I'd lie for hours in a darkened room, just wallowing. That's such a great word for it, so perfectly descriptive. Whatever idea I came up with to get out of this situation seemed doomed. I couldn't be gay and happy at the same time, in spite of the dictionary definition that begged to differ.

I knew that lying in a room with the curtains drawn was no solution. I had to tell someone. I sat down and wrote two letters. One was to an old school friend from Cape Town, the other to my cousin, Ricardo, who was roughly the same age as me and a university student in Durban.

My school friend was a very beautiful young woman, whose company and attention was much sought after among my peers. She would later have a brief career as a TV actress. Her reply was immediate and to the point: 'No problem,' she said. But was I absolutely sure about my sexual orientation? And if I wasn't, would I like to sleep with her to make certain? Even in my exaggerated state of emotional flux, I could see the funny side of that. I could just imagine the cachet this kind of offer would have had among my old schoolmates, who would have given their favourite testicle for a chance like this.

Of course, I respectfully and gratefully declined, but was touched by her unique gesture of support. She and I would remain friends for the ensuing decades. She is still living in Cape Town, married and the mother of a teenager.

Ricardo wrote back to me saying, 'Guess what? I'm gay too.' At last a real, empathetic ally in this personal awakening. But, in truth, I needed someone there and then to share my thoughts with. I looked around. About 90 per cent of the footy-loving lads of Botha House where I lived would probably have beaten me up for having the temerity even to raise a subject like that with them, let alone admit to being a homosexual. After all, as everyone knows, talking about gay issues with other guys is tantamount to suggesting they're gay as well.

The few who had somehow managed to find a room at the inn without being obsessed with sport I didn't know well at all. There were yet others I regarded as friends, but that brought with it new tensions. What if I was misjudging their apparently liberal outlook and found instead that my revelation would put undue pressure on our friendship?

It eventually boiled down to one person, a Zimbabwean friend. I got the feeling he was – like me – a bit of a square peg in a round hole. He was a soft-spoken, gentle kind of a guy, open to many different ideas and not easily offended. And, I mused, perhaps, just perhaps, he was sensitive enough to be gay, or at least in the grey zone. A nice fantasy, I thought. He'd had the odd girlfriend. But then, so had I.

So, one day I asked him to set some time aside because I wanted to tell him something important. It was commonplace for mates to get together in each other's rooms for coffee and a chat. I fumbled about a bit but eventually had to bite the bullet. 'I'm gay,' I said, as simply and straightforwardly as I could muster. It was the first time I'd actually uttered the words out loud to someone who didn't know and the relief was immediate. He was very understanding and supportive, but it was obvious to me – without any words being spoken to this effect – that he was definitively heterosexual. Even more sobering was his next response. After a few days to let things settle, he came up with a suggestion. He wanted to drag me off to see one of the student counsellors. These were not university staff counselling students, but undergrad psychology students who did counselling as part of their practical course work. And when I say 'drag' I mean that in the literal sense. I remember him grabbing me by the arm and trying to physically pull me all the way to the Psych department. I resisted like a pig being led to the slaughter and proved too strong for him. That, perhaps, was a pity, because it probably would have speeded up my dealing with those messy sexuality issues. But no, I was having none of it. No way was I going to discuss my situation with some stranger who, for all I knew, was going to have a good laugh with his mates at the pub afterwards about the poof he was counselling. I simply had no idea how these things worked, no conception about privacy and trust in that kind of professional situation.

Gradually, I started telling my closest friends and my black secret slowly changed to shades of grey. Astonishingly enough, not one single person I've told – then or since – has rejected me or walked away from our friendship. That's a wonderfully gratifying thought, which speaks eloquently about the calibre of friends I have had over the years.

So, looking back, it was a double whammy for me. I was dealing with the racial adjustment of life at a white university and making new friends across the colour line, while at the same time being hit with this mind-altering reality of being gay. I suppose part of me always knew I was gay, but I certainly didn't accept it. Like most other people in this kind of situation, I thought it was just a phase I had to pass through as I progressed toward adulthood. I dabbled with girlfriends. Sincerely, I might add. In case you're wondering, let me be clear: it was all romance and no sex. There is no way on earth I would have been capable of faking my way through that minefield, had it ever become an eventuality. I'm not sure what those girls were thinking but perhaps I got away with the no-sex approach because I was a reserved, polite young man, far removed from the grappling, groping types some of my heterosexual friends probably were.

I suppose I always felt like something of an outsider. I was English-speaking in a community that spoke mostly Afrikaans; I lived in a largely Third World country when I regarded myself as something of a global citizen;

I was gay in a straight world; a person of colour in a society dominated by white racists.

The second time I came out, if indeed it is possible to come out twice, was in Sydney in the 21st century when I was interviewed by *TV Week* magazine. As the relatively new presenter of the late news on SBS, I was, of course, eager to build a profile by making public appearances and saying yes to virtually all interview requests. Over coffee in Potts Point, the reporter casually pointed out to me that there was an Anton Enus listed as a silver medal winner at the 1998 Gay Games in Amsterdam. 'Was that you?' he wanted to know. The question shook my equilibrium a little as I had assumed the interview would just be about the usual publicist-inspired material.* However, since I had put no restrictions on what kind of questions I would be taking and since he had clearly done his homework, I felt he deserved an answer. And I'm not in the habit of lying, so I had no option but to come clean. 'Yes,' I said, 'I won a silver medal in the squash championship.' Once again, this 'coming out' proved to be completely unremarkable. It was buried in a half-page column some-where in the middle of the magazine, completely overwhelmed by reports on Ramsay Street or whatever the soapie focus of that week was.

It wasn't until *Good Weekend* magazine, with its significant readership in the biggest Australian markets, interviewed Roger and me for its *Two of Us* feature that anyone took any notice. All the attention, I'm pleased to say, was positive. Literally for years afterwards, people would stop me in the street and say how much they'd enjoyed reading about our love story. SBS management, not surprisingly (given the generally supportive environment that existed there), had no quibbles.

So I have always thought that I've lived a charmed life, protected from some of its extremes by an unseen guardian. How else would one explain all the good fortune I've enjoyed: a rewarding career on two continents, a marvellously contented home life, the opportunity to explore and talk about literature at writers' festivals, a love of sport that has given me exciting experi-ences in beautiful places. I am not an activist in any substantive sense of the word. My role, as I see it, is to use my public profile to speak up where and when I can, bearing in mind that my contractual obligations preclude partici-pating in controversial or political public discourse. I like to think that my conduct as a figure in a trusted public role serves by example to make it easier for others to be out and proud. It seems to me the least I could do.

---

* The reporter has subsequently pointed out to me that he had in fact cleared this question with my publicist beforehand and I accept that.

After all, others made it easier for me. Such as my dear friend, Edwin Cameron, who bravely spoke up as a gay man living with HIV/AIDS on the eve of public judicial hearings as he sought appointment to the highest court (this was in a TV program I was producing – not an easy thing to ask of him). And Zackie Achmat, an outspoken activist who shamed the South African government into providing anti-retrovirals to people who couldn't afford them. And Simon Nkoli, a fellow runner, who worked tirelessly and quietly to raise awareness of gay-related issues in the townships of Johannesburg. And Graham Flax, my dear friend, serving on committees organising various sports events, fundraising, negotiating with contacts at the Federation of Gay Games to get (democratic) South Africa admitted. We put on fun runs, tennis tournaments, swimming carnivals, weekend hikes, even tea dances. We provided a home, a safe playground, within which we saw people blossom and flourish. Sadly, we said farewell to Graham just before Mardi Gras time in 2013. He was brutally attacked in his apartment in Sea Point, Cape Town, and left for dead.

When I think about visibility in our community, I hope we don't lose sight of what's at the heart of our overall campaign: to make life easier, more inclusive, more rewarding for all individuals. My friend Graham Flax and his gentle laughter form my template for measuring what we're capable of.

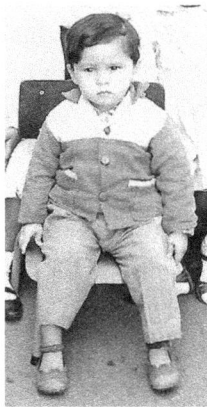

'I'm movin' up, nothing can hold me down, I'm gonna get to . . .'

Sally Goldner

The lyrics of Dreamworld's 1995 track 'Movin' Up' seem pretty apt as a way of starting my story. It was released the year I came out to myself and then gradually began coming out to others. I will always remember 27 April 1995: an issue dominated by a huge question mark finally moved into answer mode. For years, I had the image in my head of 'looking like a woman' and 'living as a woman' (my words to myself, for better or worse, in the first part of my life) – yet I didn't know what to make of it. Was I imaginative? Creative? Something else?

To some people reading this in 2018 and beyond, you're thinking, 'Huh, what?' For someone born in 1965, like myself, there was no internet, no social media or search engines. If I had sent a telegram to someone somewhere saying 'assigned male at birth stop think I'm female stop', I doubt I would have received a positive response. So I lived the first 29 plus years of my life knowing something but not knowing what to make of it.

I spent all 13 years of schooling at an Anglican boys' school – hardly a positive environment for a nice Jewish girl. It's a school that even in recent times has been in the news for the wrong reasons, such as sexist content from students on Instagram, and a counsellor saying boys who are bullied should 'toughen up'. It was like that in my time there from 1970 to 1982.

There was also a huge emphasis on sport, academic competition and (Anglican) religion. From an early age I had one eye weaker than the other so they were not in sync – not good for batting at cricket. I only realised later I have one leg shorter than the other and am a 'deep processing' person. So my resulting lack of football prowess due to not being a 'reflex' person added to my problems.

As well, there were the stupid remarks when returning to school after absence for the High Holy Days: 'Oh, you were off counting your taxes again.' To be fair, most of the religion taught by the school did focus on the true spirit of Christianity as taught by Jesus. Parables such as 'lay down your life for your friends' and the one about a rich man finding it hard to enter heaven were largely emphasised over the technicalities of the Old Testament. But constant bullying from most of the class in Years 7 and 8 tore apart my self-esteem, which was only held together by a reasonable academic record. The bottom line, however, is that the isolation and my need to survive school influenced my life for a long time afterwards (and still does) to a point where it was no longer serving me.

Being Jewish meant Sunday school, leading to my bar mitzvah at age 13. Again, lack of understanding of the truth about myself meant that the 'coming of age of a Jewish boy [sic] into a man' had no meaning for me whatsoever. Also, I received a very limited idea of what it was to be Jewish, for example 'donate money to Israel' did not mean anything to me.

To tidy up the first part of my physical life, on leaving school I studied commerce, majoring in accounting. I went to work as an accountant and, from 1989 to 1994, worked for a very difficult manager until I reached burnout. I quit work and travelled for three months, which relieved the short-term stress but also allowed what I had largely buried about gender to surface. I tried to get the information I needed to understand myself but to no avail. I then saw a psychiatrist who tried an aspect of conversion therapy on me and now we're back at 27 April 1995.

With the help of a wonderfully supportive friend, I had tracked down a psychologist who had completed her Masters in gender and sexuality. In the first session I gave my life story in the first 20 minutes, to which she replied: 'Has this ever been described to you this way? Some men are masculine then feminine. Some need to be female and that's called transgender'. Mega-sized light bulb moment. So that's why I hadn't fitted at an all boys' school! I remember driving away once the session was over and having to pull over. My mind was reframing 29 plus years within this new paradigm. The past made sense; for the first time I could focus on my future.

I lived nearly the next three years occasionally going out as female but still identifying mostly as male. My personal identity label during this period was *cross-dresser*. In regard to my sexual orientation, I still thought I was only attracted to women. In 1997, a moment of clarity emerged and I realised my truth: I was attracted to people regardless of gender. The only term I had at the time was bisexual; later I heard pansexual and now use bi/pan as my label. Dare I, as a nice Jewish girl, say 'gender, schmender'?

In early 1998, the façade of trying to live or identify as male simply dissolved. I reached the point of realisation that my identity was female and I needed to live as female for the sake of my own health and wellbeing. I started on hormones later that year and the feeling of finally seeing and feeling my body become what it needed to be was highly exciting. As with anything, it's always good to be in the present moment rather than be overly focused on the end point. This in itself led to an issue. Both of what is now called the trans and gender diverse (TGD) communities and broader society were still seeing TGD in very binary terms of transwomen only being 'real' (urk) if they had completed surgery or, to a lesser extent, were aiming for surgery. I was told I had 'stopped' or 'slowed down' because I wasn't desperately seeking a date for surgery. Thankfully, another helpful counsellor asked me a very useful question: 'Any person has any operation to make themselves happier and healthier. Will gender surgery do that for you?' My answer then and now: 'No'. I had reached the end (internally) of my gender and sexual orientation journeys. I had the bases for myself in these two areas. Having clarity in these areas enabled me to look at other parts of my life, including spirituality.

As mentioned, I had previously been turned off from Judaism by what seemed to be limited attitudes regarding money and also an anti-progressive bias. In 1998, I was fortunate enough to meet empathic people from the Jewish Lesbian Group. They were highly inclusive and welcoming to me as a transwoman and, in particular, attending the Jewish lesbian Seder was a wonderful experience filled with good principle, good humour (and good wine). The sense of connection with progressive-minded Jewish people was very welcome. Over the years I have been asked what Judaism means to me and it often comes back to that sense of community and connection above anything else. As someone who had previously experienced much isolation and emotional abandonment, this was something to treasure.

I see myself as a very spiritual person rather than being tied to a religion or a 'denomination' within a religion. I've looked into Wicca, paganism and a range of goddesses from other faiths and, while incorporating some bits and pieces from those faiths, I have ended up still with a connection to Jewish community. If there was a bump in the road, it was that at times I have witnessed incredibly high levels of chauvinistic behaviour in Judaism and Jewish male-identified people. It has been largely Jewish women who have kept my sense of connection.

Perhaps the best moment, the real sense of peace, came at the first ever Melbourne Pride Shabbat service in 2014. Being called up to read a short piece of the Scriptures was a long-delayed bar mitzvah at age 48. The sense of connectedness both within and to the outer world that evening was huge and I have really felt settled in this area of my life since then.

My spirit is broad and multifaceted, and spirituality encompasses much more than religion and needs to include all of this person. I believe in a universal power, creative force, love, spirit – call it what you will. In many ways we cannot see this; for me, it is there. Believing in it is faith. I am in that sense, to use a term that seems largely forgotten, a theist. I believe in *a* force, not the God of the Jews, Allah etc. I am happy with that, it works for me, and hopefully enables me to strengthen others. Every individual, however, has a different journey to travel and can only work out faith for themselves.

There are other parts of me that make up this whole spirit. I was always aware I was an introvert; like many introverts I had been judged for being 'too quiet' and 'not outgoing enough'. The two books *Introvert Power* (2008) by Dr Laurie Helgoe and *The Introvert Advantage* (1998) by Marti Olsen Laney were helpful in beginning to counter the negative beliefs I had taken on board. I realised it was fine to want time out to recharge and be by myself. Later, Susan Cain's fabulous book *Quiet: The power of introverts in a world that can't stop talking* (2012), led me to reclaim this part of me as the huge positive that it is. In a similar vein, I stumbled onto the Highly Sensitive Person (HSP) trait in 2005 while viewing the blog for a fabulous book called *The Career Guide for Creative and Unconventional People* (Eikleberry, 1995). A quick run-through of the self-test at hsperson.com and I realised this was a part of me. I never liked noisy environments, hated being rushed and having too many things to do at once. Yet, parallel to the introvert trait, I had been told I 'couldn't handle pressure', was 'withdrawn' and 'shy' and should 'toughen up'. Again, having accurate information helped me first eliminate negative beliefs about myself and then see this trait as the amazing gift that it is. I have huge insight and foresight into situations that often many others do not. As someone with a dry sense of humour said to me, 'It's an in-built nonsense detector' (they used a different eight-letter word to 'nonsense' which I have politely avoided). Sadly, people who are brought up on so-called left-brain and logical thinking still ridicule my approach to life; again, difference not being valued.

At the time of writing, as a deep-processing introvert, I believe strongly that we need some deep thought to counter the rise of right-wing, including anti-LGBTI, attitudes occurring in Australia and many parts of the world. Our own rainbow communities have not been good at valuing diversity time and again. Attitudes to TGD people have improved but there is still much work to do, especially for those of non-binary identity. Bisexual erasure and biphobia are still common. To use the language of Twitter, #binarybusters are still needed. Linking it all, in the same way that society puts expectations on us about gender identity, gender expression and sexual orientation (and sex characteristics for intersex people), society also puts expectations on people around neurological processing.

As someone whose traits differ from neurological expectations, I have huge empathy for those on the autism spectrum. A gathering of friends from one area of my life during 2016 to discuss autism made me realise autism is simply another way of looking at a situation parallel to HSP. Yet society overwhelmingly sees autism as negative or in deficit terms. A child experiencing autism is drugged because they want some time out and don't look people in the eye – goodness me. And this issue, while not affecting me personally, is of relevance as there is a strong correlation between TGD and autism and also bi and autism. I know there are bi and TGD people who are willing to speak up about this; let's hope they can lead the way in both the rainbow communities and broader society toward autism being valued for what it is.

Another area where we need legal and social progress is people working in the sex industry. It says how deeply gendernormativity and heteronormativity run that I, like many others, thought sex work was largely cisgender females servicing cisgender males. I had been aware of TGD in sex work for a long time, but thought it was a small part of the industry. My understanding of sex work has expanded rapidly in the last three years, both that its nature is very broad, for example bodywork and somatic counselling, and also that, according to Vixen Collective, more than 60 per cent of people working in the industry identify as LGBTIQ+. Our rainbow community will need to be truly inclusive of all those working in the industry if we are to achieve equality.

Another area for consideration is age. It is great that there are increasing numbers of programs and research pieces looking at the needs of rainbow seniors (let's group seniors as aged 55+) and youth (under 30). Society does tend to have a belief that those in the middle cohort (30–55) can easily look after themselves. While there is evidence that gays and lesbians in the middle cohort are doing reasonably well, for TGD and bi people, especially those outside larger cities, it is still far from a bed of roses at the point of coming out. Also, many middle cohort TGD people have faced significant rejection, abandonment, ridicule and similar and, while 'coming out' is a good thing, there is often a huge amount of emotion buried underneath. We will need to look at ideas to habilitate 30+ TGD people to live a full life.

I am one of those people with stuff buried underneath. At the time of writing, I have what could be called a body image issue. The years of bullying and ridicule about sport at school have left me with very negative beliefs about how my body coordinates. The distress from that bullying that has been buried for so long comes up when I exercise in any form. I have tried a range of forms of therapy to deal with this and, as yet, no success. Meantime, my weight continues to increase which is not healthy (and lots of clothes don't fit). Sadly, some people snipe at me rather than asking about the deeper issues, which doesn't help. It's a reminder that the effects of gender stereotyping and transphobia (and other prejudices) can run deep and in very subtle ways that society often can't, doesn't and won't see.

In 2006, while working with a life coach, I undertook an exercise to identify my values. Perhaps unsurprisingly, my biggest value turned out to be diversity. That value guides me – and it needs to guide the rainbow communities to greater heights in the future. Further, to quote Albert Einstein, 'the significant problems we have cannot be solved at the same level of thinking with which we created them'. While we can be hugely empathic and understanding of the difficulties faced by LGBTIQ+ people and the resulting internalised prejudices, we are all going to need to reduce the internalised prejudices we have if we are going to work together more effectively to overcome the rise of anti-LGBTIQ attitudes and progress to legal, social and all forms of equality. Imagine if every one of us eliminated one per cent of any negative ideas we had taken on board! What would the positive effect be for our communities? And what if it was two per cent? Five per cent? Ten per cent? Most of all, if people in positions of prominence and influence in the LGBTIQ+ communities eliminated even more, what would this do for us all?

The future is in our hands. We can keep progressing with persistence, growth and effort. When we value all the diversity under the rainbow, we can tap into all our strengths. The quicker we start doing it, the quicker we will all be better off. And we will all keep 'movin' up'.

Mixing Things Up Through Art

Carl Gopalkrishnan

I have known for a long time that I mix things up. I collapse time and space with the stroke of a brush. I mix colour, thought, energy and dream-like processes, and they all come out at once. It's not logical to others, but to me, well, it makes perfect sense. Despite the mythology, artists do real work. Over the years you delve deeper to focus on quality, on resolved pieces, and on completed thoughts.

All this makes perfect sense because this mixing began with my life. I'm a middle-aged gay male, and a lapsed Catholic. I'm also of Indian and Chinese heritage, was born in the UK, and grew up in Sweden before coming to Australia. I began working as a typographer and designer after studying graphic design in Perth, Western Australia. At the same time, I completed a BA in History and later received First Class Honours in Sociology. I have worked in many worlds. So I mix the worlds of academia, art, politics, music and the company of strangers. I didn't take the traditional road in my art practice and my painting technique is influenced by outsider traditions. My Indian and Chinese heritages instilled in me a respect for art that is inspired by a Spirituality of Ages rather than religious doctrine. That's the easy mix.

As a queer-identifying man of colour with multiple geopolitical and sexual identities, I have found myself directly affected by the political climate of the last two decades. After 2001, and for the first time, I started looking *outside* myself to use what is *inside* me to create an alternative to the narrative of the War on Terror. That narrative always insists that I use my cultural heritage to position my loyalties in a dangerous time. I also questioned my queer identity. As I aged, the queer community failed to diversify and grow. It tacitly accepted deceptions like pinkwashing as a form of queer internationalism. Mixing mediums, ideas and ideologies on the canvas has been my way of challenging these false victories.

This intermixing has renewed my passion for excavating stories from a blank canvas. For three decades I've been exploring the small gestures we select to define ourselves and the historical turning points that shape us. If nothing else, I'm happy if my life leaves a paper/paint trail for someone else to make sense of, because I learn so much from practising my art. I learn that living life itself is also about putting down the paint – good or bad – having to work with it and make it work, and accepting the temporal nature of that time and place in your life. Painting art or the art of life requires little acts of commitment to complete the story. It also needs research and contemplation. I paint even when I'm not painting.

I like to reach across dividing dogmas. I've presented my art at international intervention workshops in the UK, painted portraits of leading quantum physicists, and I've developed my ideas on how cultural politics and technology are changing the human story and the power of creativity to affect social change. Cultural relevance and cultural safety still don't get mixed into mainstream ideas of same-sex identities. LGBTI culture and politics still promote ethnic assimilation into an established visual gay identity. Yet the opportunities to form unique identities, or fusions and collaborations through being LGBTI and also multicultural, exist. A genuine queer internationalism is not about being told, 'This is *you* because that's how being gay is defined by *us*.' I see that paternalism today as quite nationalistic. I want to see a queer culture rich in the historical sexualities of Muslims, Indians, Pakistanis, Jews, Thais, English and people from different parts of Asia. At the moment, the language preferences LGBTI communities over multicultural communities. But we want to see both there because we live in both. Until we understand the diversity of sexuality in those cultures, it's hard to talk about other cultures positively in terms of sexuality. We need to hear it so we can be the bridge between communities. That's our role. We're a bridge.

Between 2008 and 2012, I created an exhibition with the Western, 'old school', queer culture of vintage Broadway and Hollywood musicals. I called it *The Assassination of Judy Garland*. I used Judy's life as an internal narrative arc, a reflective tool, as part of my personal response to the 9/11 consciousness we inhabit today. To me, she is more than a gay icon. She represents the best and worst of America – and their inevitable interoperability. I also had no difficulty with being sympathetic because I can't *not* be sympathetic to one side of Judy without acknowledging the damage on the other side. That damage is now in full view under President Trump.

I also used French medieval epic poetry – *chansons de geste* – roughly translated as 'songs of heroic deeds' because they were used at that time to support the political narratives of the Crusades in ways that reminded me of how many Hollywood products support the War on Terror. So the queer lens

I created for these paintings is a prescription lens made for a specific time and place. And this lens acts as a screen to both hide and reveal motivations and desires, as much as the screen icons I reference.

People seem to forget that queer theory breathes within a time of terror that smashes lenses and burns books. But I could not find a queer framework that helped me to paint what I saw. I no longer understood what I call the new normative queer, and so I returned to what I knew was 'naff' and 'old school'. I allowed myself to visually linger in the Hollywood of the 1930s and 1950s. I felt quite alienated from the new normative queer climate influenced by a hyper-masculinised LGBTI culture that was becoming increasingly nationalistic in its desire to go beyond its backroom history into the light of mainstream acceptance.

Screen culture has a power equal to that of the *chansons de geste*, which could inspire entire populations to lay down their lives through songs orally memorised and sung from village to village in the time of the Crusades. I took away from these paintings a deeper appreciation for how our intermixed queer histories have become silent pictures that sit patiently and move slowly behind the interactive and hyperactive edges of this new normative queer. So while I reference moving pictures, the surreality in my paintings is happening on the silent screen inside us. Applied to the bigger stage, this queer screen can affect the small gestures that lead to momentous global change. We should respect that power.

The painting here is an example of my 'mixed up' art:

Four Horses Running Wild (2012)

This painting is a 100% subconsciously created self-portrait. The energy of the Four Horses of the Apocalypse is how I experience the stories playing out in our phase of history. The biblical narratives of the Book of Revelations collapses time with Hollywood of the 1940s and the present into a continuous experience. History is not tone deaf and, like a DJ mixing songs, the mix up of perspective anatomy with folk art, expressionism, pop art screenprints and Byzantine biblical frescos on the canvas is the soundtrack of my generation.

Adoptee Diasporas and a Queer Jew
The precariousness of the 'I am'
Anne M. Harris

> [Roots trips] reveal the impossibility of ever being fully integrated, of having anything that constitutes both an outer and inner place where I belong. – Yngvesson (2003: 17)

Introduction

This chapter is about cultural and sexual diversity and belonging, but it is also about its impossibility. Is it useful or possible to define 'culturally diverse', or 'queer' for that matter, beyond one's own personal definition? For adoptees, the search for belonging is literal and is almost always tied to questions of race, culture, gender and sexuality. Going home is impossible; indeed, even searching for home can be crushing. Yngvesson reminds us that 'roots trips' and reunions often bring a 'loss of bearings' which 'involves the discovery of a self both familiar and strange, me and not-me' (2003: 9), unsettling the idea that such journeys are inexorably toward wholeness, as popular narratives and wish-stories would have us believe. 'Roots trips,' she tells us, 'reveal the precariousness of "I am", the simultaneous fascination and terror evoked by what might have been, and a longing for the safety of home' (2003: 9).

When I was a kid I used to sit on my bed and talk to my brother Michael via a string telephone (string for the wire, two paper cups for the handsets). We talked about our birth families. We were adopted through what they now call a 'closed' adoption process, so we never knew anything about our birth families until, somewhere around my 30th birthday, I went knocking on the closed door of my birthmother's house in San Jose, California. After years of searching (pre-internet) for my birthmother, of adoptee support groups, magazines, tragic short stories about alcoholic, suicidal or otherwise bad-ending stories about people like me, I finally broke down and hired a private detective known only as – true story – Mister Big.

Back then you had to talk to people by phone. There was no internet, no Skype. Even on a holiday weekend, after two days Mister Big had found the names, phone numbers and addresses of my birthmother, her three siblings and parents. He wouldn't release the information to me until I had paid him the (then exorbitant) sum of $2000, so of course I paid.

After a year of being hung up on by my birthmother, I decided to try my birth grandparents, who still lived near my adoptive parents' house in upstate New York. Giving up on phone contact, we decided to go in person. One visit home, my girlfriend Vanessa and I drove there and sat in their retirement apartment parking lot for several hours before finally knocking on the door. My grandmother (*babci*, in Polish) answered, and after an over-long stutter, and in desperation at her non-recognition, I shouted, 'I'm the one who kept calling you last month!'

A looked dawned across her face. We laughed nervously. She wagged an aged but strangely terrifying finger in my face. 'Oh boy, you are really gonna get it! Well I guess you better come in then.'

She stepped aside. Not exactly the tearful joyful reunion I had imagined. I stepped in.

'Hey!' she screamed over the television to the man sitting at a card table smoking, watching the baseball. 'Hey, who do you think this is?!'

He took one look, expressionless, and faced back to the TV. 'I got a pretty good idea.'

We sat.

Two things about my grandmother: we had a lot of the same mannerisms and we had exactly the same laugh (I was 29, she was 83). Vanessa said it was a good case for nature over nurture; it broke my heart. That visit she showed me a photo of my grandfather in Poland in a yarmulke. She denied they were Jewish, so I let it go. For queers and migrants and adoptees and refugees and so many of us, the stories of our lives don't always match the knowing of our lives, the rivers that run beneath what is obvious, visible or intelligible.

When I was about 10 or so, my mother went to work as a secretary at a Jewish synagogue near where we lived. Despite being a devout Roman Catholic, she had a great passion for comparative religions. She taught me that Jesus was Jewish and we should respect them for that, and she taught me that Jewish people were devout, had contributed enormously to world culture, and that they had a great love of learning. She also taught me that Barbra Streisand was Jewish and the stereotypical large Jewish nose was very resonant for singing and so there were a lot of good Jewish singers, like Neil Diamond, whom she loved. If my mother's positive biases toward Jewish people were largely stereotypical, they were at least a counter-narrative to the largely anti-Semitic context in which I grew up.

I loved the synagogue where she worked. I went to work with her when I could and have vivid memories of playing piano in the back room of Rabbi Kiefer, the kind young man who led the synagogue and who fed me my first lox and cream cheese bagel. I remember Rabbi Kiefer remarking to me how 'Jewish' I looked, which he attributed to my eyes and my colouring. My mother said happily, 'She could be, she could be. She's very good with music, so you never know!' I tried to demonstrate my resonant nose, much to Rabbi Kiefer's confusion.

My best friend in high school turned out to have a (non-practising) Jewish mother. I learnt from them about the concept of converting, but I also learnt about the ways in which Jewish and other identities hang around apart from dogma or ritual; how they can live in your blood, your bones, your stories and your food. There were jokes, food, music, unkind comments about money – little bits and bobs always attributed to her being Jewish. She loved it and celebrated her 'mutt' heritage and her mother (Gram) who was fully Jewish. We all loved it and celebrated it, mostly thanks to our mutual love affair with Barbra. From them I learnt about being culturally (if secularly) Jewish.

But we were mostly working-class white Christians, so when I moved to New York City at the age of 18 to go to university, I couldn't believe my luck. In case you've been living under a rock all your life, New York City is pretty Jewish. The food, the accents, the histories, the art, the language. When I finally encountered a Catholic from Brooklyn Heights who talked like *them*, I said 'Why are you going to church if you're Jewish?' He laughed and told me it was a New York accent, not a Jewish accent – but to my ears, they were the same. I loved my Jewish friends because they were loud and they argued – at dinner tables, in cafes, in love. I had already spent a lifetime being shushed. I thought surely I had found my people.

I don't know why people always thought I was Jewish. I even thought of converting – I went to a progressive Jewish synagogue near my house in Brooklyn for a while. Lots of gay people at that time used to go to progressive synagogues more than churches, or at least it seemed so to me. I liked the service. I liked above all the welcoming of my constant questioning. Questioning, I was told, was a sign of faith to Jews. All my life, my experience of Catholicism had been that my questioning was a sign of a *lack* of faith. So naturally I was drawn to the Jewish faith.

Then when I finally met my grandmother, she said I wasn't. How confusing. That first day sitting in her small living room, shouting over my grandfather's baseball game, I had two immediate questions for her:

Does anyone here play music?

'Music?' she said with a cynical wave of her 83-year-old hand. 'Who has time for music? Nice for you that you grew up in a family rich enough to give you music lessons while we were all slaving away trying to pay the mortgage. Good for you.'

'We weren't rich,' I said. 'We were poor. But my mother loved music and wanted us all to have lessons. I was always good at it, and so I've always thought it must be genetic.'

'How would I know about genetic music?' she said. 'We work too hard to find out if anyone is good at music in this family. Making pierogi? That, we're good at. You know how to make pierogi?'

'No,' I said quietly.

'Okay then,' she said, 'Maybe they should have given you pierogi lessons and at least you could eat.'

These are the kinds of conversations you have when you find a birth family after 30 years and expose some lies. No one is really that happy about it; tensions flare up.

'So what's the second question?' she asked.

Are we Jewish?

'Jewish!?' she said that day. 'Why would we be Jewish? What a ridiculous question.'

'Well,' I said, 'I've been told by friends who know something about Poland that this spelling Baranovski with an "i" is a Jewish spelling, and I thought you might have come here – left there – because of being Jewish. It's a logical guess.'

'Not really,' she said. 'We're not Jewish. Trust me. We're more Catholic than you can even imagine. It's impossible to know how Catholic we are.'

Awkward silence.

'Okay,' I said. 'Don't get upset. I'm just asking. Where are you from in Poland?'

'I'm from Bialystok and Antony is from Gdansk.'

I knew a bit of Polish history. It is where Solidarity and Lech Walesa were from – we had Polish refugees live with us for a while when I was a teenager. My parents were good people. They sought to do good in the world. They didn't always succeed, but they sought to, including by adopting us.

'Bialystok in the east? Like Russia?'

'No,' she said. 'Like Poland. Trust me. I should know.'

But I knew that Bialystok was a region that had been bitterly fought over, through many different waves of invaders, with victims displaced and murdered, including large numbers of Jews.

So when my grandmother finally said – one of the last times I saw her – that my people had been Jewish people, that yes we were Jewish, I just very stupidly said, 'What do you mean?'

'You're Jewish.'

'But why didn't you tell me?'

'Because we're not any more.'

And that was that.

There is a power in silence and forgetting. My views are deeply informed by my outrage as a working-class, queer and adopted person in a world of privilege. But these days I find that I'm white, work at a middle-class job, and people just don't buy it when I say I feel working class and marginalised. I understand why they don't buy it, but that's how I feel. I still feel the right-eous anger of the dismissed, the rejected, the sidelined. And yet I don't wear it so identifiably on the surface, so somehow none of it makes sense exter-nally. I am still overly concerned with fitting in, with people liking me, with being accepted – all of which I consider a legacy of my adoption experience and partly of being gay. People find that a weakness or pathetic or suspect, in a person of middle age. But I can't help it. Rage usually comes when I feel I'm being abandoned or rejected. These are things I have tried very hard to change but cannot. For me, abandonment and loss inform my identities as queer, Jewish, Polish and living outside of the USA. It is inexorably tied up in my views on culture – both my own and that of others.

Cultural perplexity

I have written elsewhere about the increasing complexity of defining culture (Harris, 2013). Through the ongoing legacies of colonialism, war and ethnic cleansing, human beings continue to move – sometimes willingly and some-times not – and in so doing continue to re/define ourselves in relation to culture, sometimes adding to its continuing dissolution, convergence and/or untraceability. These global mobilities are often governed (for the poor and those seeking refuge) by organisations like the United Nations High Commission for Refugees (UNHCR), which continue to require definitions of culture and nationhood in relatively set terms. As we know, culture and identity are seldom so fixed, and nations (including, egregiously, Australia) continue to abnegate their sworn responsibility to these cultures and indi-viduals, regardless of how we demand they define themselves.

Lauck describes a phone call to adoption writer Nancy Verrier in which she gives this advice for adoptive parents: 'They are grieving a terrible loss of the mother and of identity. Tell them to not expect gratitude from these children. They have no gratitude to give' (2011: 138). The words resonate with me. When I started working with those from refugee backgrounds in Australia, I identified strongly with some of their feelings of loss, although I knew it was irrational and there were so many differences (Harris, 2012a; 2012b). I also identified with their frequent rage about being framed as the 'grateful refugee' – an imperative required of those who have been given a so-called second chance, like adoptees and refugees. I imagined my feelings of identification were because I had emigrated from the USA to Australia and was feeling that loss, but the further I explored the feelings, the clearer it became to me that it was linked primarily with being gay and adopted. For me, being queer and adopted are inextricable; in loss, cultural and sexual diversities merge. Memory and feeling make strange bedfellows, and not always by logic. Indeed, ghost remnants and shadows from sometimes-lost, sometimes-never-there memories can cause grief, isolation and sometimes shame. For me, shame is interwoven with roots, family, sexuality and identity. Who am I, and why don't I know, and where might I find the answer? Where do I belong? Some of my tribal loss is due to the adoption narrative, in which my Polish Jewish ancestors came from eastern Europe for a better life after which my birthmother gave me up as a baby, for her own better life. But part of my tribal loss is also about my coming out in my teenage years as a lesbian and the repercussions of that within my family. My shame is also in relation to more firmly situated others. For those from cultural minorities, there is exclusion but there is also the very real possibility of inclusion. Rejection from one source (dominant races, genders, religions, cultures) opens a kind of possibility of camaraderie among others suffering similar rejections.

When I moved to the city from upstate New York at the age of 17, I thought I would find this camaraderie among other queer and trans* people and, to a degree, I did. But I also found a world of other exclusions: gender-based, politics-based, scene-based, class-based, and I certainly witnessed race-based. At some point I felt I really didn't have enough in common with other queers in the age of ACT UP as I thought was necessary to 'belong'. When I found out I was Jewish, it made me feel a sort of shame about that as well, as though I was a fake. And finding my birth family around the age of 30 and experiencing those overwhelming emotions, and the rejection of my birthmother as an adult, solidified some feelings in me that seemed like liberation at the time, but have settled more into a dull and unresolved grief.

Conclusion

If this book sits at the intersection of cultures and sexualities, it betrays a belief that such lines of flight can be mapped, their coordinates able to be found (and marked) on the map of one's identity. In such a mythical place, my intersectionality must remain unmapped. Most people who write about loss of identity and notions of 'home' through adoption write about intercultural adoption, but few like me who are adopted domestically write about the lost cultures that they can never re/trace (Harris and Gandolfo, 2013). Like my early feelings of disorientation with an LGBTIQ 'community' in New York that didn't feel as homelike as I had imagined, I have also experienced a great deal of alienation in relation to culturally diverse others since living in Australia.

Sometimes, I'm accused of being defensive, which I'm sure I often am. I'm an English-speaking, not-visibly-different adult migrant, and that matters enormously in the material conditions of our lived experiences; I respect those differences. Yet these discussions continue to feel like me justifying myself to a birth family for whom I represented something lost or unwanted; and to an adoptive family as a teenage lesbian. For me, these conversations represent something like an attempt to prove my membership, my legitimacy, my right to belong. Is it possible to consider oneself culturally diverse as a white, (now) middle-class, American woman? Is it possible to consider oneself queer today as that white, middle-class woman? It seems to me that in our efforts to belong, many of us on the margins continue to define culture and sexuality in very narrow terms, sometimes in essentialising terms, in order to find or define some parameters to our own experiences, our own identities, to map spaces for our own belonging – at the cost of excluding queer or allied others. Such behaviours risk becoming gatekeeping behaviours in which the number of potential insiders continues to dwindle until we inhabit our corridors of difference alone. For me and others populating adoptee diasporas, identity is both fixed and fluid in ways that continue to unfold.

The Brownfella and Sister Onan

Dino Hodge – Konstantino Hadjikakou

Over the years Sim and I have become steadfast brothers. We already were in our early 20s when we met in Darwin in 1983. Our Chinese-Malay and Greek-Cypriot families have defined our continuing discussions exploring generations of migrations across continents and cultures.

Darwin in the early 1980s had very few places where men of a certain persuasion could meet. There was Dix nightclub, the beats, and Darwin Gay Society – affectionately known as DGS. Intimacy between men was illegal. Pretty much everyone kept a low profile.

People looked out for each other as much as they could. Kenny was a cook at the RAAF base and needed to be back by early morning to prepare the first meal of the day. At 4.30 am, the DJ at Dix would announce 'Airforce Kenny, it's time you weren't here!' Word got around and one day Airforce Kenny was called to meet senior officers who offered him the opportunity to avoid a dishonourable discharge if he voluntarily resigned.

Beats were a key feature of life. From accounts in various court proceedings, it seems that almost every park and public toilet in the Northern Territory at some point or other was a meeting place for men seeking the company of men. The most popular beat in Darwin was Fannie Bay. It was known as 'the chapel by the sea' – a sly shot at the local cleric who was often there giving blessings on his knees. Men from all walks of life and of all ages frequented the beats. Some were gay or bi, some were drunk or high, and most were whitefellas, although a few were blackfellas.

Sim and I met through the DGS weekly gatherings held either at somebody's home or sometimes at a beach. These were opportunities to gossip over take-away dinners and one or more beers. DGS organised a volunteer phone information service, a newsletter and a monthly disco at a local bar on a Monday night. The venue depended on someone knowing someone who would accept – or at least tolerate – a bunch of poofters, and so it was always changing. Anonymity was important and DGS used pet names instead of sur-names. Someone explained to me that this would protect people should the police raid DGS.

I was one of only three DGS members from a non-English speaking back-ground. Michael was Anglo Indian and cared for his elderly mother, with whom he lived. He was called Mem-Sahib, that is, Madam Boss in British India colonial speak. Sim was Hokkien Chinese from Malaysia. He had studied computer programming at Australian National University and had a passion for languages and history. He was called Dim Sim, but not to his face. My heritage is Greek from Cyprus. I never heard whether I was called anything but I reckon they would have called me difficult – more of that later. There were no blackfellas.

The only opportunity to meet blackfellas was at the beats. My mate Gary – a Chinese Filipino Larrakia man – recalls the first time he saw me. I was sitting in the back of a car at Fannie Bay chatting with local blackfellas. Gary says he knew then that we would be firm friends. Many whitefellas enjoyed sex with blackfellas. As Lyle from Gunbalanya liked to quip about white men's obsession with black cocks: 'the blacker the berry, the sweeter the juice'. But it was a rare whitefella who would be seen in public talking with or even acknowledging a gay blackfella.

It wasn't until the late 1980s that Aboriginal people were welcomed to DGS bar nights. In those days, DGS held an annual awards night and a crowning of the Queen of Darwin. Blackfellas held their separate Black Gay Awards. Gary mentioned to me that 'You'll find more non-Caucasian guys at our dos than at the Gay Society.'

In none of these networks would you meet women. Darwin was a man's world – one that pretty much always involved alcohol and often violence. An aggressive assault at Dix upon a woman by a prominent gay man had resulted in a boycott of the venue by the lesbian community. In any case, Territory lesbians generally had broader interests than the gay men: feminism and social justice, the Working Women's Centre, services for victims of domestic violence, assault and rape, and the Pine Gap peace camp in Alice Springs. For homosexual men, much of their political agenda was simply surviving institutionalised homophobia and social ostracism.

I shared with Sim my books on feminism, gay politics and history. We talked about the dynamics of sexism and its parallels both with homophobia and with racism. Details of our family histories permeated these discus-sions. We each came from the professional middle class of a global ethnic diaspora, and our families had lived in countries under British colonial rule. Each country had achieved independence following the Second World War. In Malaya, Sim's family was an ethnic minority. In Cyprus, my family was part of the ethnic majority. Foreign imperial powers retained military bases in Malaysia and Cyprus following independence (and continue to in Cyprus). Both countries now participate in the Commonwealth Games.

South Australia – where I was born – was the focal point of Australian liberal politics during most of the 1970s. A comment by a gay activist in 1978 has always stayed with me: he told me that I couldn't be gay and Greek. Gay liberation demanded group solidarity and uniformity. Looking back, it was a mob mentality reaction against the extreme discrimination and police persecution experienced by homosexual men during the 1950s and 60s.

In the late 1970s the centre of Australian gay life shifted from Adelaide to Sydney and, to a lesser extent, Melbourne. My generation of gay men left South Australia in droves for these cities. For most of my contemporaries, 'coming out' meant abandoning one's biological family for a new life and family in the gay ghettoes. I could never picture myself in such a setting because rejecting one's blood family also meant – for me at least – removal from my ethnic heritage. Celebrating cultural diversity, yet alone understanding what we now call 'intersectionality', didn't feature much in the popular gay culture of the time.

My initial exposure to Darwin was around 1967 when I saw a Leyland brothers' home movie. Their outback camping adventures took them to Arnhem Land, where they filmed locals hunting sea turtle and then feasting and yarning around an open fire on the beach. While I couldn't follow their words, their habit was entirely familiar. Our extended family would go crabbing together and these excursions inevitably led to a beach-side festive occasion. True to one particular stereotype, I grew up surrounded by fruit trees and vegetable gardens, and the harvests were shared among families. My parents hosted gatherings of 40 or 50 people simply taking pleasure in the joy of being alive.

In 1984 I suggested to Sim that he accompany me to the National Homosexual Conference in Brisbane. The experience ignited for Sim a passion for activism and the following year we decided to organise the first Darwin Pride Festival. A few like-minded friends joined our 'Pride Collective' and we held planning meetings at my flat. DGS was taken aback. The DGS president called me to his home and explained how the high risk of a public backlash meant that the festival could not be a public event. Under no circumstances, he added, could there be any publicity or media interviews. I responded that Darwin Pride was separate from DGS and not under its control. I invited DGS to take part in the Pride planning group, and this was agreed.

The week-long festival took place in June 1985. Our posters were displayed in city mall shops. It fell to me to be the media spokesman in interviews with the ABC and the local women's community radio program. We hoped to reach as wide an audience as possible. The Northern Territory Museum rejected our request to use its auditorium for our film night as we were considered 'political', even though every other community group in Darwin that screened movies had access to the venue. I was a part-time tutor at the then Centre for Aboriginal and Islander Studies at Darwin Community College and was able to arrange access to a lecture theatre. The film night stands out for me as the most significant festival event. For the first time in the Northern Territory, lesbians, gay men and their allies came together in public to celebrate lesbian and gay culture.

HIV was emerging as an issue in 1985 and moves commenced to establish an AIDS council. It was no surprise that leadership working on this was drawn from the festival organising committee. No one was willing to be the council's inaugural president, and Sim volunteered to take on this difficult role. The fear surrounding AIDS was palpable. People were harassed and jobs were lost simply for suspicion of being gay and, therefore, a health risk. Anyone admitted to hospital with an HIV-related illness was placed in isolation and meals would be delivered outside their room. Anyone known to be HIV positive became a social outcast from both the mainstream and the gay communities.

The Northern Territory AIDS Council (NTAC) commenced operations in 1986. Unfortunately the Northern Territory Health Department thought it was a soft target and took the opportunity to siphon HIV funds for its own use. NTAC's services were developed largely due to the efforts of volunteers, especially Lori, a straight woman. Eventually she was employed as one of NTAC's two staff, and set about organising Darwin's first support network of HIV-positive people, Friends. The Council would not have survived those initial years without the support of mainstream allies.

In 1987 I left my job managing the Migrant Resource Centre and resigned from my volunteer work with the Gay and Lesbian Immigration Task Force. I was headed to Greece to study for a year at the University of Thessaloniki. By the time I returned to Darwin, Sim had moved permanently to Amsterdam. A new phase of leadership at NTAC eventually emerged with the election of Anthony Smith as president. By then I was working with the Human Rights and Equal Opportunity Commission, and I was invited to become an NTAC board member. One of our pressing priorities was to challenge the Health Department over NTAC's funding. Some strategic thinking and straight talking resulted in a meeting with departmental executives. Consequently, Northern Territory Health released full funding and overnight NTAC's staff levels increased to nine positions (six full-time and three part-time). It was a pivotal moment in the Council's history.

A greater challenge was dealing with discrimination. The Northern Territory government rejected NTAC's initial request for anti-discrimination legislation, asserting that the community had not expressed any need. NTAC formed a legal working party with Anthony, David (a lawyer), and me. We organised a Territory-wide 'phone-in' during Human Rights Week in December 1989 to gather people's stories of discrimination, and used this as a base for a comprehensive report. Our submission *HIV/AIDS, Discrimination and Law Reform in the Northern Territory* was tabled in February 1990. As well as law reforms in several areas directly related to HIV, such as the sex industry and intravenous drug-use, we called for protection against discrimination for transpeople and for full recognition of same-sex relationships.

Chief Minister Marshall Perron announced six months later that the government would introduce anti-discrimination legislation. At all of the community consultations held by the government there was consensus support for NTAC's recommendations in this area, but two years passed without parliamentary action. Rumours began to circulate that conservative government ministers would not approve the inclusion of sexual preference in the proposed new law. Both Anthony and David had left the Northern Territory, and I was no longer a board member with NTAC although I continued to participate as a volunteer. It seemed to me that NTAC's reticence to challenge the government was partly due to concern of risking its funding. And after such a long period, the new legislation was no longer a hot topic in the wider community.

A bold initiative was needed to place the issue at the forefront of news reports. I decided Darwin needed help from the Sisters of Perpetual Indulgence, and established the Northern Territory Convent of Equal Opportunity. I adopted the name Sister Onan of the Immaculate Palm. In the Old Testament, God condemned Onan to death for masturbating. I reckoned that the Sisters' mantra of 'the expiation of stigmatic guilt' was a fitting response to the parliamentarians' reservations, and it was sure to attract media attention. What I didn't anticipate was that the Sisters would be lauded.

Five Sisters made their maiden 'manifestation' at the 1992 May Day Parade, distributing information about the need for anti-discrimination legislation.

They were an instant hit. The May Day organisers invited us to bless their annual dinner. Before long we were receiving other invitations. Best of all, the media couldn't get enough of the Sisters. We blessed parliamentarians as they arrived at the parliament for the first day of the May sittings. The nightly news bulletins on all of Darwin's television stations broadcast Sister Onan discussing how anti-discrimination legislation was being delayed by homophobia, and that the Sisters were exorcising this demon from the parliament.

The Sisters had garnered public awareness and successfully pressured the government to at last declare its position. In early July, it officially announced that the draft legislation would be introduced and that Cabinet had decided that sexual preference would be excluded. It was wrong that a handful of conservative parliamentarians who insisted that they represented family values could deny the majority public position supporting the gay and lesbian community.

This was a time to call on our straight allies. Sister Onan shed her pure white robes and glamorous pink habit, and I became the convenor of the Coalition for Lesbian and Gay Rights. The Coalition organised our allies to declare their support for inclusion of sexuality in the anti-discrimination legislation. Professional bodies, non-government organisations, private individuals and representatives of the two main political parties and the labour movement supported the call. They donated campaign funds, signed an open letter published in the newspaper, spoke at public events, and wrote directly to the government. Responding to the Coalition's request, the Anglican bishop and the Uniting Church synod moderator wrote to the government supporting our case. We never heard back from the Catholic bishop.

The campaign generated widespread media coverage. The *Northern Territory News* editorialised against the government's decision being based on 'silly fears and prejudices'. NTAC declared that the decision was 'contrary to the national HIV/AIDS strategy'. The government's own Women's Advisory Council called for a reversal of the exclusion.

In less than four weeks, the government changed its position and announced it would include sexuality but with 'exemptions covering areas such as child care centres and the care of minors' – poofters can't be trusted to care for children. The Anti-Discrimination Act received assent in December 1992, three years after NTAC's 1989 discrimination phone-in. Importantly, while the Sisters retired from the campaign, they continued to manifest through a younger generation of queer activists.

The following year my oral history book *Did You Meet Any Malagas?* (1993a), about Darwin's multiracial gay community, was published. 'Malaga' is a local word for man or fella. Gary was one of the interviewees and he created the cover illustration. The book has enjoyed different readerships. In 1993 it was read mainly by a mainstream audience. Many times a white gay man mentioned to me how much he enjoyed the Whitefella's interview about life as an arts worker in a remote community and, in particular, about his blackfella boyfriend.

It was a surprise to me that not as many readers raised the book's broader themes. The Whitefella chapter was complemented with the experiences of two other white gay men: one was a linguist whose documentation of language and sacred sites was essential for land rights claims; and the other was a lawyer employed by the Northern Territory government to fight land claims. The chapters by blackfellas discussed family and cultural life, homophobia and racism in the gay and mainstream communities. More recently the book has reached a new audience of whitefellas and blackfellas. Their comments to me focus on these other elements.

Racism is a structural problem too. A decade had passed from NTAC's inception before an Aboriginal person became involved in the organisation. Gary joined NTAC in 1995 as an outreach worker from an Aboriginal Medical Service. His brief was to look at services for Aboriginal people who identified as gay, bisexual, transgender or intravenous drug users. In 1996 he broke new ground with the release of *Malaga to Malaga: Man to man – Aboriginal and Torres Strait Islander HIV/AIDS research report.* It challenged racism in both the gay community and the Northern Territory Health Department, and it provided a road map to address the deficit of HIV policies and services for Aboriginal people.

Attitudes were changing. *Did You Meet Any Malagas?* did not bring this about, but I like to think that it contributed to greater awareness among whitefella queer people about blackfella circumstances, and about working in collaboration. On a personal front, *Malagas* brought me to other knowledge. I was invited to join five lesbian and gay blackfellas (including Gary) and another whitefella in writing the seminal essay 'Peopling the Empty Mirror: The prospects for lesbian and gay Aboriginal history' (Dunn/Holland et al., 1993). These early works and my later initiatives led to the honour of being invited to edit *Colouring the Rainbow: Blak Queer and Trans perspectives*, published in 2015.

The cover of *Colouring the Rainbow* features Crystal Johnson's 2012 campaign poster. Crystal is the nation's first blackfella transperson to be elected to public office. She credits Gary as her mentor. Through NTAC, Crystal has played a key role in HIV education nationally. Her efforts on behalf of transpeople for access to services in the Northern Territory are inspiring. Brie Ngala Curtis from central Australia, also interviewed for the book, credits Crystal as her mentor. Together, *Malagas* and *Colouring the Rainbow* chart the progress and achievements of three generations of Northern Territory Indigenous LGBTIQ leaders.

The Darwin launch of *Colouring the Rainbow* was a double pleasure. The event was coordinated by the Northern Territory AIDS and Hepatitis Council, which provided the Council with a suitable occasion to confer life membership upon Gary. This recognition of his significant contributions and publications was long overdue. He is the only Indigenous person to be honoured by the Council with this award.

The publication of *Colouring the Rainbow* coincided with the 30th anniversary in 2015 of the inaugural Darwin Pride Festival. Two Darwin locals – Koulla and Matty – had approached me with the idea of an exhibition. There was a great deal of pride when the administrator (the Northern Territory's governor) opened *Pride NT: Our queer history* at the Northern Territory Library.

The exhibition traced a disparate set of disempowered and alienated groups who found common ground and, in the process, created a thriving contemporary rainbow culture. It acknowledged how social pariahs – Indigenous and non-Indigenous LGBTIQ folk – challenged unfair laws, lobbied for anti-discrimination protections, and engaged mainstream Australia in supporting our quests for full equality. It commemorated the city-wide celebrations in 2014 when Darwin hosted the third Asia-Pacific Outgames. The games' cultural festival included a Human Rights Forum, a Transactivism Conference, and a Queer Histories Symposium. The Northern Territory Library declared the exhibition one of their greatest successes ever in community and audience engagement, and subsequently set about establishing a queer archive in their permanent collection.

Developing the exhibition was, at times, emotional. Matty was one of several local artists commissioned to produce new works. His piece was a self-portrait at the age of 12 in 1992. The pubescent Matty is seated on a stool in front of a television, following an evening news report about a swarthy man dressed as a nun who was promoting human rights for lesbian and gay people. Hovering like an angel and watching over Matty as he views the news report is Sister Onan. This news report, Matty explained in his artist statement, was the moment when he understood that he belongs in a rainbow family too.

Dino in Greek 'military dress'
foustanella, *Adelaide, 1960*

God Is Mine Too

Rida Aleem Khan

Khuda Mera Bhi Hai (*God Is Mine Too*) is a Pakistani drama serial that finished with 26 episodes in April 2017 on ARY Digital. The series focused on the protagonist 'Noor', a transgendered-intersex boy who was born to an upper-class educated married couple, Mahagul and Zain. As the serial progresses, it touches upon different issues, including Zain finding it difficult to accept his child due to society defining strong masculinity scripts and gender roles. He is made to feel that having a transgender child makes him 'namard' or less manly, and this affects his honour. But Mahagul, the mother of Noor, accepts her child and decides to raise him.

Issues shown in the serial are very applicable to many societies in the world, such as the requirement of writing 'boy' or 'girl' on birth certificates. In Pakistan, some schools require birth certificates when enrolling children and checking their age and gender; and, if the child falls into the category of transgender or intersex, then schools have the right to refuse admission as such children can have 'negative influence' on other children from educated backgrounds and affect their 'normal' sexual development, which is of course false. Moreover, in the subcontinent, transgender and intersex children are abandoned by their families to the isolated corners of cities and villages where other 'hijras' hang out, especially if surgically they cannot transition to one gender. Sometimes these places are brothels, while other times they are small congested houses where eight to ten people of similar sexual and gender identities live together. Once a child reaches this place, their fate is sealed to be a sex worker, dancer, beggar or cleaner.

The most admirable element in *Khuda Mera Bhi Hai* is the solution-focused approach of Noor's mother, who chooses home schooling with the help of a teacher who is passionate about helping disadvantaged children. She enrols Noor in extracurricular activities (including the knowledge of Islam and the Quran) and, with the help of his teacher, searches for scholarships online to foreign universities where Noor can study. Along with the sexual development of Noor, he also acquires emotional maturity as he passes from falling in love to heartbreak to becoming emotionally independent upon the death of his mother. He then adopts an orphaned baby girl as his own daughter, providing her with the same support his mother gave him, thus beginning a cycle of positive change.

This drama was labelled a 'game changer' by *Express Tribune Pakistan*, followed by two more series focusing on LGBTIQP (pansexual) issues. These included a one-episode love story of a lesbian couple called *Chewing Gum*, and another serial *Alif Allah Aur Insaan* (*God and Humans*), focusing on the lack of honour and gratitude among privileged and unprivileged, and the power of malediction or curse from the victims of injustice. In particular, it explored the belief that any curse from a transgender person will come true, so society should treat them well and fear God.

It is important to point out that unlike the stereotypical perceptions of Western media, despite being a Muslim-majority country practising blasphemy laws and years of state corruption, Pakistan makes far more effort in producing constructive content for a country where 67.1% of 180 million people are under the age of 30, as stated by Stephen Cohen in his book *Future of Pakistan* (2011). Another thing to note is that the majority of Pakistani youth want an Islamic democracy, support women's rights to work, and believe that the main reasons for violence and terrorism in Pakistan have to do with injustice and poor economic conditions and not with Islam, as so often misjudged and falsely presented by Australian media and various politicians. Therefore, it is important to understand that sexual and religious identities can go side by side in certain societies, and faith can act as a tool of empowerment, equality and motivation to fight against injustice.

But what if that same faith or religion condemns the very essence of your sexuality? What if that same faith, instead of supporting you for something you are born with, outcasts you as being sinful?

And (We sent) Lot when he said to his people: What! do you commit an indecency which anyone in the world has not done before you? Most surely you come to males in lust besides females; nay you are an extravagant people. And the answer of his people was no other than that they said: Turn them out of your town; surely they are a people who seek to purify (themselves). So We delivered him and his followers, except his wife; she was of those who remained behind. And We rained upon them a rain; consider then what was the end of the guilty. – Chapter 7, Verses 80–84

In short, God told Prophet Lot to leave the 'lustful' homosexuals as well as his wife behind when the flood came and killed all.

The above happens to be the only verse of 6,236 verses from the holy Quran that vaguely touches upon the issue of LGBTIQP. Thus, it is concluded that the Quran is largely silent about this issue. Other homophobic claims are made in *hadiths*, which were written 200 years after the death of Prophet Muhammad by Persians who did not speak Arabic. Many scholars continue to challenge their authenticity. Moreover, there are countless commentaries on the interpretation of this verse as some scholars make a distinction between 'lustful' homosexuals-heterosexuals and 'love-full' homosexuals-heterosexuals, as lusting is considered a sin but loving is a virtue. Thus it is lust among the people of Prophet Lot that is considered a sin, not love. Others claim that this verse came in the context of young boys being raped by privileged men of that society, given the quote 'do you commit an indecency which anyone in the world has not done before you?', proving that the target audience of this verse must be doing something so horrific that no one has done it before them anywhere in the world. This excludes homosexuality, given the practice has been around for thousands of years. Another interpretation of this verse claims to be referring to bisexual men as it states 'surely you come to males in lust besides females'. Even though these bisexual men have the ability to procreate and choose the opposite gender or are already in a relationship with a woman, to fulfil their lust, they go after men despite having female spouses. In other words cheating and betraying their partners, or simply fulfilling their fetish costing their marital relationship.

Thus I need to be careful myself as a bisexual Muslim woman to not indulge in lust or fetish towards other women (or men for that matter), and daily there is an internal struggle or *jihad* to overcome any lustful desires. Like the great Sufi scholar Jalaluddin Rumi says, 'Virtue cannot exist without temptation and difficulties to overcome.'

And so, in 2016, the first transgender mosque opened in Islamabad in Pakistan, while a gay Imam came out in Australia, introducing the *Melbourne Marhaba* lounge for young LGBTIQP Muslims to chill in and create a sense of belonging in a society where we may feel pressure to have sex outside marriage to display our sexuality.

As I look through my pictures in Japan from 1997 till 2000, I see a little girl smiling with short hair, in collared tops and either wearing pants or shorts. I miss the good old days of watching *Dragon Ball Z* episodes at 8 pm daily in our comfortable apartment with the view of Tokyo Tower. I still remember refusing to wear *sharara* that Nani Ma (my maternal grandmother) sent me from Pakistan. It was too bright and shimmery and I never wore skirts or dresses let alone something so . . . so . . . Bollywood.

Mum and I slowly got to know the neighbours: downstairs an Indian couple, Suraj Uncle and Preeti Aunty, upstairs Mehta Uncle and Kanchan Aunty, on the left a Chinese teenage boy living with his mother, and opposite on the other side of the apartment balcony lived a little Chinese girl, a year or two younger than me, with pretty hair and chubby cheeks.

I don't recall her name but I remember asking Mum if I could go play with her when I got bored and annoyed with my brother. One day, my neighbour and I decided to go up and down the lift, which smelt so nice and I always wondered why. Maybe it was the invisible air freshener or the obsessive cleanliness among the Japanese people. Nevertheless, it pleased me. While going up and down the lift was fun, we got tired and went to the ground floor TV lounge and watched cartoons. But after some time, she did not want to watch TV. So I suggested we play 'mummy and baby', and I would be the mummy taking care of the house, cleaning and making food for her. She agreed and as I finished doing all the chores, I decided to change her nappy and so, I pulled down her panties, touched her butt twice, and pulled the panties back up.

I was six years old at the time. And this wasn't my first time. I had the same thing done to me by another Pakistani girl who was six when I was four. She looked inside my panties, copying some actor in a Bollywood movie she watched getting intimate with a female actress. Perhaps South Asian parents need to be careful regarding what their children are watching on television and learning from Bollywood movies?

Sadly, the Chinese girl told her mother what happened. I even wrote a letter to her in broken Japanese but never saw her again.

One day, in the hot heat of Pakistan, my family arrived in Multan, the city of Sufis, and my world changed. I could no longer wear shorts or pants; frocks or *shalwar qameez* was the attire for women (while my brother could continue to wear pants and shorts). I was encouraged to follow the footsteps of my female cousins. My hair grew medium-short, which I liked, and then began the era of never-ending Indian soap operas that were about love, infidelity, marriage, divorce, in-laws, ex-lovers and everything and anything to do with the heterosexual world. The conversations that Pakistani 'aunties' and 'bajis' (sisters) had were about clothes, shoes and gossip – I had no interest in any of this and was accused by all of them of being backward.

Errghhhhhhhh!!!

But all of this aroused in me desires for a man who I would marry and live happily ever after with, like Sujal and Kahish, Sumeet and Kumkum, Prerna and Anurag, Hatim and Jasmine, and the list goes on.

Religion guides us, cultural experiences shape us, but it is our own interpretation of our individual personality traits, lifestyle choices and behavioural patterns that sets the foundation of our identity.

Australia has its strengths, the multicultural, multi-flavour food, the intellectual hubs to exchange ideas, the hybridisation of clothes, shoes and accessories, and above all the opportunity to interact with the rest of the world without having to travel large distances and pay for expensive hotel bookings. We are diverse in race, in religion, in culture and in values.

However, diversity is still a controversial phenomenon given we continue to put five people from five different racial backgrounds in the same room, all thinking like a white person, and we call that diversity. We expect everyone on Collins Street to dress in Western attire when working in Australian corporate and government departments because that is 'professional', or expect everyone to have 'finger food' with champagne at events. We still have a very long way to go and while the White Australia policy is behind us, and we have opened doors for migrants and refugees, we did not build sufficient resources to appropriately cater to the needs of migrant and refugee communities. Sadly, the visa processes are longer, employment opportunities are limited and, more significantly, according to the *Migrant Act 1958* and the *Australian Citizenship Act 2007*, the Australian government can revoke citizenship, leaving more than 7 million migrants and refugees in fear of losing their identity and a sense of belonging. And yet it is Australia that will face the burden of an ageing population requiring young migrants and refugees to sustain their future.

Diversity at work, in thought and leadership is what we need. Yet, we just expect everyone to assimilate because why else would they leave their culture behind and come to Australia? The assumption that there must be nothing great about their cultures back home and there must be everything great about the Australian culture here is very much a fallacy.

The National Fear Survey conducted by researchers at Edith Cowan University in August 2007 found that many Muslim Australians are isolated and highly likely to experience discrimination due to societal beliefs that:

- Muslim Australians are potential terrorists,
- there is no place in Australia for Muslims, and
- Muslims should abandon their cultural practices and assimilate.

This is important when we consider the Human Rights and Equal Opportunity Commission (HREOC) shows that 281,578 Australian residents identify as Muslim and, of these, 50 per cent are aged 24 and under. Furthermore, the University of South Australia found that 'using household income of less than $600 per week as a benchmark, 2011 data reveal that over one quarter of all Muslim children in Australia (26.9 per cent) were living in poverty compared with 14 per cent of all children'.

I am the voice of that 24-year-old Muslim who grew up living in poverty, fighting with a society that continues to expect me to abandon my cultural practices and assimilate.

But then we need to go a few steps further, and look at what it means to be a bisexual woman in Australia. As stated in the National LGBTI Health Alliance:

- 50.6 per cent of bisexual women aged 16 and over reported being diagnosed or treated for any mental disorder in the past three years, and
- 38.8 per cent of bisexual women aged 16 and over reported being diagnosed or treated for anxiety in the last three years.

So now I am not only a young Muslim living in poverty, fear of isolation and forced assimilation, I also happen to be a bisexual woman who is suffering from a mental health condition and being treated for anxiety.

Sigh . . .

There have been times when I would ask Allah, 'Why me?' I prayed five times a day, read Quran every morning before going to school. I always did my homework and earned good grades. I wore a headscarf as per my father's wishes even though kids at school picked on me and the bullying by adults continues today, albeit for not wearing a headscarf. I advocated for justice throughout my life and only want to do service to humanity before I leave this world. Even in my darkest hours in my studio apartment of Jackomos Hall at Monash University, even during those hours of crying and suicidal thoughts, I never cut myself because Islam taught me that my body is a trust from God, and I must look after it, causing it no harm, no mutilation.

Scholarships that I earned in 2012 all went toward my private psychiatrist's fees. My psychiatrist, despite coming from a Sri Lankan background and being a female with migrant parents, happened to be white under brown skin. Upon challenging her diagnosis, she said we couldn't have a therapeutic relationship as I was always on about marriage and could be lying to her about my sexuality, given there is no record of any mental health illnesses in my family (Pakistani doctors do not keep medical records).

Assimilation has consequences. It is based on the idea that one culture or race is superior or better than another. Those who demand assimilation and those who have assimilated like the Sri Lankan psychiatrist cause damage to minorities that preserve and protect ancestral traditions and knowledge of heritage, just like the Indigenous Australians, and are willing to share their culture while being curious about other's cultures.

When my parents brought me to Australia, it was not to get assimilated and abandon my Pakistani values, nor did they intend my religious or sexual or political identities to dominate my personality, as some young Muslims consider themselves Muslims first then Australian, while other young Australians consider themselves LGBTIQP first then Australian, or feminist or vegetarian (or other ideological and political identities) first then Australian. Instead my parents brought me to Japan, and then to Australia, to shape meaningful perceptions and to be able to do a fair comparison between Japanese, Pakistani and Australian cultures, and pick the best of all worlds, all cultures and all religions and have a diverse political understanding. This is why my family accepts me for being bisexual because Allah made me this way and if Allah is the *musawir* – an artist – then his every creation is flawless and has a unique purpose. Therefore, I will always be a human first, before any labels, and my conscience and value system dominate my personality, not man-made labels for the sake of political correctness.

While my parents are under pressure from conservative Islamic clergy, they understand that while sexuality is suppressed in Pakistan or overtly expressed in Australia or the West in general, we need to embrace a middle path. We hope for a society which is free enough to explore sexuality and religious identities but modest enough to not let these identities radically drive us to bias and exclusion of those different from us. Muslim communities need to accept LGBTIQP Muslims and represent them in powerful positions, such as the advisory boards of Islamic councils, and selection-committees. And the Australian LGBTIQP community and supporters of LGTBQIP need to create a safe space for inter-faith LGBTIQP (away from harsh Facebook keyboard warriors!) where people like us don't feel the pressure to assimilate to secular values of privatising religion to the point of no religious expression in public spaces, or being accused of backwardness for following a religion and adhering to our parents' cultures. The feelings of invalidation arising from mainstream LGBTIQP community expecting me to dress in 'queer' attire or participate in casual sex to prove my sexuality, especially the expectation on bisexual women to be the door to threesomes, has to be challenged. As someone once asked me:

'How do you know you are bisexual if you have never made out with a woman?'

'When I thought I was heterosexual, I knew I desired men without needing to make out with one. Later on, when I reached clarity about my sexuality, I know I am a bisexual woman without needing to make out with both genders to prove my sexuality. I say I am bisexual, therefore I am. Just as I say I am a Muslim, therefore I am.'

'Still, how do you know you are bisexual?'

'Well . . . I did make out with a girl when I was six.'

'That doesn't count. The make out experience has to be when you are an adult.'

'No, but I want to wait until marriage because I am a Muslim.'

Or the other conversations that need to take place:

'Would you marry a woman?'

'No, because I want biological kids, but then again, the future is unpredictable. If I was to marry a woman, thankfully we have an Imam who can perform the Islamic marriage ceremony under Sharia law.'

'How will you have kids with a woman? Would you go for surrogacy?'

'No, surrogacy is a Western construct. I would want to adopt a child from Pakistan as Prophet Muhammad was an orphan and taught Muslims to help orphans so adoption is much easier under Sharia law than under Australian law. God is mine too, thus God will help me in my struggle, inshallah.'

Best of both worlds

Homesickness

Azja Kulpińska

Ten artykuł został napisany na suwerennej ziemi ludności aborygeńskiej Wurundjeri, Bunurong i Dja Dja Wurrung nacji Kulin. Te plemiona nigdy nie zrzekły się swoich ziem – zostały one skradzione podczas brytyjskiej inwazji, której skutki odczuwane do dzisiaj. Jako imigrantka, która odnalazła poczucie domu i przynależności na tej skradzionej ziemi chciałabym złożyć wyrazy najgłębszego szacunku dla członków i członkiń starszyzny aborygeńskiej: byłych, teraźniejszych i przyszłych. To jest, była i zawsze będzie ziemia aborygeńska.

This article was written on the sovereign lands of the Wurundjeri, Bunurong and Dja Dja Wurrung people of the Kulin Nations. As an immigrant who has found a sense of belonging and home on this stolen land, I would like to pay my deepest respect to the Aboriginal and Torres Strait Islander elders past, present and future. This was, is and always will be Aboriginal land.

Every time I book a ticket 'home' it's followed by a period of intense trepidation. I put the word 'home' in inverted commas because, as is the case for most immigrants, the concept of home is complicated. The moment my credit card transaction is processed I know there is no way back. I'm going back and I'll have to face all the old fears and navigate that messy territory of multiple identities again, under the careful watch of my compatriots. Do I speak my mother tongue with a foreign accent now? How many expressions and words have I forgotten and what kinds of bizarre English calques will I interlace into my speech to the amusement of my monolingual family? How will I navigate being perceived as rich by my Polish friends and family – now that I have a regular job in the community sector – who more often than not struggle to make ends meet? Is the fact I started supporting my family financially going to change the way we relate to each other? How do I translate my experience of having lived, loved, struggled and thrived in so-called Australia for the last eight years in a way that makes it relatable for my loved ones here? How do I maintain my integrity as a queer person with a lived experience of mental illness when I made a conscious decision not to reveal any of these facets of my life to my family, even though they both greatly influenced my daily life and my career path? Can I still call this place home?

Nearly two decades ago when I studied for an 'English as a Foreign Language' exam, never imagining it would become the main language of my daily expression, I came across the term *homesickness* and initially understood it quite literally as being made unwell by an aspect of one's home. Today I know that both the meanings of the term, the actual one, and the one made up by my young learner self, are relevant to my relationship to the place where I was born and grew up. Sometimes I feel them simultaneously.

It took me a long time to feel comfortable with self-identifying as queer. Where I came from, labels were assigned by others, not chosen. I was Polish because it said so in my passport. I was a woman because this is how I was read. Categories were rigid and prescriptive. Taking up any space to define myself in my own terms would be considered self-indulgent and attention-seeking. Even after moving to so-called Australia, I wasn't convinced whether my life experience was 'queer enough' as I found it hard to relate to most mainstream queer (or rather LGBTI) narratives. For example, I was not bullied at school. In fact, the silence around any non-heteronormative experiences was deafening. Looking back now I can see how my teenage self missed out on the world of crushes and dating due to the lack of language or awareness of how my sexuality could be expressed in any way other than getting stuck in a co-dependent relationship with a male classmate who grew up reassured by the patriarchal structures of his inherent superiority and entitlement to my body and spirit. If that was the world of attraction, feelings and sexuality then I didn't want to be a part of it.

I also don't have a coming out story. Sitting down with my Polish parents who never uttered the word 'sex' in front of me and turned bright red every time a kissing scene came up in a movie, revealing myself as a sexual being of any inclination would have been excruciatingly awkward to say the least. And after all, I didn't see any of my straight friends discussing similar issues with their families.

Yes, I did experience attraction to a vast array of people regardless of their gender identity and expression. Yes, I squirmed at the way heteronormativity was privileged on every level. Yes, I found the term 'queer' alluring. I related deeply to it as an adjective, in how it rejects simple classifications of identities, traverses multiple categories and affiliates with those oppressed by or uncomfortable with the dominant culture. As a noun, it resisted the norm and as a verb, it always aimed to deconstruct simplistic, rigid and prescriptive notions of identity I grew up with. Yet, it took me years to be able to fully and unashamedly identify as queer.

One of the earliest memories I have around feeling a part of the queer community is of the early 2000s. I rent a room with a friend in a dilapidated house near the centre of a medium-size Polish city. Through word of mouth we hear about the 'Equality March' happening downtown. It is not specified whose equality we're talking about (a strategic move to keep the conservative council members at bay), but everybody knows. We feel it's important for us to be there. We rip a mustard coloured curtain off our dingy room window. With the help of scissors and sharpies we turn it into a banner, and we go.

It's cold and drizzly. Unforgiving Polish November. A few dozen protesters gather at the square with their umbrellas and soaked banners demanding justice for LGBTIQ people. Surrounding us is a police cordon: stone faces, in full riot gear, some of them sitting high up on horses. They are in 1:1 ratio to the protesters. I have never seen so many cops in one place before. We know that in the previous year, the parade was officially banned by the city mayor, but took place anyway as an act of civil disobedience. The brutal police pacification that ensued was commented on even in those media outlets on the more conservative side. People were violently yanked out of the crowd, pulled by the hair, hit with truncheons, pushed to the ground with shields. Several dozen protesters got arrested. This year, my friend and I look at the tasers hanging off the police officers' waists. We look at the mustard curtain banner. We look at each other. We don't need to speak to know that it feels right to be here. We march through the city, small in numbers, but loud. Halfway through the march we see a group of right-wing youth militia – hatred on their faces, rocks in their hands. The cops place themselves between the two groups. I'm scared. It now feels like there are two groups of people hating on the small group of us marching. I'm hoping we can all make it out of here uninjured. I'm scared, but I also for the first time realise how powerful we are as a small group of people marching with our soaked banners demanding justice. I realise that they are probably more scared than we are: why else would they deploy their entire reserve of riot police? I realise that what we represent can seriously disrupt the status quo.

Not too long after this experience I migrate to so-called Australia. Being so far away from the familiar script, I suddenly feel like I have much more headspace to think about who I am, to explore my identity and sexuality. People around me seem so confident talking about who they are, what that means to them, and where it situates them in the broader socio-political context. The few times when I speak up about certain aspects of my identity, it is taken at face value – it feels strangely empowering to be able to self-define and not face harsh judgement and questioning everywhere I go. I become more comfortable identifying as queer, even though at the time I'm in a long-term relationship with a man. There are still a lot of questions I grapple with: is it okay not to be out to my parents? Does it mean my queerness is real? Why is there such a pressure on queer people to openly discuss the fact that they are sexual with their families? Why is there that hierarchy of authenticity that privileges people who are 'out' to their families? I crave conversations and perspectives that will help me make sense of my experience and I'm not quite sure where to find them.

A few years later a friend invites me to a panel discussion he is a part of titled 'Same Same But Different: Navigating sexuality, gender, culture, and religion' where some of the topics I crave to hear more about are discussed. But most importantly, I find out about a project run by the Multicultural Centre for Women's Health (MCWH) aimed at young same-sex attracted women from culturally and linguistically diverse backgrounds where we would be able discuss issues around the intersections of culture, gender and sexuality, and have a creative outcome at the end. After the discussion, I chat to the project facilitator and, uplifted by the fact that at the age of 29 I am still considered 'young' for the purposes of the project, I decide to take part.

A few weeks later we meet at the MCWH office for the first part of the *Our Voices, Changing Cultures* project – a focus group. We are about 20 same-sex attracted women and non-binary people from outside of the Anglo cultural mainstream. I know a few of them, but most I haven't met before. Everyone seems very confident in the ways they talk about their experiences. I feel so anxious that I mainly stay silent that evening, but I soak up everything that is being said like a sponge. I hear a lot of critiques of the 'coming out' narrative as a concept, which doesn't necessarily benefit people from ethnically diverse communities. Instead the concept of 'inviting in' as a strategic choice of who we might want to share the details of our sexual identities with resonates with most people. People talk about mental health and the difficulties of discussing our struggles with our blood families. People talk about how their queerness is often erased, even within the queer community when they are in long-term relationships with a man. People talk about specific gender– and sexuality-related terms from their languages they feel describe them better than English terms. The conversations continue way over the scheduled time, until it's late at night and we have to leave the building. A few months later, after multiple workshops where we keep discussing our queerness and our culture through words, sound and movement, we are ready to perform at Footscray Community Arts Centre for an audience of friends and community members. It feels quite vulnerable to reveal such personal aspects of my life on stage, but I also feel grounded by the process we have gone through together, supported by the other women and non-binary people, many of whom remain my dear friends.

The conversations I had and connections I made during the *Our Voices* project helped me not just to understand my experiences as a queer immigrant person navigating two cultures as valid, but also to find strength in creating new meanings as a response to the clash of concepts and ideas I experience. I realised that the concept of queerness as a resisting force can only maintain its radical potential if it's constantly challenged by those within the queer community who aren't served by any prescribed or institutionalised way to perform it. I have learnt to find a certain degree of comfort in ambiguity and strength in creating new meanings. Reading queer, feminist and diasporic theory has provided another source of solace. Not only has it helped me grasp some of the complex dynamics happening around me and within me, but it has also given me a sense of connection to a lineage of writers navigating multiple identities. In times when I feel confused by my in-betweenness, I read these words by a queer Chicana writer and theorist Gloria Anzaldúa:

> En unas pocas centurias, *the future will belong to the mestiza. Because the future depends on breaking down of paradigms, it depends on straddling of two or more cultures. By creating a new mythos – that is, a change in the way we perceive reality, the way we see ourselves, and the way we behave – la mestiza creates a new consciousness.* – Gloria Anzaldúa (2012: 102)

Some things have changed in Poland since that cold November in the early 2000s when I participated in the 'Equality March'. In 2017, the march in Warsaw attracted around 50,000 people. The photos that circulated on my Facebook feed looked no different from any generic pride march situated in any major city in the global west. Shoddy banners were replaced with quality rainbow flags, corporations chasing the pink dollar with the latest collections of rainbow merchandise. However, the state's position is still openly hostile and the police still sport riot gear instead of embellishing their uniforms with rainbow accessories in order to appear to be on our side. I'm connected to many queer and feminist activists on the ground via social media and I deeply admire their constant efforts at resisting the oppressive structure, imagining new possibilities and creating spaces where some of these possibilities can unfold, and all of that despite quite limited resources. I deeply admire their commitment to intersectionality and their willingness to wholeheartedly stand up for the rights of any oppressed group. Whether it's a blockade of an unfair tenant eviction, a rally for refugee rights or mass protests for reproductive rights, Polish queers will be there rain or shine. And they do it all with that amazing Polish sense of humour I miss so much.

Sometimes I feel guilty for not being there with them. Sometimes I feel guilty about my privilege of living in a country where I can have relatively stable living conditions, access to health care and job security, when I know that a lot of my Polish counterparts struggle with these. I am also aware that the place I migrated to, so-called Australia, grants me tons of privileges as a person of generic European heritage. This is not the case for my Polish friends who migrated to the UK, where they experience plenty of discrimination and xenophobia and are perceived at best as cheap, exploitable labour keen to do any job, often in unsafe conditions and below the minimum wage; and, at worst, as uncultured Eastern European hordes who need to go back to where they came from. Sometimes I try to use my privilege and translate it into material support, such as when I organise fundraisers on this side of the world to support queer Polish activists on the other side. Sometimes I'm fine with the fact that I now live here and I can focus my efforts locally.

Every time I book a ticket 'home' it's followed by a period of intense trepidation. And then by a period of intense excitement. I will see people who have known me for more than 20 years, who have seen me grow up and who I know will always support me in their own ways. Yes, they might laugh at my accent, my awkward choice of words and my 'foreign ways', but I also know that they will throw a welcome party for me that will go on for two days and they will reschedule their commitments to spend time with me. I know that I will rediscover delightful Polish idioms and sayings that don't translate to English. I know that I will be surrounded by the sense of humour that will make me laugh so hard it'll make my stomach hurt. I know that I will see new, exciting queer spaces and initiatives and incredible resourcefulness and commitment of the community organisers that allows them to create in times of scarcity. These intense conflicting emotions have become a part of me and my way of dealing with them is through accepting that my relationship to 'home' and identity will never be straightforward.

Azja with Grandpa Albin

The Only 'Dot Dot Dot' in Your Village

Benjamin Law, as told to Maria Pallotta-Chiarolli

Diversity isn't justified by one accent. Every single person is like a myriad of things at any given time. And when I think of growing up in the suburbs of coastal Queensland in the 1990s, television was pretty white and it was pretty straight. Those two things make you very aware of what normal is supposed to be, so you really do feel apart. And growing up in an especially white part of Australia kind of amplified it. When you're the only 'dot dot dot' in your village, sometimes you grow up with internalised racism or other kinds of minority phobias. You see white as being cool and you see straight as being cool and the way in which that can manifest is that you won't want to engage in Asian cultural things. Or you'll see camp people and you'll think, 'Well, I might be gay but I'm not one of those gays.' And it took a long time to get that out of my system and realise that there's nothing wrong with being camp and that it's a judgement you've been taught by straight people who potentially hate gay people. So I now say, don't kowtow to the straight or white idea of what has currency. You need to form your own identity on your own terms. And that can be really hard; but finding a community of other people like you helps.

Which reminds me of another thing that amplified feeling apart: dial-up internet was just coming in for our generation as I was leaving school. So, really, the main access point to the rest of the country, or to my idea of the rest of the country, was television. So when I'm asked about who and how I identified with other people, I think the simple answer is that I didn't. I didn't meet another gay person until I was an adult. Then I met some people online or talked to them in private, covertly. I didn't have Asian friends or any non-white friends. If you were a non-white adult, you might not have been picked on or anything like that, but you really stood out. I would hear stories about Asian suburbs in big cities and I'd think, 'Oh my god, there are Asian majorities in Australia?' I had no idea of that whatsoever.

So these days, I think queer people being online is a blessing and a curse.

It's a curse in that everything is so geared toward sex and hooking up, and the pressure or emphasis is on that rather than making friends. Whereas if you go online and access organisations, it can also be about forming community and making friends and getting resources. So, first of all, find your tribe by going online.

I think film and television are changing and I think people like Tony Ayres are at the forefront of that. It's not like he goes into his meetings and broadcasts, 'We're going to put a show on about intersectionality.' No one wants to watch a show with an agenda. The only agenda for making great art and for telling good stories is having a good story to tell in the first place and really good stories are about intensity and three-dimensional characters who embody intersectionality in some way. So what's changed is that someone like Tony has been at the coalface of making his own work for so long, he's now in a position of incredible influence and power. He is able to make those works. He is able to create the first Australian Muslim 'rom com' for the big screen. He is able to create *The Family Law* from my book, which is about a Chinese Australian kid who is watching his home fall apart and he happens to be gay as well. That's not a classic Australian story, but in a lot of ways it is and should be.

So now we have ethnics and gays coming of age in the arts in Australia who are able to be the people in power that they had to approach when they were younger. It's a game changer. For example, when I was younger, because I didn't really see any Chinese Australian representation in books or on television or film, I went to a lot of American stuff. I read a lot of Amy Tan, *The Joy Luck Club* (1989) author. And I discovered David Sedaris, whose father comes from a Greek background. He also came from a really big family, one of six siblings. And so there was all this resonance for me. Even though David and Amy come from a completely different generation, I was like, 'Oh my god, I get what they're talking about. That's not my story but it totally is my story.'

We really hoped that *The Family Law* would resonate with Asian-Australian audiences and it has reached this kind of core audience. Not just Asian-Australian representation but Asian-Australian stories are difficult to actually get right. It's one thing to be represented, that it will be a character who is part of an ensemble, but to tell the stories with Asian-Australian characters at the centre of those stories is new. So even small moments in the story, which we just wrote in because we thought they could be casual parts of a scene, become important without us intending them to be. For example, in series one there's a scene where Danny comes into the lounge where his dad is watching a Cantonese soap opera in the very early hours of the morning and eating an apple. He gives Danny a slice and they watch together. We had viewers saying, 'Wow, that's my childhood. My dad used to do that. Watch those soap operas late at night. I'd come in because I couldn't sleep, or I had to pee, and he would feed me a piece of fruit and then I'd fall asleep.' And it was just like a moment in the script that seems to capture a lot of things for a lot of people. I think that was unexpected and gorgeous.

Another example of what we didn't anticipate was how the Eurasian family across the road is this perfect mixed-race family. The perfect Eurasian children who are models, go on holidays and are into art and music. We just thought this was an hilarious juxtaposition to the Laws because the mixed-race family, they're cosmopolitan, they're cool. What we didn't realise was that's also really rare to see on screen. It should have struck me as obvious but a lot of people from mixed race families, they were like, 'Oh my god, we're on screen! And it's hilarious. I've never seen a family like mine on screen before.' We were very acutely aware that we were breaking ground in terms of Asian-Australian representation but we didn't realise that we were breaking ground in terms of having mixed-race families on TV. And the final thing I'd say is that a lot of non-Asian-Australian viewers wrote in and said, 'Thank you for representing my family.' Some people might think this is strange but these non-Asian viewers saw themselves in it. They came from a big family, or a family of divorce, or having grown up with an inappropriate father, or they were that gay kid who didn't know why he was perving on the hot male neighbour across the road. The ethnicity wasn't a barrier to empathy. It makes sense, you know, because I've been watching white Anglo stories my entire life and I empathise with those characters. It shouldn't surprise us that it happens in reverse.

Every week, I do a column in the *Good Weekend* magazine for the *Age*. I try to very casually and hopefully funnily bring in different parts of my life, different experiences I've had. To me, it's not that unusual that I'm gay and Asian, because that's what I am every day. But we have to acknowledge that having a non-white weekly column in a major newspaper is still a weirdly unusual thing, considering that the last census shows that by some measures we're more diverse than the US, UK, Canada and New Zealand. And yet, our mainstream media is just so far behind. I don't write a column every week about being gay. Sometimes I mention that I have a boyfriend because it's important in terms of how I tell the story. But some readers, especially when I started writing the columns, were like, 'Why do you have to write about being gay every weekend?' I got a bit self-conscious and I went back through my last dozen columns and I realised that I hadn't mentioned that I'm gay in any of the last two months' worth of columns. It's just that I had mentioned I had a boyfriend that week, about something he might have said, and they're like, 'Oh, that's banging on about being gay.' Whereas I don't think that Richard Glover, who is a weekly columnist, and one I really love, and who mentions his female partner in his weekly column, would raise eyebrows ever. So there is still a very acute double standard. And when I get feedback like that, I'm like, 'Well then, I'm going to mention my boyfriend more, you fuckers. Now you've made me want to make a point of it.'

To the readers and emerging younger writers in this book, I want you to feel like you're a part of a community even though you haven't met some of the key players who are no longer sidelined figures. If you speak a language other than English at home you're one in five Australians. If you weren't born in Australia, you're one of four Australians. I think the latest count is pretty much 50 per cent of Australians have at least one parent born overseas as well. Those numbers are substantial. And just because we don't see ourselves involved in the mainstream conversation, I hope this book and this conversation show that we're coming to the centre of things. I think the other thing that has really changed, and if you're reading this and you're young as well, is that you can't underestimate how much social media has changed things. Today, something like black face on *Hey Hey It's Saturday*, when I was nine years old, no one who was offended was able to reach so many people, 'That's wrong, that's screwed up.' We have that kind of fuel now to remind people that we exist and can challenge what we see, 'For us, that's racist. That is bigoted. That is stupid and that's ignorant.' Or, 'I want to see more of this on television.' You've got this direct line, which I didn't grow up with. Those conversations can be broadcast wide. It's reassuring and reminds you you're not alone just because other people dispute your feelings with, 'Oh that's not racist' or 'You're being too sensitive'.

I've been called a disgrace to my race on several occasions. And I think this is one of the difficulties and challenges. I also think it's a conversation that we should embrace. When there is so little representation and so few role models, whether it's in arts or business or the media or whatever, you're really expected to be a role model. The thing about writing stories, whether it's for television or columns about my life, or whatever, I'm not particularly interested in writing characters who are perfect. I'm not interested in writing stories about role models. They have their place, absolutely. But I'm interested in telling stories that are complex and sophisticated, about Asian Australians who are gorgeous and flawed, who fuck up. Like everyone else. I also want to be that person as well. I'm happy to fly the flag for Chinese-Australian communities, but I don't welcome being held up as a prime example of what every Chinese Australian should be, because I think that's kind of ridiculous.

It's funny that when you come from a minority background and say you're an academic or an artist, you will immediately be associated with activism. It's a light bulb moment. White people aren't really called activists unless they call themselves activists. It's just when you're of a minority background, you're immediately seen to be someone who's trying to actively be an agent of change in and of yourself. Of course I want to be an agent of change, but I don't see that as my central responsibility. My responsibility is to make art, to work on stories, and hopefully that is its own agent of change. I've been picked up on for a tweet I've sent on something that's happening in politics, 'You can't say that, Ben.' It's back to that subject of, 'Don't you know you're representing us?' Well, I think there are plenty of other Asian-Australians who agree with me on the issue, and I don't represent anyone except myself, just as white people don't represent all of whiteness. Going back to David Sedaris, he often writes about himself with all his flaws and being an idiot, a buffoon, embarrassing moments, and that's why his stories resonate with me. I don't want him as a role model; I want a sense of companionship and solidarity with him. This book's readers and writers don't need role models, but to feel that companionship and solidarity.

Tsifteteli, or Double-stringed

Anthony Lekkas

The first time I experienced any gender bending was when I was nine years old at my brother's godparents' house. We were there for a New Year's Eve house party with extended family. Naturally there was Greek dancing, a lamb and pig on the spit, lots of drinking, the adult men playing cards inside while the adult women were dancing in the backyard and preparing food. I always found my family events to be lively and festive, particularly on New Year's Eve and name days. On this particular night, as the countdown to 1985 began, my brother's godfather appeared, dressed in drag and dancing to the Greek tsifteteli in the backyard where we were all gathered. Everyone was clapping and laughing and shouting out. This was such a spectacle and I remember thinking it looked like he was having so much fun and wanting to get dressed up myself.

In 2001, I attended a family wedding in Vanuatu in a gorgeous resort in Port Vila. I had a female partner at the time and I was 25. I asked her and her friends if they could dress me up in women's clothing so that I could 'put on a show' at the wedding reception. I remembered my brother's godfather's performance and thought I could finally get my go. On this occasion, I was not disappointed. I came out to the tsifteteli music and tied the groom up to a chair and gave him a drag lap dance in front of many of our family and friends. Everyone thought it was hilarious. I had so much fun. I was pretty drunk too. At the end of this night, one of my relatives said to me, 'I've always wondered about you.' I wasn't sure what he meant exactly but this was the first time I worried about negative responses to my bisexuality. I was not out to anyone in my family. I mean, heck, I just danced around in drag, so I wasn't exactly trying to stay invisible either.

I had already been secretly sleeping with men and transwomen for casual sex since I was 20 and never ever imagined telling my family. They had only ever known me to have female partners. My partner 'Mary' (pseudonym) at the time was my high-school sweetheart and our parents knew each other from within the Greek community schools in Melbourne. They had all imagined that we would get married and have a family. I felt some pressure to do so since our relationship was very 'public' in our social networks. I did love her, but her family was quite religious, Greek Orthodox, and although my family was less conservative, there had never ever been any conversations or positive remarks or obvious representations of queer identity in my family of origin, childhood experiences and early adult family life. So I had no way of framing my secret sex life or giving a name to my sexuality that made sense.

Mary and I had already been talking with her parents about getting engaged. I felt that getting married would get rid of any desire I had for men or transpeople and also help me to conclude that my sexual behaviour was just a phase. The more we talked about getting married, the greater my desire to pursue other men for sex. I secretly started to see a psychologist for my private struggle. It was there that I decided I would break up with Mary. This was difficult because she didn't see a separation coming at all. No one did. I wanted to tell her about my sexuality but I wasn't sure if I was gay or trying to sabotage our relationship with infidelity because of my pre-existing anxiety about marriage, since my parents' marriage was a traumatic example to work with. I shocked everyone with my decision to separate from Mary, except my therapist. My mother and sister were hoping for more children in the family. I still feel guilty about my mother not having more grandchildren. She often reminded us of our 'jobs' as men to have families of our own. She was one of nine children and my father was one of eight.

I went on to have other relationships with men and women. Every relationship I have had since Mary I have come out as bisexual very early. I've been surprised and very touched by how supportive and affirming my (ex-)partners have been. Yet Mary was the first and last Greek partner I have had. I miss how familiar it can feel to be with someone from your own ethnic culture, but I don't miss the pressure that comes with having to perform our culture in very specific heterosexist ways. I'm now 40 and looking back I'm glad I didn't come out to Mary or my family because I would not have been equipped for their responses.

I came out to my biological family when I was 35. I was in a relationship with 'Colin' (pseudonym). He's Anglo Australian and had been out since he was a teenager, and his family was very supportive. He lived a very gay life I guess. Colin encouraged me to come out to my family because he wanted our relationship to be more meaningful, involving our families. I needed to take it slowly with my family but Colin felt like he had 'been-there-done-that with the coming out stuff' and eventually we couldn't find an agreed pace for our public relationship identity, so we decided to break up. Although I did come out to my family while I was with Colin, I noticed that my family stopped asking me questions about my love life and my social life generally. I know my family loves me but their lack of interest and inquiry into my life indicated to me that they were struggling to come to terms with my disclosure. Their distance made it difficult for me to initiate conversations around it and so we all moved on as if I had never said anything. Some people might find constant questions and scrutiny into people's personal lives intrusive. In my family it's how we show love, care and interest.

This is all a work in progress with my family. I now let my LinkedIn profile do some of the work as I know my family members view my profile and can see that I work in queer spaces, I co-host a bisexual radio show, and do some work for Bent TV. I always attend queer rallies and I post comments on queer news on social media. The queer, bisexual and poly communities have become new, vibrant and supportive forums for me to process and develop my sexual identity and how I want to love and be loved by others.

I have a queer social network that I now consider my family also. I am proud of my Greek culture and my mother, and I still love to sit in her backyard, eating fresh salad from her vegie patch, drinking beer and listening to Greek tunes, yet the elephant in the room remains.

Conversation with my Grandmama

Mei Tze Ling

Ah Po, Ah Kung*
In Sibu, Malaysia
we, your grandchildren, mostly overseas
our mothers, your daughters too, are overseas

reminiscent of the past
of the times I spent with you

of you so versatile, knowledgeable and wise
so adult whilst I was young, twelve or thirteen
coming on my bicycle to visit you
when I have available time
seemingly very often
the cycle along Lanang Road
sometimes being chased by dogs

Grandmama
we have to grow up
you older and having joint pains

Grandpapa older too
you fainted in the shop in town
as you do your daily shopping of vegetables and meat,
gave us a fright
I love you both

---

* Ah Po Ah Kung: Grandma and Grandpa in Hakka

We talked about my lesbian existence
I asked when I will get my gold in dowry
you said I should get married to a man
I crushed your objections
and said we have been over that,
I will not change
I asked for fairness in my dowry
I want my gold as in Chinese tradition

yet you accept when I told you my girlfriend is Teochew
you asked who cooks
I replied she does
I joked 'she does the ironing as well'
Grandma said 'you must be the man'
I said 'no, we look after each other and share chores'
You listen you understood

you thought I would get AIDS for being a lesbian
I want to explain to you, I am an HIV/AIDS educator

you are so far away
we miss you
my mother and I

I thought to myself
how many of us (SAL or Sydney Asian Lesbians) are here
with ties and roots elsewhere too
with a past and culture so different
from today

Myra with her mother in the Philippines
Kimmy and her Grandpapa
Poznan who recently arrived

I miss you, my Grandmama and Grandpapa

today
practising softball at Marrickville Park
Dragon Boat training at the Drummoyne Sailing Club
having noodles
going to Thai Thai or having Indian   .

today

Conversation with my Grandmama
speaking my dialect

First published in: Ling, Annie (1992). Mei Tze is also my name.
PMT Publishing: Sydney.

Hyperreality

Lian Low

Hyperreality was a monologue I wrote in the mid 1990s, when I was just coming to terms with my lesbian sexual identity. At the time, the only training I had in playwriting was a devout attention to diarising my day-to-day experiences, which I began when I was 14 and continued all the way to the end of high school. Through various interpersonal interactions at school and university, I was constantly reminded of my foreignness, my heavy accent, my un-Australian migrant body. On top of that I bottled-up my intense crushes on women. And I was painfully, painfully shy.

At the end of high school, I saw an advertisement for the Irene Mitchell Inaugural Short Play Competition in the *Age*. I'm not sure what compelled me to submit. I had no role models in my family who loved literature as much as I do. However, I'd just completed high school co-aceing the 'advanced' English Literature class with another classmate. I had a knack for language, and so I submitted because I felt like I had a good story to tell. I didn't think twice that in 1996, on a predominantly white theatrical stage, judges may not be so kind to a Chinese-Malaysian Melbourne-based migrant lesbian coming out and being infatuated with kd lang.

There were 100 entries in the competition, judged by the *Age* senior critic, Helen Thomson, and journalists John Mangan and Pamela Bone. I won the Under-25 category, was awarded $1000 and a rehearsed playreading at the George Fairfax Studio, Victorian Arts Centre. When it came to casting, the producers had to fly a WAAPA (Western Australian Academy of Performing Arts) based graduate actor, Fiona Choi, to perform. There wasn't an Asian-Australian actor in Melbourne they could find to play an 18-year-old Chinese-Malaysian-Australian woman. Two decades later, Fiona Choi now plays Benjamin Law's infamous mother in the acclaimed television series, *The Family Law*. She's now surrounded by talented Asian-Australian actors from a range of ages and genders.

But, since writing the play, what hasn't changed much is homophobic and transphobic social mores. While anti-discrimination laws exist, social attitudes haven't really shifted. In 2013, a report called *Growing Up Queer*, on issues facing young Australians who are sexually diverse and gender variant, found:

> *Almost two-thirds of the 1032 young people who completed the survey experienced some form of homophobia and/or transphobia, with some experiencing multiple forms of abuse – 64% had been verbally abused, 18% physically abused, and 32% experienced other types of homophobia and transphobia. Schools were identified as the major site in which homophobia and transphobia prevailed. Peers were most frequently the source of this homophobia and transphobia, but for many, it was the homophobia and transphobia perpetrated by some teachers that had the most profound impact in their lives.* (Robinson et al., 2013: v)

I feel lucky that my favourite teacher in high school, my literature teacher, who I'd showed my finished draft to, didn't humiliate me about the content of my play. My gratitude for this crucial turning point in my life still remains. While there was no talk about sex and sexuality within my family context, writing about it was a way of making sense of the largesse, wonder, pain and beauty of the world of sex, sexuality, passion and love. And being true to myself.

HYPERREALITY DRAFT 3.0

Cast:

GIRL/WOMAN – A young Chinese woman, 20s

VOICE/MONSTROUS-GHOST-LIKE FIGURE – GIRL/WOMAN's mother, 50s.

Setting:

The GIRL/WOMAN's bedroom; her sanctuary. *kd lang, Tracy Chapman and Buddha posters cover* **GIRL/WOMAN**'s *four bedroom walls.*

Time:

Mid 90s. kd lang, Melissa Etheridge and Tracy Chapman have just burst onto the mainstream music scene to critical acclaim. There is also a new flourishing of queer representation – films like *Incredibly True Adventures of Two Girls in Love* and *Go Fish* have mainstream releases.

Lunch time

GIRL/WOMAN *has just had a very stiff Saturday lunch with her mother. Mother asks her to clean the room. G/W storms into her room, yells, 'Leave me alone-lah, okay or not, Maaa?' Agitated, she walks into her room, flustered. She's struggling with living with her mother, but she's too scared to leave. She picks up the remaining kd lang posters on the table and sticks them on the* *wall. She looks in the mirror, annoyed with her pimply face. When she finishes sticking up the posters, she walks around agitated for something to do.*

GIRL/ WOMAN:

Do you want to know how . . . *bored* . . . whatever . . . I feel? I'll tell you.

I'm waiting, just waiting, waiting to bleed.

Sounds stupid right? Who waits to bleed?

My boobs and tummy are so swollen, and my face is all pimply, I just wish it would come!

Imagine the inconvenience of waking up and then finding your groin and undies in a red pool. Like I'm a murderer. Of my own body. I hate my period. I really, really hate it. I wish I didn't have periods.

(Talks like an advocate)

Boys don't have periods

Boys can piss standing up

Boys talk and people listen

Boys can get drunk and go topless and no one cares.

Boys can hold hands with girls in public

Boys can kiss girls in public.

But I can't. I'm not supposed to, because *I'm a girl.*

G/W puts on kd lang's 'Constant craving' and rocks herself.

Actually, I'm just waiting, waiting for love to happen. Fall into my arms one day, like a miracle. Like *kd lang.* I've videoed her whenever she's on TV, cut-out articles about her from random magazines.

(Reminisces)

Ingenue her first big hit album, was my first album. I have *Ingenue* on cassette and CD! I also have *Salmonberries*, her first film. And I have all her country and western albums!

When she was on *Hey, Hey It's Saturday*, I sent the producers a drawing I did of her, but I didn't get a response.

(Addressing audience . . . support) Oh, dear Lord Buddha, my darling baby brother **tapes videos** of kd for me.

(Addressing herself . . . struggle) Doesn't he know that she's, you know, one of those? I don't like saying lesbian. To me, it sounds wrong, dirty, perverted.

(Addressing audience . . . support) But dear, dear, dear Lord Buddha, you know a month or so back I was watching the Pride March, and there I saw my darling baby brother in the crowd as well. Then, at the Melbourne Queer Film Festival he was in the audience. He is one of the most supportive brothers in the world. I can't believe how supportive my baby brother is, that I would just keep bumping into him at all these queer events I'm at.

G/W hunches over on the bed.

Today is boring. The waiting. The nothing. (*checks undies*) Like my boring love life.

(*Falls onto bed star-shaped*)

(*Conversationally*)

But two weeks ago, it was the most exciting day of my life. (*bubbling with excitement*)

My uncle, Roger, had invited me to the NGV cos there was an exhibition of gamelan instruments, and he knows I'm interested in this. I arrive a bit early, and wait by the waterwall. My uncle arrives. With him, his housemate. This housemate of his is everywhere with him – at all the family birthdays, Christmases, Chinese New Years. The only thing they don't do together is go to the same church. I don't really like my uncle's housemate Dickie. He's always very awkward around me, a bit cold. He doesn't really talk much. Actually, my uncle doesn't really talk much either and is awkward, and can be a bit cold. They both have the same personalities.

Anyway, hanging out with them is NOT the most exciting thing that happened to me. *Please!* We were in front of a Picasso, when just beyond a wall cavity, I spied *kd* with her *girlfriend*.

I stifled a scream and smiled goofily at Roger and Dickie.

'What is it?' my uncle asks.

I just smiled. I couldn't speak. Then Dickie says, 'Oh my god, Roger, it's kd lang.'

The three of us huddled to the wall cavity. (*G/W appears to hug her uncles*) I wanted to run and touch kd, but I couldn't.

I wanted to hold kd's hand. I wanted to be her girlfriend.

A loud voice interrupts the **GIRL/WOMAN**'*s engrossed self-chatter . . .*

VOICE (*off-stage*):

Oiiiiiiii! Come and help wash the dishes!!

GIRL/WOMAN:

Wait . . . laaah . . . O.K.??? (*Angry*)

GIRL/WOMAN:

So, anyway, after the gallery visit, my uncle Roger, his housemate and I part ways. I was on a hunt for an SLR camera, and I swear, dear Lord Buddha, it was *fate*.

G/W hears a noise outside her door. She quickly jumps into bed, grabbing a book about kd lang to read. Her door creaks quietly open, not long after, and then shuts. After a few minutes, G/W jumps out of bed.

GIRL/WOMAN:

My mum can be *sooo* annoying. Why is she always checking on me? Where was I?

Argh, I think I'm about to have my period.

*GIRL/WOMAN runs out of her bedroom to go to the toilet. Lights go dim and the audience sees a **MONSTROUS-GHOST-LIKE FIGURE** entering the room and cleaning things up. The **MONSTROUS-GHOST-LIKE FIGURE** exits as G/W enters her room. **GIRL/WOMAN** walks in slowly – preoccupied. She is oblivious to any changes to her room.*

GIRL/WOMAN:

I don't feel too good. Still no blood. I think I'll just relax and play some kd lang. See you later, dear Lord Buddha.

GIRL/WOMAN looks for her kd lang videos. She suddenly realises that things have been re-arranged in her room. Her face contorts in panic and she loses it. She runs out the door and slams it behind her. She yells off-stage.

GIRL/WOMAN:

I saaaaiiid don't come into MY room without MY permission!!!!!! Why can't you just leave me alone?!!! Why don't you listen to Me??!! Listen to ME . . .! Leave me alone!!!

*GIRL/WOMAN locks her door. Loud yelling and banging can be heard on the other side of her door. **GIRL/WOMAN** ignores the yells, the yelling stops.*

GIRL/WOMAN:

(reminisces)

Dear Lord Buddha, it was fate because I met this beautiful girl in the camera shop at The Glen shopping centre. I wanted to drown in her almond eyes. I didn't, *couldn't* listen when she explained the fine technicalities of the camera to me. All I saw were her hands, her slender fingers, the way her mouth moved. Inside I was screaming, can you please teach me – *[softly aside]* touch me . . .

(to audience)

I remember her explaining and re-explaining how to focus a few times. I must have looked really vague. She went on about deep focus, wide focus – while I got very unfocused.

Now I remember an interesting technicality – she reminded me of this other person I was majorly magnetised to. *Same attitude and personality –* a boy; but I can't imagine sleeping with a guy. Just doesn't feel natural. There are so many guy meets girl love stories. Feels like everyone wants romance in their life, Hollywood-style. Nothing different.

Oh well, what do I know? I never seem to have any luck with girls. Oh dear Lord Buddha, where can I go to find answers? How can I tell this girl I like her? What do I do? Will she go out with me? But, she's so handsome, and I just feel ugly, trapped and I still live with my parents.

I wonder what would happen if my badminton buddies from the M'sian society or my M'sian Christian friends knew.

Or maybe they wouldn't care.

Maybe they would be supportive.

Like my brother who is always at a queer event where I'm at.

Or Dickie who is always asking me about volunteering for something gay.

Or, or, no way . . .

The problem, Lord Buddha, is that nobody talks about love or sex in my family. It's about who is sick or well, or dying, or money, or who married who, who has how many children, what job they got, or how big is their house or car.

But, you know, as I told you, Dickie, my uncle's housemate is at every family function, and at every family function my dad's second cousin's wife, who I also call aunty asks him every single time, 'You're so handsome, so when are you going to get married?' She also asks my uncle, me and my brother the same question. Then she'll look at me, shake her head and say, 'Aiyah, why you cut your hair so short, what a shame.'

Every time.

Kd's 'Constant craving' plays softly in the background.

GIRL/WOMAN:

Oh, hang on a sec, I think . . .

G/W dives under the covers and masturbates to relieve her pain. One hand pulls the covers down, and she reaches out, looking at her hand, relief and content on her face.

GIRL/WOMAN:

It's come.

End play.

Lian Low by Hayden Golder

'And does he have a girlfriend?'
Jack Migdalek

Being different is one thing when points of difference are respected, or at least accepted. But when being different is scorned, ridiculed, or sidelined, then it's something else again. Mainstream Australian society promotes and upholds gender behaviour that is fundamentally heteronormative. This is reflected in the manner and deportment of prominent figures in public arenas such as schools, politics and mainstream cinema, television, sport and advertising (Migdalek, 2015). Those who do not behave in gendernormative ways tend to be trivialised, if not actively denigrated. This can impact on the social and emotional state of those who are not inclined to behave according to validated standards of behaviour. So too, gender norms promoted in ethnic and religious communities to which we belong can have a profound impact on our sense of belonging. To not toe the heteronormative line in ethnic/religious communities can be alienating. This essay reflects on my own journey – as a Jewish homosexual male of European heritage – and ways in which my ethnic/religious enculturation stalled my coming out to family and community. While my personal journey is unique to my own circumstances, I hope this narrative might be encouraging, entertaining and enlightening for others.

My parents are Eastern European Jews who, having survived hostile persecution and hatred fanned by the Nazi regime, emerged from concentration camps in Poland and Slovakia. Still in their teens, they eventually managed to migrate to Australia, which is where they met. Australia represented hope for a new life and liberty, where being Jewish would not incur discrimination. It wasn't long before they married and started a family.

As children we attended state schools near our home. As far as discrimination goes, I faced nothing, nothing, nothing like what my parents had. However, I was always aware of being different to most of my peers, even well before becoming conscious of my sexual orientation. Being different by way of cultural origin and religion frequently made me feel self-conscious, and not always in a good way. I vividly recall school lunchtimes during the 1960s, and being acutely aware of how unique the cuisine was that my mother packed me off to school with. My irregularly shaped rye bread sandwiches,

filled with various Euro delights, looked and smelled very different to the perfectly square, perfectly white sandwiches that emerged from most of the other
students' lunchboxes. Question to self: what is more perfect about a square
slice of white bread than an irregular oval shape slice of *off-white* caraway rye?
The 'imperfect' shape of the bread I ate and the peculiar smells that permeated
from the wax paper food wrap as I opened my lunch each day (garlic, pickled
cucumber, caraway) drew unwelcome attention from other students ('Whoa,
who farted?'). I felt envious of my classmates' short and simple surnames and
their sandwiches, which drew no attention and fit so perfectly into the square
paper bags or lunchboxes from which they emerged.

Looking back I realise that in those days it wasn't desirable to stand out
for being different. It was a source of amusement for my classmates to hear
teachers fumble and/or joke over pronunciation of long Euro surnames such as
my own (often substituting multi-syllabic Anglo alternatives that stuck). You
were either a girl or a boy and, in the schools I attended, girls played rounders
and basketball and boys played football and cricket; girls did needlework on
Wednesday afternoons and boys did woodwork. We had school breaks at
Easter and Christmas and, even though not Christian, I marked those holy
days by default. In short, there were many indicators that enforced for me that
being a male of Euro and Jewish origin, and not being a fan of football, cricket
or woodwork, meant I was different to most of the other male students and
teachers in my school environment.

Things have changed somewhat in most schools and schoolyards. Nowadays
it's not uncommon for kids to eat lunches that vary enormously: some eaten
out of boxes or bags; others wrapped in flour-cakes, lettuce leaves or dried
seaweed. Many of these exotic foods have become fashionable, raising the
status and making it easier for those whose parents pack these treats for them.

Feeling different to so many of my peers for reasons of cultural and
religious origin, the last thing I wanted was to feel even more different to
everyone for reasons pertaining to my sexual orientation. And so, I tried to
conceal such aspects of who I was within mainstream Australian contexts
such as my school, and also within religious and family settings. Sadly, I con-
cealed these aspects not only from others, but also from myself.

We were not a religious family but we did adhere to certain Jewish rituals
and traditions. We attended an orthodox synagogue, although only three or
four times a year. Like other religions, Judaism specifies certain roles and
rituals for males and females, enforcing the notion of male and female being
positioned in binary opposition. In orthodox traditional synagogues, such
as the one my family attended, the congregation was divided according to

biological sex: males led the service and prayed downstairs; females were relegated upstairs. Men wore skullcaps on their heads, and those who were married wore prayer shawls on their shoulders. This made the single male easy to spot for those who gazed across the congregation. There, until well into my 30s, I would've been the subject of consideration of mothers and grandmothers seeking out a nice Jewish boy for their eligible daughters and grandaughters: *He's a nice boy; I know his parents; Lovely family; And does he have a girlfriend? I don't think so; I know the sister, I'll ask her.* Well, I did indeed fit all those criteria: nice, Jewish, male. What is more, I was single. But alas, I was also gay . . . and closeted.

Nowadays women in synagogue surveying the nice, single, Jewish males below, will very possibly qualify, *He could be gay.* However, back then 'gay' was not openly discussed . . . or considered. It was also untenable that a gay would attend synagogue or keep the Jewish traditions.

I was a docile young male. I understood that I was a male-child and that particular behaviours and pastimes were deemed appropriate for boys to pursue. And so, out of love and obedience, I tried earnestly to fulfill my family's desires for, and expectations of, me. For example, I took up soccer in my father's footsteps, which I remember both disliking and not being good at. However, not wanting to disappoint, I didn't voice my aversion to playing. It was only after some time when my father, who must have sensed how mis-matched soccer and I were, asked how I felt about his favourite sport. It was then that I came clean – not quite the same as coming out – and was relieved to be able to stop going.

I sensed that there was a lot at stake for boys or girls should they transgress from the clear demarcations of what was appropriate activity and behaviour for each, such as boys taking up 'girlie' pastimes like sewing or dance. So I never thought to take up an activity such as dance . . . which I only did many years later – but that's a whole other story (Migdalek, 2015).

Many conversations in my family and community commenced with the phrase, 'When you are married . . .'. The expectation was that I would not only marry, but marry a girl, and marry a Jewish girl at that. Fulfilling this brief was also what I, as the dutiful son, expected for myself. I attended a Jewish youth movement which I greatly enjoyed and had a small but close group of pals. However, looking back, everything in those social environments also reinforced heteronormative hopes and expectations of marriage . . . to a Jewish girl. That I wanted those outcomes for myself too stalled my coming to terms with my sexuality. Indeed, along with my buddies at the time, I attended loads of dances and social events in order to meet girls. I even had a long and meaningful heterosexual relationship through my late teens and early 20s. When I think back, I realise that this relationship could easily have led to marriage. I am thankful that it didn't eventuate, even though it would no doubt have made many people happy . . . at the time.

Homosexuality was neither visible nor discussed in my family. When I became aware of what homosexuality was, I understood it as a major negative, and something that might cause shame to family members of the identified homosexual. Even when the realisation that I might be gay dawned on me, I tried to maintain a relationship with my girlfriend, with the notion of fulfilling the hetero happily-ever-after dream my family and community espoused. A few homosexual encounters had me thinking for a while that I might be bisexual, but when such encounters far outnumbered my straight encounters, I finally faced the fact that I was more gay than bi or straight. From that point, it was a combat between who I was and a dreadful fear of shaming my family if I were to come out. This saw me spending a half-year in Israel, two years in England, and six years in Japan. While these experiences were enriching and unforgettable, I can also see that taking these journeys was a means for me to be away from my family and community, and my consciousness of their expectations for me. Physically distancing myself from my family was a way to continue to *appear* as they desired me to be.

It took me a long while to come to terms with my sexuality and to stop loathing myself for not being able to comfortably live the straight dreams that those I loved had for me. I relate all this as a cisgender, Jewish, gay male under pressures to conform to particular societal and cultural norms. I can only begin to imagine the impact that the same pressures must have on individuals who do not comfortably identify with their natal sex.

I returned from six years in Japan and it didn't take long for family friends to mention single Jewish girls whom they thought I might want to meet. In a panic, I began to consider departing to live abroad again . . . more to facilitate not facing my family than a desire to do more travel. As with so many other stories, when I finally plucked up the courage and came out to my family and friends, it was not as dramatic or horrid as I had feared. Many were immediately accepting. Some took longer to adjust to my confession. In time, things found a way of panning out. My family and I remain incredibly connected and close. I have a wonderful partner. He may not fit the bill for what my family and community desired for me – he is neither female, nor Jewish – but he respects and embraces my cultural and religious background. My parents, siblings, cousins, nieces and nephews adore and see him as very much a part of our clan.

I look back on my experiences and discomforts as a gay Jewish male growing up within a close-knit community. It is all too easy – from my current happiness – to adopt the catchphrase (after the It Gets Better Project, 2010) and advise young ones who may feel out of place or oppressed in their families or communities that *it gets better* as they get older. Such rhetoric may point toward a brighter future. However, advising young ones to 'suck it up' now in the knowledge that things will improve in time, is not really all that comforting in the present. It is surely preferable for a young person to feel accepted and worthy of respect for who they are within their own community in their here and now. The alternative is spending years harbouring feelings of guilt, shame and/or secrecy, which will ultimately impact on the individual's social and emotional wellbeing.

Looking back, it saddens me that I did not feel able to come out earlier than I did. I put a great degree of energy into what I thought a straight son should be, due to consequences I feared had I been seen as and/or recognised as gay. Even though I don't fear the same consequences as I did then, my sense of homosexual self is entrenched and a constant force in my consciousness in most situations and contexts. I do still feel awkward about 'flaunting' my sexuality in the Jewish community. For example, my partner and I were recently at a Jewish wedding and found ourselves exiting the dance floor when up-tempo music changed to slow-dance. It is difficult to articulate why we felt uncomfortable at the prospect of dancing in one another's arms among the many straight couples doing the same. The discomfort – despite knowing better – can be understood as a resurfacing of ways in which I *used* to think males should behave. In time, that 'scar tissue' (Migdalek, 2014) may stop surfacing. Maybe, in time, at our own Jewish wedding.

Docile boy with flower

The Rise of the Queer Muslim

Alyena Mohummadally

Saying 'I am a queer Muslim' in 2018 doesn't bring with it as many raised eyebrows as it did at law school in Canberra in the year 2000. At that particular time in my life, any time I said I identified with a faith and a spirituality I was asked questions as to 'how?' . . .

Fast forward to September 11 in 2001 and the beginning of outright Islamophobia and I then had to move from questions about the 'how?' to the 'why?'. This meant the conversation would be more phrased to me as: 'Why would you choose to identify with a demonic, barbaric, backward, offensive, oppressive and evil religion?', to use a few choice epithets. Very few people who challenged me ever bothered to hear me when I talked about my faith, my family, my community and how we too do not condone violence, especially senseless acts and the killing of innocents.

There were times I feared being open about my faith, especially when I was judged by how I looked – 'Middle Eastern' – and therefore instantly assumed to be an 'other'. I am an 'other'. But I am a Pakistani-Australian queer woman who chooses what labels I want and I get pretty angry when labels I do not want are given to me. Perhaps I shouldn't use 'angry', it makes me sound a bit like those crazy Taliban people who have a lot of anger doesn't it? Yes, using humour comes easily to me; part defence mechanism and part natural response.

My faith is important to me. I need to have someone to thank and, just as importantly, someone to yell at when life does not go according to plan. I tell people I've had my tumultuous coming out journey twice: once as queer and once as Muslim. I embrace the two and it's the only way I can truly be happy. I'm aware that when I acknowledge that the two facets to me are equally important and evenly complement one another, I feel peace. I've had my days of doubt where I believed that I had to pick one world over the other, to be queer and not Muslim, or Muslim and not queer. And I have tried. To live in either of these two worlds as dictated to me. But I fit firmly in neither but clearly cross both in how I live, love and feel. And I have a community that is queer and a family that is not, and both love and support me. So I am one of the lucky ones, yes? But it wasn't always so easy . . .

As young as 13 or 14 I knew I was attracted to women. But what complicated it for me was an attraction to men as well. I wanted to be 'one way' only growing up in the late 80s/early 90s. No such luck and throughout university I felt confused and lost, unable to find a world that I believed in – I wasn't completely straight but I didn't really understand what it meant to identify as queer either. Faith sometimes helped. I would convince myself of the old adage 'God made me this way' (and so there!). But I would also feel guilt and confusion as my understanding of homosexuality or any non-heterosexual activity was that they were 'haram' or forbidden. I spent many years facing and running away from that guilt and confusion. Eventually it was finding and becoming a part of an eclectic group of ethnic queers, bis, gays and lesbians that helped me find peace.

I moved to Melbourne from Sydney in 2004. It was a cold July, I had no job, but I did have a Masters at Monash to focus on. I had been active in queer politics at both the University of Sydney as well as at the University of Technology Sydney and also volunteered in my final year of law at the HIV/AIDS Legal Centre. Being Queer Officer at a university for two years meant I sought out LGBTIQ organisations for support or to support them. I was a quiet Muslim but a loud and proud queer. At uni I didn't mention my faith as I was afraid that I'd be the only one and then be targeted by extremists. The fact that I had never had any contact with extremism didn't soothe me; I truly believed that for my own personal safety I had to be quiet about being Muslim. And so I became 'Aly M' and moved to Melbourne.

I met Maria Pallotta-Chiarolli at a PFLAG launch of her book, *When Our Children Come Out*, in Toorak in 2005. I, like many of my generation, had a massive crush on this amazing and influential academic, author and ground-breaking woman who I am now proud to call my friend and confidante. Amusingly, it is now my three-year-old son who has the crush! Maria and I connected immediately and she invited me to come and speak to her students in one of her courses. She then invited me to join the AGMC as they were planning a conference and I was welcome to become a part of it. Little did I know that I was finding a place in history. Overnight, from not knowing any ethnic queers, I now had a queer family. A Greek man. Two Jewish men. A Jewish woman. A Vietnamese woman. A Malaysian man. An Italian woman; well, two of them at the time. And we met on a Monday night and it was exhilarating. They were in the early stages of planning a conference. And I fit right in. Pakistani Muslim queer. Not out to the world but open with this group and excited.

I was given the task of publicity which I took to readily. I networked extensively and my contacts assisted in creating huge interest in the conference which was titled 'Living and Loving in Diversity' and was held in St Kilda in 2004. The energy was amazing. The atmosphere was high. Following the conference, I remember speaking with a friend and saying the one thing I was disappointed about was there was no queer Muslim speaker. And she point-blank said to me, 'Why don't you do it?' and I had no reply.

So I started speaking. Quietly at first and then more firmly. And by 2006, as 'Aly M', I had presented at many workshops and run one at the second conference as well. I also became President of the AGMC for many years and we worked hard as a committee and established our relevance in Victoria (and slowly all over Australia). I worked with an incredible group of people. And an incredible group leads the AGMC nowadays as well. We also became a resource for groups, where we would assist them in publicity, support, even funds if we could access grants.

My name is not Aly M. It is Alyena Mohummadally and I am a queer Muslim woman.

Caught Between Two Worlds
'Coming out' in Italian families
Tony Mordini

In 2013, the AGMC held a very successful event for Italo-Australian LGBTIQ people, their families and allies. The project, a collaboration between Australian and Italian academics (see Bertone and Pallotta-Chiarolli, 2015; Cipelletti, 2013), leveraged off work undertaken in Italy by *Associazione A.GE.D.O., Associazione parenti e amici di omosessuali, bisessuali e trans* – Italy's national association for parents and friends of LGBTIQ individuals.

For me, and I know for many others present, it was a day of great celebration and acknowledgment of the love, acceptance and diversity that exists in the Italian and Italo-Australian communities for its LGBTIQ family members. Many have found incredible support from their families, friends, colleagues and wider professional networks. With respect to the latter point, LGBTIQ Italians and Australians of Italian origin have made significant contributions in a number of fields including the arts, education, science and commerce.

However, besides being a joyous occasion, the event also captured the pathos, struggles, difficulties and tensions faced by many LGBTIQ Italians and LGBTIQ Australians of Italian origin. For many, the journey has been complex and difficult to negotiate. Some individuals have chosen to live in silence or in 'two worlds' as a way of appeasing the dual forces of familial and community acceptance versus that of their own attractions and volition. This is a 'tough ask' and one deeply bound in a belief system where sexual and gender diversity is inconsistent with the prescribed tenets of that belief system.

Italy is a Roman Catholic country and here I believe lies one of the greatest impediments to having a full and frank discourse on the topic of sexuality and gender diversity and to achieving full acceptance in all aspects of family, social and community life for LGBTIQ Italians and Australians of Italian origin. These religiously-rooted beliefs are deeply embedded in the Italian psyche, even if church attendance is relatively low. Traditionally, Italians have also been quite conservative with respect to understandings around gender, sexuality, marriage and community expectations. Consequently, coming out has not been without its challenges. In some cases, individuals have chosen to remain silent and not taken the step to out themselves; others have chosen to live two lives – one private, one public – creating additional layers of stress and anxiety.

Personally, I have found I do not have one life, I have *many* lives; I do not have one identity, I have many. I have become a chameleon who adapts to the situation he finds himself in. My professional identity is often masked (and quite guarded) to protect me from the risks of not being able to properly fulfil my professional roles in educational administration and the judiciary.

The private person is often a different person but again it will reflect where I am and what I am doing. At family gatherings, there is a bit more freedom but I often feel that the 'don't ask, don't tell' policy is applied. At times, it saddens me, at times it appals me, and at times it angers me. I am a son, a brother, a father, an uncle, a highly educated and successful professional, and yet I still live in a world where I need to be concerned about my personal safety and how people may view my personal relationships.

I am not alone and I know of many other sexually and gender diverse individuals from ethnic and religious communities where homosexuality, bisexuality and other forms of gender and sexual diversity conflict with their community's faith, religious traditions, conservative ideologies, social mores and family expectations. We also know that in some of these communities homosexuality is a crime punishable by death.

These socio-political factors can impact individuals on a number of levels, including culturally, psychologically and emotionally. These factors may result in individuals being shunned and isolated; the victims of domestic and community violence; and/or depressed and anxious. The health literature illustrates that social and emotional factors play a significant role in health outcomes. In my own doctoral research on the psychopathology of self-harm, I noted that same-sex attracted people are seven times more likely to take their own lives (Mordini, 2001).

Regrettably, we do not live in a world where all people, irrespective of their sexual or gender identity, have full equality under the law. And even if they do, they may still feel unable to live as they are being called to live because of family and community pressures, stigma or prejudice. The impact of such stress factors cannot be underestimated. Not all find these factors easy to navigate.

It saddens me to say that in an advanced country like Australia, issues such as Marriage Equality, safe schools (anti-bullying) initiatives and equal opportunity in employment continue to be problematic. As a result of this situation, gender and sexually diverse people continue to be over-represented in the mental illness data, have more experiences of prejudice, are at greater risk of suicide, have higher expectations of rejection, and live with higher levels of stress due to hiding and concealing behaviour.

Those who cannot (or may find it difficult to) advocate for themselves need champions who will advocate on their behalf, such as the AGMC and community groups it supports like *I Ragazzi* and *Arcilesbica Australia* which provide a specific point of reference for LGBTIQ Australians of Italian origin.

The AGMC continues to grow as a peak body, an important and credible voice, and to advocate for social and political change; change required to ensure a more equitable, egalitarian and just society.

Tony and Maria at the AGEDO event, Melbourne Trades Hall

A QPoC Manifesto
Fighting for invisibility in a world that loves to talk

Nonno and Aroosa

Story #1

Sara and I were outside the club, taking a break from the dance floor, smoking cheap cigarettes. Sara was wearing a bright red hijab. A scene photographer came up to us, and she turned her head away from him. She said, 'Tell him to go away,' so I did. Sara said, 'The last time I came to this party, they put my photo on the cover of that gay paper for the whole world to see. I didn't sleep for days worrying about it.'

Introduction

Gossip can really suck sometimes – it's pretty fun when you're doing it, but not great if you're on the receiving end. But if you are a queer person of colour (QPoC), who is not out to your family or community, gossip can have serious consequences. We are two QPoCs from Sydney who are doing our best to negotiate the tricky space between being respectful members of our communities and living our own queer lives.

Gossip can be any talk about a person's sexuality or gender identity, no matter how casual, innocent or well-intended. For example, disclosing your QPoC friend's sexuality or gender identity to another queer person might seem reasonable but can actually be unsafe. On a basic level, gossip can lead to outing, and outing can be disastrous for us.

When the queer community talks about outing, we usually mean intentional outing of celebrities and homophobic politicians. Unintentional outing of QPoCs is different – celebrity outing is a political strategy designed to advance the interests of all queer people; outing of QPoCs is often a careless use of gossip with no real purpose.

We are writing this from our own perspectives, and we certainly don't claim to speak on behalf of all QPoCs. We are from Mediterranean/Middle Eastern backgrounds, and while some of these issues will apply to all QPoCs, they are pretty specific to our communities. We have been thinking and talking about unintentional outing for the last 10 years and we want to start documenting these stories. They are hard for us to write, because the reality is these issues are complex and have a huge impact on our lives.

So why did we write this piece? Being a non-out QPoC in Sydney is kinda unusual, and we find we keep getting asked the same questions. So we've compiled the top 10 questions we've been asked with some answers that will hopefully explain things better. The point of doing this is to build a better understanding of our stories and therefore stronger alliances in our diverse communities.

'What do you mean you're not out? What is this, the 1950s?'
Being out is almost seen as a rite of passage in the gay world. Saying 'I'm not out' just prompts a whole series of questions like, 'When will you come out?' or people suggesting ways to come out – as if we were looking for advice. Rarely has someone said, 'Well, you don't actually have to be out.' For a long time we struggled with this feeling that we needed to come out as a natural part of our journey. It isn't for everyone.

The reason why we are not out to our families is complicated, and it's difficult for us to discuss. It's also private, so we'd rather not go into it. Instead, let's look at the question: why is being out a rite of passage? Why do people want to know if someone is out? What assumptions accompany these questions?

One day, someone did say to us, 'You don't have to be out.' Sekneh Hamoud-Beckett introduced us to her concept of inviting people to 'come in' (Hammoud-Beckett, 2007). It is precisely what has worked best. She explained that the 'closet' isn't a dark and scary dungeon as some Western queer politics makes it out to be. Not being out doesn't mean you're all isolated and oppressed. Rather, you bring people into your own welcoming space as and when they are ready to be part of it.

Coming out is about pushing your agenda. Inviting people to come in is about creating an organic process that comes with time and with the necessary adjustments people need to make for themselves. For many people, this can be a way to prevent the conflict, disruption and stress brought on by the pressure of coming out. That's not to say inviting in is completely free from stress and angst, but for some people it's the best option.

So when we hear that someone is not out, let's start a new pattern: rather than trying to make them fit with a mainstream Western perspective that coming out is the only way to true liberation, let's talk about inviting people in.

'You should meet my co-worker. She's from your village and I told her that I met this awesome QPoC.'

We can't emphasise this enough: never ever out someone. Just because someone is out to you, it doesn't mean they are out in every facet of their life.

Outing is dangerous and can be very destructive. And it can cause a big mess that can take someone years to undo, if that's even possible. There are cases of people getting married to prevent the backlash. Don't be responsible for another fake marriage! It's nice to get the white goods and money, but really not worth the long-term pain of having to now live a triple life. The webseries *I Luv U But* (2013) explores some of the issues around fake marriages.

Your co-worker might be really open-minded about sexuality, but you don't know anything about whether we know each other, or our family or cultural history with each other. Leave it alone.

Some QPoCs have what might commonly be called a 'double life'. We refer to it as a complex information management system. This system could mean using a pseudonym in the queer world, keeping our gay clothes/photos/love letters in the car, and having two Facebook accounts.

Having an information management system enables some people to be part of important aspects of their cultural, religious and social environments, as well as being queer. This can be stressful and painful as well as rewarding, especially as this system might be a lifelong necessity. Do not disturb this with your need to bring two people of the same ethnicity/religion together just because you know them. A lot of us try to avoid this interconnection and try to manage it by keeping it separate.

The best thing to do is *never out*. Even if the person is out, it's not up to the rest of us to make these announcements. It's that simple.

Story #2
Being from a small community, I always worry where people from my cultural background work. When I fill in forms and get to the section, 'Do you have a partner/next of kin?', I always just put my sister's name. I'm too scared to name my partner in case I get found out. As far as any government, real estate or bank is concerned, I am single.

'Surely there are other QPoCs from your community out there – why don't you come out and then you can find them and support each other?'

Just because we're from the same community doesn't mean we will get along. Of course, people will do this with the best intentions, to try and bring people together based on a commonality, but don't assume that people of the same cultural background or religious background want to hang out together all the time. It's also likely that within communities, the queer folk already know each other and they are already making individual choices about when, if and how they socialise together. This is like when your co-worker says to you, 'Oh, you're gay? You should meet Rodney from Accounting. He's gay; you guys would make such a cute couple.'

'But when you were straight, didn't you bring your partners home?'
Um, no. We didn't. In our younger, more foolish days, we may have had opposite-sex partners, flings or crushes, but they didn't make it anywhere near the family home.

In a lot of PoC communities, the whole issue of sex and sexuality is handled very differently from mainstream Australia. Sexuality is not talked about, and there are very strict rules for who can discuss what in front of whom. This is especially true for many girls, who are not allowed to date, not allowed to run around town with boys, and who have to protect their virginity. In a lot of communities, girls don't have boyfriends; they have fiancés.

In our cultures, if we were to say to our families, 'I'm gay' or 'I'm homosexual', it implies that we are having sex. The word 'sex' in any sentence is so rude and embarrassing! In fact, in some cases, the good married girls don't even talk to their fathers about being pregnant because it's telling your dad you had sex!

Of course, these standards are kinda hard to live up to, and we certainly haven't been able to do it. A lot of straight girls haven't, either. But no matter what we actually do with our boifriends, grrlfriends, tricks and lovers, we cannot discuss this with the family. It's not completely about queerness; it's more about sexuality in general.

All of this means that it's not unusual that we haven't brought opposite-sex partners home, so parents don't necessarily get suspicious and wonder if their single kids are gay. Our families are also pretty good at seeing what they want to see. This means they can pretend to ignore that their unmarried daughter is pretty butch, or that their child is exhibiting behaviour that others would identify as genderqueer. Not bringing partners home just means we are good PoC girls who are waiting until we get married, or nice PoC boys who won't bring home anything less than the perfect girl.

'Don't you feel like a teenager, sneaking around on your parents? I couldn't do it.'

Yes. It is difficult. There comes a point in your adult life when you no longer feel an adrenalin rush about being rebellious, and it gets harder and harder to sneak out of the bathroom window at midnight when you get older. (Please don't ask why I haven't moved out yet, that's another thing I can't get into right now – I'm trying to get my leg out the window without dropping my dad's bottle of Brut).

Keep in mind some of us are not doing this because it's fun and exhilarating. We do it because we don't have an alternative. Sneaking out is hard. Especially in a world obsessed with tagging and checking in and posting all over social media.

People find ways to manage their lives. Some have fake jobs they invent and are 'on call' (this sucks because it can mean having to give extra money to the folks and the uncles in the homeland!); others sneak out and try to come home before morning prayer.

Support your friends and don't make them feel any more uncomfortable about this. While you are enjoying your night out freely, they have the compounded stress about being seen by someone in the wrong place; being photographed and pasted on social media in a place where they shouldn't be; accidentally dialing their mother's mobile from a nightclub; getting into a taxi driven by their second cousin; or Mama finding that there are pillows under their doona instead of their child. It's stressful enough thinking about all of this and also having to satisfy our friends' casual curiosities about what we do and why. Have a good time and support your friend with whatever they need.

Story #3
The cute butch at the bar looked at me over her gin and tonic and said, 'You poor thing. When are you going to come out?' Earlier that night, I had spent 20 minutes putting my make up on and deciding which shoes to wear. I was having trouble with the hair straightener, and my mum helped me with it, talking about the parties she used to go to when she was younger. We sat in her room putting femininity on, just like women in our family had done for generations. How do I explain this to her? Why should I disrupt this?

'Oh, I get it. PoCs are totally homophobic, so if you came out to them, you would probably get bashed, right?'

Okay, so this actually does happen to some people. When some parents find out their kid is queer, they can react violently and irrationally. But we all know that this can happen in all communities. There are plenty of white families who react this way too. Violence is not specific to a particular cultural group; violence is about power and control, and this exists in all cultures.

Homophobia is homophobia and it is never acceptable. What we can say is that QPoCs and allies within our communities are trying to have an honest discussion about queerness and acceptance.

It's also difficult for QPoCs to air our community's dirty laundry in public. If someone is bashed by their community, then this can feed into racist stereotypes of violent aggressive PoCs. Seriously, how do you think this question would make us feel? It would make us less likely to discuss difficult family issues with you for fear of feeding your racism.

Finally, we have heard some great stories of PoC families who have embraced their queer kids and their partners. Some of it is explicit, some is unspoken, but it is all love. For some beautiful stories of acceptance, see Ghassan Kassisieh's (2011) 'We're Family Too': The effects of homophobia in Arabic-speaking communities in New South Wales.

'My parents are really homophobic too. I told them that if they didn't accept me, I would walk out of their life, and I did. Why don't you do that?'
Good for you. That's awesome that you had the strength to make this decision and stick to it. But for a lot of QPoCs, we can't do this, and we actually don't want to do this.

We're sure that it must be hard for anyone to cut off contact with their family. But for QPoCs, added on top of that is the years of training to respect our elders and put family first. And on top of that, there is the whole issue of shame, as well as the drama any family dispute will cause in our small communities. Sometimes these issues of shame can force our elderly parents to go into isolation and become completely ostracised, causing immense grief and pain. We wouldn't enjoy this.

In our communities, there is not just the nuclear family. Grandparents, aunts and uncles have a say in our lives and we are very intertwined. Walking out means losing all of those connections.

If we were living back in the homeland, then the coming out blitz might be more possible, because we would still have our food, music, language and culture around us. But in Australia, we are in the minority and our families and communities are our only link to the culture. Coming out could mean losing this link.

'If your family rejects you, don't worry. The queer community will take care of you!'

That's nice of you to offer, but it's not going to work for two reasons.

First, no matter how awesome the queer community is, it can't replace your family of origin and the culture you grew up with. The queer community can't make the food from the homeland and it doesn't celebrate our religious and cultural festivals. We love our cultures, and sometimes you really need to be around people who come from the same context and understand the depth of the connection and nostalgia to the culture and the homeland.

And second, the queer community is not some amazing haven of inclusiveness and sunshine. We have experienced a fair bit of racism from the queer community, both intentional and unintentional, in mainstream gay bars and alterna-hipster parties, and queer community organisations. And we haven't even gotten into the ways that the queer community can chew up and spit out its own members. One of the saddest examples of this is the ongoing high levels of domestic violence in the queer community. So, we don't have confidence or any expectation that the queer community will actually look after us, when it hasn't addressed its own Anglocentrism, casual racism and internal abuse.

Story #4
I met a real hot guy at the Mardi Gras party. We danced for ages then went to have a drink. He asked what my cultural background was, then he squealed, 'Oh wow, one of the ladies at my work is the same! Maybe you're from the same village. I can't wait to tell her on Monday that I met this great guy.' I froze up, then started to explain that I wasn't out to my family and I would prefer it if he didn't mention it to her. Things got a bit awkward after that.

[CLICK] 'Hey, what do you mean you don't want me to take your photo? Your outfit is amazing – I'm just gonna put it on Facebook.'

Thank you. Our outfits ARE amazing.

But don't take photos of people without their express permission. Not everyone wants their lives pasted up on social media for the world to see. Be mindful that for some people coming to a gay bar is a big risk. And they don't want to be seen by others.

We have had particular problems with the queer media. Some photographers go out to catch a glimpse of the social scene. They snap away liberally without any thought or concerns for people's privacy and the fear that some people carry about being seen. Ask before taking a photo and, if someone says no, respect it no matter how hot they are.

The presence of social media has made it even harder for non-out QPoCs to manage their lives. Just think about this: some people have to be constantly looking over their shoulder to make sure they are not being photographed. They want to enjoy the night as much as the rest of the partygoers, but they have a heightened tension and fear of being outed. When we go out, we look after each other as a group. If one of our group sees a camera taking a photo, they will turn their back or cover their friend's face. If you know your friend doesn't want to be photographed, you can be a great friend by looking out for them and making sure they are protected from the lens. If you see their photo on social media or queer media, let them know and ask the site to remove the photo immediately.

'You shouldn't worry about getting outed here. All of my friends are totally not homophobic.'
I'm sure they are not homophobic, but that doesn't mean they understand the issues that QPoCs face or why they shouldn't out people and gossip. What if they take our information and casually mention to our grandmother's best friend that they met a QPoC from the village?

We should all be able to make our own decisions about who knows what about our identity and be in control of our own information. It's not about you and how cool your friends are, it's about autonomy and self-determination.

Conclusion
By doing these things, you are committing to being an awesome friend! These two QPoCs are not looking for pity or judgement – we want you to stand in solidarity with us!

This article is for our friend Sekneh. She has been a constant support to us and many others in the QPoC community, and is a real community hero. We also want to dedicate this to all QPoCs who are finding the joy in the mix of their culture and sexuality/gender identity. Finally, thanks to the two fully sick wog boys who helped us with content and editing.

Coffee cup readings

That's Amore!

Olivia Noto

Growing up

Arches. That described many of the houses on the street I spent my youth in the European-dominated Western Sydney region of Fairfield, New South Wales, Australia. Lots and lots of arches. In many front yards, Virgin Mary statues with adorning water features would light up at dusk. Dad preferred a Roman-inspired statue of a half-naked woman carrying an urn of water among the rockery. In one childhood photo, my sisters and I stand like three statues in among the rockery, spread out across the flowerbeds. We were lined up in order, my older sister Julie on the left, me in the centre, and Rebecca, the youngest, to the right. Like a Babushka set, only with big, dark hair. I wonder if Dad's interest in gardening came from his upbringing in a small village somewhere in Sicily. His threats of calling the Mafia when I failed to clean my room were never substantiated.

Local parks felt safe, despite the swooping magpies. My sisters would sometimes join me playing soccer with the boys up on the top of our steep cul-de-sac. But mostly I'd ride my bike within a 20 minute radius of home, which, despite the proximity, failed to keep Mum's anxiety at bay. Whenever she was watching, I would race down our hilly street and brake just before colliding with the imaginary truck she swore I'd hit. Her shouts were often accompanied by flailing arms raised high above her head – typical of someone's over-zealous Nonna. Mum was Bosnian, born to an Italian mother and Polish father, whose parents were Ukrainian. When they passed away, they took with them the answers to the many questions I have about my mother's background. Why did her parents move to Bosnia? Where did they meet? Why did they migrate to Australia? I've only recently started piecing together the jigsaw with the help of Zio John, the great storyteller in the family. Forced migration between the Poles and Ukrainians was a thing after the Second World War.

In the 90s during the Yugoslavian Civil War, Mum defensively continued to identify as a Yugoslav, even after she heard on the evening news that her birth home was being broken up, reformed and renamed. I was adamant she tell me what country she was 'actually' from, not understanding as a teen how much pain such questions would evoke. She still occasionally refers to herself as Yugoslav.

Being Ukrainian/Polish/Italian/Bosnian/Australian made me as culturally diverse as our mutt of a cat, Ginger, who had hair that grew to various lengths and, despite the name, had brown, white and black patches of fur covering her otherwise ginger body.

Realisation

I probably should've realised I was attracted to girls when I played Disney's *The Little Mermaid* for the 297th time at the age of five. The scene that always got stuck in my head was where Ariel, in all her Madonna-like seashell bra glory, palms firmly placed on a sea rock, waves crashing behind her, hoists herself up singing, 'wish I could be, part of your world'. Wow. I'm not sure if it was the lyrics or the bra that inspired me the most. I suspect it was a little of both, but I did really want to be part of *her* world. A world where many seashell-clad mermaids swam around, singing and looking beautiful all day long. In my version, I'd play Eric, of course, the black-haired stud who wins Ariel's heart.

It took Disney about 30 years to release an animated film featuring a gay couple who live 'happily ever after'.

Catch me if you can!

I've never really been one to follow fads. So when everyone at primary school was watching *Home and Away*, the Noto girls remained staunch *Neighbours* fans. This left very little to talk about at recess. At lunch, we played 'catch and kiss'. I used to run far away and hide behind trees so that the boys *never* caught me. Not once. I couldn't understand why my girl friends would seem to purposefully get caught and giggle at being kissed. Yuck! All that seemed totally gross and I wanted none of it.

Gender matters

In Year 3, I came to the realisation that being the only girl who played hand-ball with the boys didn't score me any kudos in the (girl) friends department. I reluctantly went back to playing with the girls, who had by then traded in their Barbie dolls for 'elastics'. (Think a long loop of an elastic band that one would jump over while a girl at either end held it with their ankles, knees and then waists). Knowing I couldn't do a roly-poly to save myself, I generally just held the elastics and didn't really participate in what I found to be the most boring pastime. At home if I couldn't entice my sisters into a game of hand-ball, the brick wall on the side of my house became my playmate.

Queer TV

I wish I knew the 'one person in ten' statistic back then. I felt so isolated. There were no queer youth support groups or queer-friendly healthcare workers nearby that I knew of. Sydney was the only place I thought other gay people were. I got the occasional glimpse of Sydney's annual Gay and Lesbian Mardi Gras on TV. My mother couldn't understand why I would want to watch that. My sisters and I weren't allowed to travel to the city, so I thought I'd have to wait until I was emancipated, P-plates hanging off my first set of wheels, until I met anyone who felt like I did.

Although I was yet to accept my sexuality, TV offered some respite. I felt lucky that my family enjoyed watching *Ellen* with me. For the younger reader, that's *Ellen* the comedy sitcom, not the talk show she currently hosts. Ellen was the first 'out and proud' lesbian who entered my sheltered world. I was so excited when she came out on the show in the mid 90s. My heart sank when homophobic advertisers pulled funding and the show got canned. The message was clear: coming out was dangerous. It would be a few years before I saw another gay character on the small screen. When Jack from *Dawson's Creek* came out, I was relieved that his father took it well. But the hope I felt didn't quite outweigh the fear. Yet.

Cooka da pashta

Inside almost every house of my Italian, Assyrian, Croatian and Lebanese friends, you'd find a picture of Leonardo Da Vinci's *The Last Supper* in a prominent place. It often had bits of palm leaves hanging from it, the remnants from the last Palm Sunday mass sticking out from the corners of the frame. Ours hung in the kitchen, which was Mum's favourite place in the house. She cooked potato pita, cabbage rolls and my childhood fave – cheese pierogi. I slowly discovered the diverse origins of such dishes when I'd go to a Serbian wedding or Polish restaurant. Not even Mum knew whether the dishes were Yugoslav or Polish or Ukrainian; they were just what her parents cooked when she was young.

Like many European families, food brought our family together. One of my earliest and happiest memories is picking basil leaves with my older sister at Nonna's. My extended family joined in to make the long-neck bottles of pasta sauce, scooped from giant plastic drums where the sweetened red mixture bubbled.

Whenever I fly from Melbourne to visit Mum (who still lives in the area), I make a point of cooking something traditional with her. It always ends up being the highlight of my trip. I got my love of cooking from her. Today, though, I cook the modified gluten-free versions of those dishes, without onion or garlic, thanks to my restrictive low FODMAP diet. Mum thinks my life is now tasteless. It's not.

Puberty blues

My post-pubescent high school life was characterised by repressed feelings and absurd rationalising that kept me the good (that is, straight) Catholic girl everyone assumed me to be. This is despite the fact that Dad often, with admiration, called me the 'black sheep' of the family. At other times, while helping him paint a fence or shovel dirt, I was donned the 'only son in the family'. This was a big deal considering how prized male children are among the older Notos of the family – something that still grates to this day. Sexism seemed rife among the Noto men. Dad once made the mistake of suggesting to my young feminist self that the house was filthy despite having three girls. He hasn't made that mistake again.

But I digress. Repression. It felt like being a fraud. I instinctively knew I was different, but it was just too scary to face. Then Josh happened.

Josh

My only boyfriend was Josh, who I dated briefly when I was 12. I was impressed by his ability to live up to the Aussie stereotype: he had freckles, played cricket and loved meat pies so much I rarely saw him without one. We did it seven times in one night. Yep. We were at Michelle's birthday party playing spin the bottle, and the bottle I spun happened to land on Josh seven times that night. So he got seven kisses. On the cheek. In fact, it was more of a traditional Italian greeting type of kiss, cheek-to-cheek. But I think I made up for it with my loud 'mmmwwaahh' noises that I learnt from Nonna. I figured if I wasn't squeezing his cheeks red-raw and telling him how *bello* he was, I mustn't have been too bad in the kissing department . . . right?

It didn't take long before I developed a reputation as 'frigid' in high school. This suited me just fine. Once in Year 8 my girl friends, including Angelica, who I had been totally in love with since Year 3, tried to pull me around the corner of a building where I knew a group of boys, including one who I heard was interested in me, would be waiting.

I couldn't run away fast enough.

Fashion

My teenaged fashion sense left much to be desired; you'd often find me in jeans, a plain white t-shirt with a denim jacket, and my black leather school shoes. This was way before double denim was even remotely cool. My hair was so constantly in a ponytail that my friend Hayley just couldn't stand the same-old look of me anymore. One day, she ripped out my hair tie and I had to chase her around the playground, holding my ponytail with my hand until I pried it out of her hands. In hindsight, I was probably mortified I'd look too straight with my hair down and waving about like all the other girls. I didn't want to get any attention from the boys so, as well as my boring hair, I would always chose uncool tailored slacks instead of skirts with tights in winter.

Unfortunately though, learning how to be unattractive to men didn't win over the heart of Angelica.

Paul

In many ways it was Paul, my best friend for the last 20 years, who helped me to accept myself for the out and proud lesbian I've since become. Back in 1997, when the Spice Girls were releasing messages of Girl Power in their 2-inch platforms, our maths teacher brought Paul and I together with his seating arrangements. Mr Cheng once asked us to put our 'hands on top of the table' in his thick Chinese accent, assuming we were up to no good. His welcome heterosexist assumptions kept maths entertaining and us both safe in the closet. For a while, anyway.

Importantly, not everyone had a phone (not even a 'dumb' one). Facebook didn't exist yet, and it was only in my final year of high school that my parents finally relented to their nagging daughters and we got our PC connected to the internet. Actually, in all truth, we probably spent more time *connecting* to the internet than actually being connected. I didn't brave looking up anything gay-related, let alone chatting to another lesbian! So Paul was the only gay person in my teen world, or so I thought at the time.

In the same year, Paul got into trouble for tackling a bully who called him a 'faggot' one too many times. The incident taught me an important lesson – school in the late 90s wasn't a safe place to be gay. Research I'd quote years later as a teacher confirmed this.

Ana

I spent a lot of my time in Years 9 and 10 kissing my friend Ana, in my dreams of course. In real life, I'd write letters to her constantly, often not waiting for a reply before I'd get out my stationery set again. Tragically, I once let slip that

I had a dream about her where I saved her from a speeding car, only to be hit myself. As I lay on the bitumen, dying, I requested a kiss from her, and she obliged before I passed away happily in her arms. (Told you it was tragic!)

It wasn't long before Ana told Melissa about the dream, and not long after that, Ana told me she needed a 'holiday' from me because I had become so overbearing . . . The end of our friendship felt like a divorce. It took a year to the day until I removed all the photos I had of her by my bed.

The dreams, of course, only got sexier, but I rationalised them away. They didn't mean I was gay. I just missed her friendship.

Acceptance

I was 18. My reflection stared back at me from the bathroom mirror. I heard my mouth say, 'I'm gay.' Finally, after years of repressed feelings, I accepted my lesbianism. No absurd rationalising could undo those words.

You'd think that my diverse cultural background would have made me feel deeply connected to my family history but, truth be told, the moment I accepted my sexuality marked the moment I consciously played down my Polish/Italian/Bosnian, not to mention Catholic, upbringing. In fact, at a work function a few years ago, we were asked to bring in food from our cultural heritage. I brought a packet of Gaytime ice creams.

Coming out

Setting: the bar room balcony, a pleasant warm afternoon.

Props: Cheap beer x 2.

Characters: Dad (D) and Liv (L), aged 18.

L: Dad, I've got something to tell you.

D: Okay . . . Wait wait wait, let me get us some beer first. [Fetches beer. Returns.] Okay. What is it?

L: Mmmm . . . Why don't you guess?

D: [Long pause] You're pregnant?

L: Ha! No . . .

D: [Another pause] You're moving out?

L: Nooo . . .

D: [Another pause that seems to go on for eternity] . . . You're a lesbian?

L: Yep.

This was followed by 'Don't tell your mother' and 'There's no need for the whole family to know about our business.' I was crushed. According to my 18-year-old self, Dad's need to jump into the closet once I came out was a reflection of his 'wog mentality', as I offensively named it. Not leaving our 'dirty washing' on the line meant that, all too often, family secrets that should never have remained secret, did just that.

And it wasn't just about me being gay either. I hated all the false pretences, playing 'happy families'. Little did others know that mental illness plagued those closest to me. My parents' marriage was a loveless mess and would end soon after. Silence just added to the stigma for us all.

Mum's reaction was arguably more hurtful. I waited a few months before telling her, ensuring I took every opportunity to say a gay-related joke to 'test the waters'. Mum said she was 'disappointed'. Me? The high-flying academic extraordinaire who only the year before picked up awards for coming first in three subjects and second in two others? Me?! The recipient of the student-selected 'most likely to succeed' award? A disappointment?! Ouch.

In hindsight though, I realise that Dad merely pretended to be okay with it and wasn't. Our relationship deteriorated after that fateful day, and only recently has gotten back on track. Mum took the news as serious and final (thankfully there was no 'it's just a phase' talk), and her acceptance of that reality meant that she had time to grieve what she thought she'd lost, worry about me getting hurt, and has grown to love every partner I've brought home over the years. Her willingness to grow and learn has brought us closer together. She's wonderful and I feel very blessed having her in my life.

I also feel very fortunate being in the position to take my family, including my two beautiful sisters, on this journey with me. It hasn't always been easy, but we're more connected now than we've ever been.

Then and now
When I think back to my post-school days, I feel incredibly grateful for all the amazing career opportunities I've had to date. My most recent dream job was working with the Safe Schools Coalition Australia team at the Foundation for Young Australians. Previously, I've taught English, Visual Arts and Sexuality Education in rural, regional and metro regions of New South Wales and Victoria, across the public, independent and Catholic sectors. I've facilitated a group of young people to share their coming out stories in schools.

Every one of these opportunities has helped to make me the resilient, brave and proud lesbian I am today. I look forward to returning to the classroom and teaching again soon, and doing my bit in making school that little bit safer and more inclusive for all students, including LGBTI+ kids and those who love them.

The year now is 2017. I'm 33. And rather obviously pregnant. My beautiful partner Sandra and I are very excited about meeting the wonderful future addition to our family; as are Mum, Dad, my sisters, all my zias and zios, my numerous cousins, all my second cousins (it's a BIG family!), my former workmates and friends . . .

The last time I visited Mum a few weeks ago, she insisted I sit and relax while she taught me to cook another traditional dish. (She doesn't know the real name for it, but we call it 'dunka' and yes, it's delish!) Last Christmas Eve, I joined my mother-in-law for a rather quirky midnight mass that I'll never forget. Nanna, who's adopted me as her own granddaughter, taught Sandra and I how to knit. The baby's blanket is almost complete, with booties to follow. We visited her yesterday while hundreds of queers marched proudly for the annual Pride March.

Culture. Food. Family. Sexuality.

They all spring from love.

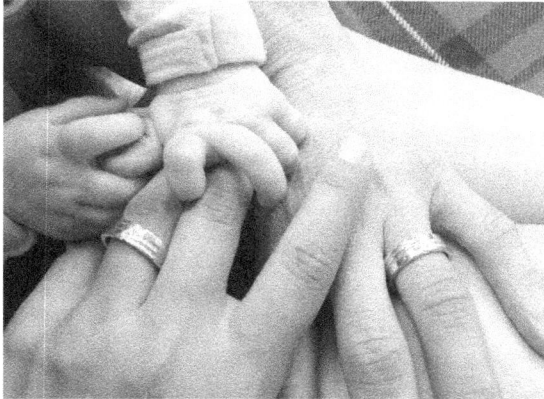

Our baby

The Science of Hairy Legs

Gary Paramanathan

Vishnu sat there, in Year 8 English class. He was yet to appreciate the smell of men, stuck in an all boys' school, smelling sweat and the occasional farts – he could think of nothing worse. He looked out into the distance. His view of a fig tree, thick, stretched out with hard branches and a veiny base, didn't go far enough. He wanted to be somewhere else, somewhere safe. Maybe a co-ed school, with girls he could talk to and maybe hide among. A school where sports and spitting were banned, and books and breasts were in.

He'd often see the girls from his sister school at the train station. They were so enigmatic, even those who were screeching for attention from the boys. The ones he was most interested in were the girls on the other end of the spectrum, doing everything they could to hide under the radar and fly home as soon as possible. By *fly*, take the express train, and by *under the radar*, unbeautify themselves. Vishnu wanted to be them, to hide out wherever they all went.

This idea of women hiding from men was a concept not far removed from Vishnu's memories of his homeland. As a child his parents would take him on annual trips to Sri Lanka, namely Colombo, where he spent much of his time going from relatives' house to house. He was eight, not yet sexually developed, but able to comprehend beauty and the effort to achieve it. He recalled a trip to the Royal Botanical Gardens in Peradeniya. A group of university students were on a trip together. He recalled how handsome all the men were, how they all wore bright coloured t-shirts, skinny jeans and fake designer label shoes. He also recalled how plain all the women were. How they kept their hair in plaits or tied back, wore long skirts, and didn't show any cleavage. They kept bright colours off their rack. Never had the human species so clearly reflected the animal kingdom than in his homeland. It was as if they had designed themselves on the male peacock, wearing its full feather regalia, and the female having none at all.

So when Vishnu started school in Sydney, he didn't understand why the boys and men didn't make an effort with the way they looked, and even the ones who did make an effort tried so hard to hide the effort. This is when he felt noticeably different to the rest of the boys. He wanted to dress up, wear bright colours and be noticed. None of the other boys wanted that. He was old enough to know he was different, but he wasn't sure what the difference was. Was it because he was Sri Lankan or was it something else?

As he sat there in English class, now refocusing his eyes on the clock ticking away above the board, Vishnu thought of his couch. He couldn't wait to get home. When he would finally make it back to its safety, he would shower, get into his pajamas, flip flops and open his favourite book. Currently it was a book about a teenager who was on the edge of a breakdown.

Vishnu was a fan of television, but the presence of his aunt in the household made TV-watching very difficult. She would always be lurking in the background somewhere and just as a kiss or some sexually explicit content appeared on screen, she would appear. It's as if she craved it and it would draw her to it. She had given Vishnu a few subtle hints about his TV habits. With Vishnu failing to respond, it had culminated in the final showdown where she walked in on one very explicit SBS Friday night movie. She stormed the room, grabbed the remote control from Vishnu, turned the TV off, and threw the remote back at him. 'You are no different to your uncle.' The uncle she had divorced.

The next day, his aunt accused him of looking at porn on the television. His parents, trying to appease the feelings of a broken heart, concurred that Australian TV was too soft-core pornographic, and banned Vishnu from watching anything that was not pre-approved by them. They had formed their own censorship board, in house, like many brown households. This censorship came in the form of the weekly TV guide, which Vishnu would sit with for a good two hours, scrolling through each page, reading each night's programming and circling the shows he wanted to watch. He would then submit this to his parents, who would look over it and then approve of most, but not all shows, making the occasional arbitrary rejection to enforce their power. He would watch the approved shows, with his aunt still glaring at him on the odd occasion.

Vishnu wasn't so oppressed outside of home. He always found a way to get what he wanted, and that was through books. He'd learnt that you could go to a public library and borrow just about any book you wanted, and he had come across some pretty heavy stuff, like Christos Tsiolkas's *Head On*. His parents only ever saw his books as educational material, and no censorship was ever implemented.

As his body began to change physically, his parents didn't bother with any talk to explain the changes, and his school hadn't kickstarted its sex education yet. He had, however, figured everything out using the internet, his friends and the library, where he would find the occasional sexually explicit book, read it over and over, and run the images through his head. Sitting at the study desk on level one, he was running his own Friday night SBS movie in his head.

Vishnu did once approach the topic of puberty with his family, one night at a family gathering. He was, as usual, keeping himself entertained playing video games with his cousins. He decided to get himself a glass of Coke. He happened to walk past a group of relatives, all women including his mum. They were talking about body hair. He heard them talk about the frustration and annoyance of having facial hair, and having to constantly shave, wax and epilate it away.

'I am so hairy, especially since I have menopause. Look, I have to wax this chin hair all the time,' said an aunt pointing to her chin.

Vishnu smiled, looking at his aunty, and said, 'Oh, I am getting hair on my chin too. Even under my stomach and around my *kunju*. Isn't it odd, Aunty?'

Kunju meant penis.

The entire group went silent.

His mother's jaw was wide open; the ginger black tea she was sipping on may as well have been oozing out of her lips.

She quickly composed herself, and said, 'Oh, sweetie, you can't talk about those things. They are not anyone's business.'

She got up and ushered Vishnu away. She looked at him directly in the eyes and said, 'Don't ever talk anything about your *kunju* to anyone, anymore. Please!'

Vishnu was 11 at the time. That was his entry into understanding human sexuality: you cannot talk about it. So he shut up, and he would never bring it up, but for the fact he went to a boys' school. The boys spent half the time talking about cars, cricket, curry and the other half talking about vaginas and penises.

When Vishnu turned 14, he was starting to feel the effects of puberty, beginning with a general sense of unrest and disassociation with his environment. He was starting to look at men like he had never before. He would often ride his bikes past the footy park, and just stop and stare. His aunt did once walk past as he sat by the park looking at the men playing footy. 'What are you doing here? I thought you were studying at the library.' Tall and slender, he appeared like a spotted cheetah taking its rest, before riding to the library which inadvertently became his solace.

Vishnu refocused his eyes to the board, and his mind back to the class. The clock still hadn't ticked over to the hour. He was tired and he was unfocused. He reminded himself that he had one mission. He was to ace all the school exams, win the praise of his family, fly under the radar with the boys, and get himself into a good university, where he could start his career as either a human rights lawyer or a philosopher. Then he could crack the code to a meaningful life. Till then, he had to keep his head down and soldier on.

The bell rang. It was a glass of cold water to his thirsty ears. As the class of students packed up, Vishnu put away his textbook and notebook; both had been carefully wrapped in thin plastic film. He was off to Science class next, his favourite subject. Vishnu had cut out pictures of his favourite animals and human inventions, and glued them onto his notebook before the plastic film was applied. He thought it'd be interesting to juxtapose the natural perfection of animals with the human perfection of machines.

No one else in his class got his intentions, except for Nathan.

Nathan was an Italian Australian, who also grew up in the local neighbourhood. As Vishnu performed his culture of playing cricket and eating curry, Nathan performed his culture of playing soccer and eating spaghetti meatballs. Nathan was handsome, physically mature for his age, and relatively fit. He was also a bit of a talker.

Nathan had spotted Vishnu's notebook first week of class. He walked past Vishnu as he was unpacking. 'Oh my god, did you do this to show how different but also similar animals are to machines?'

'Yes,' Vishnu's eyes lit up, 'I did.'

'Man, that is amazing. I love your work.'

Vishnu's throat went dry all of a sudden, 'But I'm boring though,' he said.

'What?' said Nathan, then proceeded to rattle off all the information he knew about sabre-toothed tigers and the telephone. Vishnu still felt awkward. It had been an unnecessary remark, one of many he found himself making as he grew into puberty.

Vishnu walked out of English class and toward the Science lab across the quadrangle, where he knew his friends would be playing handball, a popular game in his school.

As Vishnu was walking down the pavement, past the fig tree, he noticed Karthik walking toward him.

Karthik was an effeminate boy, something that Vishnu tried very hard not to be and, for this reason, he avoided Karthik at all occasions. Vishnu knew that any relation could be guilty by association.

The boys would often mock Karthik as he walked past them. 'Oh Karthik, your legs are rubbing together so closely, what have you got between them?'

'Oh Karthik, are you walking over to the girls' school and finally enrolling yourself?'

And that one magic bullet to the heart: 'Fag.'

Vishnu had heard that word thrown around at him a number of times, but always jokingly. He played cricket, hockey and touch footy for the school. While he was always petrified by the idea of catching or hitting any three versions of a leather ball, he had taught himself that the best way to not be bullied is to butch it up. That little girl in him could never come out, at least till he crossed the finish line to Year 12.

As Vishnu walked past Karthik, he avoided eye contact. 'If you don't see him, he won't see you,' he thought.

Karthik did see him.

'Hi Vishnu.'

'Hey K.'

'Are you doing that Science comp Mr Sillett set up?'

'Yeah, I think so.'

'So why don't we do it together? We are the two best Science kids in school.'

As Vishnu was about to respond, a group of Year 8 students walked past, his peers but not necessarily his friends. Nathan was in the group.

'Yeah maybe,' Vishnu said awkwardly, hoping the boys wouldn't notice him.

'Yeah we'd be great together. We might even go all the way to state,' said Karthik.

One of the boys turned around and said, 'You mean you two are going to get married?'

Another one said, 'Who's going to wear the sari?'

The first boy, Joe, then said, 'Vishnu, you are becoming a fag.'

Vishnu died a thousand deaths. It was a Mortal Combat style KO to the throat. He had to respond.

He looked at Karthik, then he glanced at the boys.

'The only fag here is Karthik. And maybe you Joe, the way you keep looking at him.'

'Shut the fuck up,' said Joe. The rest of the boys laughed, including Nathan.

Karthik shook his head. He was disappointed in Vishnu, and hurt. This was his life in high school: a daily set of microaggressions.

'Bye fag,' said Vishnu, and grinned at the boys as Karthik walked away. Vishnu took a silent, long breath. He was relieved but numb.

Vishnu walked himself to Science class. He got his books and pencil case out, laid them neatly on the table. While the rest of the class flowed in, he took a sip of water from his water bottle in his bag.

Just as Vishnu's mouth drained out the last bit of water, Nathan walked through the door. He saw Vishnu and smiled.

Vishnu didn't want any more embarrassment, so he quickly looked at his books and opened a random page.

'Hi mate.' Nathan stood next to him. 'Can I sit next to you?'

'Sure!' Vishnu felt like one of those girls at the train station, smiling on the outside but screaming inside.

'Ready for the Science exam?' asked Nathan.

'Aren't I always?' Vishnu said and laughed awkwardly.

'Well, I might have to copy off you then,' laughed Nathan.

'You can if you want.'

'Ok maybe I will.'

'What's in it for me?'

Nathan looked at him and smiled. 'You know I've been shaving my legs for soccer. They are really smooth.'

Vishnu looked at Nathan's legs, his shorts now hiked up to mid thigh from sitting. Nathan was right, his legs were very smooth. 'Oh, I thought you just didn't have hair.'

'I do, a lot of it, but not anymore. You want to touch it?'

Vishnu looked at Nathan, he looked out into the class. Everyone was busy doing their own thing. The teacher was writing up the agenda for the class. He was all alone in a crowded room, just with Nathan. He looked down at Nathan's legs, then looked at Nathan.

'Okay.'

He put his hand on Nathan's left thigh, and ran his hands up to the edges of the shorts, then down to the knees again.

'Yeah they are super smooth,' said Vishnu laughing.

'Nice right? It's so much better.'

Vishnu looked at his own hairy legs.

'Don't worry, I still have hair elsewhere,' said Nathan.

Like an express train leaving the station, Vishnu's heartbeat began to pick up speed.

'If you ever want to see sometime. Maybe come over after the Science exam.'

Vishnu gulped the saliva that had built up in his throat. 'I'd love that!' He wasn't sure if his mouth had any liquid to lubricate his words. He could feel the pores of his underarms opening up, excreting stress sweat.

'Maybe we can go for a skinny dip in the pool.'

'Oh, that'd be cool,' said Vishnu. He was screaming inside. This is going to be amazing, he thought.

Finally, he'd made a connection at school that could be so much more than he imagined.

Nathan looked at Vishnu, intensely, taking a good long pause. He leaned over, placing his lips near Vishnu's ear.

He whispered, 'I knew you were a faggot.'

La Dolce Vita

From Australian Italian to Italian Australian

Vic Perri

It all started with the mantra, 'Always remember, you're Italian!'

My dad often said this when I used to disapprove of his constant display of Italian pride.

'No I'm not, I'm Australian,' I would defiantly reply. Not even knowing what might define Australian.

He continued with, 'If we go back to Italy, you'll come with us.'

Of course my final response before storming off would be, 'No way, you can go back if you want, I'm staying here,' – without thinking if it was even feasible at my age.

I can't remember how many times this confrontation would happen. I was in my early teens and I thought I was the only kid with this problem. I would eventually find out I wasn't and that this conversation between Italian immigrant parents and Australian-born kids was repeated in many Italian households across Melbourne.

My 'obligations'

'Hey, where do you think you're going? We have to stuff the salami!'

This was the cry from my parents, warning me of my job for the weekend: salami making. Sure I loved eating salami, as many people do, but this meant I was to hang around the house the whole weekend because I had to put in the work to help make it happen. It became embarrassing. Other kids would come around to see if I wanted to go out and play and I couldn't, explaining what I had to do. 'Salami? Ah, what a wog!' If it wasn't salami, it was pickling mushrooms or eggplant. To me, it wasn't an activity that celebrated my rich cultural background; it was a tedious job.

English was not the first language used in our household. As a result, I was the official interpreter. I remember 'responsibilities' such as going to the bank with my mother. She would make me explain to the staff what her issue was and then they would respond through me. My mother would ask in Italian, 'Well, what did they say?'

'Oh, I'm not really sure but I *think* it was . . .' would be my response.

'What do you mean you're not sure?' prompted my mother.

'OUCH!' I would feel a pinch on my arm – and in front of the bank official! 'Sorry Ma, but he's using some words I don't know.'

She would reply in frustration, 'Why do we bother sending you to school to learn English then?'

Now, you tell me. How is a kid in his early teens supposed to understand concepts such as state tax liabilities?

This constant back and forth between wanting to satisfy my desire to belong to the local culture I was born into, going to school, playing with my friends, and the attention I had to pay to the demands of my parents and 'family' obligations, was emotionally draining. There was this ongoing tension between not only having to fulfill my responsibilities but also demonstrating my willingness to participate in the overt pride of my cultural background and, well, just being happy doing what 'I' wanted to do. In fact, I was feeling that the two could only ever have been mutually exclusive.

You see, I was torn between two worlds: the life of *la famiglia, la comunita*, living and participating in Italian cultural customs and traditions while trying to fit in with my 'Anglo' friends and enjoy the things they were doing.

If that wasn't enough to deal with!

This unworkable paradigm became even more problematic when I realised I was sexually attracted to other guys. Hearing the standard Italian mantra, 'Of course you'll get married and have kids!' began to grind me down emotionally. I wanted to be able to express my hidden feelings to my family and to the world but I knew I just couldn't. If I said anything about my differing sexuality, my parents would have 'killed me'. I seriously imagined they would throw me out of the house and onto the street. And who else was there to support me as a young teenager? I felt totally alone.

So, not only did I have to deal with the enormous gulf between the cultural traditions that my family forced upon me and those that dominated Australian society, but at the same time I also had to deal with having a different sexuality from both the expectations of my Italian family and my Australian-born friends. I didn't fit into either camp.

So, who am I?

When I started to deal with my sexuality, a wonderful stage in my life began. As soon as I turned 18, I ventured out and visited a gay bar for the very first time. I began to meet the most wonderful people, making friends and having an adult social life. It was literally the very first time I felt a sense of belonging. I found plenty of support where people accepted my sexuality. However, it still wasn't complete. It was a world where my Italian background was not respected as an aspect of my life and in some cases it was actually fetishised. At times it was almost as if it was a commodity to be used rather than respected. They were my friends but it didn't stop them from ridiculing me at times with generalisations about Italians and so I was put into this stereotype. To some, this could have been seen as something to have fun and play along with but to me it wasn't good enough. I wanted to be accepted as a whole person. So this seemingly new sense of belonging wasn't totally real.

Still not fitting in

Sure, it was a relief that I no longer felt isolated. I had an outlet that involved other people where I could express my sexuality. However, it was a vulnerable time because I felt the guilt of failing my family's expectations. When I was a kid I was too busy rebelling and not caring, like most kids, about what my parents thought. But as I matured emotionally, not only did I want to be happy but I actually wanted my parents to be happy, too. But happy knowing who I really was. It was difficult because I couldn't freely express with my new gay friends the challenges that my cultural background presented. When trying to have some serious conversation with my Anglo friends about some of the issues I had to deal with at home they would laugh, 'Yeah, yeah we all had it hard at home. Coming out is tough regardless of what nationality you are.' Yes, it can be hard regardless of one's cultural background, but I still felt I had different issues to my Anglo friends that made it even harder for me. It was difficult to explain the differences.

This need to fit in, to belong to my peer network, continued to affect my quest for true and meaningful happiness. Then one day, Dad said, 'I'm visiting the relatives in Italy, want to come with me?'

I thought about it, with slight indifference I might add, and asked, 'Are you paying?'

Dad replied, 'Yes.'

'Then sure,' I quickly responded. It was a free trip so how could I say no? That was the only reason to go, I would tell myself and my friends.

What were my expectations before the trip? I don't think I had any. I thought I'd go with an open mind to see what would happen. Well, who would have thought! We spent four weeks travelling through the cities of Venice, Florence, Milan, Genoa, Turin, Rome, Naples and finally settled for the last couple of weeks in the province of Calabria where most of our relatives lived. I have to say, I had the time of my life. The beautiful sights, the history, the delicious food and having the opportunity to immerse myself in the rich Italian culture through my relatives was an experience I'll never forget. So, how did I come out of it at the other end?

'You've changed!' my dear old friend Giovanni noted a few weeks after I returned home. He was of course referring to my new attitude and how I had accepted my Italian heritage with a new robust sense of pride. *Oh Dio mio*, I was beginning to sound just like my father! My dad saw it as a vindication, my mother would simply laugh. I didn't only start accepting my heritage, I began to wear it as a badge of honour. I started bragging about being Italian.

That was back in the 1980s. And while I was beginning to feel better about myself and my identity, I could only genuinely share it with my friend Giovanni. He was the only other Italian gay friend I had. I was having a great life but it hadn't truly become meaningful. Another piece of the puzzle needed to be put in place.

Well, finally!

Fast forward to the 90s.

I remember going out one night to a gay bar and I ran into an acquaintance who was also from an Italian background; in fact, Calabrian, so an even stronger connection. There were a few other guys there who were also of Italian background. Before we knew it there were about a dozen of us drinking together. We were recounting stories of our childhood. Of growing up, going to school, rebelling against our Italian background and trying to fit in with our new world. Wow, we shared so much. It was an amazing experience. Who would have thought? I had never ever felt so truly open about my feelings. I was able to express my gayness with an Italian flavour and have absolute empathy and non-judgment from the group around me. I knew that at home I couldn't be gay. And out on the 'gay scene', I couldn't be too ethnic. But that night, that moment, for the very first time in my life, I could be me. This was my tribe. I could be Italian and gay at the same time.

What became of that night for the group as a whole? Well, the Southern

European and Latin Gay Men's Group (SEALGM) was born. And if you want to read more about this group, check out my second piece later in this book.

It opened another chapter in my life!
The years rolled on and while SEALGM began to wind down, as community groups can naturally do over time, I started to volunteer for the Victorian AIDS Council/Gay Men's Health Centre. They were beginning to recognise the importance of supporting the many members of the queer community who were from different cultural backgrounds. I was an active member of the Italian and Gay group which was supported by them at the time. Because of my active involvement and growing presence at the organisational offices, I was contracted for three months to conduct a needs analysis of queer members of the community who were from diverse cultural backgrounds, including Indigenous queers, and those both out and not out. I did this alongside a colleague who focused on Asian communities. I explored their issues within the queer community, how they felt about service provision and their interactions in their own ethnic communities. After three months and a list of recommendations, I was asked to fill the newly developed position of Cross Cultural Worker and implement the very recommendations I had written in the report.

A new decade and a new audience
I wrote a paper in 2000 for the Italian Australian Institute's inaugural conference *In Search of the Italian Australian in the New Millennium*. The stream, coordinated by Maria Pallotta-Chiarolli, of which my paper was to be a part of, was titled, *You Can't Be Gay, You're Italian!* (Perri, 2000). It was an exploration of the sensitive and controversial issues experienced by many Italian Australians who identify as LGBT and/or living with HIV in relation to the Italian, queer and wider communities. The very issues I have been writing about right now in this piece. Here was our opportunity to raise awareness among the business, academic, political and cultural Italian community leaders. My response to the stream title was reflected in my own presentation title: *I'm Italian and YES I'm Gay*.

Having lived as Italian and gay and writing about it in the queer community for a number of years now, I was finally given an opportunity to formally talk to the Italian community in a public forum. Was I nervous? You bet. I had thoughts of people sitting in the audience recognising me and then talking to my family about it. It wasn't really that I was afraid to be outed to certain members of my family who didn't know. It was more about the gossip that could have been generated in the community. All I could think of was them saying, '*Che vergogna!*', 'How shameful!' I was dreading words such as those getting back to my family and causing embarrassment or even shame. I truly cared about that and did not want to hurt them.

So, how did I speak to them without the fear of them using their prejudices against me and not truly listening to me? I had one strategy that I thought would surely work. I started my presentation discussing how easy it was to be proud of being Italian. What a beautiful country, generous and loving people, and a fascinating culture. Who wouldn't be proud! And as a gay man I wanted to feel a part of that. I was proud too. While I did then give an insight into the challenges of dealing with my sexuality, I made sure that they knew I was proud of my Italian heritage and loved my family at the same time. In order to get them to understand and accept me, I strategically reminded them of the words of one of the keynote speakers earlier in the conference: *To be an Italian you don't need a passport, you need a heart.*

The talk was well received by the audience and at the end, without wanting to encourage stereotypes, an older woman with the persona of a 'nonna' in the way she dressed and her manner, came up to me and said, '*Bravo, ti complimenti*' (I compliment you). That was such a highlight for me at this very important historical conference.

Time for a new approach

By now, much was being achieved for people of differing sexualities and genders from diverse cultural and linguistic backgrounds in terms of support on an individual/group level with a variety of community groups operating. But there was a gap. There was no national framework to draw good policy from. It was thought that a formalised national entity could not only provide support to the many groups but also seek funding in order to support the various initiatives, and enable all groups to work together and share the benefits.

Key volunteers representing a variety of groups came together and decided that a more cohesive approach was needed. The AGMC was born. Our vision was to provide a national support network for all multicultural groups and to educate queer and ethnic communities. For the queer community, the focus was on raising awareness around cultural diversity and addressing racism. For the ethnic communities, it was about the stigma around diverse sexualities and genders and addressing homophobia.

I was very proud to be a part of this committee and its achievements. I was a key member in coordinating the inaugural and world-first national AGMC conference in 2004. My responsibilities included helping develop the program, co-chairing, rapporteuring and publicity. Due to the success of the conference, we decided to hold another one in 2006. The conferences provided a rare opportunity to bring together people from different sexualities and cultures in a unique space. Sure, there have been many queer or sexual health conferences with streams dedicated to these issues, but never had a whole conference on this scale been held in Australia, and as far as we knew, in the world. I was immensely grateful that my own personal lived experience of being Italian and gay as well as my cross-cultural work had me well placed to contribute to the success of these conferences.

And then a book

No, I didn't write an autobiography, even though it has been suggested on more than one occasion. I contributed a piece to a book. Having written many articles for various queer press and community resources and having the enriching experience of organising and presenting at conferences, I was asked to contribute to the book, *When Our Children Come Out: How to support gay, lesbian, bisexual and transgendered young people* (Pallotta-Chiarolli, 2005). It's a valuable guide for those whose lives are affected by a young person coming out. Particularly for families. My piece was titled *Expressing My Gayness with an Italian flavour* (Perri, 2005). I wrote about my own story of growing up and dealing with my sexuality in the context of an Italian background. My message to parents was clear and simple: if your child opens up and talks about feeling different in regards to their sexuality or even gender for that matter, the absolute best thing you can do is to support them. Complete acceptance and a willingness to understand, even though it may be difficult, will make the road ahead so much easier. For both yourself and your child.

At 55, I am quite content when I look back at my life, even though I can look at it in two ways. One that is full of challenges. Growing up in Australia with Italian immigrant parents but dealing with my sexuality, which, according to many in the Italian community, didn't even exist. Then expressing my sexuality comfortably but still not feeling whole as my cultural background was more of a novelty than a legitimate part of my identity. But the life I choose to focus on are the positive changes I created as well as the opportunities that were given to me that provided irreplaceable and memorable life experiences. All of this has also allowed me to meet the most wonderful people along the way. That's what I remember. From this Australian Italian who defied the expectations of family and community and travelled a different road to become a gay Italian Australian, life for me has been *la dolce vita*.

My communion, 1969. Being the dutiful son and fulfilling my obligations.

Dear Sophie

Corey Rabaut

To my dear Sophie,

My darling daughter, one day you will be old enough to read this. You have a blood line of people who have taken steps in our lives to make sure that not only our lives are better, but lives of others are also improved. I have learnt from our family's past and my own life experiences and hope that you will too. To help you guide your way through life, I am taking this opportunity to tell you how I found my feet.

I feel my understanding of race politics was taught from my parents. My mother – you call her Ma – was born a coloured South African and she moved to Australia during the apartheid era. My father – you call him Papa – is a Mauritian man who also moved to Australia, not knowing a word of English, in his younger years. In our household growing up it was not unusual to hear my parents discussing race politics. They would discuss their own experiences along with passing comments about the current state of play in Australia. Neither overtly described themselves as activists; however, their words, although they may not have meant it, influenced how I thought. I remember as a high school student writing to the principal about forced participation in sporting activities. I believed that students in the senior years should not be required to play in sport when the time should have been self directed. I believed it would encourage ownership over how we spent our time. In hindsight, I am a big supporter of sports in schools and it should be encouraged. I remember my colleagues in my high school job nominating me to speak to my employer about issues we were facing. It felt natural to me and I did it with ease. My activism started long before I consciously understood there was a name for it.

In my early years at university, my understanding of activism became sharpened. At this point in my life, not only did my understanding of race politics stay active, I began to understand the fluidity of my sexuality. Being a person of colour was always easy to understand: I was clearly brown skinned, our surname Rabaut is distinctly Mauritian, and I enjoyed all the food and the music that came along with it. Sexual identity was not as easy to understand: the 'typical' music was different; taste in clothing was different, just to name a few bits. The LGBTI community was not anything I really grew up with, however there was a desire to understand it, to even be a part of it. There was difficulty in marrying the different social identities of race and sexuality. While my cultures are important to me, both have a deep belief in religion. South Africa also has the additional issue of outrageously high HIV rates. During this time all these things always ran through my head: going to hell, HIV, or being a cultural outcast.

Race and sexual identities are not mutually exclusive. In fact, my experiences in how they interrelate influences my activism. For instance, HIV impacts both South Africa and the LGBTI community more than other areas; lives are severally impacted and, in some cases, unfortunately lost. Marrying these identities became easier over time. I once took a trip to South Africa and spoke with a now deceased auntie. She was described by others as an activist in her own right. She was a lesbian who fought against the apartheid regime. Our conversation was quite simple; she said it was important for her to fight for equal rights regardless of colour or sexuality because it was simply the right thing to do and there is a conflict in those identities only if you allow it. Her words resonated deeply with me. They were confident and clear, and I started taking ownership of my life and social change.

As time progressed I felt an increased responsibility to continue the work of campaigning for equality. It felt like a natural progression that I would involve myself in student politics where I met good comrades. After a number of conversations with my friends, I decided to run for Queer Representative of the Student Union. This experience had its highs and lows. The university where I completed my undergrad degree was a conservative campus, so it was not unusual for people to assume I was working on multicultural events and not campaigns for sexual diversity rights. The surprise or occasional discomfort from people did not bother me as I considered myself a fairly resilient person. The highs far outweighed the lows: the friendships and the fun and belief in contributing to social change.

I have spent most of the last decade (at the point of writing this) working in the union movement. On a day-to-day basis, I engage with workers on campaigns and work with them to resolve their issues in the workplace. I have been fortunate enough to be able to continue work with people of diverse identities. I recall providing assistance to a male same-sex couple, who adopted an infant, in accessing enhanced paid leave, which would otherwise only be available to a mother who birthed a child. I also recall working with the local Indigenous community in their issues at the workplace. My activism extended outside of the union: I volunteered with Maria Pallotta-Chiarolli for a number of her university classes in discussing how these social facets inter-relate and about my life experiences. On many occasions my struggles have been a catalyst in working with others in achieving social change.

Society, including myself, makes assumptions. People assume gender, sex, race, sexuality to name a few. My experiences provided me with opportunities to challenge assumptions but, more importantly, to challenge my own. I have learnt to bring together all elements of my life and use it as motivation. So Sophie, I am sure you will go through your own life challenges. Some will relate to identity and some won't. In sharing this story with you, I hope to provide you with some insight of who I am, but also to pass on lessons I have been taught. Learn from our past, be proud of it, but do not be defined by it.

Love from Dad

Special thanks to my parents Desiree and Jean-Claude and my sister Chantelle.

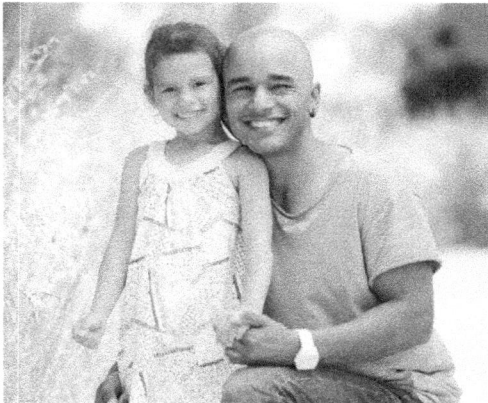

Not 'Norm' Enough,
Not 'Queer' Enough

Raven

Coming from a Maltese background, having a Catholic upbringing and education, as well as an obsession with Disney cartoons, meant that I was taught two so-called absolutes: genders were binary, and heterosexuality and monogamy were the norm.

When I was in school, I had crushes on boys and girls. I thought I was just weird.

As a teenager, I was fascinated by the subversive and by things that challenged social norms. In particular to alternative and goth subcultures and to body modification. I remember watching *The Rocky Horror Picture Show* and it blew my mind. For the first time I can remember, I saw a person in Dr Frank N. Furter who behaved and looked in a way that was true to themselves but completely 'out of the box' by society's standards. Figures like David Bowie and Marilyn Manson also gave me an idea that maybe gender and sexuality can be fluid and beyond strict boundaries, and maybe you do not have to be or look the way you are told. These were some of the catalysts in my life that encouraged me to explore feelings I just was not brought up to know, let alone understand.

I cannot remember exactly when I learnt the word 'bisexual', but once I did, it completely resonated with me. For me, being bisexual is about having an attraction to people of my own gender and of other genders and I use the terms bisexual and pansexual interchangeably.

Coming out as bisexual was a huge deal for me. It ended my relationship of five years, led to experiencing being with a woman for the first time, and exploring the queer night life. I found some amazing friends during this time, people I am still close to now. However, I also found some negative responses from people within the queer community because apparently I was not 'queer' enough. The most common responses were 'you're actually just a lesbian', 'bisexuality does not exist', 'you need to choose between being straight or gay', 'you can't say you came out because you're not gay'.

Following the break-up with my partner, we ended up getting back together and married. After a few years of marriage, we decided to separate and focus on ourselves. We are still really close and I hope that at some stage we can reconnect.

I have found acceptance from my ex-husband, friends and immediate family in regard to identifying as bisexual. But my ex-husband's Greek family and my extended family have been far from accepting.

The negative and hurtful reactions I have experienced from people who I opened up to about my sexuality, and hearing about what my bi friends have been through, have encouraged me to be an activist and be actively involved in the bisexual community. I feel that the more people understand bisexuality the more we are seen and respected in the community.

Being part of a queer choir has been another way for me to be an activist and fight for equality. It is definitely difficult for people to ignore all the rainbows and loud voices!

The second journey I am on now is being polyamorous (poly).

Coming out as poly is a separate journey for me to that of coming out as bi. I found from speaking with people both in and out of the queer community a common misunderstanding that if you are bi than you must also be poly. Actually, not all bi people are poly, and not all poly people are bi.

For me, poly means being open to dating and being in relationships with more than one person. My relationship with each partner is a separate experience and one which is not emotionally or physically shared with other partners. However, there is a lot of open communication so that we are aware of others that we are dating.

Through coming out as poly, I found two common issues have come up: jealousy and shame.

When first exploring poly, I would feel quite jealous about a partner being with someone else, and would worry that they would lose interest in me. However, those feelings are now a rare occurrence. I think part of this has been that my view of relationships has changed quite drastically. I used to consider a relationship as a situation where my partner was in a sense mine, and so for them to be with someone else took away from their attraction or love from me. Now I see that when I am with someone they are giving me a gift of their time and affection, and I am grateful for those moments. When they are spending time with someone else, that does not take away from their relationship with me. Also, I feel good when I see that my partners are fulfilled and happy. If our relationship comes to an end I would feel sad, but ultimately I would rather see them happy than continue a relationship that was not meant to be.

Communication is something which I have found has also helped to overcome jealousy as jealousy often comes from making assumptions about how the other person is feeling. For me it is vital to continue to check in with each other and communicate about our feelings. I find it liberating being so open and honest with partners, especially around attraction to others. It is something that I do not feel was encouraged in the 'monogamous world' I was living in. In that world a) women should not find anybody else attractive but their partner and b) if they did find someone attractive, they should not tell their partner.

I find that shame is the more challenging issue that I am yet to overcome. Being poly is inconsistent with the relationship values I was taught to aspire to as a child: namely that a woman gets married to one man, full stop. Shame and fears of rejection by my family, peers and colleagues, means that at this stage I am only open to my partners, my brother, and some of my friends.

The recent Marriage Equality debate in Australia brought up a lot of discussions among my family, my ex-husband's family, friends and colleagues. Although a lot of the discussion was around sexuality, the topic of polyamory would come up generally. From those discussions I do feel that at least some of my family may accept me being poly, however, I am not yet ready to have that discussion. If I was to get back with my ex-husband, I feel that his Greek family would not be accepting at all. As I work in the legal field, I am concerned that coming out may have a negative impact on my career. This is mostly from my own feelings of shame and belief that in our society, there is a lack of understanding and acceptance of poly relationships.

Although my life is a bit of a dichotomy at times, and although I am not yet completely 'out of the closet', I am extremely happy and proud to be part of the rainbow family. In the words of Dr Frank N. Furter, 'don't dream it, be it'.

Raven as a doll

what's your flavour?

Adam Ridwan

my lips taste sweet.
but don't eye off my hips as if a slice of cake.
sexual desire (or lack of desire) for skin colour does not equate
to your craving for desserts.
ethnicities reduced to a fucking carton of Neapolitan ice cream
melt underneath the white gaze.
my bones touch tender.
but I am not a prime cut of butchered meat.
you use your preference as another deft tool of discrimination.
my blood oozes in the same way as the cow,
and when you stick the knife in I stay conscious to hear you
chew my rare, pink flesh.
my skin runs smooth.
but I won't slide down your throat, I'm not a glass of merlot.
I do not exist to make you feel good at parties
or fulfill your perverse desires for an exotic blend.
my body bruises a deep shade of grape when you reveal
I'm just the flavour of the month. X

Photo by Stacey Johnson,
Stuz Photography

We're All Mongrels

Wil Roach

No one's pure. We're all mongrels. We're all mixed. White people jumped all over the world, you think they didn't jump into bed with the Africans? What nonsense is that? I'm collaborating with another writer to tell the story of a black man who was deported for theft from the UK to the penal colony of Australia in 1796. There were 11 African-American slaves or ex-slaves on the First Fleet to Australia. You never see any depiction of this. The First Fleet is always presented as completely white. They never show the fringes. A descendant of two of the 11 African-Americans has written a book in the form of poetry explaining their amazing story (Johnson, 2017).

My father, the family historian, told me we are descended from the Yoruba in Nigeria. I always remember this Nigerian guy in London on the Tube who kept staring at me. He followed me, and in London if someone starts following you, it's like, 'What do you want?' When I got off the train he was shadowing me. I thought, 'Well, he must give up in the end' but he didn't. I thought, 'Stuff this,' and went up to him and said, 'Why are you following me?'

He said, 'Are you from Nigeria?'

I said, 'I believe I have descendants from the Yoruba.'

He said, 'Oh, have you ever been to Nigeria?'

I told him that I've never been to Nigeria but my ancestors were part of British slave ships that ended up in Trinidad, and a bunch of them escaped into the hills. My father told me that our family had inter-married with the Yoruba. I have facial features similar to those of the Yoruba nation. There was a significant presence of Ibo and Yoruba people before Trinidad's independence and there are close bilateral ties between Nigeria and the UK.

Dad told us some slaves had run away into the dense forest areas and established their own communities. I remember being awestruck by a BBC doco in the early 1970s on this same group. They had kept their customs and didn't have much to do with Trinidad and the colonial authorities, even after independence was granted by the British in 1962.

As well as my Nigerian heritage, I have two great-grandmothers who were white and two grandmothers descended from the First Peoples of America. On my father's mother's side, I am sixth generation descended from Samuel Brown (who was white) and Jeanette Brown (a First People's woman). They met at Theological College in Manhattan, New York, fell in love and got married. They were missionaries who arrived in Trinidad in the 1840s before slavery was abolished in the United States in 1864. They set about building churches, orphanages and their children and children's children were encouraged to marry ex-slaves. The descendants branched out into education, politics, law, the army and the police.

On my mother's father's side, I'm descended from people deported to Barbados for penal servitude from England, Scotland and Ireland. So I carry that ancestral past in my DNA as well. My surname is Roach, an Irish name from Cork. My previous partner of 10 years was Irish. He was an O'Keeffe. I went to Ireland and looked up the map. There's a river in Cork and on one side it's the O'Keeffes and on the other side it's the Roaches. Roach comes from the French La Roche, from white ancestors who bought a slave plantation from a French count.

I was brought as a baby to London by my mum. My dad was already there. He had gone to England first at the invitation of his sister's husband. He checked it out and wrote to Mum: 'This is a racist country and the English don't like the coloured man and I feel the same about them. I won't stay. I will return to Trinidad'. Mum wrote back telling him how pleased she was with his decision.

Then in January 1962, Dad changed his mind and decided it was safe for Mum and I to travel. We left Trinidad on 13 August 1962 and arrived, as fate would have it, on 31 August, the very day the United Kingdom granted Trinidad independence.

I grew up in northwest London, moving in with Dad's sister and brother-in-law, plus my four older cousins. Our family was allocated a small room with a hole in the window on the ground floor of the house in Kilburn. For me it was a cold, dark room. I was the youngest in the household, my parents had to work, and that meant before attending school I was looked after by a succession of childminders. It was disturbing for me and I was often on my own. I had to make my own play and entertainment.

Dad and Mum spent the next 35 years in London. They decided in the early 90s that once they reached retirement age they'd return to Trinidad. But by then, Mum didn't want to return as her 'boys' lived in London and she didn't want to be separated from us. Dad, on the other hand, always said he was 'existing' in England, and yearned to return to the land of his birth. As an agriculturalist he had a deep affinity with nature and growing food in a sustainable way. So, once they reached retirement age they returned to Trinidad, to their hometown Tunapuna, to redevelop Mum's family property. My parents lived upstairs with their youngest son, my brother, his wife and two grandsons, until Mum died in 2000 and Dad in 2008.

When I was growing up, Dad told me stories about how racist people are. Then I got to experience it myself; starting in school and continuing in the workplace. It didn't stop me. I soon learnt to tell by people's body language whether they were accepting, fearful or uncomfortable. You learn to do this when you come from a society like Britain, which to me is the home of racism, which they exported all over the world in many forms. I can tell when someone's setting me up to fail or shutting me down. It's like I read people. When I'm with my ethnic white boyfriend, they just talk to him until he says, 'Wil's my partner,' but they still continue talking only to him. I just walk away but my boyfriend gets very agitated.

Of course, I have my prejudices too. I can look at a person who is not the same colour as me and make assumptions. But you just open yourself, put your preconceptions to the side and say, 'Okay, we're here. What do we need to do?' When Australians say, 'Oh, you're English', I say, 'I'm not English. I have English ancestry, but I'm not English.' When white people tell me I don't look gay, I ask, 'What's a gay man supposed to look like? Like you?' They define and construct what gay is and what it isn't. And when my partner and I hold hands, other black men are horrified. They can't believe it. They look at me, stare at each of us, then us together.

I've been in Australia for a number of years now. We need more light shone on all our mongrel stories. Here are two of my childhood memories.

Skin protection

I first became aware of my skin colour when I was about six years old. I knew my skin had to be protected from harsh English weather – rain, hail, sleet, snow, ice – with a product called Vaseline. My body had to be protected at all times but more so during winter with a heavy coat, hat, gloves (which I hated so I compromised with mittens which allowed my fingers to poke through), shoes or wellington boots. Mum and Dad repeated that if I didn't protect my hands and feet I would get chilblains. They didn't explain how you got chilblains but I found out many years later. Your hands or feet itch and blister because of a temporary loss of blood supply to the extremities of the body.

I ignored my parents and never got chilblains until I went to college! I have the scars to prove it.

One morning, Mum was getting ready to send me off to school, which was around the corner from where we lived in Kilburn. She checked and rechecked my clothing and whether I had enough Vaseline on my face. I assured her I did but she took my face in her left hand and turned it from side to side. I just hoped the ordeal would be over quickly. Then she gave me my dinner money and just as I put it into my pocket, she said: 'Son.'

Me: 'Yes, Mummy?'

Mum: 'You do know you will always have to work 10 times as hard as your white school friends.'

Me: 'Yes, Mummy.'

That was it. Mum never mentioned it again but I pondered the words she'd used for colour: black and white. I thought about the amount of effort required for me to do something. I thought no further about this but it wasn't long before the truth of her words became brutally apparent to me.

The kiss

Julie looked at me intensely. There was nowhere for me to hide. It was now or never. Julie confidently spoke: 'You have to kiss me now, that's the rule.' I thought to argue but aged six this did not seem possible against the determined passion of a six-year-old girl. I prepared myself to kiss her.

The kiss had come about because Julie dared me to do it. Julie was a friend and we went to the same primary school, St John's. She lived locally and her mum was friendly with my mum. Julie always seemed keen to touch my skin, which wasn't white like hers. I tried to show her that her touching left me uncomfortable. I'd move away from her but she'd just follow me anyway. Julie began to suggest we play her version of kiss-chase – where one child hides and the other has to shut their eyes and then look for the hidden child. If they fail to find them, the loser gets to kiss the winner.

One school day afternoon, she said we should play kiss-chase. I demurred saying, 'We'll get into trouble,' but she insisted. I followed her slowly while looking around for teachers or other children, hoping that we'd be stopped or questioned. Julie found an empty classroom full of grey metal chairs, tables and wooden cupboards. Now I understood there was no escape but hoped that a teacher would walk in and scupper Julie's plan.

No teacher or other child appeared. Julie said, 'I'm going to hide and you need to count to 10 but shut your eyes.'

I said, 'Okay,' crawling under a nearby table which could take my sizeable frame. I was nervous but, hoping to get this over with, I stayed where I was. I counted softly to myself: one, two, three, up to ten, and then opened my eyes from under the table. I looked around. There was a closed door leading out of the classroom to another classroom. I wanted this game to be over and the quickest way was to let Julie have her one kiss and be done. I stayed put and she joined me under the table. She placed her face close to mine and said, 'You have to kiss me.'

I said nothing, closed my eyes, pursed my lips as I'd seem them do in films, and moved my mouth closer to hers.

Then in a second it was done. I had kissed her but in that moment, a thought came to me: 'I don't like kissing girls. I like boys.' That was it. That's when I first knew I liked boys. I told no one. It took me another 14 years to act on that thought.

Wil unhappy in primary school, 1971

Excerpt: *These Wild Houses*

Omar Sakr

As-salamu 'alaikum.

I won't keep you long.

First, I acknowledge the Gadigal people of the Eora Nation, on whose land the majority of my poetry was written.

Now you are about to read the poetry of an Arab Australian, which is a rare thing when it shouldn't be.

Now you are about to read the work of a queer Arab Australian, which is a rare thing when it shouldn't be.

Now you are about to read the life of a queer Muslim Arab Australian from Western Sydney, from a broke and broken family – not rare, but it should be.

This is not a definitive statement on Islam.

This is not a definitive statement on Arab identity, not Arab Australian identity, not bisexuality, not even Western Sydney.

It is a statement – an exploration of me and what I've seen.

The only thing I ask of you is that you do not stop with me. Discover the other diverse writers and poets in this country – find us, find our books. We're here, and we're growing.

Call Off Duty

Salaam, brother. I am rekindling
when last we met: your body knotted
into a fist around the controls; screen aglow.
'Search & destroy,' came the instruction
and your fingers fired, the machine gun
your only avatar on screen. It speaks
in bursts of you, and men fall prostrate
as if praying, echoes of the azan
bowing on the air.

The fading sound

called for submission, but though I've seen
your head hit the mat in the unfolding
choreography of prayer, the blaze within
you never dimmed even for a moment,
not then, not now, as duty urged
you to kill with such ease then laugh
at your victory, glee and vitriol flowing
from your lips.

Samson, our dog

gambolled wildly at our feet, fur unshorn
and gossamer thin, fey-lit with ghost light.
Sweat gleamed on your brow, and you growled.
Occasionally, face set, hackles raised.
Only when your phone pulsed and sang
God's song did you press pause, then turn
to see if I'd wash with you.

I demurred,

and you laughed. 'Still on the fence? No?
What are you then?' I didn't answer, brother,
busy submitting to struggling, to overcoming
reality. Salaam, I accept you'd prefer
the fantasy of death and fury given form
than to speak to me; I too barely know
the comfort of family, or how to sow the fields
between us with things green and grateful.
Salaam, I know when you discover my secret
loves, I will lose yours, and the ache of knowing
it gnaws at my bones, this loss I have
yet to bear.

Salaam is knowing

your hatred is foretold, inscribed in Arabic,
in the holiest of text; it is knowing the morning
will dawn when you pretend not to know
my name, when you won't look at my way.
Salaam is loving you anyway, I'd rather
fold myself into a supernova's flare
than submit to this, it's that hard to think
of a life long without your laugh. But

the day is accumulating, driven closer
with every poem I write like this & I write
every day, even now, snug in the corner
as you play on cold, serene in the chaos
of your virtual world.

                                    Brother, salaam

I must ask: if I cover my body in verse
you cleave to, will you see me then? Maybe
later, when you honeysuck the East, your mouth
gracing the Earth, you will know me in full
or at least make the effort to try. Some would
say that if ours is peace – accepting paths
twinned from the start are set to part – I should
make war and gut your wisdom,
the weave of your life. I'm not sure
if you would survive the breaking
of all that you think you know. This is me,
brother, mine, saying I forgive you
for all that is to come, and hoping
at last for salaam to exist between us in
this life, or the next

                                    as the light tapers

out, I hit 'send' on this letter of years
in the making. You reply: 'Don't be
silly. I'll always have your back.'
And everything I thought I knew
broke into a sound like prayer.

Sex, Politics and Pastizzi
A Maltese migrant in Sydney

Michael Schembri

1 May 1986. I was 24 years old when I arrived in Sydney. My luggage consisted of clothes and books. It also included my parents, a brother and a sister.

I brought with me another type of luggage: 24 years of living in Malta.

I was born in 1961 in the British colony. When I was three, my country nominally became independent, though still ruled by the British queen and a British governor-general. The British controlled the banks and the media, the airport and the harbours. Britain and NATO retained their military bases on our land.

I was a Catholic in a country where the church was feudal and reactionary and fought tooth and nail against the labour movement. The same year I was born it imposed an interdict on the Labour Party, making it a mortal sin, inherited for seven generations, to support the party in any way, even just reading its papers. My first existential dilemma: was my inherited sin first generation (my father) or second (my grandfather)?

I was a very capable altar boy and I didn't mind sneaking the occasional sip of wine when filling the ampoule for mass. Atheism knocked religion out of me at age 18.

At age 10 in 1971, I celebrated Labour's electoral victory. I celebrated Malta becoming a republic in 1974. I celebrated Freedom Day on the 31 March 1979, when the last of the British troops left the islands.

I brought with me to Australia eight years of left-wing political activism, first with the Socialist Youth (Labour), then with the Communist Youth and Party; and five years of student politics at university, partway through which I parted ways with the Communist Party, supported a teacher's strike against the Labour government, and was barely saved from reactionary disillusion by briefly turning to Eurocommunism.

I gave the go-ahead to my father to apply to migrate to Australia.

I left Malta nominally a heterosexual – albeit a non-active one.

Now to unpack my luggage . . .

Family does matter, but . . .

For the first six months in Australia family provided my sole social network. Luckily it was a reasonably sized extended family: my mother had three brothers and sisters and their families. To my surprise I looked forward to doing the family social rounds. I acquired quite a reputation for making a decent cup of tea. Remembering how much milk and sugar they all preferred was quite a feat.

Though it might seem contradictory, I subscribed to the radical, left critique of the family which, among other things, posits that the nuclear family under capitalism reproduces the heterosexual norm, thereby making it oppressive particularly to LGBTIQ children.

This does not mean, however, we should renounce our families. It is to say that the traditional family must be deprived of the privileges given it by the state. It is to say that legislation needs to be changed to allow for and recognise alternative forms of relations that individuals and groups choose to develop.

My experience is not uncommon among migrants. Migrant families and migrant communities often provide the first social and support network in our new country. But, proving the veracity of the critique of the family, LGBTIQ individuals very often do not find acceptance within our families. Many have found themselves ostracised by some of their relatives, while others have been kicked out entirely.

I consider myself very lucky. I came out as a gay man to my sister first. No problems there, pretty much as I expected. My father was quite another story. Though in many ways quite an enlightened man, he was still a patriarch. He couldn't stomach that his oldest son was a poof. He took it very personally, probably finding my homosexuality a threat to his manhood. He once even asked the classic WDWDW – What Did We Do Wrong? It took me a while to realise it, probably because he asked it in Maltese.

I was lucky again. My father prioritised keeping the family together above all else. Over the years he got used to me being gay. I was lucky too that I did not have to make the decision to turn my back on my father. Some 10 years after my coming out he even asked my political opinion as a gay man. Now that was impressive!

I did not expect much from my extended family in Sydney. They are largely Catholic and Liberal-leaning. My sister had told me how Uncle D, when he was once watching some news coverage of the Sydney Gay and Lesbian Mardi Gras Parade, commented how disgusting it was and that 'those poofs should have a red-hot metal stick shoved up their behind'. Spunky young woman that she was, she berated him for being such a Catholic hypocrite. Funnily enough his favourite singer was Freddie Mercury – did he not twig on to this performer's blatant and flamboyant homosexuality?

And yet I was always invited to their family parties. And, once Danny and I became an item, we were always recognised as a couple, and the invitations kept rolling in. Did any of them disparage us behind our backs? Maybe, but nothing that ever came to our notice.

Solidarity with Aboriginal Australia

In 1987 I attended the Summer Marxist School, organised by the Communist Party of Australia (now defunct.) (see *On Lesbian/Gay Liberation*, 2003). One of the sessions dealt with Aboriginal rights. I remember saying that as a new migrant to Australia I had an obligation to support Aborigines in their struggles. It was at this session that I met Bruno Di Biase, from the Federazione Italiana Lavoratori Emigranti e Famiglie (FILEF), who introduced me to the Migrant Committee for Aboriginal Rights.

On 26 January 1988 – Invasion Day, the 'celebration' of the bicentennial of Australia Day – thousands of Aborigines from all over Australia gathered at Redfern Oval. From there they marched to Belmore Park, where they were awaited by thousands of non-Aboriginal supporters, among them a huge contingent from the Migrant Committee for Aboriginal Rights. Forty thousand of us then marched up George Street to Hyde Park. Meanwhile, White Australia 'celebrated' the day on the Harbour, an event attended by 2.5 million people.

I entered the gay and lesbian movement from the Left: in May 1986 I joined the Gay Solidarity Group (GSG). Much smaller than in its early days of the first Sydney Gay Mardi Gras in 1978, its members came from a number of Trotskyist groups, including Ken Davis (co-founder of the Mardi Gras), anarchists (Peter Collard, aka Sister Mary Mary Quite Contrary) and left Anglicans (Fabian Lo Schiavo, aka Monsignor Porca Madonna, Mother Inferior and other personae). I became a Trotskyist.

It was largely through GSG that I continued participating in solidarity actions with Aboriginal Australia. GSG members had founded Gays Against Racism in 1984. It was not long lived but it did enter a walking group in the 1984 Mardi Gras; approximately half of its contingent was Asian.

This was before I arrived on the scene (and in Australia). But in 1992, in reaction to a racist, anti-Asian letter in the monthly magazine *Campaign*, Gays and Lesbians Against Racism (GLAR) was formed, with several GSG members including myself, joining.

During its short life (February 1992 to November 1994) GLAR organised a number of activities; possibly most notable was Koori Night, a concert held at the Belmore Street Theatre during the Mardi Gras Festival in 1993. A packed theatre watched a show including performances by Aboriginal singer Deborah Cheetham, the Bangarra Dance Theatre and the Indigenous storyteller Pauline McLeod. I am proud to have been one of its organisers.

Gaywaves (a gay and lesbian program on Radio 2SER FM, produced by a collective of which I was a member from 1989 to 2004), provided another venue for solidarity with Aboriginal struggles. This included covering Aboriginal events, both LGBTIQ and straight.

Gaywaves 2SER FM

So *Gaywaves* certainly suited my political and cultural inclinations. I attended my first *Gaywaves* planning meeting simply because a work colleague was himself a member and I needed company due to feeling down about a mistake I had made at work. I stuck around for the next 15 years.

The collective's constitution gave a clear idea of its politics:

We actively support and promote gay and lesbian identity and liberation. We support feminism and oppose racism.

The collective has determined that there should be a majority of women on the collective, because of the under-representation of lesbians in the gay and lesbian media, and of women in radio.

We also seek to ensure that the collective is representative of the broader lesbian/gay community (for example, people from different ethnic backgrounds, people living with HIV and AIDS, people with disabilities . . .)

Gaywaves seeks to explore the many facets of gay and lesbian life, and issues relevant to lesbians and gays, including the related struggles of other oppressed minority groups.

My first two contributions pretty much set the tone for my work on *Gaywaves*. I interviewed Cyrus Dumasia about his attendance at a conference of the International Lesbian and Gay Association (ILGA). I also wrote and read out a brief biography of Joseph Chetcuti, and I played a recording from Joseph's chapter 'Personally Speaking for Myself' from the book *Being Different* (1986).

Having a great constitution and making it real on radio can be two entirely different things. Content, to a large degree, depended on its members. Given my political background I brought more focus to Left politics, to cultural production which did not depend overwhelmingly on the English-speaking world, and to international politics. The joy and satisfaction of my experience on *Gaywaves* is that this was much encouraged by the rest of the collective.

From 1992, with the experience of GLAR, we covered issues of racism more frequently. Also in the early to mid 1990s there was a flourishing of LGBTIQ ethnic social and political organising among which was a Maltese social group (Schembri, 2000). All of this was avidly covered on *Gaywaves*.

I also had the opportunity, over the years, to interview activists from other countries, among them Owais Khan, an Indian gay activist; Aditya Bondopadhyay, a lawyer and gay activist from India; Simon Nkoli from South Africa; Ni Jia-Zhen from the Taiwanese organisation Queer & Class; Oscar Atadero, secretary of PROGAY – the Progressive Organisation of Gays in the Philippines; Roddy Shaw, an organiser of the Third Chinese Tongzhi Conference in Hong Kong in 1999; and Pedro Manzur, a Sydneysider who returned to his homeland Chile. Burma democracy activist Debbie Stothard provided us with a unique interview with a Burmese gay freedom fighter living in a refugee camp in Thailand. And any international material produced by *This Way Out*, a weekly radio production from Los Angeles, USA, which was sent out to radio stations around the world, was also aired on *Gaywaves*. I also sent our productions to *This Way Out* for international distribution.

In 1989, while visiting my partner's family in Indonesia, I had the idea of producing a regular news segment which I named *News from Asia*. An edition was broadcast on average once a month, with a total of 50 editions produced. A similar series, but with only five editions, was produced entitled *Africa Update*. All this activity meant a widening of the range of cultures, both local and international, for our Sydney listeners, ensuring that listeners who did not belong to the dominant White Australian demography felt included, and providing a choice of music that went beyond the culturally limited fare that one heard on Oxford Street or King Street.

Homosexuality and the Maltese migrant community
In 1989 I was on the phone speaking to R, who is a prominent intellectual in Maltese-Australian circles. (I have not revealed R's name because many years later, at the time that the *Maltese Herald* was celebrating its 50th anniversary edition, he wrote a lengthy letter in which he urged the paper and its readers to haul themselves into the modern era by also embracing gay and lesbian rights).We mentioned an anthology of Maltese-Australian poetry (Cauchi, 1986), at which point R referred to poems by Joseph Chetcuti, deploring that he brought homosexuality into his poetry and into the anthology. At the other end of the line R, at that time unaware that I was gay, was equally unaware of

the excitement that I felt at that point. As soon as we hung up, I rushed to pull the book out from my home library to check out Chetcuti's poems. Among them I came across this delightful little poem, and I offer here my translation:

The Inner City Suburbs
yesterday
along the length of Oxford Street
in the heart of Paddington
lived the mass of maltese-emigrants
today its denizens
are trendies, designers, gays.
yesterday, an ethnic minority;
today, a sexual minority.
for some maltese,
paddington still remained home.
14 December, 1983

The Maltese migrant community is, by and large, a very socially conservative, Catholic community. Newly arrived in Australia in 1986, I joined the NSW Maltese Australian Cultural Association. I didn't stay long. Not only because I did not drive and therefore I found it hard to travel in the Western suburbs, but especially because most of the events organised by this association were church and religion related. Not to this atheist's taste, thank you very much!

To a degree I think that this conservatism reflects the fact that the bulk of Maltese migrants came to Australia in the 1950s and 1960s. Values and customs since then have changed in Malta. However, many migrants' views of Malta and its values remain caught in a timewarp of the era of mass Maltese migration.

I had my own encounter with Maltese anti-homosexual attitudes via the *Maltese Herald* (this weekly paper unfortunately folded at the end of April 2013, after 52 years). Paul Calleja, a regular contributor to the paper and a Labour Party supporter, took objection to the push for same-sex marriage. I challenged him in the paper's letters page. After my second rebuttal he backed off. Another letter writer tried to provide Paul Calleja with some back up, which I rebutted as well (see Schembri, 2012a; 2012b). I was very pleasantly surprised that the paper's editors printed my replies without applying any censorship, as I believe that Paul Calleja was voicing the opinions of the majority of the Maltese migrant community. It is ironic that, being a critic of the mainstream gay and lesbian focus on the campaign for same-sex marriage,

I found myself defending it against the conservative Paul Calleja. Fabian Lo Schiavo, in conversation, told me he has the same experience with sections of the Italian community.

Ethnic identity: but wait, there's more

Gay and lesbian identity in the mid 90s came under sustained attack from postmodernist queer, bisexual and transgender activists. The Gay and Lesbian Rights Lobby organised a series of two fora in 1993. At one of these a transgender activist ridiculed homosexuals by calling us 'little boxes', a reference to the song with the same title by Malvina Reynolds, popularised by Pete Seeger. The new 'radical' [sic] queer movement was replicating the anti-homosexuality of the larger heterosexist community in denigrating what Craig Johnston (1999) called the 100 per centers.

At one of the three gay vs queer debates in 1995 I stated:

- I am ethnic Maltese because of white Australian racism.
- I am a socialist because I am a worker.
- I am gay because of heterosexist oppression.

The point I was making was that LGBTIQ identity is not something you can pick and choose from your wardrobe depending on your mood. Identity is a socio-political construct. An attempt to liquidate a gay identity was a reactionary political act, as David F. Greenberg put it so clearly (emphasis is my own):

> *The epistemological observation that alternative systems of classifying people are possible has little relevance to those who are now classified as homosexual. Had I been born in a different country or different era, my ideas would no doubt be different from what they are now, but that doesn't mean that at the snap of the finger I could begin thinking like a Hindu or a Medieval Frenchman. The modern Western system of sexual classification is embodied in social identities, roles, institutions, and ways of life that can hardly be abolished by an arbitrary act of will.* **Gays who tried to do so would be giving up the resources they provide for self-defense.**
>
> *The analogy with race is instructive. Racial-classification systems place people in categories on the basis of a small number of attributes. At different times and in different cultures, the choice of attributes has been differently made. The significance attached to racial membership has also varied greatly. It hardly follows from this that American blacks could or should stop thinking of themselves as blacks, or that black civil rights efforts should be halted.* (1988: 492–493)

The other underlying meaning of what I stated was that we cannot separate the various oppressions in real life. Liberation from one oppression requires liberation from all oppressions: 'The divisions between gender, class and race don't exist at the level of the everyday/everynight world of people's actual lives; to be black, a woman and working class are not three different and distinctive experiences.'(Smith in Sears and Moors, 1995: 229).

I have now spent more years in Australia than in my country of origin. My LGBTIQ politics have evolved, hopefully matured. I came to grips with and saw my way to integrating my identity as a Maltese migrant, a worker and a gay man in a capitalist, racist, sexist and heterosexist world. It is this integrated identity that helps me navigate my way through life.

That takes care of the politics in this essay's title. Where's the sex, you might ask? Don't you know that ladies do not kiss and tell?! And the pastizzi, those savoury puff pastry filled with mashed peas or ricotta cheese introduced to Australia by Maltese immigrants? To Maltese migrants pastizzi are at the heart of our identity. Although that then beggars the question: where does that leave those who are gluten-intolerant?

Michael and Jubal

Twenty Years On
A personal reflection

Budi Sudarto

Learning about sexuality

My journey began in Indonesia . . .

Growing up, I always knew that I was different from other boys. Just like other boys, I was taught to follow certain gender expectations. This includes not being effeminate, liking trucks instead of dolls, and being 'tough'. However, I was an effeminate boy, and I got teased for being 'girly'. I often encountered disapproval, albeit subtle, for not 'acting' my gender. I learned to watch my behaviour, but still, I couldn't change who I was. I remember thinking that life would be a lot easier if I was born a girl, because then I wouldn't feel guilty for my effeminate behaviours.

It wasn't until I became a teenager that I started to learn about my sexuality. The feeling of being different grew stronger, especially as other boys my age started to express interest in girls. I couldn't relate to them. I convinced myself that, if I tried hard enough, I could get rid of my attraction to other guys. Adolescence was indeed a confusing time.

I couldn't tell anyone how I felt; I was too scared. I couldn't explain to my parents because I was afraid they would reject me. As a Muslim, I was led to believe that I could not be gay because it was against my religion. It was a confusing time, and it came to a point where I simply couldn't lie anymore. Thanks to the internet, I started seeking information about gay issues. I remember sneaking to the lounge room late at night when everybody else was asleep and browsing the web, hungry for information. It was through the internet that I had conversations with other gay men around the world about being gay. It was also the first time I had an online conversation with gay men living in Indonesia. I couldn't believe my luck! The internet became my saviour that helped me to feel comfortable with my sexuality.

It wasn't until I finished high school that I finally met other gay men. The year was 1997. I thought, 'It's time.' I couldn't bear the feeling of being alone any longer. I wanted to explore. I wanted to be connected to people like myself. I summoned up enough courage and took a leap of faith.

And I'm glad I did.

I still remember the feeling of liberation and joy when I met other gay men for the first time. Everybody was very friendly and, finally, I wasn't alone. I felt a sense of connection and a sense of kinship. The only problem was, I couldn't tell my parents who I was hanging out with. At the same time, I couldn't deny my sexuality any longer. I was torn between two worlds: one filled with secrecy, the other with a sense of freedom and liberation

I entered Jakarta's gay scene, or a small part of it. I was introduced to nightclubs where gay men hung out. I quickly learnt the Jakarta gay sub-cultures, with their unique sets of language to indicate group belonging. All of a sudden, the possibilities were endless. When I caught up with my new friends, we talked about boys freely and supported each other. At the same time, social changes started to happen. I still remember reading an article about homosexuality, not filled with condemnation, but with support and acceptance. It gave me comfort and hope that, one day, all would get better.

Nine months after I came out, I left Indonesia to further my education in Australia.

Learning about 'race'

I came to Australia in 1998, a few years after Pauline Hanson made her infamous maiden speech at Parliament House, voicing her fear that Australians 'are in danger of being swamped by Asians' (Jones, 1997). I did not, however, see myself as an Asian migrant. I was an international student, and I didn't think I'd stay in Australia after my study. I didn't think much about Hanson's conservative political views as I wasn't aware of Australian politics. Plus, I was too busy finding my feet in a new country.

It was an exciting and exhilarating time; meeting new people, getting used to speaking English daily, and living independently of my family. Even though I was aware of my 'race', it didn't affect me much. I was young and naïve. My social network contributed to my lack of awareness about 'race'. I was living in a shared house with three other international students. Most of my friends were students from other countries: Indonesia, Malaysia, Singapore, the Maldives, the Philippines and many more.

A few months after arriving in Australia, a series of events made me aware of my 'race'. I realised that being 'Asian' could affect my social interactions. In Indonesia, I was identified according to my parents' ethnic backgrounds. In Australia, however, I was 'Asian'. I started to understand the low socio-political position of 'Asians' in Australia.

I began to see things differently. At times, I automatically assumed my 'race' was the reason why some people were unpleasant toward me. It could be subtle things, such as delaying serving me at the shops, or talking slowly based on an assumption that I didn't speak English. These small things added up. As years went by, I became aware of racial stigma and discrimination. I was experiencing the very same thing that Asian migrants to Australia have endured for many years.

Learning about 'race' in the gay scene

At the same time, I was becoming increasingly involved in Melbourne's gay community. I registered for a workshop run by the VAC, 'Gay Asian Proud', and met many wonderful, supportive individuals. Once again, I felt a sense of connection and belonging to a community. I felt welcomed in a new country.

My early experience in Melbourne's gay community was rather fun. I still remember the first time I attended Midsumma Festival. The year was 1999 and Commercial Road was filled with people of diverse sexualities and genders, all there to celebrate our community. I felt a great sense of joy and pride. A few weeks later, Pride March and the after party at Luna Park were something that I cannot forget. Attending a LGBTIQ festival was new to me. Again, I felt a sense of community connection and attachment.

I wasn't aware of racism in the gay community. I wasn't aware that my 'race' would, once again, affect my social and sexual interactions with others. I thought the gay community was a welcoming space. I had to learn about 'race' the hard way.

My first encounter of sexual rejection on the basis of 'race' happened online. I was chatting to a guy and the conversation became a bit, well, sexual. He asked what I like to do with guys (and I quickly learnt that 'having coffee and chat' was not the right answer) and what I looked like. After I described myself (height, weight, etc.), he asked 'Where do you come from?' After I told him that I grew up in Indonesia, there was no reply.

At first, I didn't think much about it. I often got disconnected since the only connection available was dial-up internet. However, after experiencing the same thing over and over again, I became suspicious. Why did some guys stop the conversation right after I told them where I came from? Did I say something wrong?

It wasn't until later that I realised my 'race' did affect my interactions with other gay men. As I browsed through online profiles and chat rooms, I repeatedly came across the dreaded phrase, 'No Asians'. I was being excluded simply on the basis of my 'race', irrespective of my personal qualities and attributes.

I quickly learnt that being an 'Asian' man put me in a low sexual status to other gay men. One incident in particular still haunts me. I was chatting online and a guy asked for my picture. After I sent him my picture, there was no reply. The next thing I knew, my picture was posted in the main chat room, with the statement, 'Look at this guy, isn't he ugly?' This was followed by some harsh words about 'Asians'. I left the chat room immediately. It was the first time I experienced direct discrimination from other gay men. It left me wounded.

Unfortunately, it wasn't the last time I encountered such rejection. There were times when guys simply said, 'Not interested' or even blocked my profile. Experiencing multiple rejections based on my 'race' started to chip away my confidence and esteem. I often asked myself, 'Am I ugly?'

Exposed to sexual rejection made me hate myself. I became my own worst enemy. I simply didn't like the way I looked. I avoided approaching guys in social and sexual settings, simply because I did not want to be rejected again. I often wondered whether I would have different experiences had I been born 'white'. I felt alone. It was not until at a later stage in my journey that I became aware many gay Asian men feel 'unattractive' because they do not fit with the 'white' ideal.

Without realising it, I was spiralling into self-pity and self-doubt. From the outside, I seemed happy. Inside, however, I did not like myself. I couldn't shake off the feeling of being unworthy and undesirable. Such was the negative impact of racist ideologies on my wellbeing.

However, I did maintain an active involvement in the gay community. I was a volunteer facilitator for VAC for many years. I also volunteered for the Midsumma Festival and Melbourne Queer Film Festival. I became an active member of the Monash University Queer Department. Despite the rejection from other gay men, I still felt a sense of belonging to the gay community. Indeed, I met a lot of people who seemed to accept me irrespective of my skin colour. It wasn't in the community that I felt rejected; it was in the sexual scene where I felt that I did not belong.

Re-learning 'race', regaining strength
I went through a period of not liking other gay Asian men due to internalised prejudice. I did not actively seek friendship with other gay Asian men. Instead, I often envied some Asian men who seemed to have plenty of 'white' friends or who were in relationships with 'white' men. At the same time, I often looked disapprovingly at those who I considered to be perpetuating the stereotypes, and distanced myself from them. Indeed, there was a period in my life where I was agreeing with the comment, 'There are too many Asians

here tonight.' I was trying to blend in with the gay white culture; I felt a need to belong to the majority, and I did this at the expense of marginalising my own community. This form of 'distancing and affiliating' (Han et al, 2013) was my way to manage stigma.

I started seeing the light at the end of the tunnel during my postgraduate study. I started a project to explore gay Asian men's lived experiences in Melbourne (Sudarto, 2004). I was curious whether they felt the same way I did.

During my research, I encountered many scholarly articles that helped me to change my perspective about my 'race'. I still remember reading *Multicultural Queer: Australian narratives* (Jackson and Sullivan, 1999) for the first time. I found voices from other multicultural LGBTs. Personal stories from Tony Ayres (1999) and Kent Chuang (1999) really resonated with me. The voices of gay Asian men in Damien Ridge, Amos Hee and Victor Minichiello's study (1999) gave me an understanding that I was not the only one who felt disconnected from the mainstream Melbourne gay scene.

Things started to make sense.

I started to view my 'race' differently. I became aware that there is nothing wrong with my 'race'. Being 'Asian' does not automatically make me unattractive to others. I learnt the socio-historical construction of gay Asian men's sexuality in the Western gay community. I came across the term 'sexual racism', used to explain sexual rejection and sexual objectification on the basis of racial stereotypes (Caluya, 2006).

As I began to understand the way racial hierarchy affected my social inter-actions, I gained an understanding that sexual rejection on the basis of my 'race' is not a reflection on me as an individual. I regained my confidence, one step at a time. Slowly, I built resilience. I started to embrace my 'race' to manage stigma.

I also started questioning the structures that contribute to the persistence of whiteness in the gay community. I became aware of the oversupply of 'white' bodies in gay culture, from magazines to pornography. It made sense that I often felt bad about my Asian body, because I did not fit with the 'white' ideal. I started to embrace my skin. I started to feel comfortable about being 'Asian'. I had to teach myself to embrace my own community, the gay Asian community.

I began to embrace the variety of individuals, personalities and sexual roles that exist within the gay Asian community. Through Gay Asian Proud, I started to build racial and cultural pride. I also began to challenge sexual racism by questioning my own racial preference and sexual desire. I was sub-scribing to the 'racial sexual hierarchy' by placing white men as the most desirable sexual object (Jackson, 2000). I made both conscious and sub-conscious decisions to not be attracted to other Asian men. I was, as the derogatory term called it, a 'potato queen'. It did not matter how good looking the Asian men were, I was ignoring their sexual advances and directing my attention to 'white' men (even when they were not interested).

As I felt comfortable with my own identity, I became sexually interested in other Asian men. I still remember my first sexual encounter with another Asian man. It was liberating because I was no longer limiting my sexuality. It was challenging because I had to also question my racial preference, ana-lysing whether my 'taste in men' had been influenced by the concept of 'white beauty'. Don't get me wrong, I still find 'white men' sexually attractive. The difference is, now I also find men of different racial backgrounds 'hot'. No longer viewing white men as the only desirable race remains my way to negotiate stigma and challenge the concept of 'white beauty'.

As I reflected upon my journey, it dawned on me that Asian-white pair-ings are not the norm; I was simply overlooking Asian-Asian desire due to the internalisation of 'white beauty'. I've talked to many Asian men who desire other Asian men due to shared cultures, values, and identity. Indeed, I've been in an intraracial relationship, and it really opened my eyes about the beauty, and appreciation of, Asian men and Asian cultures. I began to shed internal-ised stigma and oppression. I became content with my culture, religion, and sexuality; I've accepted who I truly am.

I also took time to talk about sexual racism to my peers. There have been a few heated discussions on the topic, where some individuals of various racial groups were upholding their 'rights' to have a racial preference. Indeed, some men were very defensive, indicating that their 'preference' is not racist, just as they are not sexist for preferring men.

It's always interesting to hear people's responses when a minority group questions the privilege of the majority group, as we are not meant to chal-lenge the status quo. Some may consider these responses as examples of racial microaggression, 'everyday exchanges that send denigrating messages to people of colour because they belong to a racial minority group' (Sue et al, 2007). I do believe that most of these men are not aware that stating their 'preference' only reaffirms the minority status of gay Asian men. However, I've learnt to gain strength from such comments, deflect the negativity, and continue the discussion with my peers.

To my peers, I often explain that the task of eliminating sexual racism is not about persuading individuals to find racial minorities sexually attractive. Instead, it is about informing people of the harmful effects of phrases such as 'no Asians' or 'Asians do not reply' on gay Asian men's wellbeing. I often drew a correlation between exposure to homophobia and being the subject of racist ideologies; both are designed to undermine a specific group of people in society and reaffirm the power of the majority group. Indicating a personal preference therefore is more than just making a clear statement about what, and who, someone likes and doesn't like. It becomes a tool to reaffirm the message that one racial group is seen as more attractive than others. For me, it is a reminder of the persistence of racial prejudice and discrimination that I've experienced in Australia.

In my current role as Gay Asian Proud convener, I've been able to share my thoughts in several community newspapers (Cook, 2012; Sudarto, 2013). Such debates are much needed to inform, and change, the community's attitudes to 'race'. After all, we want to create an inclusive rainbow community. I often say to people, 'race' and racism are ongoing issues in Australian society; we simply have to continue engaging people with the topic.

Finding my kin

It was at the inaugural AGMC conference in 2004 that I found allies. I was able to share my opinions with like-minded people. All of us were there to celebrate cultural and racial diversity, and to closely examine the influence of race, culture and religion on the LGBTIQ community, especially for ethnic minority LGBTIQs. I felt a great sense of belonging. I felt empowered. I felt that I'd finally found my kin.

However, it was just the beginning.

At the AGMC Forum in 2007, it became clear to me that we needed to do more than just have internal discussions. Those who attended the conference were already supporting multiculturalism in the LGBTIQ community. However, how do we engage and inform the wider community about the harmful effects of racism, racial stereotypes and racist ideologies on our wellbeing? How do we go beyond political correctness to empower people to end racism in our community? How do we celebrate multiculturalism and challenge racism without being told to 'shut up' and 'get on with life'?

My activism has become part of my healing process, as well as rebuilding my sense of self. People often think of activists as constantly angry and argumentative. My way to approach the issue is by establishing dialogue, sharing knowledge, and having conversation based on respect. My current involvement with AGMC has enabled me to do so, building a bridge to create a truly inclusive LGBTIQ community, one step at a time.

The future is bright, and I've seen progress in the LGBTIQ community.

I've witnessed many people of all racial, cultural, and religious backgrounds stand up against racism in the LGBTIQ community. I've seen a lot of work done to ensure multicultural and multifaith LGBTIQ are not forgotten. I've engaged in discussion with young people of multicultural backgrounds who are dedicated to embracing and celebrating our identity in our many communities; the LGBTIQ community, cultural and religious community, and the peer network. All of us have become part of a social movement that embraces diversity in all of its different shapes, colours, and identity. The work is ongoing, because we don't want to be silenced any more.

It has been a privilege to be part of such a movement, as I gain strength, knowledge, and wisdom from my peers. I believe that we have several choices: we can either be angry, be compliant, or be agents of change. My contribution to this book is about creating change, sharing a personal story that can hopefully inspire and empower others to feel comfortable, and celebrate our unique identities. I'm still learning, growing, gaining knowledge and wisdom every day. It never stops, and my own personal journey continues . . .

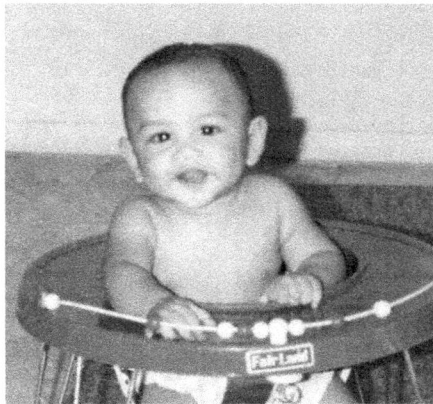

A Typical Australian-Asian Girl

Judy Tang

I was a typical Australian-Asian girl and, in fact, I reckon I still am today. I have loving parents who migrated from Vietnam after the war to begin life anew in Melbourne. They both found work as manual labourers and, before long, saved up enough money to buy a little place in Thornbury, which was traditionally an area where there were more Greeks and Italians (I still remember having my first souvlaki – it was spiritually transcending!). But I digress . . . as I was saying, I did well at school with my parents' constant reminder that they arrived in Australia with nothing and, therefore, education was everything. I learnt to play piano and, later, the violin. I got into university. Got good grades there. I had my first crush on a girl at uni.

Wait, what?

Yeah . . . I had my first crush on a girl at uni. So as every new lesbian uni student would do, I searched and found the Melbourne University Queer Lounge. However, I very soon noticed that it was NOT a place that a typical Australian-Asian girl would ever venture into. I mean, for starters people put their feet with SHOES onto the couch! And there were always people there – you know what that means right? It means that these people did not attend class. It means they *wagged* (I know, I know – I still get some jitters recalling this). I suppose I also quickly noticed that I was only one of three Asian people there.

Nevertheless, I decided that these were 'my people', so to speak. I had just discovered my sexuality and I'd be damned if I didn't explore it and understand the spectrum, the rainbow, and anal beads. So I persevered. But something was off – I felt like I was trying so hard and I still felt isolated. The people in the Lounge were friendly, but I felt as if no one really understood me or had similar interests. It was not my interest to go out to the local pubs after class – I preferred cafes or restaurants. I felt as if I was not legitimately queer if I wasn't out and proud, and I felt as if no one understood the importance of family to me and how that influences the way I approach my daily life.

Then one day someone from YellowKitties came along and said, 'YellowKitties is an Asian Queer Women's group.' Wow! I joined the next day. I was the youngest member, but I didn't mind at all because the first few events were all food-related. I felt . . . relaxed is the best way to describe it. It wasn't as if I had everything in common with other YellowKitty members, but I suppose I had more in common with them and so it made it just that wee bit easier to be myself.

Story 1: My first coming out
I introduced my mum to my then girlfriend as my friend (I know, I know – as if all mothers would ever fall for that). The next morning, she asked me if I liked her, and I am a terrible liar, so I told the truth – I said yes. She proceeded to run to her bedroom and cry for the next few days. After this, she attempted to threaten our mother-daughter bond by saying she was considering moving to Brisbane as she could not face anyone about this. And yes, my first thought was, 'Why do you have to run away from me?' and my second thought was '. . . and why Brisbane?!'

Story 2: Judy returns to the closet
So more days passed with my mother's threats to hide in Brisbane. Then my father took me aside one day and said, 'I don't understand, but I accept – because you are my daughter and I love you very much.' And yes, I cried. He then said, 'Er . . . but, could you please pretend to be straight?'

I stopped crying as he quickly explained, 'Just pretend to be straight until you move out of home.'

'. . .'

'I love you very much, but I also love your mother very much. I also happen to sleep next to your mother every night. And for the past few nights she has been talking nonstop at me about you being gay. You know I work very long hours and I just. Really. Want. To. Sleep.'

I laughed and agreed to his request, because I love my parents very much and my father did work very long hours. Later that day I told my mother straight up, 'Okay Mum, I'm straight.' She sniffed once, looked at me, and never cried again. It was that easy.

One of the members I first met was Peggy, who I still love to dub the 'matriarch' of YellowKitties. Without her and her partner Leo's welcome and persistence, I truly believe the group would not have lasted to this day. Currently YellowKitties stands strong with over 100 members – and we still welcome more! So thanks Peggy!

It was also Peggy, in 2004, who asked whether I wanted to join the AGMC Conference (AGMCon) team, collected by Cinzia Ambrosio from Arcilesbica, as their web developer. I was still a university undergrad at the time studying psychology, but it was a hobby of mine to make simple websites. It sounded interesting, so I said 'Sure!'

It was one of the best decisions I've ever made.

The first time I attended an AGMCon planning committee meeting, it was the most overwhelming thing I had experienced in my young years. Imagine about 15 older LGBTIQ community leaders, each representing their own cultural support/social group, crammed into one room. My eyes widened as I kept silent.

I expected much hand gesturing. There was much heated hand gesturing.

I expected loud, passionate voices interrupting one another. There was so much noise at times my ears rang a little.

I expected that the meeting was most definitely going to be longer than the intended 90 minutes. It lasted a bit over two hours.

And I loved it.

Don't get me wrong, I still had some reservations that this conference would never be organised in time (especially since the committee once spent 30 minutes arguing whether we needed tablecloths or not), but it was so much fun, lively, and the dedication to the cause for equality was palpable.

Long story short – the conference was a massive success! And it was so heartening to see so many people from different cultures and faiths in the one place to discuss all things LGBTIQ and cultural.

Story 3: Why the AGMC is needed
After the conference, we held a dance party – United We Dance. And – this is a very sad, but true story – I was manning the ticket booth with another person, and two Caucasian young men came in and asked what was on. When we responded that it was a multicultural dance party fighting against stigma/racism, one man turned to the other and said, 'Nah – no wogs,' and they left. Racism exists within the LGBITQ community and I can tell you it frustrates a lot of people who are multicultural and LGBTIQ. It boggles us that if the community has experienced stigma/homophobia/biphobia etc. for being different, how could a LGBTIQ person treat another with stigma for being different? This is one of the many reasons why our AGMC is still so relevant today.

After the conference, the committee decided to form a council to continue the mission of advocacy for equality for people from multicultural and/or multifaith background who also identify as LGBTIQ. Thus the AGMC, under the leadership of its founder Cinzia, was formed. I remained in the group for a while longer, but eventually left due to my (now postgraduate) university commitments.

Now, I'm not sure exactly when, but maybe two years after this, I received a phone call from Alyena Mohummadally, who at the time of the conference was a university student like me. Now that I think about it . . . how did she get my number? Oh well, I'll figure that out another time. In any case, Alyena called. Apparently AGMC had dwindled in passion and was at risk of disbanding. Alyena understood the importance of such a group and she was calling upon anyone she could find to help her continue AGMC. Also there were not as many women and no Asian representative on the committee. I was a bit unsure, as this meant I could possibly be dealt with more responsibility in a smaller committee, but I said yes. And so I returned to AGMC.

I have to admit, another reason I returned to AGMC at that time was because I had recently found a girlfriend and realised there were limited services and support for multicultural LGBITQ individuals, let alone their families, to access. I was about to move out of home (*see Story 4*) and was frantically preparing my second coming out (*see Story 1*). I knew that we had to set the groundwork for other people who needed this support.

Alyena kept the AGMC ship running for a few years, with the tireless help of John Tzimas from Greek and Gay, and the ever perky and amazing Maria Pallotta-Chiarolli. Really, I was part of the Committee but I still don't think I did much during that time, other than update the website and online content as much as I could while finishing my doctoral thesis.

Alyena eventually decided to step down as the head of AGMC as she felt the Committee was stagnating and new blood and leadership was needed. It was then that I had the fortune of meeting Dr Tony Mordini. He initially joined through I Ragazzi and had the experience of sitting on multiple boards and committees, so it was a no-brainer and super exciting that he stepped up as the President of the AGMC. For me, the original AGMCon committee built the boat, Alyena set it sailing, and Tony pimped the ride.

Story 4: Judy's Second Coming (Out)
So Melbourne City decided to open a couple's register, and it was open to same-sex couples! How cool! And hey – it's affordable too – only $50! Cheap! Cheap! Those were the exact words I exclaimed to my girlfriend. After noting that my 'proposal' was lacking in romance, she agreed to register with me. Yay!

We filled in the forms and sent it off. My residential address? Well, still my parents' home but I was going to move out in a few months with my girlfriend. The postal address on the form? My girlfriend's house.

Murphy's Law – where did they send the register confirmation letter? My parents' house.

I came home late one night (still my parents' place – keep up with me, yeah?) and found the opened letter on my desk in my bedroom. My mother, like other Asian mothers I'm sure, will open letters if they look like a fine or something like that (it's as if they are genetically programmed to want to be the first to know how many demerit points their children receive). And of course the letter had the Melbourne City Council logo on it.

That's not the worst of it. As I lifted up the letter and began to read . . . dear heavens, it was the GAYEST THING I HAD EVER SEEN.

'Dear Judy – CONGRATULATIONS!!! We are sooooo excited to celebrate your GAY relationship with our total GAY acceptance of you and your GAY partner. Come to the CBD and register asap! WE LOVE THE GAYS!!!' is pretty much a summary of that two-page letter. The only thing missing was rainbow glitter.

In any other circumstance, it would've been a great thing to receive. But they got the address wrong and they just announced my GAY to my mother. Surely this time she would threaten to move further north, like Darwin.

I called my girlfriend, who told me to relax and just wait till the morning and see what happened. So I did. The next morning, my mother sat sullenly in the lounge and refused to look me in the eye. My dad looked at me and shrugged (gee thanks, Dad). These were her first words to me:

'Why did you lie to me?'

I chose my words carefully, 'Well, you weren't exactly happy with the truth the first time I told it to you, and I want you to be happy, so I chose to say what you wanted to hear.'

'. . .'

'. . .'

'. . . Do you really like her?'

'. . . Yes.'

I could see she was also choosing her response. 'Well, then you have my blessing. Just don't lie to me again.'

'. . . Okay.'

And that dear friends, was my second coming out.

But it was not the most memorable part – that was when immediately after-wards, my mother wanted to have the 'last word' as it were, so she huffed and said, 'And since you now want to be so grown up, from now on you can do your own laundry.' Really, you can't make this stuff up (she still did my laundry despite her words).

We had additional committee members come and go, but Tony increased our profile and also our opportunity to network and advocate more widely within the LGBTIQ community, within some cultural communities and with local government and councils.

By now, I had been with AGMC for over 10 years and I was (finally!) settling into my skin and my life. When Tony decided to step down due to his busy schedule in 2016, I was hesitant, but still had sufficient confidence to hold the AGMC torch. My goals from here? Well, to turn AGMC into a fleet of ships. We have much to do and I hope, with your support, we can make Australia a truly open and friendly place for all its people – regardless of culture, faith, gender and/or sexual orientation. I hope AGMC can extend its reach to all states and their rural and remote communities. Get in touch with me – I'm friendly and nice – honest! Just ask my mum – who still lives in Melbourne, by the way.

Uni graduation and AGMC commencement!

Degenerate: Ari middle-aged

Christos Tsiolkas

Aim for the middle of the bloody toilet bowl

– Aim for the middle of the bloody toilet bowl.

Tate's voice is quiet but firm, as it always is when he's giving Ben instructions.

– Alright, got it. Get off my fucking back.

I groan, slipping in and out of sleep. I keep my eyes shut, hoping that in doing so I can coax sleep back.

– And don't swear at me, I'm your father.

Sleep is gone.

– Good luck with that, I call out, Is there coffee?

I hear Tate laughing. And then a beat: a snicker from Ben. It feels like a victory.

My eyes are open. There's a huntsman crawling across the ceiling. As if conscious of me, of my every movement, as if it sensed the flicking open of my eyelids, the insect halts its wandering. I remain still myself, a battle within me, between my wanting to sink back into dreaming and the urgent pressure on my bladder. The desire to piss wins. I jump out of bed and as I do so, as my feet hit the floor, I let out a groan. I know this sound, it's the exact same sound my father made when he was working in his garden, squatting in the veggie patch, lashing the bean stalks to the rods and getting up on his feet. He would let out that exact same groan, hand to his hips, massaging the pain.

I am my father's son. I've inherited his dodgy hip.

I pull on trackie dacks, slip on a dirty T, walk into the kitchen. There's coffee brewed, the smell bitter and welcoming. Ben is on a stool, his head bowed over his phone, madly scrolling. Tate too, standing by the stove, is peering at his phone. I grunt my good mornings and make my way to the loo. My flow is strong and long and as I'm pissing, looking at the tiles, I notice the splash of urine. When I'm finished I grab at the toilet paper, scrunch it up and scrub the tiles. Ben is 15 and his aim is hopeless. And he never fucking cleans up after himself. I toss the paper into the bowl, think for a moment: Do I flush? Is that a waste of water? Am I contributing to the sinking of another South Pacific island? The paper uncurls, floats on the surface of my urine. I flush.

I pull out a stool and sit opposite the island bench from Ben, who's still obsessively flicking on his phone. Tate leans across and gently pats my shoulder, hands me a cup of coffee. He never kisses me in front of his son. A hug maybe. I'm the same. It is awkward when Ben's staying over. Like we're the guests, like we have to be on our best behaviour.

– What's so interesting?

Ben doesn't look up.

– There's been a terrorist attack in Paris.

– Bad?

It's Tate who answers.

– Really bad, mate.

My phone is on the bench, recharging. I lunge for it, five missed calls. One from Alex, one from Peter, one from Mum and two from Johnny. Twelve text messages. I fire up Google. A bomb in a stadium, shootings at cafes and nightclubs, young kids slaughtered at a rock concert. None of us are talking, our heads bowed over our phones. I can't make any sense of it. I don't know how to make any sense from it.

– Your coffee's getting cold, Ari.

Tate is beside me. His arm lopes across my shoulder. I smell him, the sweat of night and the sweat of morning. Acrid and warm, lulling and intoxicating. I glance up and Ben's still head down over screen. As I look he stretches his arm and his baggy t-shirt flops down over one shoulder. A hint of tawny fuzz on his pale white skin. Overnight, as if it has sprouted there overnight. The stir in my crotch. A city has been made an abattoir halfway across the world, my lover is standing next to me and I'm thinking of what his son looks like naked.

I grab my phone.

– I'm turning on the TV.

The curtains are drawn in the lounge room and it's dark and chilly. I pull them open and the warm rays of sun flood the room, bash against my eyes. I switch on the idiot box, press the button on the remote for the ABC. The sound is a din and I fumble, mute the remote. I watch the images. Talking heads. Unsmiling and grim. Young adults crying. Stern French police. A con- stant scroll of words rolling across the bottom of the screen. Of death, of mayhem, of fear. I stand there, just watching, images bleeding into images, remembering why I hate television. Why I detest it. The real cheapened, the real being made unreal. A girl on screen is shaking: her crying, even in silence, animal and raw and unceasing. I breathe in hard, wanting to squash the tears already forming, wanting to deny television's noxious hold on me. I wipe my eyes. I call Mum.

– Ari mou, Ari mou, Ari mou, her voice a lowing wail, Are you watching? Can you believe what's happening?

– I know, Mama, it's terrible.

– They're fucking animals, Ari, why do this? Why butcher these young children? Why don't they shoot the politicians that created these wars? They're cowards, they're degenerate cowards. If they had guts they'd be shooting Obama and Merkel, Cameron and Erdogan. But they're degenerate, so they shoot children.

Such a strong word, such an unusual word for my Mum to use. *Degenerate.* She's right but I can't quite take a grip of that word. I need to file it away, look it up, pinpoint its exact meaning.

– Are you there?

– Yes, Mama, I answer in Greek, I'm still here.

She's crying now. She's probably looking at the same images I'm looking at. Mesmerised, not able to look away. Ben has come in, plonks himself on an armchair, sits there cross-legged. His hand reaches out to me. I hand him the remote and he unmutes the sound. I walk into our room, sit on the bed and look up. The spider has vanished.

– Have you spoken to your sister?

– I'll call her.

– I'm going over. Can you come?

I fucking hate those terrorists. Blowing up the world, blowing up my weekend.

– We've got Ben this weekend. We've got shopping to do.

– Please, Ari mou.

Her pleading makes me a child. I want a cigarette. I need a cigarette.

– Okay, Mama, in Greek again, I'll meet you at Alex's. Give me an hour.

I search my jeans pocket, find a squashed packet of Peter Stuyvesant and head into the kitchen. Tate's on the phone, English and Tagalog, he too is speaking to his mother. He notices the packet of fags in my hand, and frowns. He indicates the clock on the wall. My rule, I've been trying hard to keep to my rule. No fags until six pm. But today the world's blown up. Today doesn't count.

I mouth: I need one. And I gently brush my lips against his stubble. His

256

frown vanishes and he grips my hand, brings it to his lips. I leave him talking to his mum. I walk out into Tate's garden.

You're born a gardener

You're born a gardener, I do believe that. Our father kept tending his garden, his veggies, his herbs, his flowers and that small square of lawn, almost up to the end. I made a habit of passing through with the van every day when he was ill, and I'd hear him before I got to the back door. His coughing, that wracking terrible churning from his lungs that sounded as if all his demons were fighting to make their escape, to surrender his now failing body. I'd try to help, with the pruning or with the weeding, but that only made him laugh and that only made his coughing worse. He'd wipe the spittle from his chin – those last months, as the illness worsened, his land would be covered with spit and gobs of phlegm – and wheezing, he'd say, struggling for breath: None of my children are gardeners.

I gave up trying to be of assistance, I have no green thumb at all. And I think he preferred it that way, my just being there, making him a coffee, helping him back to the house when his strength gave way. And finally it did; all his power and his heft, all his manhood, the cancer sliced it all away.

Tate's garden is small, even smaller than my mother's garden in Richmond. But it is neat and it is ordered. He's built a bin for the compost and he's even fashioned a small pond, a kidney shaped pool in which three or four goldfish lazily swim. Tate knows the name of every flower and every shrub. I know what a rose is and I probably can guess what's a hydrangea and what's a carnation. But that's about the extent of my knowledge. And like my father, Tate glowers if I ever try to help. You're a useless gardener, Ari. Tate says that to me and I hear it as the voice of my old man.

This last week summer has settled. The breeze from the north is hot, not warm, and the smell of cat piss and cat spray is everywhere, as if the animals have all awoken from hibernation and are leaving their mark on the new world. I look down at the squashed cigarette packet in my hand. Should I? Should I not? I think of the drive from Mordialloc to Alex's place, the long dull stretch of the Nepean Highway to Punt Road, and I tap the packet, release a cigarette into my hand. And then the arguments when I get there. Osman screaming at Belgin, Belgin screaming at her dad. Alex screaming at Osman to stop screaming at Belgin. Osman quoting Karl Marx and Belgin retorting with some bullshit quote from the Qu'ran. And Alex, giving up, falling silent in their small kitchen, crossing herself and whispering to the Panagia. And then there'll be Mum in the mix.

I grab the lighter from off the deck table and I light the cigarette. The harsh burst of smoke fills my lungs and then the gentle rush of the nicotine in my blood. I smoke slowly, standing on the narrow bluestone path that cleaves the garden in two. I can hear the beginning ring of the railway crossing. I try to hear the sea, four blocks back. But there's only the clanging of the shutting gates and the low drumming of the approaching train.

I know I should ring Johnny and I know I should ring Peter and I probably should ring Alex and tell her that I'm coming over. And I haven't even looked at my messages. But I don't want to do any of that. I don't want to speak to anyone, I don't want to communicate with a soul. I bring the cigarette to my mouth, I suck it in deep. Even with the low hum of the cars and the trucks on the highways; the screeching to a halt of the westbound train; the squawk and cries of the birds in the trees from next door; the occasional bark of a dog; and also, a portend of summer's arrival, the dull thump of a bat whacking a cricket ball from the oval across the road: there's sound but it is sparse and in between it all is the silence of the suburbs. The quietest place on earth.

The screeching of a sliding door.

– You okay?

– Why?

Tate points to my nearly finished cigarette.

I shrug.

– I've got no willpower.

His laugh is deep and joyful and he's behind me, he steals a nervous glance toward the glass door but Ben must still be in the lounge and Tate slowly rubs his crotch against my arse.

His voice, in my ear, it makes me shiver.

– That's a fucking understatement, he whispers, you've got no willpower at all.

His voice, I first fell for his voice. Sound, I travel and go forward through sound.

I take his hand, lazily but deliberately, I lay it over my crotch.

– I have to go to my sister's, Mum needs us. She's pretty upset.

At this, Tate lifts his hand, moves away from me. I stub the cigarette end into the charcoal stained ashtray we bought in the airport in Barcelona. He sits on one of the deckchairs, pulling his knees up as he does so, and I see the swing of his cock as he sits. His voice, then his eyes, and then his cock. That's the order in which I fell in love with him.

He is playing with the cigarette packet, tossing it from one hand to the other.

– She's not the only one who's upset.

I draw in breath. Not now, I don't want to deal with his cool and analytical dissecting of my family. Every point he'll make will be right and every point he raises will make no difference. I am a son and a brother.

I squat beside him.

– How's your Mum?

He sniffs, shrugs his shoulders.

– She's okay. She's been trying to contact Marie, a good friend of hers in Paris but has heard nothing back yet. She'll call me back later.

I've only met Valerie three times but each time I have been impressed and a little cowered by her self-possession. Tate's mother is tiny, not even five feet, but her presence makes her seem a giant. She lives in Sydney and Tate's father has retired in Perth. I like Valerie and I get along really well with Ray. Unlike his ex-wife, he hardly speaks. And he's comfortable in the silence.

– Have you called Alex?

– Not yet.

– And does she want you all over? It's Saturday, Ari. We were going shopping with Ben. Remember?

I eye the cigarette packet. I want another. I stand up, clenching my teeth so I don't make that groan, so I don't reveal my weakness.

– I'm sorry, Tate. I'll go over to Alex's, I'll spend some time with Mum and then I'll meet you at the shops.

– And what time will that be?

– I don't know what fucking time that will be.

I do it, I get surly.

– Anyway, Ben doesn't want to spend time with me. He wants to spend time with you.

Tate has chucked the cigarettes back on the table. He taps his knee.

– I think all this scares him.

Does he mean us arguing? And then I remember. Young people and kids getting gunned down at a gig in Paris. The Eagles of Death Metal, that was part of the endless scroll on our screens. They slaughtered them at a concert for the Eagles of Death Metal. As if the Eagles of Death Metal had anything to do with Islam or the Middle East.

I'm scared of what's being released inside me. Fucking Muslims.

– What?

I can't look at Tate.

– Mum's fearful that it's going to mean a rise in racism and Islamophobia. It's going to be a very difficult week for her.

I still can't look at him. There's nothing I can say now that won't have the potential to ignite an argument. Tate is calm as he speaks. I try to resist but I find myself resenting that quiet and that certainty in his voice. Valerie works for the Equal Opportunity Commission. So he's right, it will be a hard week for her. Jesus, it's been a hard decade for her. But his quiet and his certainty separates us, reveals the distance between our worlds. At this moment, and I know only in this moment – I know that I won't, that I must not feel this way tomorrow, I promise myself I won't feel this way tomorrow – I don't give a flying fuck if some Mussie girl gets her veil ripped off on a train. That isn't a bullet to the head. That isn't being mowed down while you're out with friends having a drink. That isn't being shot in the back while you're in a frenzied and terrified mob, trying to find an exit.

– I should head off.

Tate starts tapping the table again.

– Please, just spend some time with me and Ben.

Mum's voice on the phone. Scared, she sounded so scared.

I try to make sense of it for Tate.

– I'll be back, mate, this afternoon, I promise, and I'll stay the night. But Mum's real upset. I heard it in her voice.

No answer. Those beautiful perfectly round eyes, the dark lids but the cool grey colour, they communicate nothing.

I inhale again and I try again.

– It's 'cause it's Paris, I'm sure of it, you know what it means to her.

The doctors told Dad that he had lung cancer and two months later he and Mum went to Greece; he needed to see his family there, he needed to say his goodbyes. But on the way they stopped in Paris for five days. It was the first time they were in a city that wasn't Australian and that wasn't Greek. And they loved it. They did all the dumb-fuck touristy things, they were always chaperoned and they didn't need to speak a word of French. But they loved it. Mum confessed to us: I think it is more beautiful than Greece.

Tate nods but his eyes are still cold.

– My mother has friends in Paris, my mother's lived in Paris.

And again the separation between us. *Your* mum was a pampered rich girl, *your* mum grew up with nannies and servants in Manila, *your* mum travels the fucking world. Your fucking mother is nothing like my mother.

I lean down and kiss him on the brow. As I do his eyes quickly dart to the door. Always, every time, the shadow of Ben.

I grab my keys, I grab my phone and wallet. As I pass the lounge room,

I poke my head in. The television is still blaring, the images are still rolling and Ben is still looking down at his phone.

– I'm off, Ben, I'll see you in the arvo.

He says something, I can't catch it. He doesn't bother to raise his head.

I miss Johnny, how he can crack me up

I miss Johnny, how he can crack me up. With some friends you don't need to explain anything, you have the shorthand and the history, the common vocabulary and your own unique dialect to make yourself known. I have that with Johnny and I have that with Betty. But he's up north – I'm a wog surfer-chick, Ari, he will call down the phone – and Betty is in Barcelona.

I've swung into the driver's seat of the van but I haven't started the ignition. I've been checking my phone. Betty's sent me a text: I love you, in Greek and Catalan – she'd slit my throat if I mistook it for Spanish – and then the words: *meanwhile, elsewhere in the world*. She's attached a screenshot of carnage and fire on a city street. I zoom into the image and it is of a bombing in Lebanon. Politics, always the politics. She'll be screaming about politics till the day she dies and even on her last breath she'll be collecting the sinned against and casting us remaining sinners down into the fiery pits. Her message has made me feel guilty, ashamed for how I let the slimy digital ooze emanating from the television and phone screens fortify my prejudices, steel my wrath, give an adrenalin kick to my fears. But the next message I open is from Johnny and it cracks me up. It makes me laugh and laugh. His message reads: *All You Need is Love!*

It's a cartoon of the Prophet Mohammad and Jesus Christ. It's a few simple charcoal lines, quick brushes of colour wash over the figures, but it is beautiful and perfectly executed. The two prophets have their arms around each other and they're kissing. Mohammad has his eyes closed in ecstatic bliss and Jesus is looking at him with real love. I want to send the cartoon to everyone, I want to send it out to the world. I send it to Betty. And then, as I'm about to put away my phone, I know I've relented. From my laughter and my glee I sense that my resentment and surliness is slipping away. I will forward Johnny's text to Tate. I'm sitting in the van, it feels like ages, my fingers rubbing up and down the keypad. I type: *This made me laugh*. I pause. I type: *I love you*. And then I delete those three words. I type: *Love, Ari*. I delete that, it sounds fucking moronic, as if we are besties not lovers. I type: *I'll see you in the afternoon, I love you, sorry for being a dick*.

I send Tate my words and the attachment.

With an almost brutal twist, I turn on the ignition. My phone on silent – my phone is always on silent – and I slam it into the glovebox.

I know nothing about cars. After all these years of driving, if I were to break down on the Nepean Highway or on Dandenong Road, I'd be fucked. I was never into cars, never that kind of guy. But I don't need to know their anatomy, what goes on under the hood and how the oil and the petrol circulates and keeps the body moving. And these days, half the engine a computer, I've got no chance of understanding at all. But though I am respectful of the vehicle I drive and I am conscious of my technical ignorance, I am happiest when I am alone in my van. I never use the phone. I play music, I play it loud, I watch the city become a movie, the stimuli of surge and movement, the symphonic charge that it's my city. When I was young I claimed I'd never learn to drive. I was a city boy and cars were the symptom – indeed, if not the cause – of brain-dead suburbia. I look back on that kid, so bloody arrogant and so bloody scared, and part of me wants to slam his face hard into a brick wall. Again and again. Grow-the-fuck-up-you-selfish-prick. And part of me wants to take his hand. Whisper to him: You don't have to be so angry.

He'd fucking hate me. He wouldn't listen.

I know what I'm doing. I'm entering my film of my city and I am separating from the world. There's a mix CD I made for Tate, old soul and new soul, the Supremes follow Janelle Monae who follows Amy Whitehouse who follows Otis. Music I will never stop loving, music that will be my soundtrack till the day I die. I know this. This is still the only thing I really know: that the music I love will be my last and final and remaining solace. Jill Scott, her voice flooding the stereo, riding and conquering the staccato hip-hop beats, she is singing about shame. I turn the volume up, weave and steer into the traffic, watch the towers of the city getting closer. A group of good-looking Chinese chicks are waiting for the lights as I cross Alma Road. They are giggling, laughing, talking furiously; taking advantage of the dawning of summer in their tight pants, their short skirts, wearing their wrap-around sunglasses.

I know that despair has settled on cities halfway across the world, I know my city's peace and calm and lassitude is not earned, not deserved. But I'm singing at the top of my lungs.

The track falls away and in that short looping moment, the breath between the last song and the next, I recall looking up a word, on the phone, just before I read my texts, just before I had set off. I had looked up that word my mother had used, *degenerate*. I can see the words burning into consciousness. *Having lost the physical, mental, or moral qualities considered normal and desirable; showing evidence of decline.* All true. The terrorists: they're definitely degenerate. Europe: degenerate. The USA: degenerate. The Middle East: degenerate. Australia: yes, a million times yes, we're degenerate.

But the sun is warm. And the music is good. Fuck them all. I'm happy, I'm outside not inside the world and I'm happy.

This is a SFW version of Christos's story. The full version is NSFW, school, church, temple or mosque.

'Boys of the Parish'

A poetic journey around sexual identity in Australia and Italy

Paul Venzo

The period of my sexual coming of age coincided with significant political and social events: the AIDS crisis, the fall of the Berlin Wall and the Soviet Union, the Tiananmen Square massacre, the first Iraq war, the early stages of the technological revolution in communications and the height of globalisation. In Australia, this was also the period in which gay rights, activism and identities began a kind of flourishing, spurred on by the AIDS crisis, state-based law reform and the influence of Western culture in which non-traditional sexual identities were becoming increasingly visible. Apart from this broader cultural and political background, it is also true to say I came from a working-class, Catholic background, was born and raised in a regional town, the son of a migrant father and an Australian mother.

I mention these contexts because any identity, sexual or otherwise, connects the self with the society, culture, history and behaviour that circulate around it. Poetry has been the primary means through which I have mapped this relationship between myself and the different spaces – real, imagined and psychological – that I inhabit. This has always gone hand in hand with my Australian-Italian identity, especially because writing poetry requires me to think closely about language and how much it shapes and interprets identity, putting us into the world through words.

Through poetry I have recorded and analysed the physical and psychological movement between two cultures. This chapter is, therefore, a poetic journey; a kind of personal, literary cartography that maps how, where and when I am in the context of my own experience of cultural hybridity, as someone who has long considered themselves a kind of insider/outsider, a 'familiar stranger' who is at once at home in, and foreign to, their environment (Venzo, 2014). To begin this journey, then, I want to take you with me, back in time to inner city Melbourne, in the early 1990s:

12 lines too late

We sat in the window of Ti Amo and drank
black coffee. I remember your Yank smile, wide
as a prairie, and your problem skin.
The place was full of students and stank
of our cigarette smoke. Outside we tied
up our bikes, a pair of metal lovers, next to the bin.
We hung out for a week and then you went off
to Queensland, or some other, warmer place.
That's where Misty recognised your face –
was it Fraser Island? – and within days
had sent a letter to reveal you liked me, after all.
My black bike leans, unlocked, against a wall.

During the early 1990s I spent much of my time in the environs of the
University of Melbourne, first as a student and then as a teacher. Melbourne
in this period was an intense microcosm of queer politics and activism around
AIDS and gay rights, and I became involved in several small groups that protested and staged fundraising events in support of these issues. Feminist,
post-structuralist and queer theories permeated my studies in literature,
cinema and art, and my university work synthesised with a period of my life
in which I was testing the edges of my sexual identity.

Carlton is the suburb next door to the main university campus, and this
'little Italy' nurtured my strong desire to connect with the culture and language of my father. My favourite hangout was a place called Ti Amo, a little
trattoria that served cheap, hearty, Italian food like pasta fagioli and baked
ricotta cheesecake, vino rosso in small tumblers, and thick black espresso
coffee. I was studying Italian and the proprietors kindly indulged my rather
rudimentary attempts to converse with them.

One day over lunch I found myself next to a young American tourist and
we got along well. His name was Kenneth and he was spending a few weeks
in Melbourne, living with friends. Over the next few days we would meet for
coffee at Ti Amo. It was a safe space for me; I felt at home there, and with
my dark, Italian features I could even say that I looked like I belonged there.
Ken was tall and thin like I was. He had red-blonde hair and still suffered
from teenage acne. He was shy and softly spoken. I didn't care – to me he
was sexy. He had strong arms and the lean muscles of his chest were barely
hidden by his t-shirt. Before I could summon the courage to tell him how I
felt, Ken left to continue his travels around Australia. This was in the days

before easy access to email, before mobile phones were ubiquitous and inexpensive. Staying in touch, let alone seeing each other again, was unlikely. It was many months later that I discovered he had liked me too. I think of this poem as a record of the disconnectedness that I felt at that time, the inability or unwillingness I had to commit to a particular version of myself, lest that not be acceptable or desirable to others.

From the distance of time I can see how important the setting for this poem is. I was still learning to speak Italian, having never learned it at home with my father. I had not yet been to Italy; I did not know my relatives there. I had a vague sense of what it must be like, what it *would* be like, so I searched out the people and places that fitted that imaginative space for me. I felt a strong desire to belong, at the same time as I was developing an acute sense of in-between-ness. My shyness with other men was part of that. I have consistently negotiated between fixed identities: not quite Italian or Australian, not quite a country boy but not a city person either, a Catholic who is anathema to the religion in which he has been raised, a gay man who has never quite fitted the stereotypes that identity seems to require of him.

In my late teens and early 20s I was caught in my own particular obsession/fascination with my father's home, his origins and 'original' culture. When I finally reached this 'homeland' for the first time in 1996 I discovered that it was in many ways as I had imagined it to be, and in other ways utterly different. People did not speak the textbook Italian I had learned at university, and so I started from scratch, losing my plummy accent and taking up the inflections of the young people who became my friends. My family in Italy were, of course, as ordinary in their tastes and daily rituals as my family in Australia, and yet I was entranced by the culture that surrounded them: rich with art and music, fashion, food and sex.

Despite the relative obscurity in which gay people conducted their sexual lives in Italy at that point, this was of course an opportunity for me to experience my sexuality in a different cultural context, outside the familiar frames of reference provided by Melbourne, my then home.

Diluvio
The rain from Sotto Gouda punches the horizon
Bruises the sky. I bolt for the last bus to Feltre,
Miss it, watch its blue arse wagging goodbye
As it turns towards Limana. My expletives are
Drenched in the cats-and-dogs downpour;
I am stranded and the payphones are constipated

266

With coins. A likely lad in a battered Opel
Cruises once, twice, and pulls up. As he leans across
To open the door, I can see the dark, moist fur of his armpit.
He's a barracks boy. I get in. He clamps a paw on my wet,
Denim thigh, guns the accelerator. His fingernails
Are as clean as the hour after a storm.

Belluno is one of the least known and most beautiful cities in Italy. Medieval in origin, it was once under the protection and control of the Venetian Republic. It is situated in an area known as the *prealpi*: the gateway to the soaring peaks of the Dolomite mountains, and these indomitable, granite monoliths rise around it, reminding its inhabitants of their alpine identity. I know this city and this region very well: many of my father's family settled here after the war, clustered about the village of Pieve di Limana, on the banks of the Piave river. When I first began to spend time there, I would often take the bus into Belluno, to have some time to be alone, to sit, drink coffee, smoke and write.

In those days, young Italian men were still required to do military service, and Belluno was home to a large barracks where members of the famous Alpini soldiers were stationed. They are notable for wearing the *capello Alpino*: a green felt hat with raven feather and pom-pom inserted into its brim. I felt a great affinity for these young soldiers, recalling my father's nostalgia for his own time as an army officer. He struck a dashing figure in his uniform, surrounded by the handsome, well-groomed men of his regiment, in grainy black and white photos from the early 1950s.

Pier Vittorio Tondelli, one of the Italian writers of the post-modern era who has most influenced my own writing, captured the erotic world of the military barracks in his 1982 novella *Pao Pao*. He described something that I came to know from personal experience: that the concentration of small groups of young men away from home adds a frisson of sexual energy – and an undeniable homoeroticism – to the environments they inhabit. Every space has its own sexual geography: from the home to the public sphere (Alley, 2016). Today, with the prevalence of geo-positioning technologies, the (homo)sexual geography of towns and cities is, in many respects, mapped online. Apps such as Grindr, Scruff, Recon and GayRomeo allow men to locate and interact with each other, in search of sexual/social interactions, predicated on identity markers such as age, taste, looks and so forth. This was not always the case. Until recently, real space – parks, public toilets, bars, clubs, saunas, even department stores and indeed train stations – were where men located other men to initiate sexual contact. The encounter in the poem

'Diluvio' is one such instance in which I recognised this liminal quality, this particular kind of in-between-ness, in another person.

Dustbin Circus
A travelling circus in a vacant lot
outskirting Vittorio Veneto.
Gypsy wagons, dust kicked up in little coughs
of brown smoke and lantern light.
The music of a whirly-gig.

The ring-master, a fat French clown
bow-tied and tipsy,
steps us up onto rickety benches.
Stringy-haired girls trot a pony
while even chickens stunt for money.

Crowds gasp at the fakery
of a broken, flaming trapeze.
A wiry acrobat feints his death with
a ta-da dismount. Feet-stamping encores,
and hats filled with clinking lire.

Later, my mate is asleep by the fire,
belly full of bread and cheap red.
I chat with an unshod boy: the ratty son
of the acrobat. His junkie mother
scratches her arm, thin as a sparrow bone.

She flinches when Daddy
and I strike up in English.
Richard: an ex-army, ex-addict Pom.
Dried out he joined the circus, and now
turns new tricks from an old dog.

Getting late, I wring out my mate
for the long drive down the valley.
Richard complains at my leaving,
wants my number scribbled on his hand.
I roll my own act onto the autostrada.

A week later, a phone call.
Keen for more bread and circuses
for its good-bye slap-up do
in a villa that once boasted a Count,
I head off in a prize-fighting Fiat Uno.

Torches, drumming, pipes and
flag throwing. Something
rose-fleshed roasting on a spit.
Children eating dry cake.
Prosecco, golden in glasses.

Richard reels me out of the circle,
wraps me in his jig, dances me
to the edge of the music, to the steps
of a kitsch caravan. In the dim light
his kisses molest my mouth.

His stubble scrapes off a layer
of my inexperience.
His lust is a ramrod pegging out
a tent of illicit possibilities.
Outside, a creeping footfall breaks us.

Weeks later, Barcelona. We reconvene:
Harriet, Michele, Richard, his wife, her kid,
the rat, the fat French clown
and God knows who else
tumble out together to a magic show

where a man balances a pool-table
on his head. Absinthe and hash
and these hangers-on intervene
in a private duet of brief touches
and sideways glances.

Of that night all I'm left
is a faded t-shirt swiped
from Richard's bag.

Dead-end searches on the internet –
an open matrix for a heavy fall.

The poem above had its genesis in one of my many journeys to northern Italy during my 20s. It is set in the outskirts of Vittorio Veneto; a town on the site of a decisive military victory in Italy's march toward independence and unification. On the spur of the moment I went with friends to see a gypsy circus. This was not the slick operation we have come to expect from the grand tents of Cirque du Soleil. This troupe performed tricks on horseback, flung themselves about on a trapeze with no net, and scratched out frantic clown music on squeaky violins and tuneless brass.

Over the next few months I found myself getting to know Richard: a married, ex-heroin-addict turned trapeze artist, whose wife, Mercedes, was part of the circus team. Through Richard I discovered that sexual identity is not static. It does not always fit into fixed identity categories, and all sorts of people have all sorts of ways of expressing desire. This realisation freed me to consider my own heterosexual tendencies and to allow different 'versions' of my identity, and particularly my sexual identity, to co-exist.

My short relationship with Richard formed part of a kind of sexual coming of age, in which I realised that sexuality is inextricably caught up with the different social, cultural and linguistic environments in which we move. At the point in my life in which the poem was written I had become a kind of nomad, in constant movement across identifications with more than place, time and community. I was like a tightrope walker: my arms outstretched, trying valiantly not to let my body lean too far one way or the other, always looking to move ahead but drawn, by some inescapable force, in two directions at once.

The new millennium saw the focus of my relationship to Italy change. In the year 2000 I took up the offer of an internship with the Peggy Guggenheim museum in Venice. I rented a room in an apartment in Dorsoduro, near the Ca' Foscari University, and for three months I worked in the museum; giving tours, running errands, researching, and meeting artists and students from around the globe. This period of time led to the creation of an indelible bond with Venice: a cultural and physical environment like no other. Venice suits my sense of in-between-ness, having itself a dual identity as something that exists between the land and the sea, between history and the present. It has always been multicultural, since its infancy as a marshy republic to which exiles and traders were drawn in their many thousands.

Venice has traditionally been associated with death, decay and sexual debauchery – particularly so in the work of foreign writers who have taken it as a creative locus. During the glory days of the republic Venice was well known for its prostitutes and for the profligate sexual freedoms associated with the annual Carnivale. However, this sexual geography is now mostly hidden. Prostitution, sex parties, swingers groups, free beaches . . . these are things which, if they exist at all, are located on the mainland; the industrialised peninsula that funnels tourists into the main islands of Venice.

The homosexual subculture of Venice is similarly invisible to most people. There is no gay venue in Venice proper. However, its labyrinthine streets and waterways create a kind of playing field for unexpected encounters and hidden meetings. Insiders speak of the *ragazzi del parrocchio*, the 'boys of the parish', who can be seen wandering the Frezzaria in the late evening; a kind of urban cruising that is augmented by contemporary technologies such as mobile phone apps that are designed to facilitate casual sexual encounters. I have tried to capture this sense of a hidden but ever-present eroticism in my poetry. For me, Venice is a sexual space, marked by its history but also by the modern desire to appear 'family friendly', to put on a façade of moral rectitude encouraged by local political and religious interest groups.

The boys of the parish

In summer, after dinner, the boys of the parish
wander towards Rialto, along the narrow street
they call the Frezzaria. Now and again eyes lift
and meet each other, in silent recognition.
We don't have a fixed spot: no bar, park,
nor bridge. Ours are typically Venetian meetings –
made in passing, sudden, hasty – they
are materialised in glances, reflections, footfalls
in quiet corners that, at this hour, are almost empty.
Just so I meet a guy in Campo Santo Stefano
who is carrying home his shopping. After brief,
whispered greetings we find ourselves in his flat.
An hour passes and we're sweaty from the exertion
of guessing the hopes of a stranger's body.
More pleasurable are the minutes spent lying
on the carpet, listening to the last symphony
of voices, carts full of goods and rubbish,

and the bells of midnight that ask us:
who will spend the night alone, and who
sees themselves running through the piazza,
hurling themselves onto the last boat for home?

Now in middle age, I have developed a relationship with the Fondazione Cini, an organisation that fosters scholarship in the arts, with a focus on Venetian history, writing, music and architecture. The foundation is located on the island of San Giorgio. The façade of its magnificent church designed by Palladio faces across the 'kiss of the bay' (*bacino*) to Saint Mark's Square. During my time at the Fondazione I have been inspired by the history of 'foreign' writers who have taken Venice and the Veneto as a creative topos. For me, this writing – much of it in English – reflects my own sense of in-between-ness, of being 'in translation' across my dual identifications with one place/space and another. Searching for an appropriate poetic form with which to write into this tradition, I found myself coming back time and again to the sonnet. The sonnet is originally an Italian form (meaning a 'little song') and yet in English we associate this form primarily with Shakespeare. However, it is the work of Petrarch – who was personally connected to Venice and northern Italy – that comes to mind whenever I use the sonnet form to write into and about my own connection to this area.

In the Petrarchan sonnet, the first eight lines set out an idea or problem, and after the 'turn' or break, the final six lines offer an alternative viewpoint or (re)solution. For Petrarch and his humanist imagination that sought to reconcile his sense of self with the prevailing religious and political environment in which he lived, this form allowed him to consider and 'turn over' the significant events and problems of his life, including his sexual/romantic fascination with his muse, Laura.

Sonnetto per Paolo

Di notte c'è un buio attraente
nei giardini di San Giorgio Maggiore.
Si vede, vagamente, le stradine
che vanno al teatro all'aperto –
ormai ricoperto di erbacce –
oppure per la viletta vecchia dove
i nespoli fanno amore,
i loro rami carichi di frutta.

Altrove ai confini dell'isola
sono i posti più scuri, in cui
due ragazzi possono togliersi
un po' i vestiti, sentendo l'afasulla pelle,
il bacio dell'umidità,
il primo tocco della stagione.

Sonnet for Paolo
At night there is an enticing darkness
in the gardens of San Giorgio Maggiore.
Just visible are the little paths
that lead to the amphitheatre –
now overgrown with weeds –
or around to the old villa where
a pair of loquat trees make love,
their branches heavy with fruit.

Towards the edges of the island
are the darkest places, in which
two young men might undress,
feel the nocturnal heat on their skin,
humidity the season's first fruit,
held wetly to their lips.

Beyond the narrative of this poem, the way that it is written in English and Italian is best described as 'simultaneous self-translation'. This means I am both the author and the translator of the two poems, which are not written one after the other but rather at the same time. In so doing I am able to better explore the poetic voices that exist for me in each language, identifying and even revelling in the similarities, differences and slippages that occur between the two 'versions' of myself.

My poetry is often 'in translation', as I am. In fact, I would say that the ways I have enacted my sexual life as a man are shaped almost predominantly through this rubric of being across cultures and languages. The Italian-Australian scholar Rosi Braidotti (2011) has theorised the notion of subjective nomadism: a kind of shifting across planes of selfhood. While this idea might upon initial consideration seem like a battleground of belonging and alienation, I have recognised, over time, that this kind of nomadism has its own consolations, and its own pleasures. I think of my poetry as islands within a broad archipelago of life-writing; they represent small 'ecosystems' of memory and imagination across which I travel. This process enables me to set myself adrift from fixed notions of self and sexual identity, shaped by the environments in which I roam.

Paul in Bassano del Grappa,
his dad's home town

The Experience (a political song)

SIM Victor (MUSIC and YOGA Nidra)

I tried to make a change
was known as a fighter
but after a while
the in-vitality took over

suffocated by lack of human rights
each day it got harder just to survive
grassroots orgs ain't got enough control
so its best leaders sacrifice for the common goal
there's a lot of people
more political than me
but you don't need to be a doctor to know we aren't free

Guruji Swamaji
It's all the same
She'll accept both of them as her name
I looked to him
coz all have something to teach us
He looked to me
coz I'm a child of the universe

Here at the ashram
since new year's day
I've left my community
but not to run away
coz middle class lied and lower-class delusions
so off many went to neo-liberal lives
some may have some sincere hopes
but nevertheless often half-assed allies

Hard to manage when subjugated
Costs and benefits never weighed, hidden enemies rumours made
Costs and benefits never weighed, hidden enemies rumours made
Costs and benefits never weighed, hidden enemies rumours made
Costs and benefits never weighed, hidden enemies rumours made
Costs and benefits never weighed, hidden enemies rumours made

Tried to make a difference
for seven years
I stayed on that journey
despite all my fears
Tried to make a difference
every day and night
. . . because it was right

coz it's hard for most to meet their basic needs
even millionaires are scared to see why
coz help one, help all outside of the bloodline
and in this system, you'll be like us lower class

I know that so many women deserve better
I know that workers deserve their rights
I know that poverty don't need to be
and I know imperialist wars can end

I know that races and faiths can coexist
I know that transphobic deaths need to stop!
I know our environment needs love
and I know this culture could better consider health

Let's change the world so death don't seem like freedom
oppressed can't be choosers if not contributing to change
we need a revolution on multiple levels
inner individual, outer micro, macro, global

as long as we ain't got
democratic centralism
we'll be governed and given
oppression, depression

issues outside of and inside of our heads
and it'll be harder to get out of bed

so I left my community
just for a little while
went to an ashram
to re-build a tenacious fire
I left my communities just for a little while
came to an ashram to rebuild a tenacious fire

Every day I'm haunted by the truth I know
and acknowledging what's real
Values Driven is the way to go
it's the closest thing to happiness in times like these

coz the experience of oppressed demographics matter
The experience of oppressed demographics matter
The experience of oppressed demographics matter
The experience of oppressed demographics matter
The experience of oppressed demographics matter
The experience of oppressed demographics matter
The experience of super oppressed demographics matter

For the audio of this song: https://store.cdbaby.com/cd/simvictor4

Finding Nevo

Nevo Zisin

When I was born, I was named Liat. Liat is a Hebrew name that my mum felt very strongly about, one that I grew to feel a deep connection with. It translates loosely into English as 'you're mine'. It was a special message from my mother to me. Those series of letters somehow became defining to who I was as a person.

Some transpeople hate their birth names. There is a lot of associated trauma and distress and many refer to it as their 'deadname'. It is considered an act of transphobia to use someone's birth name without their consent. I have had mine used many times without consultation, in interviews and articles and by people who have decided it is too difficult to adjust to a new name. That name being used as a way of invalidating my identity has caused a bitter rift in my relationship with those people. Though truthfully, I love my birth name. Revealing that name to people is a recognition of closeness. So by choosing to include my birth name in this book, I am allowing you to see a very guarded part of me.

There will always be a part of me that is Liat. I think of her almost as a little sister, and sometimes I miss her. When I refer to my past self, sometimes I use 'she' pronouns and sometimes I use my old name. By no means does that give permission to anyone else to do the same. I exclusively use 'they/them' and 'he/him' pronouns now and that is what I expect people to use when referring to me in the past. I know this sounds confusing, but I think it's okay to have a different set of rules for myself in relation to my gender and past than I do for others.

There is a part of me that wishes I could have kept my birth name. But as time went on, my name felt distant. I started to see it as a 'girl's name' rather than my name. Out of the mouths of those I knew would not accept me it felt like a slur, an insult and total invalidation. When people said that I would always remain Liat to them, it felt like they would never see me for who I truly was, just merely the performance I had been. Once my name became my insult, there was no getting it back.

I spent a long time deciding on a name for the new me. It's difficult to choose your own name. I started making lists and searching Hebrew baby-name books. It was important to me that the name would be Hebrew as my Israeli heritage is central to my identity. I thought about Lior – close to my name; maybe too close. It would feel strange correcting people. Also, it's a gender-neutral name and it was very important to me to have a masculine name (whatever that means!). I read my list of new names to Tia, my partner. She didn't like any of them. But they were Hebrew and probably sounded very foreign and strange to her. I would have loved my mum to be a part of my name-choosing process, except she was not ready to face the reality of my transition.

I went away for the weekend to a Hebrew camp organised by my school, in which Israeli leaders came to teach us about topics relating to Israel. I asked one of them what her favourite Hebrew boy's name was and she said 'Nevo'. And something about it felt right. I also loved that it could be short-ened to Nev for those who couldn't correctly pronounce it. I told my close friends and Tia and I started living more comfortably in myself.

But my mother didn't know my name. I left the house and was Nevo, authentically and truthfully, and at home I was Liat, quiet, sad and hidden. Eventually my mum found out my new first name and I gave her the oppor-tunity to choose my middle name. That is how I became Nevo Amiel Zisin.

If it wasn't for the youth movement, Habo, I think it could have been easy for me to reject my Judaism, move north-side and assimilate into the queer community. I'm grateful that didn't happen. My Judaism is important to me; it's integral to everything I am and it's my community. Despite differences in ideologies and understandings, I trust the Jewish community. I know that should I ever need it, the Jewish community will be there for me.

My life has always revolved around community, and still does. Being raised with many wonderful people in my life has made me feel an important sense of belonging. Engaging in transgender and feminist activism within the Jewish community is vital for me. I have had many young queer Jewish people message me and ask for my help. I have loved being in Habo as a leader. Educating kids on essential and critical issues has made me a better person. I run programs on gender and sexuality, polyamory, privilege, femi-nism and other issues and there is plenty of space for me to do that.

The queer community is also integral to my existence. I could not comfortably assimilate into the Jewish community without embracing my queer identity. My queerness bleeds into my political position on many issues. In recent years, other trans and gender diverse people have been a lifeline for me in times of dysphoria and depression. Seeing people transcend gender binaries and fight to take them down fills me with inspiration and hope. I am surrounded by incredible activists changing the world. It helps me to keep going.

The queer community is not without its issues. I have spent a long time, and imagine I shall spend a long time in the future, trying to navigate my place in this community and within its politics. I have seen and experienced things that have made me feel unsettled. We need to find ways of engaging in political discussions that don't isolate people if they aren't knowledgeable enough, or happen to make mistakes. Similar to the Jewish community, I feel a responsibility for the problems that exist here. I am committed to changing it for the better, and also taking a step back on issues that don't directly affect me in the hope of supporting those who are affected.

It's amazing to be a part of two incredible communities. I am abundant in love and support. But sometimes, being part of both communities at once can feel tense. It doesn't always feel like I truly belong anywhere. My queer family will never understand what it means to be Jewish, and how I connect to my Israeli identity. At the same time, the Jewish community will never fully comprehend my life as a trans, queer, polyamorous person.

I am always trying to find ways to bring the communities together in my life, but often I am balancing the two on opposite ends of my identity and city – quite literally! I drive from the south-eastern suburbs to the northern suburbs multiple times a week. I still live with my mum. I am grounded in a community of Jewish people at my workplace, in my neighbourhood and at my movement. I feel like I am always explaining my identity in both worlds. But it's a process and I wouldn't change it. I have also made queer Jewish friends who feel similarly, and we are trying to navigate these two identities together. I hope I'll maintain balance between the two without having to compromise either, because they are both integral to who I am.

Excerpted with minor modifications from the autobiography Finding Nevo *by Nevo Zisin, 2017, Black Dog Books, Melbourne, Australia.*

Nevo Zisin – living their best life

Multicultural Multifaith LGBTIQ Group Snapshots

This section is a collection of short pieces from the multicultural groups that have been involved with the AGMC and/or advocate for specific cultural and spiritual queer communities. Please go to the AGMC website for full details about these groups, or go to the AGMC Forum to add your own group or to add any groups we've missed. Please use the Forum to update us on any of your group's future activities: www.forum.agmc.org.au.

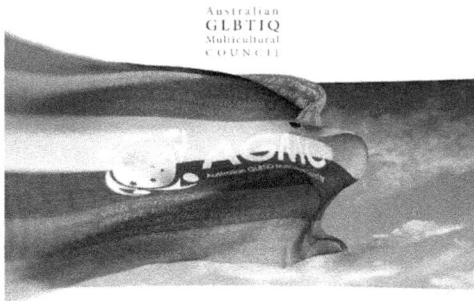

Earlier AGMC logos

Acceptance
Reconciling faith and sexuality
Benjamin Oh

Acceptance is a welcoming ministry of LGBTIQ Catholics, their families and friends, affirming their dignity and Catholic faith. It was founded in Sydney in 1972 by Garry Pye. By the mid 1980s, Acceptance had grown into a national organisation with chapters in Brisbane, Sydney, Canberra, Melbourne, Adelaide and Perth.

A national coordinator office was established in 1981. National conferences commenced soon after Acceptance Sydney was established, being held every two years for over 20 years.

Acceptance also supported other gay faith groups. The establishment of the Metropolitan Community Church in Sydney had its genesis in a visit to Sydney in 1974 by the Reverend Troy Perry from Metropolitan Community Church, USA. Garry Pye invited Troy, and Troy and his partner stayed with Garry in his house in Paddington.

Acceptance was also a founding member of the Gay Christian Network established in 1984.

Entering 45 years in ministry, Acceptance is an incorporated body managed by members for members, governed by a board of management committee.

A fundamental challenge for most gay Catholics is reconciling their faith and their sexuality. Garry experienced this struggle. Acceptance, therefore, has both a personal and a societal dimension. This is the reason why Garry Pye chose the name 'Acceptance'.

In Australia, groups of gay men and women began meeting in each other's houses for a monthly mass in the 1970s. Priests were invited to celebrate this mass, sometimes travelling long distances. At that time it was difficult for LGBTIQ Catholics to participate openly in the church, but the priests at these masses preached a gospel message that welcomed them as loved people of God.

Homosexuality in the 1980s was still illegal and opportunities for gays and lesbians to meet and socialise were limited. As Acceptance grew it needed a larger place for the gatherings and weekly mass. With a broadening range of activities – the establishment of a professional telephone counselling service, a choir, women's spirituality group and, for a while, a medical clinic – the pressure for more space grew.

Over the first two decades in Sydney, Acceptance moved to a number of venues around the inner city area. Sadly, due to the strong opposition of the Catholic Church in the Archdiocese of Sydney, Acceptance was not able to celebrate mass in a Catholic church until 1990.

With the assistance of other faith groups, and the links with other gay support groups established following the discovery of HIV in the mid 80s, Acceptance has been able to celebrate a weekly mass continuously since 1972. Acceptance advertises regularly in the gay press and the weekly suburban newspapers.

In describing the activities of those early days, the late Garry Pye said:

We have mass celebrated every Friday . . . Followed by a social hour of wine, coffee and conversation. We have recently started Human Rights Relations Groups, which are going well and looks like one way that our members can help themselves and others. We have social evenings, barbecues, theatre parties, prayer services. We have also started a monthly newsletter. [The newsletter was called Insight.]

Members of Acceptance marched in the first 1978 Mardi Gras protest parade and they have continued to march in every subsequent parade. In the mid 1980s, Acceptance formed as a separate group and entered a float into the parade.

A charity that has been supported by Acceptance for many years is Stanford House. Established by the Daughters of Charity nuns, it opened in August 1991 and provides supported accommodation for people living with HIV/AIDS.

Reinforced by official statements issued by the Vatican in 1975 and 1986, the Australian Catholic Church position remained opposed to the goals of Acceptance. In the 1970s and 1980s, members of Acceptance prepared many submissions to the church. In Brisbane, the Archbishop agreed to establish a formal dialogue group with Acceptance. Discussions also occurred with other priests and bishops. In South Australia, we remember the empowering work of Father Maurice Shinnick, including the publication of his book, *This Remarkable Gift: Being gay and Catholic* (1997), with the strong support of Archbishop Leonard Faulkner.

While the official position remains unchanged, Acceptance and its members remain confident in their faith and that the gospel values will lead to change.

At the Global Network of Rainbow Catholics' inaugural assembly, Acceptance Sydney was represented by board members Matthew Ng and Benjamin Oh, and by a member of the Acceptance Sydney community, Tim Smyth. Benjamin Oh is a member of the Board of Acceptance Sydney. Acceptance Sydney's members extend beyond the area of Sydney and include informal and formal membership. Formal members are paid voting members who participate in the decision-making of the organisation.

Acceptance offer thanks to the many members who have contributed to our history and this snapshot, which by no means is exhaustive or complete.

We pay tribute to the pioneers, advocates, leaders, lay, religious and ordained sisters and brothers whose tireless ministry and advocacy has led the positive social changes we continue to see being advanced today.

For more on Acceptance history and membership, please visit www.gaycatholic.com.au/history

Aleph
At the convergence of queerdom and Judaism
Michael Barnett

In 2003 I received an invitation to become involved in a conference to promote queer multiculturalism. I received the invitation through my involvement with Aleph Melbourne, then a social and support group just for gay and bisexual Jewish men, although now it is fully inclusive of all LGBTIQ people of Jewish heritage and their allies.

While the circumstances of the invitation are vague in my memory, I do recall that it was with excitement and enthusiasm that I accepted it and offered to get involved in the project. What is most memorable for me was meeting Cinzia Ambrosio, the driving force behind this visionary concept. Cinzia's passion and positivity were most remarkable. I don't think I'd met anyone before who just made things happen with remarkable clarity, integrity and brazen chutzpah. It really was eye-opening and awe-inspiring watching her in full flight.

And so it was that Cinzia brought together a vast and diverse team of people from every end of the queer and multicultural spectrum, with the vision of putting together a conference the following year. What I do remember of this time was the number of person-hours we collectively contributed and the tireless dedication to bringing the inaugural AGMC Conference to life at the St Kilda Town Hall in October 2004. It was quite an unstoppable force, and with Cinzia at the helm driving the project, her vision was being realised.

Just from my perspective, as a representative of Aleph, together with many Jewish volunteers, it was an exhilarating experience. And from the Jewish perspective, perhaps the icing on the cake was Rabbi Jonathan Keren-Black's presence among the many speakers. He delivered a presentation on how it was okay to be Jewish and queer. Hearing this from a rabbi was a rarity, and very welcome. While the progressive Jewish perspective is more accommodating of diversity, the orthodox Jewish perspective was diametrically opposed and my upbringing had been immersed in this less accepting perspective.

Other Jewish speakers at the conference included Adelaide Jewish

Lesbians activist and writer Margie Fischer, co-founder and producer of Feast queer arts and culture festival in Adelaide (see Knight, 2017), and Yiddish lesbian Hinde Ena Burstin. This was definitely the convergence of queerdom and multiculturalism, and it was very, very good.

The 2004 conference was a huge success and it brought together many great people to form a new community shared by both common and disparate cultural experiences. New friendships were made and old ones strengthened.

The following year the AGMC formed. The organisational structure was formalised, strategic allegiances were made, and a vision of bigger and better things was being set in place.

The next big project was the second conference in 2006, this time at the Northcote Town Hall. Again I was involved, maintaining my presence on the committee as secretary and representative of Aleph. Again, many months of planning and hard work went into bringing this conference to life, and it was a huge success, in quality if not in numbers. It was a major achievement and, considering the size of the organisation behind it, quite remarkable.

Perhaps most memorable for me from this conference was hearing addresses from both Graeme Inness and Michael Kirby. Also memorable was having my mother, Naomi Barnett, join a panel of parent speakers. She made me very proud.

Through my involvement in both conferences, and a number of smaller events, Aleph and I have been able to contribute toward the goals of Cinzia's vision. I sat on the committee for five years and gave many hours in a voluntary capacity to help make our diverse communities a better, more accepting place.

The AGMC has travelled for over a decade and it has come a light-year. I am honoured to have been part of this very important organisation, to have been part of Cinzia's vision and family, and to have made so many wonderful friends and companions over the years.

Over the years, I have seen the tide of intolerance change in the Jewish community and, increasingly, being queer is becoming accepted as normal. Not to say this is universal across the Jewish community; far from it in fact. But where there was once a lack of acceptance and understanding in some areas, now there is a desire to know more and to welcome with open arms.

Much work remains to be done to break down the barriers of ignorance and fear that prevent some communities from treating queers as equals. Pressure needs to be applied to community leaders. Politicians need to be lobbied. Education and quality research are imperative. And lastly, and most importantly, children need to be given role models of love and unconditional acceptance, to show them that all people are equal, irrespective of their religious background, cultural identity, gender expression, intersex status or sexual orientation.

In September 2013 my partner Gregory asked me to marry him. I accepted and we made plans to get married once the law changed in Australia. However, we later decided to get married in New Zealand, given there was no prospect of Australia changing the law any time soon. Together with a dozen of our family and friends from each side we declared our love for each other, and were married in a civil ceremony in picturesque Queenstown. Little did we know that the Australian government would pass Marriage Equality legislation in December 2017.

Whilst the passage of Marriage Equality in Australia allowed unwed same-sex couples the right to get married, we were not able to marry owing to having previously married under New Zealand law. Despite this, we had a recommitment ceremony on 10 February 2018, in front of friends and family, on Australian soil. We renewed our vows, cut a cake, danced a waltz, shared food and music, and celebrated our love, equally, and now legally recognised.

For Gregory and me, this brings to an end 13 years of intense activism. Rivalling the monumental achievement of seeing Marriage Equality become law was seeing the leadership of David Marlow and the Jewish community declare their support for Marriage Equality, at both state and national level. I often wonder if this would have come about without Aleph nipping at their heels. We will continue fighting for equality for all, but for now are satisfied with this outcome, despite the devastatingly damaging process the Australian government forced upon the queer community.

Aleph reached a significant milestone in 2015, being the 20th anniversary of the group's founding. To mark the occasion we embarked on an ambitious project, to make a documentary to capture the group's two-decade journey. With a generous grant from Glen Eira Council and funds donated by members of the community, we began a year-long process of sifting through archival material, interviewing group members, and enduring a painstaking production process in the making of 'Aleph Melbourne: Celebrating twenty years'. Testament to the success of the movie was acceptance to a range of film festivals both here and abroad, including the Belfast Human Rights Film Festival, the St Kilda Film Festival and several festivals in New York City.

In closing, it would be remiss not to mention two very important people who were and remain part of the AGMC family. One is Rochelle Millar. Rochelle was a dear friend to all and she lit up all of our lives. Rochelle succumbed to cancer in 2006.

The other is Bridget Dunn, life partner and best friend of Cinzia. Bridget was also a fixture at all AGMC events and she also lit up the room. Sadly Bridget also succumbed to cancer and died in 2012.

We will all miss Rochelle and Bridget forever. Our lives are diminished in their absence.

Michael and Gregory getting married in New Zealand

ArciLesbica

Not the only Italian lesbian in Australia

Elvira Andreoli

'Mamma mia, sono una lesbica!'

Growing up, I remember thinking I was the only Italian lesbian in the world. So I became very much indoctrinated through culture and religion into the understanding that I would one day get married, have children and never tell anyone – least of all my mamma! I thought maybe I'd tell the priest on my death bed or something dramatic like that.

Fortunately, thanks to ArciLesbica Australia, it did not turn out that way.

In my early 20s I heard about a group of Italian-Australian women who had started a social support network for LGBTIQ Italians. When I finally had the courage to call the number to find out what it was all about, I was greeted by a very friendly and warm voice quickly inviting me to a 'bring a plate' night. Then I found the courage to front up.

Immediately I felt like I was catching up with long lost friends or cousins. Apart from one person who I knew from a totally different circle of people, I didn't know anyone, yet immediately I felt safe and comfortable – I felt like these people were part of my mob.

I remember the food being way too much, the laughter being loud and the connections swift! We all poured out stories about being Italian and gay, about our parents, our culture, our fears, our joys, and so much more.

And so that was my first understanding that I was not the only Italian lesbian in Australia!

For a number of years I was involved in Italian social nights, dances, celebrations, picnics, marches, quiet 'bring a plate' nights and more. I was part of a women's musical trio, I Vagabondi, with Rita Leuzzi and Donata Biancofiore, playing and singing Italian traditional folksongs, often with feminist and/or queer twists to the lyrics! The connections at the time were invaluable for us all in different ways – it was a great opportunity to celebrate our culture in a safe yet familiar space.

Apart from the long-term friendships gained over the years, my favourite part of being involved in ArciLesbica Australia was when the new and shy people would come along – clearly new to the whole Italian-and-gay thing. It was very rewarding to see them make connections and open up to like-minded people. It was also particularly rewarding to receive phone calls from women who were in difficult situations, women I never got to meet, women who just wanted to talk to someone, to have someone say, 'It's okay that you are a lesbica, there are many Italian-Aussie lesbicas just like you. ArciLesbica, I Ragazzi, and I Ragazzi Girls are tools through which to connect with others just like you.' These friendships, partnerships and deep connections formed over the years are invaluable and have been pivotal for so many.

The ArciLesbica Origin Story

Stud Rd, Rowville, Victoria, pm, early 2002:

'Lara, this is Cinzia Ambrosio. I was told via the Italian and gay men's group that you were also interested in starting an Italian lesbian group?'

'Cinzia, no not interested but keep me in the loop regarding events and stuff'.

'Can I ask why, Lara?'

'I'm just too busy now and my life is undergoing change at this moment'.

'No worries and hope to see you around at some of our events'.

E mo?

'Betty (Greek Lesbian group) – what should I do?'

'Cinzia, hold an event and go from there. Desi and I will come for support'.

'Okay, I'll organise a dinner and invite the women on the list. Thanks, Betty.'

Lygon St – *mah* where else? Our first social event in March 2002 at the yummy restaurant Il Cammineto (it has since then ceased operation in Lygon St, but still operates from Moonee Ponds . . . *se non mi sbaglio*).

At that event: Silvana Giordano, Frances Indomenico, Grace, Lina, Sam, Mary, Lucy, Jen, Betty, Desi and Cinzia. The event enabled us to put faces to 'contact details', chat and eat yummy pizzas. Some of the women were timid, others boisterous as only some wogs can be, but we were determined to create and sustain a positive and safe space to celebrate our existence! The night ended with questions about whereto from here.

The whereto from here?

Our name: ArciLesbica Australia

(Pronounced ArchiLesbica. Definition *arch*: chief, superior [Oxford Dictionary, 1990] *lesbica*: lesbian.)

The name ArciLesbica was chosen in honor of our lesbian sisters in Italy (arcilesbica.it). We thought it was very apt and described, somewhat, who we were and are: Italian lesbians. Two women provided the initial euros (we got this money back after the group had some funds – we're not that generous!) to have our organisation listed in lesbian and gay publications, such as *Lesbians on the Loose* (*LOTL*) (lotl.com) and the then *Bnews* (now *Southern Star* – sstar.net.au).

We produced a quarterly members' newsletter, *Malafemmena* (bad woman – tongue in cheeky!), organised bocce afternoons, picnics, pasta sauce-making days, go-kart racing, in-house get-togethers and the main event: our annual dance held mid-year. We are also very active, politically speaking!

I dedicate this contribution to my old friend Franca whom I met through ArciLesbica Australia. Franca was an older Italian lesbian who served very much as a cultural mentor for many of us, providing support and advice, and sharing her own story. In 2015, Franca passed away after a long illness. She was very much a strong and endearing character in the Italian LGBTIQ community.

ArciLesbica picnic, left to right: Crescenzo Rillo, Elvira Andreoli and Franca

Australian Catholics for Equality (ACfE)

Broadening representation in public discourse

Benjamin Oh

Australian Catholics for Equality (ACfE) is a grassroots collective of Australian Catholic Christians sharing news, information, resources and advocating for the rights and dignity of LGBTIQ members of our community.

Our members and supporters come from the broad spectrum of the Australian Catholic Christian community. We celebrate the gifts and the lived experiences of LGBTIQ Catholics, our friends and families. Together, we campaign on issues including homophobic, transphobic discrimination and intersex exclusion; safer and inclusive schools and parishes; Marriage Equality; age discrimination against older LGBTIQ Australians; the plight of LGBTIQ refugees and asylum seekers; and family and domestic violence stemming from homophobic and transphobic violence.

We seek to broaden Catholic Christian representation in the Australian public discourse in enhancing a more affirming, diverse, authentic, inclusive Catholic perspective, especially on issues concerning LGBTIQ Catholics, our families, friends and allies.

We promote and encourage leadership that celebrates the lived experiences, as well as the value and gifts of LGBTIQ people. We affirm leadership that serves to empower LGBTIQ people, the poor, the marginalised, and also to advance the loving care of our environment and communities.

Australian Catholics for Equality is a multi-platform organisation with an active online forum where activists and organisers from across Australia meet, discuss and coordinate.

Benjamin Oh is the current chair of the Advisory Board. He founded Australian Catholics for Equality in 2014.

http://www.australiancatholicsforequality.org.

Gay Asian Proud
Making our communities a better place for all

Budi Sudarto

Gay Asian Proud (GAP) and the AGMC have worked together and with multicultural communities to create a safe space for multicultural LGBTIQ. Our aim is to ensure that no one feels they have to choose one community over the other. We strive toward the celebration and inclusion of our unique identities, to live without fear, and to love without barriers.

We would like to congratulate the AGMC on its almost 15th anniversary. Their dedication and hard work have resulted in many achievements, ensuring that multiculturalism is celebrated as an integral part of Melbourne's LGBTIQ community. GAP and the VAC have been proud supporters of the AGMC since its inception in 2003. What started as an organising committee for a conference on multiculturalism in the LGBTIQ community has become an influential organisation advocating for greater social inclusion irrespective of sexuality, gender, race, ethnicity and religion. This is in accordance with VAC values of upholding social justice for all.

Both GAP and the AGMC continue our collaborative approach to addressing the many issues faced by multicultural members of the LGBTIQ community. Gay Asian men in particular often experience sexual exclusion and/or objectification. Ongoing exposure to racial prejudices often result in feeling isolated and alienated from the mainstream LGBTIQ community. This has a detrimental effect on our health and wellbeing, for example through internalised stigma and low self-esteem. Expressions such as 'no Asians' and 'can't even speak English properly' are just some examples of the persistent racial discrimination that exists in the LGBTIQ community and Australian society at large.

Community education, public forums and conferences, and ongoing dialogues through social media are just some ways that we educate and empower the community to say 'No' to racism. We are advocating for a cultural shift within the LGBTIQ community.

Stigma and prejudice also exist within our own cultural communities.

Homophobia, biphobia and transphobia often result in double discrimination, where we feel discriminated against on the basis of our diverse sexuality and gender identities as well as our cultural identities. We constantly have to navigate multiple identities, which can be a daunting process that negatively impacts our overall wellbeing.

It is through active collaboration and shared vision that we continue our work, irrespective of the many challenges we face. Even though there have been many positive changes in both the LGBTIQ and cultural communities since 2003, there is still more to be done. We want to ensure that our voices are heard and not silenced. We strive toward creating a better world for the younger generation, including LGBTIQ international students, and we can achieve this by laying a strong foundation embracing our uniqueness instead of focusing on our differences.

Congratulations AGMC. We look forward to continuing our partnership in the years to come. Together, we can make our communities a better place for all.

At the time of writing, Budi Sudarto was the Peer Education Coordinator at VAC with a multicultural portfolio, including running Gay Asian Proud and maintaining partnership with the AGMC and other multicultural LGBTIQ support groups.

Gay Asian Proud
is a social
group for gay and
same-sex attracted
men of Asian
backgrounds.

We meet once a
month in a welcoming
and supportive
environment.

Partners and friends
are welcomed.

Want to find out more?
Contact 9865 6700
peer_ed@vicaids.asn.au
vicaids.asn.au/peer-education

@peer_ed_vicaids

Victorian
AIDS Council /
Gay Men's
Health Centre

Budi's treasured possession – signed by Penny Wong!

GLBTIQ Interfaith Intercultural Network
Advocating against discriminatory practice
Benjamin Oh

The GLBTIQ Interfaith Intercultural Network (GIIN) is an advocacy network that speaks on the basis of conscience with the authority of our diverse lived experiences of the consequences of religious, cultural and civil (legal) forms of discrimination. We know that once a precedent of discriminatory practice has been created, it can be extended to discriminate against additional groups. We do not wish for that to happen.

GIIN was founded in 2015 and brings together Australian leaders and organisers of LGBTIQ and ally community groups that are faith led or culturally led. Our network consists of leaders from organisations and groups not limited to:

Asian Australian Alliance – Asian Australian Rainbow Alliance

Uniting Network

Trikone Australasia

Muslims Against Homophobia

Marhaba Melbourne

Rainbow Catholics InterAgency for Ministry

Arab Council of Australia

Sydney Queer Muslims

Rosh Pinah: Orthodox Jewish Network

Dayenu

Metropolitan Community Churches

Equal Voices

Benjamin Oh, first person, front row left

Greek and Gay Support Network
A voice for equality and recognition

John Tzimas

Over more than 21 years, the Greek and Gay Support Network (GGSN) has been a voice and a source of support for the Greek LGBTIQ community, putting on events such as the annual United We Dance. This is our way, as a united multicultural community, to give back to the LGBTIQ community that has supported us all and to show everyone that regardless of our cultural and spiritual backgrounds, we can work and party together in harmony.

The GGSN has had a role on the AGMC, has worked with other multicultural organisations in Melbourne, and has organised events that educate, raise awareness, and celebrate. It comprises the Greek and Gay Group (GGG – the guys' group) and Greek Australian Lesbians (GAλS). In 2003, GGG and GAλS were invited to join the AGMC committee and be the voice of the Greek LGBTIQ community. John Tzimas and Betty Mathiopoulos represented the groups until the conference in October 2004. Being part of this committee was a very rewarding experience for the individuals involved and our groups received exposure. We found that we were not alone with the myriad issues we experience as LGBTIQ Greeks; people from many other cultures had similar experiences. We learnt from each other's experiences and reported back to our groups on how others were facing the same issues.

The conference committee encouraged us to communicate with other Greek organisations and community groups in Melbourne and develop stronger ties with the Greek press and peak organisations. At the time some of these were more encouraging than others.

This is how our relationship with the AGMC began. It didn't end with the conference however. Over the last 14 years a Greek voice has nearly always been on the AGMC Committee and it is with pride that we have been given the opportunity to be involved in its extensive work for the AGMC. We have given our time to assist at AGMC events but it hasn't been a one-way relationship; the AGMC has assisted us with securing space and exposure at

Midsumma Festival, Pride March and ChillOut Carnival days. Without the financial contribution made by the AGMC we may not have been able to have a presence at these events. In addition it was always great to work with the other groups at these events and even compete over who had the best music and desserts. We had an amazing time.

So where are we all now and where are we going? In 2013, we Greeks officially took on the challenge of Gay Marriage at Pride March with our slogan 'Και στα διχα μας' (Best wishes on our wedding day). Our committee is expanding with new and fresh faces, our membership has increased to more than 300, and the support from our membership is growing. GGSN is still heavily supported by VAC and our relationship with the AGMC is also strengthening. Our presence on Facebook continues to grow as does the interaction via our website www.greekandgay.com. We have also established an online forum to support members as the need arises.

Our 21st anniversary took place in 2016 and for the first time in our history we celebrated with a very successful Greek Dinner Dance. Three hundred and thirty members, family and friends partied like only Greeks can; an amazing night was had by all. The coming years will see us venture into new territory. We are planning to work with other local Greek organisations to reduce the stigma still experienced from our own Greek community. It's a huge challenge but one that we are determined to take on.

Where do we see ourselves in 10 or 20 years time? It is really our hope that the need for a group like ours will have disappeared. We hope that by then there will be no discrimination against LGBTIQ individuals and, in particular, we hope and pray that by then the wider Greek community in Australia has embraced its LGBTIQ brothers, sisters, children and parents. Some of us may even be grandparents by then and wouldn't that be an amazing way to celebrate our achievements. Those who have come before us deserve a very big thank you; without their outspoken voices we wouldn't be where we are today. Should life not eventuate this way, then we Greeks will be there to keep pushing the message for equality and recognition for who we are – proud Greek Australians who happen to identify as LGBTIQ.

Finally, on a personal note, my involvement with the AGMC covered a 10-year period. Once we incorporated I signed on as Vice-President and later became Treasurer. The AGMC has taught me so much over that time, including appreciating other cultures and diverse opinions on both LGBTIQ and multicultural issues; dealing with government agencies; and organising conferences, forums and other events. AGMC involvement has also given me an avenue to tell my story of growing up as a Greek gay guy, and has given me the strength and support to grow even further and start breaking down the barriers within the Greek community.

GΑλS — GREEK AUSTRALIAN LESBIANS

GGG — GREEK and GAY GROUP

Helem

For peace and acceptance

Adam Messede

I have always hoped that, in my lifetime, I will see peace and acceptance, not just in the Arab LGBTIQ communities but all around the world.

I first got involved with the AGMC in April 2003. John from the Greek and Gay Support Network introduced me to the AGMC. At the time I was involved with the original Arab and Gay group, which ran until 2008. We then re-established Helem Melbourne in 2012, which received much appreciated support from the AGMC. Helem meets monthly and supplies a safe and comfortable space for any Arabs from the LGBTIQ community to voice their opinion or concerns.

The AGMC has given us support, confidence and friendship. It has provided information on how to set up the group and network with other LGBTIQ groups or events. The committee has also been very generous in supplying a fully functioning website for the group.

The AGMC has been important to me personally. I arrived from Lebanon in 1994 as a married man and have a 24-year-old son from the marriage. I have been proud to be a paying member of AGMC for the last 12 years.

While it is still early days, we now have a global website, which means we now have a global voice and can reach out and support many Arab people in the LGBTIQ international community.

I Ragazzi
Establishing and supporting the Italian group
Tony Mordini

The AGMC has provided valuable support to I Ragazzi, from helping to establish this important Italian support group, to breathing new life into it and setting it up for a bright future.

I Ragazzi represents the gay Italian men of Melbourne. The AGMC was instrumental in helping the group establish, find a voice, and build its presence in the Italian community, the LGBTIQ community and the wider community.

The group became involved with the AGMC through the Greek group, which reached out and encouraged them to create their own group and build a presence within the LGBTIQ community. Initially this was done through an approach to Marco who then brought others into the group, including 'Merlot', David, Angelo and Joe. Some of the Italian lesbian women were also helpful in getting the men's group started.

The AGMC has helped to advertise I Ragazzi events and, through its networks, connect Italian men to the group. Through the AGMC, the group has been able to tap into funding which has helped with events and printing resources. The AGEDO project was a very successful example of the AGMC working closely with the Italian LGBTIQ community. AGEDO (*Associazione, parenti e amici di omosessuali, bisessuali e trans*) is Italy's national body of parents and friends of LGBTIQ individuals. It plays a key role in supporting this community through education, support and advocacy. On the day of the workshop, which included food and dancing to Elvira Andreoli's 'I Vagabondi', a video – *Due Volte Genitori* (*Twice Parents*) by Claudio Cipelletti – was used to provide a series of Italian narratives. A group of parents spoke about the journeys they and their children went through. Ultimately they had to start again as parents (as the title indicates) to re-connect with their children and embrace a fuller and more nuanced understanding of their identity. These narratives provided insights and helped to illustrate that ultimately our children deserve love and acceptance irrespective of their sexual or gender identity. Our role as parents is to support them through their journey and be the best ally we can be.

The AGMC also helped to connect I Ragazzi to other groups, such as Helem andAleph which, through Michael Barnett, has provided assistance with publicity materials.

Without the AGMC, I Ragazzi would not have formed and would not have had publicity, access to funding and moral and other support. The AGMC has, for example, linked I Ragazzi with media agencies such as *Southern Star* and JOY FM, and gay men's health advocates such as the VAC.

Photo by Rob Chiarolli

Jewish Community Council of Victoria LGBTI Reference Group
Advocating for equality and inclusion

Doron Abramovici

Over the past decade, the Jewish Community Council of Victoria (JCCV) has been developing strategies, resources and responses that aim to end discrimination and promote equality and inclusion.

Under the direction and chairmanship of former president, John Searle, and at his invitation in 2009, Julie Leder, Andrew Rajcher, Sally Goldner, Nathan Rose and I joined the first LGBTI Reference Group established by a Jewish community roof body in Australia. The JCCV set up this group to ensure that the voices of LGBTI Jews in Victoria are heard and represented, and to support the eradication of discrimination and vilification.

The LGBTI Reference Group's first report in 2011 spoke to a wide array of Jewish school principals, community organisations and rabbis, and recommended strategies to minimise discrimination and vilification in extension to existing policies by focusing on the damage caused by intolerance and vilification to people's mental health. Most community leaders, including orthodox leaders, were able to distinguish between their personal religious beliefs and their professional conduct. This was a significant shift to a decade prior.

Two years later, under President Nina Bassat, AM, the JCCV encouraged affiliates and other organisations within the Victorian Jewish community to endorse the 'No to Homophobia' campaign with about 26 Jewish community organisations signing up to the campaign. A year later, the JCCV was awarded a HEY grant from the Youth Affairs Council of Victoria and in 2015 President Jennifer Huppert oversaw this project. This also marked my first year as a board member of the JCCV with responsibility for the Social Inclusion portfolio. With David Marlow as Executive Director of JCCV, the project produced three key outcomes:

- a diverse community forum represented by LGBTI panelists with 80 attendees, followed by breakout sessions

- a youth group JADE and video competition for students and young adults
- a community LGBTI services directory.

Also in 2015, Keshet Australia, a Jewish organisation that provides educational outreach on LGBTI issues, became the first LGBTI organisation to be admitted to the JCCV as an affiliate.

In 2017, the JCCV issued a statement in support of civil Marriage Equality and was delighted by the enactment of civil Marriage Equality legislation before year end. Today, the JCCV's role in advocating for LGBTI Jews and interfaith relations is paramount as inclusive practices, while monumentally accepted, may not be fully embedded. The JCCV looks forward to further discussions with members of the LGBTI community, interfaith community and politicians on all sides with respect to the significant, non-partisan issue of equality and inclusion.

JEWISH COMMUNITY COUNCIL
OF VICTORIA INC

Jewish Lesbian Group of Victoria (JLGV)

Honouring and celebrating diversity

Hinde Ena Burstin

The Jewish Lesbian Group of Victoria (JLGV) began meeting in 1992 and has been a ground-breaker and an inspiration ever since.

JLGV was the first Jewish LGBTIQ group in Victoria. From the beginning, we were passionate about honouring and celebrating diversity, both within our group, and among lesbian, feminist and LGBTIQ communities. We were active in lesbian multicultural groups InterNESBian and DARE, and in the 'Sappho was a Wog Grrl' conference in 1995. We initiated and facilitated a range of multicultural lesbian events, including the Multi-Culti Lesbian Party in 2001, and presented many workshops and conference papers on cultural diversity and countering discrimination.

JLGV was the first Jewish group to march at Pride March and Mardi Gras, the first LGBTIQ group to have a visible presence at the Jewish community's annual festival, 'In One Voice: Concert in the Park', and the first group to hold public events within the Melbourne Jewish community on LGBTIQ issues. Our presence as an out-and-proud group has inspired other culturally and linguistically marginalised (CALM) lesbian groups, as well as other Jewish LGBTIQ groups, including Aleph Melbourne, Dayenu and Keshet.

As our twentieth anniversary approached in 2012, we realised that our many acts of courage needed to be celebrated and preserved. We produced the documentary film *It's Who We Are: Celebrating 20 years of the Jewish Lesbian Group of Victoria* as a record of our ground-breaking achievements as a grass-roots collective of Jewish lesbians who challenged and changed Jewish, lesbian, queer and feminist communities, and created a community for ourselves. Our film is a joyful celebration of our culture, our community and all aspects of who we are. Our world premiere at Melbourne Queer Film Festival in 2014 played to a full house. *It's Who We Are* has since screened as far afield as the United States and India. Sharing our stories can increase awareness and create powerful connections across communities. This passion for connection across our differences is at the core of our involvement in the AGMC.

When the AGMC was established, JLGV played an active role through the invaluable contribution of the late, great Rochelle Millar (*a'h*), a much-loved and highly committed representative of our group. Rochelle was one of the principle advocates of the AGMC, serving as a conduit between JLGV and the AGMC.

JLGV has contributed significantly to the AGMC, and particularly to the 2004 AGMC conference, 'Living and Loving in Diversity'. Rochelle was a key player in the organising group and a tireless worker for the AGMC and the conference. We also contributed Jewish humour to the conference through group member Hinde Ena Burstin's performance, *Boobas for Babies*, playing a Jewish grandmother fighting against the (then) ban on assisted insemination for lesbians.

JLGV has participated in the AGMC stall at the annual Midsumma Festival, and has contributed recipes to the AGMC cookbook. JLGV members have been among the few lesbians to attend the United We Dance parties.

The AGMC is an umbrella group for diverse LGBTIQ CALM groups and provides an invaluable resource in connecting individuals with groups. It can also be a powerful lobby group for our communities. JLGV commends AGMC for its ongoing work and recognises the significant contribution being made by the dedicated volunteers who make up this organisation. We would like to see the AGMC focus on women's issues and resources, and involve more women in the organisation.

We hope that the AGMC will continue to be bold in educating and agitating for the rights of LGBTIQ and CALM groups and issues within the community. We hope too, that the AGMC will remain a strong advocate, speaking out fearlessly against the oppression of LGBTIQs that is being enshrined in legislation and in practice in many countries around the world. The AGMC has an important voice to raise in highlighting the persecution of LGBTIQ asylum seekers, and demanding freedom, safety and an end to human rights abuses, for all asylum seekers. This is a crucial role of the AGMC today and into the future.

In a time of backlash against LGBTIQs and against cultural diversity, we all need to ensure that our needs and our issues don't disappear from the agenda. We believe this book will be an important community resource. We hope it will also reinvigorate much-needed discussion on cultural diversity and discrimination. JLGV looks forward to many more years working on these issues with the AGMC! We hope the AGMC will continue to exist *biz 120* – until 120!

In loving memory of dynamic JLGV founding member Sara Elkas (1949–2017) and dedicated JLGV member Rochelle Millar (1952–2006).

Sara Elkas and Rochelle Millar

Keshet

A safe environment for LGBTIQ Jews

Jonathan Barnett

Education is critical to challenging discrimination and promoting under-standing within families and communities.

Keshet Australia is committed to challenging the ongoing prejudice and discrimination within the Jewish community, helping Jews who may or may not feel able to come out. We have an array of engaging education campaigns and initiatives for, and developed in partnership with, Jewish communal organisations, especially schools, youth movements, aged care homes, and synagogues.

Our primary goal is to help nurture, protect and provide a safe environment for LGBTIQ Jews, children and adults. We need to do this to keep families together. We need to do this to keep our LGBTIQ Jewish friends within Judaism (no matter what their affiliation) and not drive them away.

Children

We offer educational programs to teach rabbis, educators and youth leaders how to support LGBTIQ Jewish children.

Parents

Keshet Parents helps families learn to work with and embrace the hopes and dreams of their LGBTIQ offspring, and to deal with the challenges of being parents of LGBTIQ children.

Community

Keshet Australia's community focus is on educating the Australian Jewish community about LGBTIQ Jews; about their needs, issues, desires and strivings as they try to remain part of our Jewish community.

We also work with and support the following groups:

- Keshet USA (keshetonline.org) – the home of the Keshet group in the US

- OrthoGays (orthogays.tripod.com) – online home of Orthodox gay Jewish men
- OrthoDykes (orthodykes.org) – online home of Orthodox Jewish lesbians
- Building LGBTI connections with Israel (awiderbridge.org)
- Twice Blessed Online Resources – archive and list of resources on Jewish LGBT topics (onearchives.org/twiceblessed/)
- World Congress of LGBT Jews (glbtjews.org)
- International Association of Lesbian and Gay Children of Holocaust Survivors
- Dayenu (dayenu.org.au) – group for Jewish gays and lesbians and their partners, friends and family, Sydney
- The Shefa Network (shefanetwork.blogspot.com.au) – a site that brings together 'dreamers from within the Conservative Movement' and provides extensive LGBTQ resources
- TransTorah (transtorah.org) – supports people of all genders to fully access and transform Jewish tradition, and helps Jewish communities to be welcoming sanctuaries for people of all genders.

Keshet קשת — WORKING FOR GLBT IN AUSTRALIA

LGBTIQ+ Latin Americans and Hispanics in Australia

'respeto y la diversidad'

Cristian Cortes Garzon

Cultural and community groups can provide a place of belonging and give voice to marginalised people. A relatively new cultural group, LGBTIQ+ Latin Americans and Hispanics in Australia, has been very active in advocating for the rights to freedom, equality and self-expression.

The LGBTIQ+ Latin Americans and Hispanics in Australia group started as a project early in 2015. Our members come from different countries in Latin America and are of diverse ages, genders and sexualities. We have created a permanent working group to build connections, provide information, make referrals to support and community services, and to identify issues that our community faces in Australia. This committee aims to build connections with other community organisations and to grow our capacity to advocate government, businesses and mainstream NGO partners.

The group's first official activity was our inaugural meeting in July 2016 at the Multicultural Hub in Melbourne. This was a very important milestone and all attendees were motivated and eager to engage. At this first meeting we discussed the purpose of the group and listened to the needs of the community. Through this process, some of the needs which were identified and with which we now work to meet include:

Having a place: to meet new people, socialise, share food, dance, celebrate Latin-American culture, maintain Spanish proficiency, and network. We aim to support our members and represent and promote Latin-American culture while providing a space to socialise and have meaningful conversation.

Be a community: to have our voice heard and to promote Latin-American culture in the wider community. This involved the creation of a representative body that advocates, participates, organises and builds on the strengths and experiences of Latin people by Latin people. In forming a community, the members expect to feel supported while also providing support for those who need it, such as new members and international students, which in turn creates a strong sense of belonging.

Resources: this includes forming an LGBTIQ+ advocacy and representative body, having a newsletter and an orientation guide to provide information about studying, work, taxes and visas, as well as creating an introduction to coming out.

Events: organising social events, activities for the social good and opportunities to educate the Latin and wider community about Latin-American and Hispanic LGBTIQ+ issues. Some ideas for activities are a same-sex salsa and a Latin queer dance night held at gay venues, a Latin-themed community dinner, Spanish/English language tutorials, a potluck sharing food from Latin-American countries, casual coffee dates with other LGBTIQ+ Latin Americans and outdoor activities.

Other needs: consultation meetings when advocacy opportunities arise, making relationships with other organisations, such as LGBTI and Latin-American organisations.

Political involvement: one of our members from Mexico, Asiel Adan, gave a strong and moving speech at a memorial service in Federation Square, remembering the predominantly Latin and Hispanic LGBTIQ+ victims of the Orlando shooting massacre. Some other members have been quite vocal at Latin-American multicultural communities speaking on SBS radio in Spanish and Portuguese.

We also organised the first protest from an LGBTIQ group from Latin-American and Hispanic backgrounds in Australia. The group gathered in Federation Square on the 19 August 2017 to demonstrate the unity of the LGBTIQ community and its allies. We were protesting for the rights to freedom, equality and self-expression. The gathering aimed to advocate, show solidarity and to act as a call to arms for the promotion of LGBTIQ rights in all Latin-American countries, Australia and around the world.

We expect the group to grow and will keep organising activities. Hopefully in the future we will be able to apply for funding and develop further activities for this population in Victoria and Australia.

'Que viva la paz, la tolerancia, el respeto y la diversidad.'

Website: www.lahrc.net; Facebook page: https://www.facebook.com/ LAHRCAustralia

Muslim Collective
A Muslim voice on contemporary issues

Reem Sweid

Muslim Collective's (MC) mission is to embody and be an effective voice of the traditional Quranic ideals of human dignity, egalitarianism, compassion and love for all humanity and the world. Any interpretations of the Quran or *hadiths* (sayings of the Prophet Muhammad) that contradict the divine message of love, kindness and mercy are incompatible with Islam.

We are part of a global community of Muslims. MC is an entirely grass-roots and volunteer-run organisation. The first ever MC was set up in the USA in 2007. Since then chapters have opened all over the world. In Australia, MC is a thriving community of Muslims which aims to establish and nurture vibrant Muslim communities across the country by creating opportunities for religious discourse, volunteer and community activities, and cultural events bringing together the arts, spirituality and social activism.

MC is a progressive Muslim voice on contemporary issues. We voice our perspectives by participating in civil discourse, engaging with the media and government entities, and by partnering with both Muslim and non-Muslim progressive organisations.

People often wonder why we use the term 'progressive' to define our values. What does 'progressive' even mean? And how does it reflect what we stand for? The Merriam-Webster dictionary defines the adjective *progressive* as: moving forward; happening or developing gradually over a period of time; and using or interested in new or modern ideas especially in politics and education. As Muslims for progressive values, we apply the progressive approach to understanding the Quran and the *hadiths*. For example, in relation to gender equality, we believe the Quran was leading the way in emancipating women (for example by giving them agency, rights to inherit and divorce). As Muslims we should continue on this trajectory of emancipating women just as our ancestors did with attitudes toward slavery.

Using a *progressive* approach to understand our *deen* means we continually return to the intentions and values that the Quran was espousing: compassion, justice, kindness, modesty, benevolence. By approaching our texts this way, we believe that rather than holding Islam back by insisting practices and beliefs stay stagnant, we are in fact being true to its message and *progressing* the religion so it can stay relevant to all humankind and for all times.

We promote theologically sound frameworks for Islamic liberalism. We seek to reinvigorate the Islamic tradition of *ijtihad* (critical engagement and interpretation of sacred texts) and intellectual discourse. We do this by collaborating with religious scholars and developing position papers on theological issues that are accessible to a wide audience. We call for critical engagement with Islamic scripture, traditional jurisprudence, and current Muslim discourses. We believe that critical thinking is essential to spiritual development.

We accept as Muslim anyone who identifies as such. The veracity and integrity of that claim is between the individual and God, and is not a matter for the state nor an issue other individuals can or should judge. We welcome all who are interested in discussing, promoting and working for the implementation of progressive values – human rights, freedom of expression, separation of religion and state – as well as inclusive and tolerant understandings of Islam. We believe that freedom of conscience is not only essential to all human societies but integral to the Quranic view of humanity. We believe that secular government is the only way to achieve the Islamic ideal of freedom from compulsion in matters of faith.

We affirm the equal worth of all human beings, regardless of race, sex, gender, gender identification, ethnicity, nationality, creed, sexual orientation, or ability. We are committed to work toward global societies that ensure social, political, educational and economic opportunities for all.

We support freedom of expression and freedom of dissent. No one should be legally prosecuted, imprisoned or detained for declaring or promoting unpopular opinions whether political, artistic, social or religious, even when that expression may be offensive and that dissent may be considered blasphemous. We affirm that one's religion and belief system are not the exclusive source of truth. We engage with a diversity of philosophical and spiritual traditions to pursue a more just, peaceful and sustainable world.

We are committed to social, economic, environmental justice and ethical treatment of animals. We believe that the full self-realisation of all people, in a safe and sustainable world, is a prerequisite for freedom, civility and peace. We support efforts for universal health care, universal public education, the protection of our environment and the eradication of poverty. We repudiate violence, whether on an individual, organisational or national level.

We support women's agency and self-determination in every aspect of their lives. We believe in women's full participation in society at every level. We affirm our commitment to reproductive justice and empowering women to make healthy decisions regarding their bodies, sexuality and reproduction.

We endorse the human and civil rights of LGBTIQ individuals. We affirm our commitment to ending discrimination based on sexual orientation and gender identity and we support full equality and inclusion of all individuals, regardless of sexual orientation or gender identity, in society and in the Muslim community. For example, MC provided postal addresses for Muslims feeling at risk if they voted Yes for Marriage Equality in their family homes.

In 2017, MC received a grant from the Multicultural Affairs and Social Cohesion Division (MASC) in the Victorian State Department of Premier and Cabinet. The purpose of this grant was to improve the understanding of the unique service needs and delivery requirements for vulnerable members of the Muslim LGBTIQ community, and how LGBTIQ and Muslim support services can best support the LGBTIQ Muslim community. In conjunction with the AGMC via its queer Muslim members and their wider networks, and with AGMC committee member Maria Pallotta-Chiarolli as researcher, interviews were conducted with LGBTIQ Muslims and LGBTIQ Muslim community leaders, and the report *Safe Spaces, Inclusive Services: Service access and engagement by LGBTIQ+ Muslims* (Pallotta-Charolli, 2018) is now available and being put to good use.

Muslim Collective.
Reason · Compassion · Progress

Queer Muslims in Australia Yahoo! Group

A first in Australia

Alyena Mohummadally

The Queer Muslims in Australia Yahoo! Group wouldn't exist if it wasn't for the AGMC. That I'm sure of. And I can be sure because I founded the Yahoo group in 2005.

Once I became part of the AGMC and started speaking out publicly, I knew I needed a group to also be there for me and others. So in 2005, a friend and I created a Yahoo! group. We made a blurb. Invited people we knew. Allowed for anonymity. And over the years I refined it with many different moderators – even creating a code of conduct that members had to agree to before signing up. The Code of Conduct accepted and celebrated, for example, that Muslims from Pakistan would and do have a culturally different understanding of the religion to Muslims from Indonesia. Or Lebanon. Or Iran. And so on.

This group was also important because if you Googled 'Queer Muslims in Australia' before 2005, only groups in England, Canada and the USA would come up in your search. No Australian groups. I knew I couldn't be the only queer Muslim in Australia and by creating the group and spreading the flyer among my contacts, people started joining and continue to do so till this day. We aren't a huge group, roughly 200 members, but we come from all over Australia.

Since 2014, new queer Muslim groups have started up in Australia. I support this as the more groups, the more voice we have. Groups like Imaan, Marhaba Melbourne, Sydney Queer Muslims Facebook, the Inner Circle, the Global Queer Muslim Network and many others are standing up to conservative Islamic interpretations of the Quran.

More Imams are coming out as gay and preaching that homosexuality isn't condemned in Islam. They push for a more liberal interpretation of the Quran and empower mosques to welcome sexual minorities. Nur Warsame is Australia's first out gay Imam. He is the convener of Marhaba in Melbourne, a social support group established in 2014, which focuses on the welfare of

LGBTIQ Muslims and has an increasing number of members from across Australia and New Zealand.

I am ready to 'retire'. To close the Yahoo! group down. With the expansion of the internet, do we really need the Queer Muslims in Australia Yahoo! Group anymore? But every time I get close to removing this online, safe cyberspace, I have messages sent to me asking me not to. Reminding me that online safe cyberspaces are just as needed as public spaces. That for some queer Muslims, the Yahoo! group is the only space they have to be themselves and meet others online. The Yahoo! group knows that I speak publicly, that I have been filmed on mainstream media, that a Google search of my name can link to the group. But the online group space they know is still safe, as no details of members are ever shared and you can use a pseudonym to join up.

And so the Queer Muslims in Australia Yahoo! Group continues to exist.

Website: https://groups.yahoo.com/neo/groups/queermuslims/info

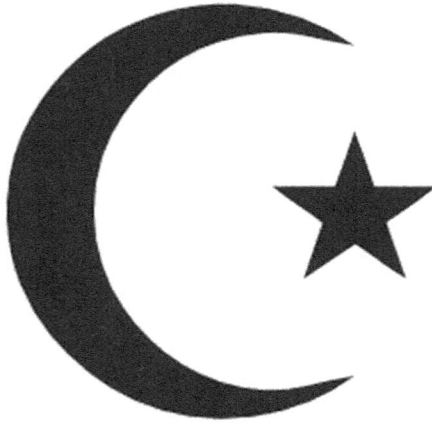

Rainbow Catholics InterAgency for Ministry

Equality and justice for LGBTIQ Catholics

Benjamin Oh

Rainbow Catholics InterAgency for Ministry (RCiA) was founded in 2015 to build relationships and dialogue, pray, educate and advocate for human rights and for full equality and justice for LGBTIQ Catholics, their families and allies in the Catholic Church and in the Australian community.

LGBTIQ Catholics continue to face discrimination within our Catholic community. While RCiA works for reform from within the church, following the Gospel and Catholic social teachings, we oppose all forms of discrimination against LGBTIQ people.

Members of RCiA are clergy, religious and lay people in active ministry and working with LGBTIQ Catholics, their families and allies. Our members work together to provide multi-agency support, share resources, celebrate the gifts and uphold the dignity of LGBTIQ Catholics and their loved ones.

Currently RCiA membership includes three LGBTIQ Catholic organisations and four working groups for inclusive parishes and safe schools; pastoral networks; parents, families and friends; and policy and dialogues.

I am the founder and chair of the RCiA. There are currently 10 co-convenors representing the various stakeholder Catholic groups.

At the historic world-first Catholic apology given to LGBTIQ people through a lamentation liturgy. From left: Benjamin Oh; Justin Koonin, AIDS Council of NSW president; Chris Pycroft, Gay and Lesbian Rights Lobby (GLRL) co-convenor; and Father Peter Maher, St Joseph Catholic Church Parish Priest.

Rosh Pinah
An affirming Orthodox Jewish network
Valuing lives and loves

Gavriel Ansara

As founding coordinator of Rosh Pinah, I would like to offer this information and reflection.

Rosh Pinah is an Australian network for Orthodox and/or traditionally observant Jews who have same-gender loves, trans and/or non-binary gender experiences or identities, and/or intersex bodies. This includes people who describe themselves as LGBTI, non-binary, as well as people who feel these terms are not culturally appropriate to describe their relationships, bodies, genders, and lives. Our name comes from the Hebrew word for cornerstone, from this line in Tehillim (Psalms) 118:22, translated in English as: 'The stone the builders rejected has become the cornerstone.'

Orthodox Jews of same-gender loves, of trans and/or non-binary experience, and those who are intersex people are the cornerstones who have inspired our religious and communal leaders to develop their compassion, moral courage, and *halachic* (Jewish legal) skill in finding liveable solutions for communal inclusion. We are not the rejected stones, but spiritual human beings who are essential partners in joining and healing Klal Yisrael (our entire people).

We live a *halachic* Jewish lifestyle. We defy the stereotypes about us in both LGBTIQ and Orthodox Jewish spaces. Many of us are from Edot HaMizrach and Sefardic backgrounds; we defy the stereotypes that all Jews are white Anglo or European. We range in skin tone from dark brown to olive to those of us with variable skin tone from brown to pale depending on the weather and season. We come from every region in the world, from Africa to Asia to South America. We create an affirming existence and support each other in living authentic, sacred lives. We are not a contradiction. We are your people, too. Come listen to us and value our lives and loves. http://myroshpinah.org.

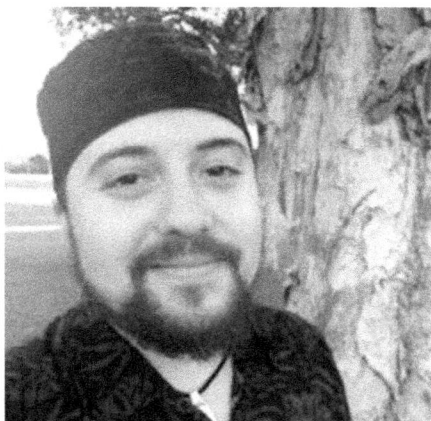

Southern European and Latin Gay Men's Group
The beginnings of a movement (1990–1995)

Vic Perri

The beginning

A chance meeting in a nightclub in the early 1990s sparked the development of an idea and then the reality of a group supporting gay and ethnic communities in Melbourne.

The first of its type in Australia and believed to be the first internationally, the Southern European and Latin Gay Men's Group (SEALGM) was a social and support group for gay men. The aim was to provide a safe and confidential environment for gay men from southern European and Latin backgrounds. At regular meetings we discussed our health and wellbeing and organised socials events for the gay and ethnic communities.

The objectives of SEALGM were to:
- improve our own self-esteem and confidence in being gay and from a non-Anglo background
- reduce stigma and discrimination in the queer community through our own educational and social events
- reduce stigma and discrimination in culturally diverse communities in the same way.

It was 1990 in Mandate, a popular gay men's nightclub, where I bumped into an acquaintance. We were speaking loudly in order to hear ourselves, as one does in a club, and as if by osmosis, one, then two, and then even more of our friends and acquaintances joined in. The conversations developed into banter, with all of us realising that much of what we were talking about was growing up as kids with Italian immigrant parents.

The quirky thing was, although we spoke English for most of the conversation, we would break into Italian words and phrases – from the Calabrian dialect we grew up with – for the fun of it. It wasn't deliberate or planned, we were using words that just seemed funnier and had more emphasis in Italian. And as you can guess, they were often swear words or the phrases our parents used when they scolded us. Every time someone recounted a word or phrase we would all break out in laughter. They were moments that brought feelings of nostalgia, and sometimes the anger and frustration we had felt when they happened. But recounting them among peers and being able to simply share them somehow made all the pain and hurt from the past heal. It was group therapy happening right there and then in a gay club. Who would have thought! We realised that not only were we in a gay club sharing our obvious commonality of sexuality, but our Italian-ness brought us even closer together.

What happened that night was to spark off an era not experienced before in Melbourne's gay community. A movement began for gay men of diverse cultural backgrounds.

A short time later we realised that the bond we had so beautifully demonstrated that night at the club should continue. The wonderful and insightful Charlie Dinami took the initiative. He decided that we should meet again; not at the club but for dinner at his place. It was a private and safe environment. Without the distractions of the noise and crowd, we were able to discuss issues seriously. We thought we could continue as a group and we discussed what this group might look like. We thought it would take the shape of a more formal social and support group.

Of course, we needed a name. And what simpler and more descript name than the 'Italian and Gay' group. Naturally we were curious if any other group such as ours existed. We found nothing else existed in Melbourne, which was not surprising because if it did we would have been in it already; we found nothing interstate and, to our surprise, nothing overseas in other comparable immigrant populations such as the US, Canada or England. Wow! Were we the first ever gay group in a western country of an Italian, or for that matter, any culturally and linguistically diverse background?

It didn't take long, however, before our Greek and Maltese friends, with either envy or simply seeing an opportunity, told us that as they didn't have anything themselves and with too few numbers to create their own group, they wanted to join ours. We thought, why not? Obviously we couldn't call ourselves an 'Italian' group anymore so we decided to call it 'Southern European and Gay Group'. But just as quickly, our South American friends also wanted in. Well, how could we say no to our Latin brothers? So we changed our name once again and we were finally called Southern European and Latin Gay Men's Group.

And what a productive group we were. Not only did we provide the necessary and much-wanted peer support for each other, but we decided to do much more. We saw ourselves as influencing the wider queer community. We realised we could potentially change some of the racist attitudes that we knew existed in our community. We decided what better way to make our debut on the queer scene than to create a space at an ALSO picnic at Fawkner Park in 1991. This was the forerunner to the Midsumma Festival.

Of course our space at the picnic was not your run-of-the-mill stall with brochures and cards. We decided it had to be an outdoor café complete with tables, chairs and red-checked tablecloths. We even had long strips of flags from a range of countries hanging from the branches of surrounding trees. People could buy European delicacies, such as cannoli, crostoli, baklava and tyropiakia, as well as fruit and, of course, freshly brewed coffee. Running a café requires many productive hands and so naturally we invited our partners to help us. We made aprons with big letters sown on the front: S.O.W. And if you looked a little closer, you could make out that it was an acronym that actually read: Spouse Of Wog.

Our café was something the queer community had not experienced before. Not only could people enjoy our food, but we were able to talk about our cultures in a social and relaxed atmosphere and in a way that gave insight and understanding of what we were all about. We saw this as a useful way of raising awareness, educating and, hopefully, addressing racism. We were planting the seeds of acceptance and understanding.

Another activity we conducted was a party at the local and popular Laird Hotel. We transformed the bar into the reception room of a Roman temple. A friend worked in props at a television station so naturally we went to town on the decorations. We had white columns holding up white sheets hanging from the ceiling. A statue of David in one corner, a Venus de Milo in another. The Laird Hotel had never seen anything like it. We charged a $10 entry fee. And what did our guests get for $10? With the wonderful support of the owners of the establishment, Ron and David, we set up a mini cooking station in the courtyard and served up fresh bowls of spaghetti bolognese. So for $10, guests could drink as much beer as they wanted and we provided the food. It was such a hit! We called it 'Pasta Bust'; a take on the popular Beer Busts that were happening at the time.

'Tracks to Our Routes – Tramming Ethnic Melbourne' was a tram ride that some lucky members of Melbourne's queer community would never forget. As the marketing at the time suggested, we had them 'rolling down the aisle' as we viewed such Melbourne landmarks as Franco Cozzo Furniture Emporium in Sydney Road, Brunswick. We cruised for kilometres, viewing fleeting but tasteful window displays as we continued along Sydney Road, and we marvelled at the streetscapes of 'award-winning' architecture in Preston and

Thornbury. For dinner we made a quick stop at a pizzeria in Lygon Street and picked up our pre-ordered pizzas. The food was washed down with a choice of Chianti, Lambrusco and other popular European wines.

And so, from the pioneering young gay men of the early 90s followed a rich tapestry of increasingly confident gay men and lesbians and, indeed, all genders and sexualities, weaving through the complexities of life to establish support networks and safe spaces for people of diverse sexualities and cultural backgrounds.

Trikone

From San Francisco to Sydney – supporting South Asian LGBTIQ

Alan Maurice

Founded in 1986 in the San Francisco Bay Area, Trikone is the oldest group of its kind in the world. South Asians affiliated with Trikone trace their ethnicities to Afghanistan, Bangladesh, Bhutan, Fiji, India, Maldives, Mauritius, Myanmar (Burma), Nepal, Pakistan, Sri Lanka and Tibet.

Trikone Australasia is a Sydney-based community organisation that provides social support and a safe, nurturing environment for LGBTIQ people of South Asian origin living in Australia. Trikone organises events, hosts meet-ups and plans social outings to encourage networking within the group and showcase South Asian talent to help nurture pride and confidence. Trikone opposes discrimination based on race, gender, class and other identities. We work with the LGBTIQ South Asian community in Australia and other social and political NGOs (both South Asian and otherwise) around the world.

I started the group in Australia in 2007. Today we have 263 group members, 349 friends and supporters and an active Facebook page, 'Trikone Australasia'.

I have been out since 1992. For years I focused inward and enjoyed the new experience. Before coming out, I was married to a wonderful woman and we have two grown sons. My background is Indian and I've been in Sydney since February 1977. It wasn't until 2006 that I started to wonder why I seemed to be the only South Asian 'gay in the village'. So I started a quest to find others. I stumbled onto my first Indian lesbian and she led me to find a tiny three-sentence advert about a South Asian gay group meeting. I rushed there to find it was disintegrating. So I set about looking for like-minded people from this group and we formed Trikone.

It's been a slow and gradual growth and awareness. Many South Asians are not happy to be out and proud for many reasons, like family, culture, discrimination and self-loathing. The very few I did meet felt ostracised and usually racially vilified. I knew I had to change this. I have always had a strong sense of justice, and the rest is history!

In 2017 we celebrated our tenth year of Mardi Gras parades, Bollywood dance parties, dinners, picnics, stories of sharing and a string of annual theatre productions for the Mardi Gras festival – all sell-out, which is pretty amazing for a small group of volunteers and little funding.

I can't begin to tell you about the satisfaction and blessing this journey has been for me personally, to know that I have made a difference in the lives of a few. Very rewarding.

Website: https://trikone.org.au/; Facebook page: https://www.facebook.com/ TrikoneAustralasia

YellowKitties
Showing up for Asian lesbians
Peggy Iu

Arising from the recognition that there was a lack of social groups for Asian lesbians, YellowKitties was formed in 2000. Answering an announcement on JOY FM for an expression of interest in setting up an Asian lesbian group in Melbourne, I attended a meeting with around 20 others. Between 2003 and 2016, with the help and support of my partner, Leonore, I took on the responsibilities for keeping the group running.

The founding principle behind the group was to provide a social space for Asian lesbians, their partners and friends. Since then, YellowKitties has expanded to include a broader range of sexual identities. Even in the early years, YellowKitties engaged with Gay Asian Proud and held joint social activities. YellowKitties thrives on the diversity of cultures and ethnicities across Asia, including those born outside of Asia.

For members of YellowKitties, our relationship with the AGMC has broadened our exposure to other cultural groups. It has given us opportunities to participate in events such as celebrating Passover with the Jewish group and playing bocce with the Italian group. There were grand ambitions and great achievements. The AGMC conference, United We Dance, AGMC trivia night, the multicultural cookbook and carnivals are highlights of our involvement with the AGMC. The challenge is to build on these achievements and expand advocacy activities to include the broader ethnic community group and the general Australian community.

Printed on a sticker on my fridge is the phrase: 'The world is run by those who show up'. It reminds me daily that there will always be a need for advocacy. The AGMC and its ambition have relevance today and will continue to have relevance in the future. We, as a community, cannot expect other people to advocate for us if we don't make an effort to advocate for ourselves.

2017 IDAHOBIT reception at Government House, Victoria.
Left to right: Shermain, Judy, Peggy and Leonore.

Author Biographies

Patrick Abboud is an award-winning television presenter, journalist, documentary filmmaker, commentator, emcee and diversity champion. Currently his unique storytelling reaches millions on SBS's *The Feed* where he presents and directs long form documentary, celebrity interviews and unique mini docs. Pat has co-hosted and directed content for the world's largest LGBTIQ live event broadcast, the Sydney Mardi Gras, for the past five years. He speaks Arabic, German and English and his storytelling has been nominated for the Walkleys, the Kennedys, the Amnesty International Media Awards and the United Nations Media Awards. He won the 2017 LGBTIQ Trailblazer Award and he was named the 2016 Broadcaster of the Year at the LGBTIQ Honour Awards. Contact: patrick.abboud@sbs.com.au.

Doron Abramovici is the Director for Social Inclusion and Community Engagement at the Jewish Community Council of Victoria.

Asiel Adan is a Mexican, non-binary doctor and writer. Their work focuses on the intersection of race, culture, gender and sexuality. You can contact them at asiel.yair.adan@gmail.com.

Faustina Agolley is a TV broadcaster, actor, producer, writer and DJ. Her family heritage is of Chinese and Ghanaian descent. Faustina hosted Australia's flagship music program *Video Hits*, as well as *The Voice Australia*, the *Sydney Gay and Lesbian Mardi Gras* and worked alongside Oprah Winfrey on her *An Evening With Oprah* arena tour across Australia and New Zealand as her touring DJ. In 2017, Faustina made her stage debut in the Sydney Theatre Company and Melbourne Theatre Company co-production of *The Father*. Her written work on LGBTI issues has been published in *The Huffington Post*, *Sunday Life* and *The Women of Letters*. www.faustina.co.

Mama Alto is a gender transcendent diva, cabaret artiste, jazz singer and community activist. She is a non-binary trans femme person of colour who works with the radical potential of storytelling, strength in softness and power in vulnerability. Fierce, femme and fabulous, she has been lauded as 'divine' (*Havana Tribune*, Cuba), 'near flawless' (*Age*), and 'a knockout' (*Herald Sun*). She has performed across Australia and internationally, and is the winner of the GLOBE Awards Artist of the Year 2017, the Melbourne Fringe Awards Access Victoria Award for Outstanding Access and Inclusion 2016. www.mamaalto.com; facebook.com/mamaalto; Twitter @ MamaAlto.

Elvira Andreoli has worked for 17 years for an ethno-specific aged-care provider as a case manager and rostered duty intake worker. The ethics by which she works mirror how she lives her life: advocate and provide a voice for people who are challenged or silenced in some way; and do this with pride and, where possible, a smile on your face. Elvira is actively involved in music projects promoting the enjoyment of Italian folksongs. https://www.linkedin.com/in/elvira-andreoli-b637a3b1.

Gavriel Ansara (PhD and MSc Psychology, MCouns) founded Rosh Pinah. He received the American Psychological Association's Transgender Research Award for his significant and original research with the first published study of cisgenderism. A polycultural psychotherapist and relationship and family therapist at Imanadari Counselling and Ansara Psychotherapy, he received the University of Surrey's Vice Chancellor's Alumni Achievement Award for his outstanding contributions to international human rights and social justice.

Tony Ayres is an award-winning showrunner, writer and director in television and feature films. He is also one of the founding members of Matchbox Pictures. Tony is the co-creator and executive producer for *Glitch* and creator of *Nowhere Boys*. Other EP/showrunning credits include the feature films *Ali's Wedding*, TV series *Wanted* and *The Family Law*, and mini-series *Seven Types of Ambiguity*, *Barracuda* and *The Slap*. contact@matchboxpictures.com.

Ayman Barbaresco, who is known as 'the busiest man in Melbourne' to his friends, has always had a passion to work in the community sector and has recently enrolled in a Bachelor of Social Science. Through his intersectional life experiences, Ayman invites you to jump in the passenger seat as he takes you on a whirlwind tour of his life, showing you that life is to be lived with passion and excitement today, as we never know what tomorrow holds. www.aymanbarbaresco.com.au.

Jonathan Barnett is President and Founder of Keshet Australia, Inc. Jonathan is the President of Progressive Judaism Victoria and an active member of Temple Beth Israel. He is a former treasurer and member of Keshet USA and former President of Congregation B'nai Shalom in Massachusetts. https://www.facebook.com/KeshetAU/; http://www.keshet.org.au.

Michael Barnett, at the age of 26 in 1995, broke open his closet doors and accepted himself as a gay man, embarking on a journey that would set him up to be a dedicated, passionate and controversial activist, fighting for equal rights for LGBTIQ people, combating youth suicide and challenging religious oppression and influence in government. Michael is convenor of Aleph Melbourne, a social, support and advocacy group for queer Jews. michael@aleph.org.au; www.aleph.org.au.

Roz Bellamy is a Melbourne-based writer, teacher, activist and workshop facilitator whose work has appeared in *Archer Magazine*, *The Big Issue*, *Daily Life*, *Everyday Feminism*, *Junkee*, *Kill Your Darlings*, *SBS* and the *Huffington Post*. Roz's work was shortlisted for the Scribe Nonfiction Prize in 2014 and she won the Stonnington Prize for Poetry in 2016. To read more of Roz's work, please visit: www.rozbellamy.com.

Maria Bololia's professional experience includes small business management in the natural health sector, youth development, women's refuge work, facilitation Fit 2 Drive and L2P learner driver information sessions, leadership, community events and recycled fashion workshops. She has been involved with the LGBTI sector since the 1980s, including participating in radio programs on 3CR for lesbians. Maria has facilitated LGBTI professional development sessions for the youth and education sectors, established a Gay Straight Alliance at Princes Hill Secondary College, and introduced the first SSA Expo in Melbourne attended by youth from 20 different services statewide: mumalio1964@gmail.com.

Tony Briffa is both Maltese and Australian, and the world's first elected intersex politician, having been elected as Councillor (2008, 2012 and 2016), Deputy Mayor (2009, 2010 and 2017) and Mayor (2011). Tony stresses that intersex is about biological sex, not gender identity or sexual orientation. For more information about Tony, visit www.briffa.org.

Hinde Ena Burstin is a founding member of the Jewish Lesbian Group of Victoria. She was a member of the editorial collective of the online anthology *Jewish Lesbians Down Under* (http://jlgvic.org/anthology.html) and of the film production collective for *It's Who We Are: Celebrating 20 Years of the Jewish Lesbian Group of Victoria*. Hinde Ena is a bilingual (Yiddish and English) writer and performer with an international following. She is a white woman who aims to use her power and privilege to fight for social change. A feisty feminist, daring dyke and a vocal and passionate campaigner for social justice, she has initiated many community education initiatives to fight against anti-Semitism, racism, sexism and homo/lesbophobia. Her essay, 'Looking Out, Looking In: Anti-Semitism and racism in lesbian communities' appeared in *Multicultural Queer: Australian perspectives* (1999).

Paul Capsis has had an extensive 35-year career as a performer, singer, actor, writer, in Australia and internationally. Most recently Paul performed his personal piece *Angela's Kitchen* at the Malta International Arts Festival 2017. He has worked on stage and film, in concerts, cabarets and theatre, and his play was published in 2012 by Currency Press. He has won numerous prestigious awards.

Carolina lives in Melbourne, Australia. She can be contacted via Maria Pallotta-Chiarolli: mariapc@deakin.edu.au.

Paula Carpio is a 30-year-old professional, born Catholic in the Philippines and living in Melbourne.

Shanton Chang (PhD) was born in Kuching, Sarawak and went to Singapore when he was 11 years old. At 21, he moved to Perth, Western Australia, for his education. He then moved to Melbourne in 1997 where he currently lives and works. He truly believes that Melbourne is home, and it's the one place where he has spent most of his life.

Joseph Carmel Chetcuti is a practising barrister and solicitor in Victoria and a registered migration agent. *Il-Ktieb Roża: Dnub, diżordni u delitt? (The Pink Book: A sin, disorder and crime?)* (1997), the first book on homosexuality in the Maltese language, and *Queer Mediterranean Memories: Penetrating the secret history and silence of gay and lesbian disguise in the Maltese Archipelago* (2009), the first book in English on homosexuality in Malta, attracted wide media coverage and drew the ire of Malta's conservatives. He is a 78er and his most recent book is *Sydney's First Gay Mardi Gras: What brought it on and how it changed us* (2017).

Margherita Coppolino is one of Australia's best-known and most influential disability and diversity consultants. With an outstanding network of contacts in government, business and social justice organisations, Margherita has a proven ability to inspire and influence a wide range of stakeholders on disability and diversity issues. In 2003, Margherita was honored with an Australian Centenary Medal for her contribution to women's and disability rights. In 2010, Margherita was invited to be the keynote speaker at the Women with Disabilities Leadership roundtable at the World Bank in

Washington DC. In her spare time, Margherita plays bocce, takes photos and is on various boards and committees.

Franco Di Chiera helped establish the first gay radio show in Australia, *Gays Weekly*; made the early gay coming out classic *Waiting 'Round Wynyard*; made the first subtitled film at the Australian Film Television and Radio School, *La Scala, Lo Scalone*; and his series *A Change of Face* is considered of one of SBS's most influential programs. His multicultural series *Under the Skin* won Best Miniseries at the AFI Awards. He has directed and produced drama and documentary and held numerous senior screen industry positions including Development Executive at Screen West, Commissioning Editor at SBS Independent, Executive Producer at Film Australia, Director of the WA Screen Academy, Edith Cowan University and Development and Investment Manager at Film Victoria.

Anton Enus has been a news presenter and journalist for 20 years. He has been with SBS World News Tonight for the past five years, after a 15-year career in radio and television with South Africa's national broadcaster, SABC. Anton's achievements include the CNN World Report Award for best international report and the Bokmakierie Award for current affairs. Enus was a founding member of South Africa's gay and lesbian sports movement in the early 1980s and was on the organising team that guided the country into the Gay Games for the first time in 1994. From a 'coloured' background, he has also served on committees aimed at reconciling Johannesburg's multicultural gay and lesbian communities.

Cristian Cortes Garzon grew up in Santiago de Cali, Colombia. From an early age he was involved in the community, participating in folk dancing groups, as well as support groups for disadvantaged LGBTI communities. Cristian currently works with Living Positive Victoria and is the founder of LGBTIQ+ Latin American and Hispanic Community.

Sally Goldner has 20 years' involvement in Victoria's LGBTIQ communities, including with Transgender Victoria, co-facilitating Transfamily, presenting 3 CR's *Out of the Pan* and as treasurer of Bisexual Alliance Victoria. She is a life member of four organisations, was 2015 LGBTI Victorian of the Year and joined the Victorian Women's Honour Roll in 2016. The focus of an autobiographical documentary *Sally's Story*, she is an educator, speaker and MC (in contrast to her accountancy training) . . . and watch out for more! www.sallygoldner.com.

Carl Gopalkrishnan (aka Gopal) has been a practicing independent visual artist for over 30 years. Born in the UK in 1967 and based in Melbourne, Australia, Carl explores society's unconscious narratives using metaphors through a queer cultural lens. A self-taught painter with a background in design, he mixes academic study and research to create works on canvas, photography, drawing and printmaking. Published in literary journals, he crosses between his day-job in policy with his painting and social commentary. He has held five solo exhibitions in Australia, participated in group shows internationally, and presented his art at conference workshops on international intervention: www.carlgopal.com.

Anne Harris is an Associate Professor and Vice Chancellor's Principal Research Fellow at RMIT University, and an Australian Research Council Future Fellow (2017–2021). She researches in gender, creativity, diversity, performance and emerging digital ethnographies; is a native New Yorker and has worked professionally as a playwright, teaching artist and journalist in the USA and Australia. Some of her intercultural collaborative arts based research can be seen at www.creativeresearchhub.com.

Dino Hodge – Konstantino Hadjikakou – is an Honorary Senior Fellow with the University of Melbourne's Centre for Indigenous Studies. He has a PhD in history and is author/(co)editor of six books, four of which consider themes of Indigeneity and social justice across either health, education, or queer studies. Dino is a life member of the Northern Territory AIDS and Hepatitis Council (2014), and a recipient of the Northern Territory Human Rights Social Change Award (2017).

Peggy Iu was born in Hong Kong, and her family emigrated to Sydney, Australia in 1979. Her family settled in a middle-class suburb. Attending the local primary school, she and her brother were the only Asians enrolled at the school. It was during university that Peggy started connecting with the LGBTIQ community. Over the last 30 years, Peggy has been involved with Sydney Asian Lesbians (SAL) both as a regular member and as the co-convenor. She also founded the first lesbian Dragon Boat racing team in Sydney, *Connecting Cultures*, which competed in the Australian Dragon Boat racing scene for three years. In 1997, she and her partner Leonore relocated to Melbourne. Peggy and Leonore celebrated their 25th anniversary in 2016.

Rida Khan is 24 years old, born in Pakistan to a Baloch father and an Urdu-speaking mother. Like most educated Pakistanis in Australia, her parents migrated to Australia for better education and employment opportunities. She grew up in Horsham near the Grampians and went to a local country school. She moved out of home at 16 and has been living independently in Australia since and has worked in a variety of multicultural, multi-spiritual and gender diverse projects. Today, she identifies herself as a Pakistani-Australian-Baloch-Muslim-Sufi-Bisexual girl, finding her place in a label-obsessed society and advocating for justice, equality and the right to nurturing relationships and safe homes.

Azja Kulpinska (she/they) is an immigrant from Poland currently based in Narrm on the lands of the Kulin nations. Azja is a writer, zine-maker, Theatre of the Oppressed practitioner and community mental health worker. Azja has facilitated dialogical theatre and zine-making projects in Australia, Solomon Islands and Poland that explore narratives around identity, queerness, migration, displacement, mental health intersecting systems of oppression and other topics. azjakulpinska@gmail.com.

Benjamin Law is a journalist, columnist, TV screenwriter and author of *The Family Law* (2010), *Gaysia: Adventures in the queer east* (2012) and *Quarterly Essay 67: Moral panic 101* (2017). He's also the co-author of *Shit Asian Mothers Say* (2014) with his sister Michelle, and the sex and relationships advice book *Law School* (2017) with his mum Jenny. *The Family Law* is now an AACTA-nominated TV series for SBS which he created and co-writes. You can find him on Twitter and Instagram at @mrbenjaminlaw.

Anthony Lekkas is a counsellor who has worked in the mainstream and queer not-for-profit community services sector for 13 years, as well as in private practice. Anthony is a member of the Melbourne Bisexual Network, a bisexual peer-led activist and advocacy community group aimed at improving the mental health and wellbeing of people who identify as bisexual, pansexual or non-monosexual. Anthony is also a co-host on the *Triple Bi-Pass* show on JOY 94.9 FM, Australia's only radio show dedicated to presenting bisexual content. linkedin.com/in/anthony-lekkas-32864752; joy.org.au/triplebipass.

Mei Tze Ling is a health professional working in Sydney and can be reached at mtling@mtling.com.au.

Lian Low writes across spoken word, performance text and creative non-fiction. From 2009 to 2016, Lian undertook various editorial and board member roles with *Peril* magazine. Publications include *Growing Up Asian in Australia*, *Griffith Review 49: New Asia Now II* and *ArtsHub*. In 2015, she was a recipient of a Wheeler Centre Hot Desk Fellowship and also a City of Literature Travel Fund. Find her at http://lianlow.weebly.com.

Alan Maurice has worked for 'a lifetime' in the University of Technology, Sydney, research and finance sector. He also is a director at a number of small non-profit organisations, mostly within the LGBTIQ area. He also promotes Indigenous women in song. Recently he has left full-time work to focus on his passions of ending racism and discrimination and to date the rewards have been fantastic.

Adam Messede is a gay man who arrived from Lebanon in 1994 and started the Gay Arab Group in 1999, refreshed as Helem in 2012.
helemmelbourne@gmail.com;
https://www.facebook.com/helem.melbourne.

Jack Migdalek's (PhD) background is in drama, dance and physical theatre. He has worked as a performer, writer, choreographer, director, and educator in Australia, the United Kingdom, and Japan. Jack is a drama lecturer at Trinity College, the University of Melbourne. Publications include *The Embodied Performance of Gender* (2015).

Alyena Mohummadally is a Pakistani-Australian queer Muslim woman who spent many years as a community legal centre lawyer before recently retraining as a primary school teacher. She founded the Queer Muslims in Australia Yahoo! Group in 2005 and has been published in journals, books, articles, spoken at conferences, workshops and has had documentaries made on her queer Muslim advocacy.

Tony Mordini (PhD) is a first-generation Australian born of Italian parents who migrated to Australia in the 1950s. He knows first hand what it means to grow up between two cultures and has leveraged off this in his academic and professional activities in education, community services, public health and more recently, the judiciary. Additionally, Tony has been very active in the LGBTIQ, multicultural and Indigenous communities. This has included presidencies of two AIDS councils and the AGMC.

Nonno and Aroosa are two western Sydney ethnic queers, who specialise in a variety of techniques in winning bill battles. According to their coffee cup readings, they are due to have some big happiness enter their lives, in six weeks, six months or six years.

Olivia Noto is a queer feminist, and at the time of writing, a very happy stay-at-home mama. She enjoys being creative and going on adventures with her beautiful family. Her eldest daughter Sunny is of the Bearded Dragon variety. She has facilitated, taught, researched and project managed her way around New South Wales and Victoria, Australia. You can read her contribution titled 'Sleeping with a Mosquito' in W. DeJean and J. Sapp, [Eds.] (2017), *Dear Gay, Lesbian, Bisexual, & Transgender Teacher: Letters of advice to help you find your way*, North Carolina: Information Age Publishing.

Benjamin Oh is the current Chair of the Australian Catholics for Equality Advisory Board, and Founder and Chair of the Rainbow Catholics InterAgency for Ministry.

Maria Pallotta-Chiarolli (PhD) is an academic-activist-author at Deakin University, sitting on the committees of the Gender and Sexuality Studies Network and the LGBTIQ Network. She is also an independent researcher and consultant; a founding member of the AGMC; sits on two Victoria Police Priorities Communities Reference Groups, the LGBTIQ Reference Group and the Multicultural Reference Group; and is a member of the DHHS LGBTIQ Working Group. Her current research is '"Mobs and Wogs": Family Histories of Indigenous People with Southern European Heritage', addressing the contestations and confluences between migration and colonialism. Author and editor of 14 academic and non-academic books, Maria has won two Lambda (LGBTIQ) Literary Awards in the USA and been shortlisted for a third. She has also won an Australian Book Design Award and been shortlisted for a NSW Ethnic Affairs Commission Award.

> http://mariapallottachiarolli.com.au;
> https://deakin.academia.edu/mariapallottachiarolli;
> https://www.researchgate.net/profile/Maria_Pallotta-Chiarolli.

Gary Paramanathan works at the intersection of arts, culture and community. He's always written, but isn't always read. Born in Sri Lanka and raised in Australia, Gary trained as a filmmaker, and has written and directed a number of short films, written feature essays and recounted personal narratives. This is his first published work of short fiction. Gary can be contacted at gary@colourfest.com.au.

Vic Perri is a Health Promotion Officer at Living Positive Victoria and provides comprehensive information and guidance on the management of HIV with a focus on peer support, education and training. Vic has been living with HIV for many years and has written articles as well as produced and presented community radio and television programs on HIV, sexual health, sexuality and cultural diversity. For more information and to view videos of Vic's projects and publications: linkedin.com/in/vic-perri-836461a8.

Corey Rabaut has spent his adult life working in the union movement. Before the birth of his daughter, he spent significant time in parts of Africa experiencing the culture and contributing to the community. His commitment to progressive politics is driven by his love for his daughter and nephews, so they can live in a better society. He can be contacted by twitter at @coreynr or by LinkedIn.

Raven is of Maltese heritage and Australian born. She is a member of a number of LGBTIQ community and advocacy groups, and identifies as bisexual and polyamorous. Raven is a lawyer and enjoys singing, drawing, and creating goth and alternative dolls.

Adam Ridwan's dad is from Padang, Indonesia; his mum is from London, England; and he, himself, is from wherever the red wine happens to be. A psychology graduate of ANU, he currently works in marketing for Expedia by weekday and plots QPOC revolution on weekends. He's a self(ie)-love fanatic on his Instagram (@adamredwine) and you'll find his off-beat tweets at @adamridwan. Brown and queer, no fear.

Naya Rizwan is a 26-year-old student born Muslim in Pakistan.

Wil Roach is a proud Londoner born of Trinidadian parents in the Port of Spain and now living in Sydney, Australia. He found his calling in community activism, as Community Development Worker for London local authorities and actively involved in the London Labour Party. He also had a heartfelt involvement in the mental health system as it affected young black men who were disproportionately locked up in secure asylums. He is a writer of essays and currently working on a memoirs project covering the period of the mid 1960s to early 1980s, as well as a performer of his own poems and short stories. If you wish to contact Wil: wilfred.roach@gmail.com.

Omar Sakr is an Arab Australian poet whose work has been published in English, Arabic, and Spanish. His poetry has or will soon feature in *Griffith Review, Meanjin, Overland, Wildness, The New Arab, Mizna, Antic*, and *Circulo de Poesia*. He has been anthologised in *Best Australian Poems 2016* and *Contemporary Australian Poetry*, and his debut collection *These Wild Houses* was shortlisted for the Judith Wright Calanthe award. He is the poetry editor of *The Lifted Brow*. http://omarsakr.com.

Michael Schembri is an advocate with the Finance Sector Union in Sydney. A supporter of the Trotskyist Fourth International, he is a staunch supporter of the Palestinian struggle for national liberation. He has lived with his partner Tjing Heng Oey (Danny) since 1997 and is the proud father of two gorgeous and adorable Shetland sheepdogs. He writes an occasional blog – http://www.il-kecwiel.blogspot.com – in Maltese and English.

Budi Sudarto is a Diversity Trainer and Consultant at Ananda Training and Consultancy, specialising in the intersection between culture, religion, and LGBTIQ identity. Budi obtained a Master of Arts degree from Monash University in 2004, and his thesis explored the lived experiences of gay Asian men in Melbourne. Budi is the incumbent AGMC Vice President, and the convener of Gay Asian Proud. contact@anandalearning.com.au and www.anandalearning.com.au.

Reem Sweid is a Muslim woman of Syrian background, Social Policy Officer, PhD candidate, and Founder and most recent past-president of Muslim Collective in Australia. She has worked on more than 10 projects on subject matters including social cohesion, multiculturalism, countering violent extremism, and past adoption practices.

reem.sweid@muslimcollective.com.

Judy Tang (PhD) is a neuropsychologist at the Jurmaine Health Service, President of the AGMC and sits on a number of advisory boards. She has been named a Multicultural Champion for the Victorian Multicultural Commission.

Christos Tsiolkas is the author of *Loaded*, *The Jesus Man*, *Dead Europe*, *The Slap* and *Barracuda*, and of the short story collection *Merciless Gods*. He co-wrote *Jump Cuts: An autobiography* with Sasha Soldatow, and his most recent work is *On Patrick White: Writers on writers*. His work has been adapted for cinema, television and for the stage. He is also a playwright, scriptwriter, film critic and essayist. Christos doesn't believe in trigger warnings.

John Tzimas has been an active member of the Greek and Gay Support Network since 1988. In addition to GGSN, John continues to assist the AGMC as and when required, is a committee member of the Eurovision Fanclub of Australia (OGAE Australia), and works part-time as an accountant. For more information visit www.greekandgay.com.

Paul Venzo (PhD) is a writer and academic living in coastal, south-west Victoria. A lecturer in writing and literature with Deakin University, his research and creative practice revolve around the study of subjectivity and identity, often linking sexuality with the contexts of place and language. His poetry, in translation across Italian and English, allows him to explore connections to both Australia and Italy; the source of inspiration for much of his creative writing.

Sim Victor has been very reconnected with music the past four years, and with fulfilling carer work. Born in Australia, with Indian heritage, he is a (trans) man who wrote this song a few years ago during his later youth years. He fulfilled active roles for several years that have helped the LGBT+ populations such as being on the 2013 GLBTI Ministerial Advisory Committee. He also did four years of voluntary full-time work at YGender which he founded and was the key driver . . . luckily it seems sustainable now with a skilled new generation behind the scenes. During those four years, till age 22, only far-left socialist-feminist people like Alison Thorne who founded organisations like the VAC could guide Sim and support him on such a pioneering journey. Now aged 26, still playing music, he returns to the community with Yoga Nidra facilitator accreditation. https://www.facebook.com/sim.victor.music.

Annette Xiberras is a lesbian Wurundjeri Tribal Elder with a Maltese immigrant father. She is Managing Director of Urban Colours Arts Cultural Heritage Consultancy, and has held the Victorian Aboriginal community-elected Chair of the Victorian Traditional Owners Land Justice Group for the past six years. https://www.urbancolours.com.au.

Nevo Zisin is an activist, educator, public speaker and the author of *Finding Nevo*, a memoir on gender transition. They run workshops and professional development in schools and workplaces around gender inclusivity. They identify as a non-binary, transgender person and are a contact point in the Jewish community for other children and families confronting issues of gender and sexuality in their own lives. Contact: nevozisin@hotmail.com; https://twitter.com/FindingNevo1; https://www.instagram.com/nevozisin/; https://www.facebook.com/nevozisin.

References

Alley, J. (2016), 'Queer Space', *The Wiley Blackwell Encyclopedia of Gender and Sexuality Studies*, John Wiley and Sons Ltd, http://onlinelibrary.wiley.com/doi/10.1002/9781118663219.wbegss336/abstract;jsessionid=EC761FAE06AC72056DDF199D10DCD7E3.f04t02?userIsAuthenticated=false&deniedAccessCustomised Message.

Anzaldúa, G. (2012), *Borderlands: The new mestiza*, San Francisco: Aunt Lute Books.

Ayres, T. (1999), 'China Doll – The Experience of Being a Gay Chinese Australian', in P. A. Jackson and G. Sullivan (eds). *Multicultural Queer: Australian narratives*, New York: The Haworth Press.

Beckett, S., Mohummadally, M. and Pallotta-Chiarolli, M. (2014), 'Queerying Muslim Identities' in A. Ata (ed) *Education Integration Challenges: The case of Australian Muslims*, Melbourne: David Lovell Publishing.

Bertone, C. and Pallotta-Chiarolli, M. (eds) (2015), *Queerying Families of Origin*, London: Routledge.

Braidotti, R. (2011), *Nomadic Subjects: Embodiments and Sexual Difference in Contemporary Feminist Theory* (2nd Edition), Cambridge: Columbia University Press.

Buttrose, I. (2001), *A Passionate Life*, Sydney: Penguin.

Cain S. (2012), *Quiet: The power of introverts in a world that can't stop talking*, New York: Crown Publishers.

Caluya, G. (2006), 'The (Gay) Scene of Racism: Face, shame and gay Asian males', *Australian Critical Race and Whiteness Studies Association e-journal*, 2(2), http://www.acrawsa.org.au/files/ejournalfiles/80GilbertCaluya.pdf.

Capsis, P. (2012), *Angela's Kitchen*, Sydney: Currency Press.

Cauchi, M.N. et al (1986), *Irjieħ: Antoloġija mill-Awstralja*, Melbourne: Maltese Literature Group.

Charman, K. (compiler) (1982), *The Little Blue Book for Girls: Health and sexuality resources guide for young women*, St Kilda South: Youth Affairs Council of Victoria.

Chang, S. and Apostle, D. (2008), 'Recommendations from the 2004 AGMC Conference', *Gay & Lesbian Issues & Psychology Review*, 4(1): 56-60.

Chetcuti, J.C. (1986), 'Personally Speaking for Myself', in G. Wotherspoon (ed), *Being Different*, Sydney: Hale and Iremonger.

Chetcuti, J.C. (1997), *Il-Ktieb Roża: Dnub, diżordni u delitt* (*The Pink Book: A sin, disorder and crime?*), Marsa, Malta: Stamperija Inprint.

Chetcuti, J.C. (2001), 'Maltese Community Life in Australia' in J. Jupp (ed), *The Australian People: An encyclopedia of the nation, its people and their origins*, Cambridge: Cambridge University Press.

Chetcuti, J.C. (2009), *Queer Mediterranean Memories: Penetrating the secret history and silence of gay and lesbian disguise in the Maltese Archipelago*, Carlton North, Melbourne: Lygon Street Legal Services.

Chetcuti, J.C. (2018), *The First Sydney Gay Mardi Gras: What brought it on and how it changed us*, Carlton North, Melbourne: Lygon Street Legal Services.

Chuang, K. (1999), 'Using Chopsticks to Eat Steak', in P. A. Jackson and G. Sullivan (eds), *Multicultural Queer: Australian narratives*, New York: The Haworth Press.

Ciccotosto, E. and Bosworth, M. (1990), *Emma: A translated life*. Fremantle: Fremantle Arts Press.

Cipelletti, C. (2013), *Due Volte Genitori* (*Parents Reborn*), http://www.duevoltegenitori.com/eng-home.htm.

Cohen, S. (2011), *The Future of Pakistan*, Washngton DC: Brookings Institution Press.

Conigrave, T. (1995), *Holding the Man*. Sydney: Penguin.

Cook, R. (2012), 'Gay, Asian and Proud', *Melbourne Community Voice*, 25 July, http://gaynewsnetwork.com.au/readonline/archives/mcv603/files/4.html.

Couros, P. and Hodge, D. (ed) (2016), *You're Not Alone: 30 years of AIDS councils in the Northern Territory*, Darwin: Northern Territory AIDS and Hepatitis Council.

Di Chiera, F. (1994), 'Interview with Andy Lloyd James, General Manager SBS Independent', in *Encore*, 18 April–8 May edition.

Dunn/Holland, W., Fletcher, M., Hodge, D., Lee, G., Milera, R.J., Saunders, R. and Wafer, J. (1994), 'Peopling the Empty Mirror: The prospects for lesbian and gay Aboriginal history'in R. Aldrich (ed), *Gay Perspectives II: More essays in Australian gay culture*, Sydney: University of Sydney.

Eikleberry C. (1995), *The Career Guide for Creative and Unconventional People*, Berkeley, California: Ten Speed Press.

Friedrich, O. (1972), *Before the Deluge: Berlin in the 1920s*, London: Harper and Row.

Friggieri, Oliver (1980), *L'Istramb* (*The Odd Fellow*), Malta.

Greenberg, D.F., (1988), *The Construction of Homosexuality*, Chicago: The University of Chicago Press.

Hammoud-Beckett, Sekneh (2007), 'Azima ila Hayati – An invitation in to my life: Narrative conversations about sexual identity' *The International Journal of Narrative Therapy and Community Work*, 1: 29-39.

Han, C.S., Proctor, K. and Choi, K.H. (2013), 'I Know a Lot of Gay Asian Men Who Are Actually Tops: Managing and negotiating gay racial stigma', *Sexuality & Culture*, Doi: 10.1007/s12119-013-9183-4.

Harris, A. (2012), '(All the) Single Ladies: Diasporic women are doing it for themselves', *Australian Feminist Studies*, 27(72): 157-170.

Harris, A. (2013), 'Ethnocinema and the Impossibility of Culture', *International Journal of Qualitative Studies in Education*, DOI: 10.1080/09518398.2013.775377.

Harris, A. and Gandolfo, E. (2013), 'Looked at and Looked over, or: I wish I was adopted.' *Gender, Place and Culture: A journal of feminist geographies*, ?:1–15.

Hassan, R. and Lester, L. (2015), *Australian Muslims: A demographic, social and economic profile of Muslims in Australia: Report from University of South Australia*, https://www.unisa.edu.au/Global/EASS/MnM/Publications/Australian_Muslims_Report_2015.pdf.

Helgoe, L. (2008), *Introvert Power: Why your inner life is your hidden strength*, Naperville, Illinois: Sourcebooks.

Ho, K. (2017), *Cultural Diversity in Australian Theatre*, independently distributed PDF.

Hodge, D. (1991), 'One Little Jurisdiction: Anti-discrimination initiatives in the Northern Territory: August 1989–February 1991' *National AIDS Bulletin*, 5(2): 27–29.

Hodge, D. (1993a), *Did You Meet Any Malagas? A homosexual history of Australia's tropical capital*, Darwin: Little Gem Publications.

Hodge, D. (1993b), 'Activism in the Top End', *National AIDS Bulletin*, 17(7): 12–14.

Hodge, D. (1995), 'Malagas at Work: Aspects of a Northern Territory oral history project', *Oral History Association of Australia Journal*, 17: 20–24.

Hodge, D., Smith, A., Patterson, D (1990), 'HIV Status, Sexuality and Discrimination: Whose turn to (en)act?', *National AIDS Bulletin*, 4(6): 48–51.

Holt, H. (2016) 'Queering the Archive at the Northern Territory Library' *Incite*, 37(1/2): 18–19.

ILGA World Congress (2003) *On Lesbian/Gay Liberation*, http://www.internationalviewpoint.org/spip.php?article177.

iluvubut (2013), retrieved from http://iluvubut.tv.

It Gets Better Project (2010), http://www.itgetsbetter.org.

Jackson, P.A. and Sullivan, G. (eds) (1999), *Multicultural Queer: Australian narratives*, New York: The Haworth Press.

Jackson, P.A. (2000), '"That's What Rice Queens Study!": White gay desire and representing Asian homosexualities', *Journal of Australian Studies*, 24(65). Doi: 10.1080/144430500097387602.

Johnson, J. (2017) *Dark Convicts*, Perth: UWA Publishing.

Johnston, C. (1999) *A Sydney Gaze: The making of gay liberation*, Glebe: Wild and Woolley.

Jones, G.W. (1997), '"Australian Identity": Racism and recent responses to Asian immigration to Australia', *Working Papers in Demography*, 71. https://digitalcollections.anu.edu.au/handle/1885/41468.

Kassisieh, G. (2011), *'We're Family Too': The effects of homophobia in Arabic-speaking communities in New South Wales*, Sydney: ACON/Lesbian and Gay Anti-Violence Project; http://www.wearefamilytoo.com.au/Arabic%20Report_March2012.pdf.

Knight, D. (2017), 'Margie Fischer's welcome home Feast', *Adelaide Review*, November 6; https://www.adelaidereview.com.au/arts/performing-arts/margie-fischers-welcome-home-feast.

Laney, M.O. (2002), *The Introvert Advantage: How to thrive in an extrovert world*, New York: Workman Publishing.

Lauck, J. (2011), *Found: A memoir*. Seal Press, New York.

Lee, S. (1986), 'A Journey with Support' in G. Wotherspoon (ed), *Being Different*, Sydney: Hale & Iremonger.

Lee, S. (2014), 'Oral History Interview with Graham Carbery and Gary Jaynes', *Australian Lesbian and Gay Archives*, Melbourne: ALGA accession no 2014-0032.

Ling, A.(1992), *Mei Tze Is Also My Name*, Sydney: PMT Publishing.

Lui, N. (2014), 'Is Australian Theatre Racist?', *Guardian*, June 12 https://www.theguardian.com/stage/australia-culture-blog/2014/jun/12/is-australian-theatre-racist.

Mendelsohn, D. (2000), *The Elusive Embrace*, London: Vintage.

Migdalek, J.(2014), 'Mincing, Striding, Stomping, Gliding: Messing with gender choreographic taboos', in M. Pallotta-Chiarolli and B. Pease (eds), *The Politics of Recognition and Social Justice: Transforming subjectivities and new forms of resistance*, New York: Routledge.

Migdalek. J. (2015), *The Embodied Performance of Gender*. New York: Routledge.

Mohummadally, A. (2012a), 'I Am a Queer Muslim', *ABC Big Ideas*, https://www.youtube.com/watch?v=i7MuTSiq1Ko.

Mohummadally, A. (2012b), 'Pride and Prejudice', *Daily Life*, http://www.dailylife.com.au/life-and-love/real-life/pride-and-prejudice-20120228-1u0ki.html.

Mohummadally, A. (2013a), 'I thought I was the only one', *Overland*, https://overland.org.au/previous-issues/issue-210/feature-alyena-mohummadally.

Mohummadally, A. (2013b), 'The Impossible Dream', in L. Gahan and T. Jones (eds), *Heaven Bent: Australian LGBTI experiences of faith, religion and spirituality*, Melbourne: Hill of Content.

Mohummadally, A. (2014), 'People Like Me' in A. Pajalic and D. Divaroren (eds), *Coming of Age: Australian Muslim stories*, Sydney: Allen and Unwin Publishing.

Mohummadally, A. (2016a), 'A Rainbow Is Political', *Comment*, https://www.sbs.com.au/topics/sexuality/agenda/article/2016/10/03/comment-rainbow-political.

Mohummadally, A. (2016b), 'Queer and Muslim: Existing within the "Other" – twice' *ABC Religion and Ethics*, http://www.abc.net.au/religion/articles/2016/06/16/4483298.htm.

Mordini, A (2001), 'Searching for Solid Ground: A study of the relationship between belief systems, self-concept and the propensity for deliberate self-harm', EdD thesis, Murdoch University, Perth, WA.

Murphy, T. (2010), *Holding the Man: Stage adaptation*, Sydney: Nick Hern Books.

National LGBTI Health Alliance (2016), *The Statistics at a Glance: The mental health of lesbian, gay, bisexual, transgender and intersex people in Australia*, http://lgbtihealth.org.au/statistics.

Neutze, B. (2016), 'Candy Bowers on Australian Theatre's White Patriarchy: Burn it down', *Daily Review*, October 19, https://dailyreview.com.au/candy-bowers/50702.

Pallotta-Chiarolli, M. (1999), *Too Busy Studying to Have Sex?: Homosexually active Asian male international students and sexual health*, report for the Public Health Unit of the Commonwealth Department of Health and Family Services, National Centre in HIV Social Research, Uni of NSW.

Pallotta-Chiarolli, M. (ed) (2008), *Gay and Lesbian Issues and Psychology Special Edition: Papers from the AGMC 2004/2006 Conferences* Vol. 4(1).

Pallotta-Chiarolli, M. (2016), *Supporting Same-Sex Attracted and Gender Diverse Young People of Multicultural and Multifaith Backgrounds: Executive summary and full research report*, Melbourne: Equality Branch of the Department of Premier and Cabinet.

Pallotta-Chiarolli, M. (2018) *'Safe Spaces, Inclusive Services': Service access and engagement by LGBTIQ+ Muslims.* Melbourne: Muslim Collective.

Pallotta-Chiarolli, M. and Rajkhowa, A. (2017), 'Systemic Invisibilities, Institutional Culpabilities and Multicultural-Multifaith LGBTIQ Resistances: Introduction to the special section', *Journal of Intercultural Studies* 38(4): 429-442.

Parliament of Australia (2007), *Muslim Australians*, http://www.aph.gov.au/About_Parliament/Parliamentary_Departments/Parliamentary_Library/Publications_Archive/archive/MuslimAustralians.

Pausacker, J. (1987), *What Are Ya?*, Melbourne: Angus and Robertson.

Perri, V. (2000), 'You Can't Be Gay, You're Italian' in P. Genovesi, W. Musolino, I. Martinuzzi O'Brien, Pallotta-Chiarolli, M. (eds), *In Search of the Italian Australian into the New Millennium: Conference proceedings*, Thornbury: Gro-set Publications.

Perri, V. (2005), 'Expressing My Gayness with an Italian Flavour' in Pallotta-Chiarolli, M. (ed), *When Our Children Come Out: How to support gay, lesbian, bisexual and transgendered young people*, Sydney: Finch Publishing.

Pitts, G. (1996), *Emma Celebrazione: Stage adaptation*, Sydney: Currency Press.

Ridge, D., Hee, A. and Minichiello, V. (1999), '"Asian" Men on the Scene: Challenges to "gay communities"', in P.A. Jackson and G. Sullivan (eds), *Multicultural Queer: Australian narratives*, New York: The Haworth Press.

Roberts, I. (2007) interview, *Advocate*, 14 August.

Robinson, K.H., Bansel, P., Denson, N., Ovenden, G. and Davies, C. (2013), *Growing Up Queer: Issues facing young Australians who are gender variant and sexuality diverse*, Melbourne: Young and Well Cooperative. Research Centre, Melbourne.

Russo, V. (1981), *The Celluloid Closet: Homosexuality in the movies*, New York: Harper & Row.

Schembri, M. (2000), 'Gay and Lesbian Ethnic Politics: A taste of things to come', in C. Johnston and P. van Reyk (eds), *Queer City: Gay and lesbian politics in Sydney*, Sydney: Pluto Press.

Schembri, M. (2010), 'My Family's Early Years', *Il-Keċwiel*, http://il-kecwiel.blogspot.com.au/search?updated-min=2010-01-01T00:00:00-08:00&updated-max=2011-01-01T00:00:00-08:00&max-results=11.

Schembri, M. (2012a), *Il-Keċwiel* http://www.il-kecwiel.blogspot.com.au/2012/09/same-sex-marriage-debate-in-maltese.html.

Scicluna, M. (2016), 'Spotlight on the Church', *Times of Malta*, 24 February.

Sears A. and Moors C. (1995), 'The Politics of Hegemony: Democracy, class and social movements' in Zavarzadeh, M. et al (eds), *Post-ality: Marxism and postmodernism*, Washington: Maissoneuve Press.

Seepe, S. (2004), *Speaking Truth to Power*, Vista University: Skotaville Media.

Shinnick, M. (1997), *This Remarkable Gift: Being gay and Catholic*. Sydney: Allen & Unwin.

Smith, A., Patterson, D and Hodge, D. (1990), 'Law Reform Submission', *Northern Territory AIDS Council*, Darwin: Northern Territory Archives.

Sudarto, B. (2004), *'Which One Is the Boat People? I Came by Airplane': Gay Asian men talk about their experiences of ethnicity and sexual identity in Melbourne*, (unpublished Master's dissertation), Melbourne: Monash University.

Sudarto, B. (2013), 'The Danger of Stereotypes', *Star Observer*, 11 July, http://www.starobserver.com.au/opinion/2013/07/11/the-danger-of-stereotypes/106498.

Sue, D.W., Capodilupo, C.M., Torino, G.C., Bucceri, J.M., Holder, A.M.B., Nada, K.L. and Esquilin, M., (2007), 'Racial Microaggressions in Everyday Life: Implications for clinical practice', *American Psychologist*, 62(4): 271–286.

Tan, A. (1989), *The Joy Luck Club*, New York: G.S Putnam.

Tondelli, P. V. (1982), *Pao Pao*, Milano: Feltrinelli.

Tsiolkas, C. (1995), *Loaded*, Sydney: Random House.

Venzo, P. (2014), 'Archipelago: A poetic journey across island of the self', Doctoral Thesis, Deakin University.

Verrier, N.N. (1993), *Primal Wound: Understanding the adopted child*, San Francisco: Ingram.

Verrier, N. N. (2003), *Coming Home to Self: The adopted child grows up*, San Francisco: Gateway Press.

Yngvesson, B. (2003), 'Going "Home": Adoption, loss of bearings, and the mythology of roots', *Social Text* 21(1): 7–27.

Zisin, N. (2017), *Finding Nevo*, Melbourne: Black Dog Books.

Maria, 1963. 'And she is going to dance, dance hungry, dance full, dance each astonishing moment' (Anne Lamott).

Wakefield Press is an independent publishing and
distribution company based in Adelaide, South Australia.
We love good stories and publish beautiful books.
To see our full range of books, please visit our website at
www.wakefieldpress.com.au
where all titles are available for purchase.
To keep up with our latest releases, news and events,
subscribe to our monthly newsletter.

Find us!

Facebook: www.facebook.com/wakefield.press
Twitter: www.twitter.com/wakefieldpress
Instagram: www.instagram.com/wakefieldpress